LIGHT FROM THE ANCIENT PAST

VOLUME I

The publishers have retained the original
page, chapter, and illustration numbers of
the one-volume hardbound edition, and have
included in each of the two paperbound
volumes the complete indexes, including the
index of scriptural references.

LIGHT FROM
THE ANCIENT PAST

The Archeological Background
of
Judaism and Christianity

By JACK FINEGAN

PRINCETON UNIVERSITY PRESS

VOLUME I

Printed in the United States of America by
Princeton University Press, Princeton, New Jersey

TO THE MEMORY OF

JESSE COBB CALDWELL

AND

HANS LIETZMANN

Preface

THE purpose of this book is to give a connected account of the archeological background of Judaism and Christianity. Within the last century and a half and largely within the past few decades, oriental archeology has pioneered a new past, in which are revealed more extensive vistas and higher cultures than hitherto were imagined. The account which can now be given of the rise of civilization in the Middle East, of the development of art, and of the formulation of ethical, philosophical, and religious ideas is of fascinating interest in itself. It is also of great significance for an understanding of Judaism and Christianity, both of which in their origin and earlier history were integral parts of that ancient world. To see that world come vividly and startlingly alive is to find biblical and early Christian history invested with a fresh sense of reality and interest. There are, moreover, many points at which biblical records and archeological discoveries are in direct contact, and increasingly in the later centuries there are many archeological remains which are primary historical monuments of Judaism and Christianity. A knowledge of these facts is now indispensable to all serious study of the Bible, and the proper utilization of the abundant new archeological materials may even be said to constitute one of the most important tasks in that study.

The presentation of this archeological background in the present book is in the form of a continuous account extending, in round numbers, from 5000 B.C. to A.D. 500. After an introduction dealing with the nature of archeological work in general, the narrative begins with the rise of civilization in the valley of the Tigris and Euphrates rivers where the origins of the people of Israel traditionally are located and where antecedents of their mythology and law are found. Then the development of culture in the valley of the

Nile is sketched, and the Exodus of the Israelites and their use of Egyptian materials in the Psalms and Proverbs are considered. Moving to Palestine, the "bridge" between these two ancient homes of empire, archeological findings are summarized, illuminating both Canaanite and Israelite times. Then the later Assyrian, Neo-Babylonian, and Persian empires are described, upon whose imperial policies the fate and future of the kingdoms of Israel and Judah depended. With the world at last under Roman domination, the cities of Palestine are pictured as they were in the time of Jesus, and afterward a glimpse is obtained of the chief places in which the work of the apostle Paul was done. In view of the great importance of the writings collected in the New Testament, a study is made of ancient writing materials and practices and of the transmission of the text to the present time. Then the Roman catacombs are investigated, together with their art and inscriptions, and a brief account is given of characteristic early Christian sarcophagi. Finally, the development of distinctive places of Christian assembly is indicated and the basilicas of Constantinian times are described—basilicas whose successors were the Byzantine churches of the East and the Romanesque and Gothic cathedrals of the West. With the clear emergence of the Christian community, centered in the place where the gospel of Jesus Christ is proclaimed, our story comes to an end.

In the earlier part of the narrative it is the broader background of the general history and civilization which is most illuminated by archeology and to which the major part of the portrayal is devoted. In the later part not only is the general history relatively simpler and more generally known, but there are also many more monuments of Judaism and Christianity themselves. Therefore in the course of the book a steadily diminishing amount of space is apportioned to the general history and a steadily increasing amount given to the specifically biblical and early Christian materials.

In order to give a more vivid sense of direct contact with the living past, frequent quotations are made from the ancient sources, and numerous photographs are presented of actual places and objects. Many of the sites are ones which I have visited and many of the objects are ones which I have studied in the museums of Chicago, Philadelphia, New York, London, Paris, Berlin, Rome, Cairo, and Jerusalem. An extensive literature has been consulted and all references cited, both ancient and modern, have been taken from personally used sources. The full title and date of each book are given upon its first appearance, with the exception of those works for which abbreviations are employed and which appear on pages xxxv-xxxvii. The maps and plans were prepared in detail by myself, and executed and lettered by Mr. William Lane Jones.

In the writing I thought often of Dean Jesse Cobb Caldwell of the College of the Bible, Drake University, who taught me the importance of history, and of Professor Dr. Hans Lietzmann of Friedrich-Wilhelms-Universität, Berlin, who instructed me in early Christian archeology, and I have dedicated the book to their memory. In the publication I was also very grateful to Mr. Datus C. Smith, Jr., former Director of Princeton University Press, for his deep understanding, constant interest, and many courtesies.

In the present second edition the structure of the book remains the same but the results of many new excavations and further studies are incorporated. Among other things there is reference to fresh work or publication relative to Jarmo, Matarrah, Samarra, Baghouz, Tepe Gawra, Eridu, Lagash, Nippur, Saqqara, Amarna, Kawa, Abu Usba, Yarmuk, Jericho, Abu Ghosh, Abu Matar, Khirbet el-Bitar, Hebron, Dotha, Nebo, Gilgal, Ai, Gibeon, Hazor, Megiddo, Ugarit, Shiloh, Tell en-Nasbeh, Shechem, Tirzah, Dibon, Nimrod, Herculaneum, and Rome; to new studies on the Habiru; to newly discovered documents including extensive Sumerian literature, the law codes of Ur-Nammu, Eshnunna, and Lipit-Ishtar, Egyptian execration texts, Babylonian chronicles, the Dead Sea scrolls, and the Nessana and other papyri; to new translations of ancient sources; and to recent researches in Egyptian, Assyrian, Babylonian, and biblical chronology. The literature dealt with extends up to January 1, 1959. Mention may also be made of my own articles on Christian Archaeology in *The Encyclopedia Americana*; on Baalbek, Babylon, Behistun Rock, Cuneiform, Jerusalem, Layard, Sir Austen Henry, Near Eastern Architecture, Nineveh, Persepolis, Petra, Ras Shamra, Tyre, and Ur in *Collier's Encyclopedia*; on Christian Archaeology in the *Twentieth Century Encyclopedia of Religious Knowledge, An Extension of the New Schaff-Herzog Encyclopedia of Religious Knowledge*; and on Achaia, Adramyttium, Adria, Agora, Amphipolis, Appian Way, Areopàgus, Athens, Berea, Beroea, Cenchreae, Corinth, Dalmatia, Elymais, Ephesus, Fair Havens, Forum of Appius, Illyricum, Italy, Lasea, Macedonia, Melita, Neapolis, Nicopolis, Philippi, Puteoli, Rhegium, Spain, Syracuse, Thessalonica, and Three Taverns in the forthcoming *The Interpreter's Dictionary of the Bible*; and Research Abstracts in Archeology in *The Journal of Bible and Religion* in October 1947 and following years. For their kindness and efficiency in everything concerned with the publishing of the present revised edition it is a pleasure to thank Mr. Herbert S. Bailey, Jr., Director and Editor, and Miss Harriet Anderson of Princeton University Press.

Pacific School of Religion   Jack Finegan
Berkeley, California

Acknowledgments

In addition to the acknowledgments made in the List of Illustrations, thanks are also due to the following for kind permission to make reproductions: to the American Academy of Arts and Sciences, Boston, for Figures 152 and 153; to the American Schools of Oriental Research, New Haven, for Figure 195; to the Biblioteca Apostolica Vaticana, Rome, for Figure 145; to the Trustees of the British Museum, London, for Figures 24, 46, 72, 74, 78, 90, 146, 147, and 149; to the University of Chicago Press for Figures 30, 40, and 43; to the Clarendon Press, Oxford, for Figures 64 and 148; to Les Éditions d'Art et d'Histoire, Paris, for Figure 82; to Éditions Albert Morancé, Paris, for Figures 42 and 49; to the Egypt Exploration Society, London, for Figures 39 and 141; to the Field Press (1930) Ltd., London, for Figures 68 and 69; to the President and Fellows of Harvard College, Cambridge, for Figure 114; to Arthur Upham Pope, Director of the Iranian Institute, New York, for Figure 87; to the Director of the Istanbul Arkeoloji Müzeleri Müdürlügü, Istanbul, for Figure 118; to Kirsopp Lake for Figure 148; to Kirsopp and Silva Lake for Figures 152 and 153; to Librairie Orientaliste Paul Geuthner, Paris, for Figure 21; to Librairie Hachette, Paris, for Figure 97; to Macmillan and Co. Ltd., London, for Figures 4, 5, and 6; to the New York Public Library for Figure 113; to Sir Humphrey Milford, Oxford University Press, Oxford, for Figures 60, 61, 62, 70, 141, 186, 190, and 193; to the Government of Palestine for Figures 190 and 193; to the Palestine Exploration Fund, London, for Figures 59 and 66; to Presses Universitaires de France, Paris, for Figure 150; to George Routledge and Sons Ltd., London, for Figure 35; to C. F. A. Schaeffer for Figures 60, 61, and 62; to the Service des Antiquités de l'Égypte, Cairo, for Figures 38 and 44; to George Steindorff for Figure 47; to Emery Walker Ltd., London, for Figure 143; and to the Trustees of the late Sir Henry Wellcome, owners of the copyright, for Figure 70. The following pictures are from books whose copyright is vested in the Alien Property Custodian, 1945, pursuant to law, and their reproduction is by permission of the Alien Property Custodian in the public interest under License No. JA-964: Figure 154, Copyright 1919 by Gesellschaft zur Förderung der Wissenschaft des Judentums, Berlin; Figure 151,

Copyright 1929 by Peter Hanstein, Bonn; Figure 76, Copyright 1938 by J. C. Hinrichs, Leipzig; Figures 84, 85, Copyright 1925 by J. C. Hinrichs, Leipzig; Figure 168, Copyright 1927 by Josef Kösel & Friedrich Pustet K.-G., Munich; Figures 41, 138, Copyright 1936 by Phaidon Verlag, Vienna; Figures 75, 134, Copyright 1925 by Propyläen-Verlag G.m.b.H., Berlin; Figures 156, 157, 158, 160, 161, 163, 164, Copyright 1933 by Verlag für Kunstwissenschaft G.m.b.H., Berlin-Friedenau; Figure 127, Copyright 1923 by Ernst Wasmuth A.G., Berlin. Because of the war and other circumstances, it was impossible to communicate with certain publishers and individuals, and for pictures used under such conditions appreciation is recorded here.

Thanks are likewise expressed to The Westminster Press, Philadelphia, for permission to derive various details of Plan 1 from G. Ernest Wright and Floyd V. Filson, eds., *The Westminster Historical Atlas to the Bible*, 1945, Pl. xvii; and to Princeton University Press for permission to quote from *Ancient Near Eastern Texts Relating to the Old Testament*, ed. James B. Pritchard, 2d ed. 1955.

Except where otherwise indicated, the scripture quotations are from the *Revised Standard Version of the Bible*, copyrighted 1946 and 1952 by the Division of Christian Education of the National Council of Churches, and used by permission. For permission to quote from *The Bible, An American Translation*, by J. M. Powis Smith and Edgar J. Goodspeed, acknowledgment is made to the University of Chicago Press.

Contents

VOLUME I

List of Illustrations

(Figures numbered 98 through 204 appear in Volume II.)

LIST OF MAPS AND PLANS

(Maps 5 and 6 and Plans 1-4 appear in Volume II.)

List of Abbreviations

AASOR *Annual of the American Schools of Oriental Research.*

AB *The Art Bulletin.*

ADAJ *Annual of the Department of Antiquities of Jordan.*

AJA *American Journal of Archaeology.*

AJP *The American Journal of Philology.*

AJSL *The American Journal of Semitic Languages and Literatures.*

AJT *The American Journal of Theology.*

ANEA James B. Pritchard, *The Ancient Near East: An Anthology of Texts and Pictures.* 1958.

ANEP James B. Pritchard, *The Ancient Near East in Pictures Relating to the Old Testament.* 1954.

ANET James B. Pritchard, ed., *Ancient Near Eastern Texts Relating to the Old Testament.* 2d ed. 1955.

ANF Alexander Roberts and James Donaldson, eds., rev. by A. Cleveland Coxe, *The Ante-Nicene Fathers, Translations of the Writings of the Fathers down to A.D. 325.* 10 vols. 1885-87.

AO *Archiv für Orientforschung.*

AP *Archiv für Papyrusforschung.*

ARAB Daniel David Luckenbill, *Ancient Records of Assyria and Babylonia.* 2 vols. 1926-27.

ARE James Henry Breasted, *Ancient Records of Egypt.* 5 vols. 1906-07.

AS *Assyriological Studies.* Oriental Institute.

ASBACH Joseph C. Ayer, *A Source Book for Ancient Church History.* 1913.

ASV *American Standard Version.*

ATR *Anglican Theological Review.*

AZKK *Die Antike, Zeitschrift für Kunst und Kultur des klassischen Altertums.*

BA *The Biblical Archaeologist.*

BASOR *Bulletin of the American Schools of Oriental Research.*

BDSM William H. Brownlee, *The Dead Sea Manual of Discipline,* BASOR Supplementary Studies 10-12. 1951.

BDSS Millar Burrows, *The Dead Sea Scrolls.* 1955.

BJRL *Bulletin of the John Rylands Library, Manchester.*

BML Millar Burrows, *More Light on the Dead Sea Scrolls.* 1958.

CAH J. B. Bury, S. A. Cook, F. E. Adcock, M. P. Charlesworth and N. H. Baynes, eds., *The Cambridge Ancient History.* 12 vols. and 5 vols. of plates, 1923-39.

CALQ Frank M. Cross, Jr., *The Ancient Library of Qumran and Modern Biblical Studies.* 1958.

CAP R. H. Charles, ed., *The Apocrypha and Pseudepigrapha of the Old Testament in English with Introductions and Critical and Explanatory Notes to the Several Books.* 2 vols. 1913.

CBQ *The Catholic Biblical Quarterly.*

CIG *Corpus Inscriptionum Graecarum.* 1828-77.

DACL *Dictionnaire d'archéologie chrétienne et de liturgie.* 1924ff.

DJD *Discoveries in the Judaean Desert.* I, Qumran Cave I, by D. Barthélemy and J. T. Milik. 1955.

DLO Adolf Deissmann, *Licht vom Osten, Das Neue Testament und die neuentdeckten Texte der hellenistisch-römischen Welt.* 4th ed. 1923.

DM *The Mishnah Translated from the Hebrew with Introduction and Brief Explanatory Notes,* by Herbert Danby. 1933.

EB *The Encyclopaedia Britannica.* 14th ed. 24 vols. 1929.

GBT Lazarus Goldschmidt, *Der babylonische Talmud.* 9 vols. 1899-1935.

GCS *Die griechischen christlichen*

Schriftsteller der ersten Jahrhunderte.

GDSS Theodor H. Gaster, *The Dead Sea Scriptures in English Translation.* 1956.

HDB James Hastings, ed., *A Dictionary of the Bible.* 4 vols. 1898-1902.

HERE James Hastings, ed., *Encyclopaedia of Religion and Ethics.* 12 vols. 1910-22.

HFDMM W. H. P. Hatch, *Facsimiles and Descriptions of Minuscule Manuscripts of the New Testament.* 1951.

HJ *The Hibbert Journal.*

HPUM W. H. P. Hatch, *The Principal Uncial Manuscripts of the New Testament.* 1939.

HTR *The Harvard Theological Review.*

HUCA *Hebrew Union College Annual.*

ICC *The International Critical Commentary.*

IEJ *Israel Exploration Journal.*

JANT M. R. James, *The Apocryphal New Testament.* 1942.

JAOS *Journal of the American Oriental Society.*

JBL *Journal of Biblical Literature.*

JBR *The Journal of Bible and Religion.*

JCS *Journal of Cuneiform Studies.*

JE Isidore Singer, ed., *The Jewish Encyclopedia.* 12 vols. 1901-05.

JEA *The Journal of Egyptian Archaeology.*

JHS *The Journal of Hellenic Studies.*

JJS *Journal of Jewish Studies.*

JNES *Journal of Near Eastern Studies.*

JPOS *The Journal of the Palestine Oriental Society.*

JQR *The Jewish Quarterly Review.*

JR *The Journal of Religion.*

JRAS *The Journal of the Royal Asiatic Society.*

JSS *Journal of Semitic Studies.*

JTS *The Journal of Theological Studies.*

KAT J. A. Knudtzon, *Die El-Amarna Tafeln.* 2 vols. 1908-15.

KFTS Samuel N. Kramer, *From the Tablets of Sumer.* 1956.

KJV *King James Version.*

KPGÄ Friedrich K. Kienitz, *Die politische Geschichte Ägyptens vom 7. bis zum 4. Jahrhundert vor die Zeitwende.* 1953.

KRAC Theodor Klauser, ed., *Reallexikon für Antike und Christentum, Sachwörterbuch zur Auseinandersetzung des Christentums mit der antiken Welt.* 1950ff.

LCL *The Loeb Classical Library.*

LLP Louise Ropes Loomis, *The Book of the Popes (Liber Pontificalis), I, To the Pontificate of Gregory I.* 1916.

LXX *The Septuagint.* Henry Barclay Swete, ed., *The Old Testament in Greek according to the Septuagint.* i, 4th ed. 1909; ii, 3d ed. 1907; iii, 3d ed. 1905. Alfred Rahlfs, ed., *Septuaginta, id est Vetus Testamentum Graece iuxta LXX interpretes.* 2 vols. 1935. *Septuaginta, Vetus Testamentum Graecum auctoritate Societatis Litterarum Gottingensis editum.* 1931ff.

MMVGT James H. Moulton and George Milligan, *The Vocabulary of the Greek Testament Illustrated from the Papyri and Other Non-Literary Sources.* 1949.

MPG Jacques Paul Migne, *Patrologiae cursus completus. Series graeca.*

MPL Jacques Paul Migne, *Patrologiae cursus completus. Series latina.*

MTAT Samuel A. B. Mercer, *The Tell El-Amarna Tablets.* 2 vols. 1939.

NGM *The National Geographic Magazine.*

NPNF Philip Schaff, ed., *A Select Library of the Nicene and Post-Nicene Fathers,* First Series. 14 vols. 1886-89.

NPNFss Philip Schaff and Henry Wace, eds., *A Select Library of Nicene and Post-Nicene Fathers of the Christian*

Church, Second Series. 14 vols. 1890-1900.

NSH   Samuel M. Jackson, ed., *The New Schaff-Herzog Encyclopedia of Religious Knowledge.* 12 vols. 1908-12.

NTS   *New Testament Studies.*

OIC   *Oriental Institute Communications.*

OIP   *Oriental Institute Publications.*

OL   *Orientalistische Literaturzeitung.*

OP   *The Oxyrhynchus Papyri.*

PATD   Samuel B. Platner and Thomas Ashby, *A Topographical Dictionary of Ancient Rome.* 1929.

PBA   *Proceedings of the British Academy.*

PCAE   Richard A. Parker, *The Calendars of Ancient Egypt.* SAOC 26, 1950.

PCAM   Ann Louise Perkins, *The Comparative Archeology of Early Mesopotamia.* SAOC 25, 1949.

PDBC   Richard A. Parker and Waldo H. Dubberstein, *Babylonian Chronology 626 B.C.-A.D. 75.* 3d ed. 1956.

PEFA   *Palestine Exploration Fund Annual.*

PEFQS   *Palestine Exploration Fund Quarterly Statement.*

PEQ   *Palestine Exploration Quarterly.*

PWRE   Pauly-Wissowa, *Real-Encyclopädie der classischen Altertumswissenschaft.*

QDAP   *The Quarterly of the Department of Antiquities in Palestine.*

RAAO   *Revue d'assyriologie et d'archeologie orientale.*

RAC   *Rivista di archeologia cristiana.*

RB   *Revue Biblique.*

RBT   Michael L. Rodkinson, *New Edition of the Babylonian Talmud.* 10 (xx), vols. 1903, 1916.

RHR   *Revue de l'histoire des religions.*

RSV   *Revised Standard Version.*

SAOC   *Studies in Ancient Oriental Civilization.* Oriental Institute.

SBT   I. Epstein, ed., *The Babylonian Talmud* (Soncino Press). 1935ff.

SHJP   Emil Schürer, *A History of the Jewish People in the Time of Jesus Christ.* 5 vols. 1896.

SRK   Paul Styger, *Die römischen Katakomben, archäologische Forschungen über den Ursprung und die Bedeutung der altchristlichen Grabstätten.* 1933.

TL   *Theologische Literaturzeitung.*

TMN   Edwin R. Thiele, *The Mysterious Numbers of the Hebrew Kings.* 1951.

TU   *Texte und Untersuchungen zur Geschichte der altchristlichen Literatur.*

TZ   *Theologische Zeitschrift.*

UMB   *The University Museum Bulletin.*

VT   *Vetus Testamentum.*

WCCK   D. J. Wiseman, *Chronicles of Chaldaean Kings (626-556 B.C.) in the British Museum.* 1956.

ZA   *Zeitschrift für Assyriologie.*

ZÄS   *Zeitschrift für ägyptische Sprache und Altertumskunde.*

ZAW   *Zeitschrift für die alttestamentliche Wissenschaft.*

ZDPV   *Zeitschrift des Deutschen Palästina-Vereins.*

ZNW   *Zeitschrift für die neutestamentliche Wissenschaft und die Kunde der älteren Kirche.*

ZTK   *Zeitschrift für Theologie und Kirche.*

LIGHT FROM THE ANCIENT PAST

Introduction

THE ancient Greeks felt themselves to be very modern and hence had a word ἀρχαιολογία which signified the discussion of antiquities. From this term is derived the English word "archeology" which means the scientific study of the material remains of the past.

Archeological interest existed even long before the time of the Greeks. In the seventh century B.C., Ashurbanipal of Assyria was proud of his ability to decipher the writing on ancient tablets, and sent his scribes far and wide to collect copies of early records and documents for his wonderful library at Nineveh. Nabonidus, who ruled at Babylon in the sixth century B.C., made exploratory soundings in the age-old ziggurat which loomed up at Ur, read the foundation records of its earlier builders, and carefully carried out restorations, giving due credit to his ancient predecessors in his own inscriptions. The daughter of Nabonidus, sister of the famous Belshazzar, shared the interest of her father and maintained a small museum in which objects of interest from earlier times were kept.

Unfortunately the "collection" of antiquities was undertaken all too often by persons of less disinterestedness, and untold treasures have been lost to scientific archeology through the depredations of robbers. An early story of papyrus-hunting, for example, concerns Setna-Khaemuast, the fifth and favorite son of Ramses II. An account written probably in the reign of Ptolemy II tells how this young adventurer of the long ago braved the wrath of the spirits of the departed to enter the tomb of a certain prince. With this prince had been buried a magic roll of papyrus, whose possessor would know what is said by the birds as they fly and by the serpents as they crawl and would be able to enchant anything in heaven or earth. After incredible adventures Setna made away with the papyrus roll, only eventually to be driven to return it to the ghosts of the dead. Unfortunately the predecessors and successors of the illustrious Setna in the art of tomb-robbing have seldom been constrained by the powers of the spirit world to replace their spoils, and so modern archeologists all too frequently have found themselves anticipated by the unauthorized efforts of plunderers before whose greed and skill not even as mighty monuments as the pyramids were secure. A commission appointed by Ramses IX to examine into the condition of cemeteries reported in part as follows: "It was found that the thieves had violated them all, that they had torn their occupants away from their coffins and cases, had thrown them into the dust and had stolen all the funeral objects which had been given to them, as well as the gold and silver and the ornaments which were in their coffins." Among the tomb-robbers who rifled so many of the graves of the kings of Ur, special ignominy should attach to those workmen who in the very process of burying Lady Shub-ad managed to loot the grave of her previously deceased husband immediately below, hiding the hole they made in the brick vault by placing over it the lady's great clothes-chest.

In distinction from the foregoing, modern archeology may be said to have had its beginning in 1798, when nearly one hundred French scholars and artists accompanied Napoleon on his invasion of Egypt. They gazed with wonder upon the impressive monuments of that ancient land, wrote out systematic descriptions, copied texts and prepared watercolor illustrations.

Early in the nineteenth century Claudius James Rich, the resident of the East India Company at Baghdad, observed in the regions surrounding that place the mounds of ancient cities and found many inscriptions. This aroused widespread interest and when the French vice-consul at Mosul, Paul Émile Botta, found Sargon's palace at Khorsabad, the enthusiasm of a young Englishman, Austen Henry Layard, was stirred. Layard's excavations, begun in 1845, at Nimrod and notably at the mound of Kuyunjik, which was the site of ancient Nineveh, constitute the next great landmark in the history of modern archeology.

The honor of beginning the scientific study of the localities and antiquities of Palestine belonged to an American, Professor Edward Robinson, of Union Theological Seminary in New York City, who on travels through Palestine in 1838 and 1852 made extensive observations and notes. Thereafter the Palestine Exploration Fund was organized in London in 1865, and its first representative, Captain Charles Warren, made a series of sketch maps of the country and, on a second expedition, actually carried out excavations on the temple hill in Jerusalem.

The real archeological work thus initiated in Egypt, Babylonia, Assyria, and Palestine, has been continued and extended into related areas by a distinguished international succession of investigators, until modern archeology has become a true science, with most impressive results.

The work involved includes the excavation of far-flung sites, the discovery and decipherment of long-lost inscriptions and manuscripts, and the study of ancient monuments and objects of all kinds. The techniques of the science have been developed slowly through actual practice and experimentation. At first attention was naturally attracted by objects of large size and obvious impressiveness but now even the tiniest pieces of broken pottery are recognized as having their own important story to tell. Early digging sometimes was done without the requisite knowledge and skill to avoid destroying much of value, but today every step is taken with the greatest care and much attention is given to the recording and preservation of the resulting finds.

The difficulties which beset the work are various. The ancient sites may be hidden beneath modern towns or be in the possession of private persons whose interests are quite different from those of the archeologists. In the case of one famous site in Palestine, Tell el-Mutesellim (Fig. 57), the thirteen-acre area was found to be owned privately by no less than ninety separate individuals from whom it had to be leased or purchased. Unexpected discoveries of great value sometimes have provoked national jealousies and led to prolonged litigation concerning the respective rights of those concerned. Again, petty officials have presented formidable impediments to the work. Friction or discontent may arise among the laborers, while wandering dealers in antiquities sometimes lurk in the neighborhood to buy from the diggers anything which those workmen may manage to steal. Many times the work is done in regions where conditions are hazardous to health, and the malarial mosquito and other scourges have often prostrated archeological staffs. Not infrequently the sites have been in relatively lawless sections where foreigners penetrated only at risk; and in modern times as well as ancient, warfare has often raged across the Bible lands.

The object of investigation is often one of the ancient city-mounds which are so conspicuous a feature of the landscape in the Middle East.[1] Such a mound is usually known as a *tell*, the plural being *tulul*. This word, which occurs in ancient Babylonia and is still in use in modern Arabic, means high, and hence is applicable to a hill or mound.[2] These ancient mounds were built up through the centuries by the accumulation of the debris of the successive cities which occupied the site. The city's own rubbish collected constantly and filled up the streets, while after each time of destruction by war or fire the new city was rebuilt upon the ruins of the old. In Joshua 11:13 there is a picturesque allusion to this situation in the mention of "the cities that stood on mounds" (cf. also Jeremiah 30:18).

When such a *tell* is excavated today, the more recent remains are naturally found toward the top of the mound and the more ancient toward the bottom. Thus in digging from top to bottom one passes through the cultural layers in reverse sequence. While a test pit or trench may be useful as a preliminary survey, or may have to suffice when more extensive excavations cannot be attempted, more effective procedure calls for laying bare a considerable portion of the mound. This is the more necessary because the strata often are not nicely differentiated like the layers of a cake, but are intricately confused. A given stratum may bend down over the edge of the hill just as the town it represents followed the natural slopes or was built on artificial terraces. Hence it is important to clear an adequate area of each stratum and to record it in its proper order. This is known as stratigraphical excavation. Sometimes the entire mound is dug completely but it is regarded as preferable to leave at least a portion where future excavators may check the results.

The process of excavating a city-mound or other ancient site may be very laborious, involving the excavation and disposal of many

[1] The term Middle East is used here as including southwestern Asia and Egypt. The same region is also called the Near East. Following the latter usage, Harry W. Hazard, *Atlas of Islamic History* (1951), defines the Near East as extending from the western border of Egypt (25° E) to the eastern border of Iran (60° E), the Middle East as stretching from the western border of Afghanistan (60° E) to the eastern border of Burma (100° E), and the Far East as continuing from the eastern boundary of Burma (100° E) across China and Japan (150° E).

[2] Other Arabic words which are frequently encountered include *ain*, spring; *bahr*, lake or canal; *jebel*, mountain; *kalat*, castle; *khirbet*, ruin; *nahr*, river; *shatt*, river or canal; and *wadi*, watercourse or valley.

tons of dirt and debris. The approach to objects of value is made with all care, and not only the pick but also the knife and brush are employed. As the various walls and structures appear they are plotted precisely and all the objects which are found from day to day are recorded with the greatest exactitude. Detailed descriptions, drawings and photographs are prepared, and thus the archeologist's conclusions are based upon a comprehensive body of detailed information.[3]

While large numbers of records and documents have been among the finds brought to light in the course of excavations, many other inscriptions have been preserved on monuments above ground. This is notably the case in Egypt where a great body of historical inscriptions provides a major basis for the knowledge of ancient Egyptian history. The transcription of these records, which are slowly perishing under exposure to the elements, and their translation and publication are among the most important parts of the archeological enterprise. Whereas the copying was formerly done entirely by hand, later epigraphic expeditions have employed more advanced methods. A photograph is taken of the inscription, and this is compared directly with the original by an artist who pencils in any necessary additions and retraces the lines of the whole. The resultant drawing is transformed into a blueprint and it in turn is "proofread" in comparison with the original by an expert in the decipherment and interpretation of ancient inscriptions. Thus the final facsimile combines the accuracy of the camera, the skill of the artist, and the reading ability of the epigrapher.

A great variety of monuments and objects fall under the archeologist's scrutiny. They range in size from the massive pyramids to small bits of jewelry and tiny scraps of papyrus, but none is neglected. Among the modern instruments which have been found useful in the study of the ancient remains is the X-ray. When an Egyptian mummy is to be studied, the X-ray makes it possible, even before the wrappings are opened, to determine the exact position of things such as jewelry which were placed with it; it is even possible to determine facts such as the cause of the individual's death and his approximate age at the time.

While aerial photography was first practiced in connection with

[3] cf. W. F. Badè, *A Manual of Excavation in the Near East.* 1934; A. H. Detweiler, *Manual of Archaeological Surveying.* 1948; Kathleen M. Kenyon, *Beginning in Archaeology.* 1952; M. B. Cookson, *Photography for Archaeologists.* 1954.

archeological work by suspending a camera from a balloon, the employment of the airplane greatly expanded the possibilities in this field. In addition to recording the progress of excavations on the ground, this made possible swift and extensive explorations of unknown areas and pictorial documentation of important sites from the air.[4] Ancient contours invisible on the ground are often seen clearly in such pictures and, if it is desired to heighten the relief effects, stereoscopic photography may be employed.[5] Needless to say, aerial photographs are invaluable to later archeological work on the ground.

Thus through the application of highly scientific techniques and by the cooperative efforts of scholars in many lands, the shattered mosaic of the past is slowly being fitted together again. Some portion of the result will be recounted in the following pages.

[4] Erich F. Schmidt, *Flights over Ancient Cities of Iran.* Special Publication of the Oriental Institute, 1940.

[5] Arthur W. Judge, *Stereoscopic Photography.* 2d ed. 1935, p.284.

I

Mesopotamian Beginnings

THE story begins in Mesopotamia. In the land which is now known as Iraq there flow two great rivers, the Tigris and the Euphrates. So distinctive is the geographical character which they impart to the region that the Greeks coined for it the picturesque name Mesopotamia, meaning "the land between the rivers." Strictly speaking this designation applies only to the upper part of the valley of the two rivers, which in similar fashion the Arabs today call al-Jazira or "the Island." In modern usage, however, the name Mesopotamia includes also the lower part of the valley and describes graphically the entire land.

The Tigris and the Euphrates take their rise in the northern mountains of Armenia where 10,000-foot peaks gather snow and rain sufficient to feed streams destined for the desert. As the Euphrates emerges from the mountains it is flowing in a southwesterly direction as if to empty into the Mediterranean, but it bends in a large circle southward and eastward, swinging toward the course of the Tigris River which is flowing down at the foot of the hills of Kurdistan. The two rivers move in gradually converging courses down across wide and undulating grassy plains which drop 1,000 feet between the foothills and a point somewhat above modern Baghdad. Watered by these large rivers, Lower Mesopotamia was probably made up at an early time of marsh, lagoon, and lake, even as much of it is yet today. Amidst the swamps and around them, more solid areas of land made possible the establishment of human habitation.[1]

[1] *Sumer.* 11 (1955), pp.5-13 (M. E. L. Mallowan), 15f. (Ralph S. Solecki), 88 (H. E. Wright).

9

While we do not know the earliest name which may have been applied to Lower Mesopotamia, by the time of the Third Dynasty of Ur the entire land was being designated as "Sumer and Akkad,"[2] Sumer being the southern region and Akkad the part farther up the rivers and nearer modern Baghdad. Later the Akkadian city of Bab-ilu became so prominent as to give its name to the entire region. Meaning "Gate of God," this name became Babel in the Hebrew language, and Babylon in Greek and Latin. Hence we now know Lower Mesopotamia best as Babylonia.

The alluvial silt of the Tigris and Euphrates doubtless built much of the plain of Babylonia, and the waters of the two rivers have always been indispensable to its productivity. The sun is blazing hot and the average annual rainfall is only six inches, but where the rivers run or irrigation canals are dug from them the soil is very fertile. Wheat, corn, barley, dates, figs, and pomegranates are grown. In ancient times an extensive system of canals irrigated the plain and it bore a dense population and was the home of great civilizations. In their inscriptions the kings of those days spoke often, and with justifiable pride, of their works in canal-building. Rim-Sin of Larsa "dug the canal of the plain, the canal of abundance, as far as the sea." Hammurabi of Babylon provided "permanent water of plenty" by a splendid canal to which he gave his own name, "Hammurabi-is-the-prosperity-of-the-folk." Sin-idinnam wrote, "Indeed I have provided waters of everlastingness, unceasing prosperity, for my land of Larsa."

But the onetime fertile gardenland became a vast desolation. The wonderful system of irrigation which the ancient empires had maintained gradually fell into disrepair and finally, with the coming of the Muslims in the seventh century A.D. and the Mongols in the thirteenth, into utter ruin. Under Turkish rule, which lasted until the British took Baghdad in 1917 and were succeeded by the national Iraq government in 1932, the land between the rivers became one of the most desolate areas on earth. Baghdad, which was founded in A.D. 762 and raised to splendor in the ninth century by Harun-al-Rashid, the famous Caliph of the *Arabian Nights*, shrank from a reputed onetime population of 2,000,000 to 300,000. Still today it is a mud-colored city on the banks of a mud-colored river. The slightest wind blows powdered mud as fine as talcum powder through the streets. Outside the city, roads of beaten mud, where every

---

[2] Samuel N. Kramer in IEJ 3 (1953), p.220 n.5; ANET p.159, etc.

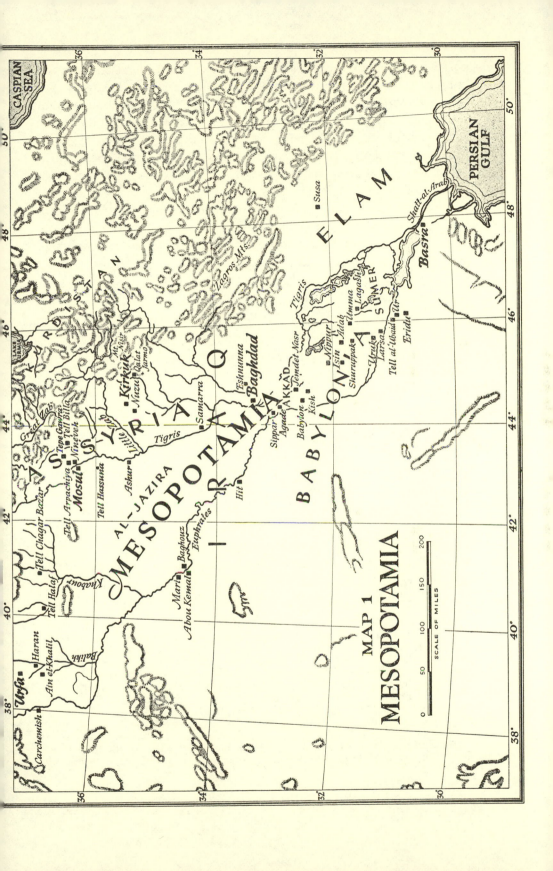

MAP 1

MESOPOTAMIA

SCALE OF MILES

0   50   100   150   200

passing horseman raises clouds of brown dust, lead among the cultivated areas. Beyond this the land stretches away, smooth as a table, brown and barren, to the sky. The city of Ur stood once upon the banks of the Euphrates but now the river has changed its course and from the summit of the ancient city-mound the fringe of palms on the river's bank is visible on the skyline twelve miles eastward. In all other directions, as far as the eye can see, stretches a vast plain of unprofitable sand. Shimmering heat waves dance over the monotonous waste, and mirages feign nonexistent waters. Here at Ur a tourist, disgruntled, wrote in the register of the mud hotel, "No wonder Abraham left; even Job would have!" But, as we shall see, in the time of Abraham the scene at Ur was far different, and no doubt it will once again become different as modern works of irrigation are carried forward.

1. THE NEOLITHIC, CHALCOLITHIC, AND LATE PREHISTORIC PERIODS,
c.5000-c.2800 B.C.[1]

EARLY VILLAGES

MESOPOTAMIA was the home of various peoples for thousands of years before the time of Abraham, and if we are to place the biblical patriarchs in their true setting we must sketch at least briefly the long historical development of which they were at least in some degree the heirs.

The earliest village settlements which have been discovered belong to the Neolithic Age and are in the northern part of Mesopotamia. One of these villages was found in 1948 at Qal'at Jarmo, thirty miles east of Kirkuk, by an expedition of the Oriental Institute of the University of Chicago, led by Robert J. Braidwood.[2] At this

---

[1] Most dates, it will be noted, are approximate rather than exact, and particularly in the earlier millenniums only the broadest chronological indications can be given. Recent discoveries have necessitated successive revisions in the early chronology of the Middle East, and in general the tendency has been toward the lowering of previously accepted dates. See Sidney Smith, *Alalakh and Chronology*. 1940, p.29; O. Neugebauer in JAOS 61 (1941), pp.58-61; Theophile J. Meek in JR 21 (1941), p.404 n.15; William F. Albright in BASOR 69 (Feb. 1938), pp.18-21; 77 (Feb. 1940), pp.25-30; 88 (Dec. 1942), pp.28-36; and in AJA 47 (1943), pp.491f. The dates given here are substantially those of Albright's revision in BASOR 88, p.32.

[2] F. Basmachi in *Sumer*. 4 (1948), pp.135f.; PCAM p.1; E. A. Speiser in NGM 99 (1951), p.46. A link between the last stage of man's life as a cave dweller and the first of his permanently established villages such as Jarmo, is provided by the dis-

site there were the remains of permanent habitations, showing that man had made the significant transition to settled life. Stone implements bore witness to a Neolithic culture.[3] No pottery was found, and it is probable that the art of making pottery vessels, subsequently so important, was not yet known. Crude clay statuettes represented the animals which had been domesticated, the goat, the sheep, the dog, and the pig. Cereals were ground between grinding stones, but the absence of stone hoes, such as appear at Tell Hassuna, suggests that the grains were not yet cultivated by human hand but simply gathered from wild growth. Primitive clay figurines of the mother goddess type attest the existence of religion or magic.

As to date, Jarmo may probably be assigned to a time not long after 5000 B.C. Confirmation of this figure has been given by an application of the Carbon 14 method of dating to snail shells from Jarmo, with a resultant date of 4756 B.C., plus or minus 320 years.[4]

TELL HASSUNA

Tell Hassuna is the name of a prehistoric site twenty-five miles south of Mosul, excavated in 1943 and 1944 by the Iraq Museum.[5] The first settlers at this place are known only from their flint or obsidian weapons and tools, and coarse pottery. Among the tools are stone axes with which they may have broken the ground in crude agriculture. A little later they had permanent adobe houses, soon numbering several rooms grouped around an open courtyard. Their pottery became much finer, and was adorned with incised or

covery in 1950-1951 by the American School of Oriental Research at Baghdad of a temporary open-air settlement of the Mesolithic Age at Karim Shahir, a little over a mile from Jarmo. Robert J. Braidwood in BASOR 124 (Dec. 1951), pp.12-18.

[3] Linda S. Braidwood in *Sumer.* 7 (1951), pp.105f.

[4] Robert J. Braidwood and Linda Braidwood in JNES 11 (1952), p.66; Willard F. Libby, *Radiocarbon Dating.* 2d ed. 1955, p.79. The Carbon 14 dating method has been developed by Willard F. Libby and J. R. Arnold at the Institute for Nuclear Studies of the University of Chicago. It depends upon the fact that in their exchange with the atmosphere, in the life process, all living things take in Carbon 14, which is an unstable or radioactive form of carbon with an atomic weight of 14. Upon the death of a living thing, this radiocarbon begins a long process of decay at a known rate. An ounce of it, for example, is reduced by disintegration to a half ounce in 5,500 years, this half is diminished to a quarter ounce in the next 5,500 years, and so on. Having determined experimentally the proportion of Carbon 14 in living matter, and knowing its "half-life" as just indicated, it is possible to ascertain the age of an ancient organic sample by the amount of Carbon 14 (measured by a radiation counter) it contains. With present techniques, the effective range of the method is about 20,000 years, with a year error in dating samples of 5 to 10 per cent. Donald Collier in BA 14 (1951), pp.25-28.

[5] AJA 48 (1944), p.371; Seton Lloyd and Fuad Safar in JNES 4 (1945), pp.255-289.

painted decorations. The development of agriculture is attested by the finding not only of more stone hand axes but also of flint-toothed sickles for reaping, and of large spherical clay grain bins sunk beneath the floors of the houses for storage. There were also flat rubbing-stones for grinding flour, and clay ovens for baking bread. Infant burials were found in pottery jars, and other jars, perhaps intended for water or food, were sometimes placed nearby. The bones of domesticated animals, the ox, the ass, and the sheep, were numerous. Beads and amulets reveal an interest in personal ornament; mother goddess figurines of clay suggest the religious or magical beliefs of the time. Such was the early farming community to which Levels i-v at Tell Hassuna bear witness. Since pottery was found at Hassuna but not at Jarmo, the settlement here was presumably somewhat later in date than that at Jarmo.

Another village which appears to have been approximately contemporary with Hassuna, although relatively poorer in its culture, was at Matarrah, about twenty miles south of Kirkuk. The excavations at this place were conducted by the Oriental Institute of the University of Chicago in 1948.[6]

Remains almost as early as those at Hassuna have been found at the famous site of Nineveh, the location of which is just across the Tigris from Mosul. A prehistoric sounding was conducted here in 1931-1932 by M. E. L. Mallowan on behalf of the British Museum.[7] A large pit was dug down ninety feet from one of the highest points on the mound to virgin soil. Underlying the later Assyrian levels a series of strata was penetrated, the lowest of which corresponded to the first settlement at Nineveh. Here were the evidences of a village which once existed on a low mound only slightly above the level of the plain. The huts of the people were represented by debris of decayed wood and ashes. Mingled with this were fragments of their handmade pottery, which was thick and coarse, poorly fired and unburnished. For the most part light gray in color, some of it was incised with deeply cut hatching, notches, and punctuations, these illustrating the earliest attempts of the potter at Nineveh to decorate his clay vessels. Elementary painted designs soon appear

[6] Robert J. Braidwood, Linda Braidwood, James G. Smith, and Charles Leslie in JNES 11 (1952), pp.1-75.

[7] M. E. L. Mallowan in *Annals of Archaeology and Anthropology, issued by the Institute of Archaeology, University of Liverpool.* 20 (1933), pp.127-177; and in *Proceedings of the First International Congress of Prehistoric and Protohistoric Sciences, London 1932.* 1934, pp.165-167.

also, and as time goes on become more common. While the very earliest level at Tell Hassuna probably precedes anything known from Nineveh, it may in general be said that the strata called Ninevite 1 and 2 are of antiquity comparable to Levels i-v at Tell Hassuna.

Yet other sites where some of the pottery appears to belong to this same period include the following: At Tell Arpachiya, north of Mosul, excavation penetrated to the tenth building level (tt 10), counting down from the top of the mound, and brought forth some incised and painted sherds resembling similarly decorated pottery at Nineveh; while in an outlying area one specimen was found just above virgin soil which was identical with the rough incised ware of Ninevite 1.[8] At Tell Chagar Bazar, a site located in the area drained by the Khabour river, Level 15 represented the first settlement on virgin soil and contained coarse pottery, with incised decoration, like that of Ninevite 1.[9] At Tell ej-Judeideh in the Plain of Antioch in Syria, excavation was carried down to Level xiv and incised ware comparable to that of the first level at Nineveh was found.[10] At Jericho in Palestine the oldest pottery appeared in Layer ix, and has been compared with that of Judeideh xiv and Hassuna i, sometimes even being regarded as slightly more primitive than the latter.[11]

The evidences of the culture here discussed thus extend from the Tigris to the Mediterranean, and reveal a village life the most characteristic marks of which are its pottery and its houses built of clay. The domestication of animals and the practice of agriculture provide the economic basis of the life of the society. Figurines and amulets attest the presence of religious and magical practices, and the burial of the dead with objects accompanying them suggests belief in an afterlife. Since the most distinctive objects of this culture were first found at Tell Hassuna, this is taken as the type site and the period is called the Hassuna period. Since no metal is found, we are still in the Neolithic Age.

A distinctive phase in the development of this culture seems to have been reached at Samarra. Samarra is on the Tigris north of Baghdad. Excavations were undertaken here in 1911-1913 by Ernst E.

[8] pcam p.10.   [9] pcam p.11.

[10] Robert J. Braidwood, *Mounds in the Plain of Antioch, an Archaeological Survey*, oip xlviii, 1937, pp.6f.; C. W. McEwan in aja 41 (1937), pp. 10f.

[11] G. Ernest Wright, *The Pottery of Palestine from the Earliest Times to the End of the Early Bronze Age*. 1937, pp.7-11, 107; pcam p.15.

Herzfeld with particular reference to Islamic ruins.[12] Underneath the pavements of the Islamic houses, however, was a five-foot layer of debris resting on virgin soil and consisting of badly preserved graves. In the graves was an abundance of painted pottery. The vessels included plates, dishes on high bases, flaring and hemispherical bowls, wide-mouthed pots, and squat jars. Mostly of medium thickness and often overfired, they were commonly provided with a slip as a base for the painting.[13] In the painted design there is an emphasis upon geometric motifs and a preference for straight lines rather than curves. The linear patterns are carried around the exterior surface of the vessels in continuous horizontal zones. Multiple parallel lines are used in many forms, and hatching, crosshatching, chevrons, zigzags, and meanders are very frequently found.[14]

Similar ware has been found at other places, including Baghouz, a site on the Middle Euphrates discovered and excavated by le Comte du Mesnil du Buisson in 1934-1936.[15] This has led some to surmise that Samarra should be recognized as marking a separate cultural phase,[16] but at present it seems best to consider it as simply representing the height of artistic achievement in the Hassuna period.[17]

TELL HALAF

The Neolithic Age, to which the early settlements just mentioned belong, was followed by the Chalcolithic or "copper-stone" Age when the peoples were moving out of the age of stone and into the times of the use of metal. In the Middle East this transition may have begun by around 4500 B.C. To the Chalcolithic Age belongs a new and notable culture which, like its more primitive predecessors, was centered in northern Mesopotamia. The first evidences of this culture were discovered at Tell Halaf. This site is in the northwest, near where the Beirut-Baghdad railway swings across the upper part of al-Jazira, and is on the Khabour, the only permanently

[12] Ernst E. Herzfeld, *Die Ausgrabungen von Samarra*, III, *Die Malereien von Samarra*. 1927, p. vii.

[13] In pottery-making the "slip" is liquid clay applied to the surface of the vessel as a decoration. It is fired, and serves also to receive whatever painting is done. J. L. Kelso and J. Palin Thorley in AASOR 21-22 (1941-43), p.106.

[14] Ernst E. Herzfeld, *Die Ausgrabungen von Samarra*, V, *Die vorgeschichtlichen Töpfereien von Samarra*. 1930.

[15] Le Comte du Mesnil du Buisson, *Baghouz, l'ancienne Corsôtê, le tell archaïque et la nécropole de l'âge du bronze*. 1948, pp.xii, 18-19.

[16] W. F. Albright in AJA 55 (1951), p.209.

[17] PCAM pp.5-8, 15; Charles Leslie in JNES 11 (1952), pp.57-66.

flowing tributary of the Euphrates in Mesopotamia. Remains of the same culture have also been found at Carchemish over 100 miles west of Tell Halaf, at Tell Chagar Bazar 50 miles to the east, and at Tepe Gawra and Tell Arpachiya 175 miles to the east.[18] From the type site this is called the Halaf period.

The first intimation that Tell Halaf was an ancient site came when native Chechens undertook to bury one of their dead on the hill and were frightened away upon digging up stone statues of animals with human heads. Baron Max von Oppenheim secured the secret from them in 1899 and worked at Tell Halaf in 1911-1913 and again in 1927 and 1929.[19] In the lowest levels were found the remains of a civilization which was much advanced over the life of the primitive Neolithic villages. The most distinctive product of this culture was its superb painted pottery. This was made by hand and among all the handmade wares of antiquity ranks as one of the best on both the technical and the artistic sides. Characteristically it is a fine, thin pottery covered with a smooth cream or buff slip on which are inimitable polychrome designs in black and orange-red paint. Many of the patterns are geometrical in character, while bird, animal and human representations also appear. Several fragments of this remarkable pottery are shown in Fig. 1. A genuine glaze paint was used, and the pottery was fired at an intense heat in closed kilns, which gave it a porcelain-like finish. Kilns of this type, making perfectly controlled temperatures possible, have been found in place at Carchemish, Tell Arpachiya, and Tepe Gawra.[20] Among the other technical developments of the time appears to have been the use of wheeled vehicles. On a painted vase found at Tell Halaf there is to be seen what, if its usual interpretation is correct, is the earliest known picture of a chariot. The chariot has great eight-spoked wheels and carries a man.[21]

Of the other northern sites representative of the Halaf period, Tepe Gawra may be chosen for description. "The Great Mound," as the name means, stands about fifteen miles northeast of Mosul and two miles east of Khorsabad. Beginning with a sounding in

[18] See e.g. M. E. L. Mallowan and J. Cruikshank Rose, *Prehistoric Assyria, The Excavations at Tall Arpachiyah 1933*. 1935, pp.17, 25, 104f.

[19] Max von Oppenheim, *Der Tell Halaf, Eine neue Kultur im ältesten Mesopotamien*. 1931; tr. *Tell Halaf, A New Culture in Oldest Mesopotamia*.

[20] See e.g. E. A. Speiser in BASOR 66 (Apr. 1937), pp.15f.; *The New York Times*, May 11, 1937, p.26.

[21] M. von Oppenheim, *Der Tell Halaf*, Pl. 51, No. 8, p.184.

1927 and continuing through seven more campaigns between 1931 and 1938, excavations were conducted here by the American Schools of Oriental Research and the University Museum of the University of Pennsylvania, with additional assistance from The Dropsie College, Philadelphia. The discoverer of Tepe Gawra and director of four of the eight expeditions which worked there was E. A. Speiser of the University of Pennsylvania.[22]

On the main mound excavation began by complete levels and was gradually restricted to smaller areas as greater depths were reached, Stratum xx being explored only by trenches. In addition, soundings were made in two regions at the foot of the mound on the southeast and northeast respectively, which are known as Area A, and Northeast Base. In Area A, Northeast Base, and Stratum xx the oldest pottery was found and was of the Halaf type. As at Tell Halaf the wares were usually thin and always very hard, having been fired at high temperatures. Often covered with a light-colored slip, the vessels were painted with geometrical and linear designs, and also with naturalistic patterns of birds, in colors of red, black, and brown.[23]

The sites thus far mentioned as characteristic of the Halaf period are all in the north or northwest, and it is believed that the original home of the Halaf culture is to be sought somewhere in the Mosul area.[24] At the same time settlement was also beginning in southern Mesopotamia.

ERIDU

The earliest site yet known in Lower Mesopotamia has been found at Tell Abu Shahrain, which is identified as the ancient city of Eridu. Interestingly enough, as will be noted later, this is the very city where the first antediluvian kingship is located by the Sumerian King List. Under the direction of Fuad Safar, excavations were conducted at Tell Abu Shahrain by the Department of Antiquities of the Iraq Government for three seasons between 1946 and 1949.[25]

The lowest levels, which probably represent a time not long after 4500 B.C., are characterized by a fine painted pottery. Shallow dishes, deep bowls, and tall goblets are among the most frequent

[22] E. A. Speiser, *Excavations at Tepe Gawra*, I, *Levels I-VIII*. 1935; and in NGM 99 (1951), pp.42f.; Arthur J. Tobler, *Excavations at Tepe Gawra*, II, *Levels IX-XX*. 1950.
[23] Tobler, *Excavations at Tepe Gawra*, II, pp.126-137.
[24] PCAM p.44.
[25] Naji al-Asil in *Sumer.* 3 (1947), p.3; 6 (1950), pp.3f., 27-33; Seton Lloyd and Fuad Safar in *Sumer.* 4 (1948), pp.115-125.

shapes found. The paint usually employed was chocolate-colored, sometimes red. Ornamental designs included checks, grids, cross-hatchings, and zigzag lines. While in the painting there is reminiscence of Tell Halaf and Samarra, in other respects this pottery is different. It appears immediately above virgin soil and continues upward through half a dozen successive levels of occupation, only then being supplanted by another kind of pottery already previously known from Tell al-ʿUbaid. Whereas the ʿUbaid pottery and related objects had formerly been supposed to represent the earliest culture that had appeared in Lower Mesopotamia, the Eridu ware is now recognized as antecedent and as the indication of a distinct and prior cultural period in that area.

Also belonging to this early period were the ruins of a small shrine, ten feet square, built of sun-dried bricks, the first in a series of no less than fourteen prehistoric temples, one succeeding the other, which were found in the mound. In some of the higher levels the traces of huts were still discernible which had been made of reeds and plastered both inside and out with clay. Although the reeds had completely decayed, the impressions of their stems and leaves remained on the inner surfaces of the two layers of plaster. Such building with reeds may well have been the very first kind of construction practiced in the lower Mesopotamian marshes.

TELL AL-ʿUBAID

Tell al-ʿUbaid (or el-Obeid) was once directly on the Euphrates, although the river has now shifted its course some distance away. In 1919 early ruins were found at this site by H. R. Hall, and in 1923-1924 C. Leonard Woolley directed the Joint Expedition of the British Museum and the University Museum of the University of Pennsylvania in important excavations.[26] This is the type site for the ʿUbaid period which must have begun around 4000 B.C. and is represented in finds in both southern and northern Mesopotamia.

The characteristic pottery found at Tell al-ʿUbaid (Fig. 2) is a fine, pale greenish ware, painted with free geometrical designs in black or dark brown. It was made either entirely by hand or on a slow, hand-turned wheel. While animal motifs were rare in the decoration of the pottery, numerous animal and human figures, hand-modeled in clay, were found.

Like huts already mentioned at Eridu, ʿUbaid houses were built

[26] H. R. Hall and C. Leonard Woolley, *Ur Excavations*, I, *Al-ʿUbaid.* 1927.

out of reeds plastered with mud. Building was also done with bricks made of mud dried in the sun. The mud-plastered walls were sometimes decorated with most interesting mosaics made of small, slender pencil-like cones of baked clay, the ends of which were left plain, or painted red or black. This usage gave the wall an almost waterproof protection and a permanent decoration, and was practiced for centuries.

Another village of the 'Ubaid period has been excavated at Telul ath-Thalathat some forty miles west of Mosul. This work was done by the Iraq-Iran Archaeological Expedition of Tokyo University under the sponsorship of Prince Takahito Mikasa and others. Dwelling houses, pottery, and skeletal remains of the 'Ubaid period were unearthed, while a larger building of the subsequent Uruk period was believed to have been a very early temple.[27]

At Eridu on the northwest side of the mound a large cemetery was found which belongs to the 'Ubaid period, as shown by much pottery of the same kind as at Tell al-'Ubaid. There were about one thousand graves here, built out of sun-dried bricks in the form of oblong boxes. After the body was placed therein the box was filled with earth and sealed with a covering of bricks. In many cases more than one member of a family was buried in the same tomb, the grave having been opened to permit the additional interment. The pottery accompanying the dead was ordinarily placed near the feet; where a second burial was introduced the vessels were put near the head to avoid confusion with the previous deposit. One unsealed grave contained the skeleton of a dog lying directly upon that of a young boy.[28]

At Tepe Gawra the Strata from xix up to xii correspond with the 'Ubaid period. In Stratum xix were the poorly preserved ruins of a temple, which was rebuilt in similar form in the next level above. In Stratum xiii, which is perhaps to be dated around the close of the fifth or beginning of the fourth millennium b.c., was an extraordinarily impressive acropolis. Three monumental temple buildings enclosed three sides of a large open court. All the temples had their corners oriented to the cardinal points of the compass, and all were ornamented with recessed niches on both the exterior and interior surfaces of the walls. Built of sun-baked mud brick, the temples were also plastered and at least in part painted. Entering the court

[27] Namio Egami in *Sumer*. 13 (1957), pp.5-11.
[28] Lloyd and Safar in *Sumer*. 4 (1948), pp.117-119.

the ancient worshiper saw on the right what the archeologists call the Eastern Shrine where traces of color suggest that the building was painted bright red; on the left the warm reddish-brown brick walls of the Northern Temple; and directly ahead the white-plastered façade and great niche of the Central Temple, the inner rooms and cult chamber of which were painted in reddish-purple. Architectural relationships suggest that the three buildings were erected in the order just named. The existence of this acropolis with its imposing places of worship, the construction of which would have been possible only through the combined efforts of a large community, witnesses to the social and religious development of the time.[29]

The 'Ubaid civilization was evidently related to a contemporaneous Iranian Highland culture which reached eastward across the plateau of Iran into Baluchistan, and it is closely associated with the findings in the lowest levels at Susa, known as Susa i.[30] The famous ancient site of Susa is in Persia, 150 miles north of the head of the Persian Gulf. Susa was explored by Dieulafoy, Houssaye, and Babin Expedition[31] sent out by the French government in 1884-1886, and in 1897 and following years was studied intensively by a series of expeditions under the direction of Jacques de Morgan and R. de Mecquenem, while more recently further work has been directed by G. Contenau and R. Ghirshman.[32] An aerial photograph of the site is shown in Fig. 3. On the principal elevation are the fortlike quarters of the French archeological expedition, while to the left is the modern village of Shush with the traditional "Tomb of Daniel."

Susa was founded about 4000 B.C. and was still a great city in the twelfth century A.D. Outside the earthen rampart of the mud village in which the earliest inhabitants lived were many graves. In them was found an abundance of fragile pottery, painted a glossy black, with decorations including geometrical patterns of triangles, rectangles, and zigzags, and human, animal, and plant designs reduced to almost geometrical forms. Galloping dogs, goats whose fore and

[29] E. A. Speiser in BASOR 65 (Feb. 1937), p.8; 66 (Apr. 1937), pp.3-9; and in *Asia*. 38 (1938), pp.542f.; Tobler, *Excavations at Tepe Gawra*, II, *Levels IX-XX*, pp.30-36, 43-47.

[30] Henri Frankfort, *Archaeology and the Sumerian Problem*. SAOC 4, 1932, p.29; Donald E. McCown, *The Comparative Stratigraphy of Early Iran*. SAOC 23, 1942, p.36 and Fig.13.

[31] M. A. Dieulafoy, *L'Acropole de Suse d'après les fouilles exécutées en 1884, 1885, 1886 sous les auspices du Musée du Louvre*. 1890.

[32] See M. Pézard and E. Pottier, *Les Antiquitiés de la Susiane*. Musée de Louvre, 1913; and the *Mémoires* of the French expeditions.

hindquarters are triangles and whose horns are sweeping semicircles, and rows of storks, whose bodies are large triangles and whose heads are small triangles, are among the conventionalized designs represented in the sophisticated art of Susa I.[33] Copper mirrors, beads of black and white limestone or imported turquoise, and little conical vases once containing green mineral paint for the eyelids, were also found. Among tools and weapons buried with the dead were stone-headed clubs and copper-headed tomahawks. Fragments of cloth also remain to indicate that these people had the art of making fine linen.

Beyond Persia lies Baluchistan, the bridge to India, where the Iranian Highland culture may even have come into contact with the culture of the Indus Valley. Baluchistan is now to a great extent desert, but many prehistoric sites have been discovered there which may be links between the civilizations of Mesopotamia and of the Indus Valley.[34] The prehistoric culture of the Indus Valley is known through the excavations at Mohenjo-daro, some 140 miles northeast of Karachi, and at other sites on the Five Streams of the Punjab. At Mohenjo-daro, "the Place of the Dead," there existed around the middle of the third millennium B.C. a planned city with broad streets, buildings made of fine brick, and an elaborate sanitary system including a bathroom in almost every house.[35]

The indications of early contact between Mesopotamia and India include such facts as the following: In the Tell al-'Ubaid period the inhabitants of Mesopotamia were making beads out of lapis lazuli, an azure blue stone which comes from Central Asia, and amazonite, a green stone which is found only in Central India and Transbaikalia. Later, in the tombs of Ur, is found the little figure of a squatting monkey precisely similar to figures unearthed at Mohenjo-daro, while around 2500 B.C. at Tell Asmar other Indian animals—the elephant, rhinoceros, and gharial or fish-eating crocodile—appear on a seal of undoubted Indian workmanship.[36]

[33] J. de Morgan and R. de Mecquenem, *La Céramique peinte de Suse, Mémoires, Délégation en Perse*. XIII (1912); R. de Mecquenem, *Notes sur la céramique peinte archaïque en Perse, Mémoires*, XX (1928); G. Contenau in Arthur U. Pope, ed., *A Survey of Persian Art from Prehistoric Times to the Present*. 1938, I, pp.171f.; H. A. Groenewegen-Frankfort, *Arrest and Movement, An Essay on Space and Time in the Representational Art of the Ancient Near East*. 1951, pp.146f.

[34] Aurel Stein, *Archaeological Reconnaissances in Northwestern India and Southeastern Iran*. 1937; and in *A Survey of Persian Art*. I, p.168.

[35] John Marshall, ed., *Mohenjo-Daro and the Indus Civilization*. 3 vols. 1931; E. J. H. Mackay, *Further Excavations at Mohenjo-Daro*. 2 vols. 1937-38.

[36] Ernest Mackay, *The Indus Civilization*. 1935, pp.170, 191-193, 199. cf. 2d ed. rev. by Dorothy Mackay, *Early Indus Civilizations*. 1948.

URUK

The story of Mesopotamia is continued at Warka, which was ancient Erech or Uruk and is some thirty-five miles up the Euphrates Valley from Tell al-'Ubaid. This is the type site for the Uruk period which occupies much of the fourth millennium B.C. If the following Jemdet Nasr period be included along with the Uruk period this entire time may be called the Late Prehistoric period since it is the last before the Early Dynastic period which is the first historic age.[37]

In the excavation of Uruk by the Deutsche Orientgesellschaft[38] the most distinctive pottery found was a red ware, running from brick-red to plum-red in color. Black and gray wares were also found; they were baked in a kiln smothered down to make the smoke penetrate and color the clay. Both of these kinds of pottery were made on a genuine spinning potter's wheel, and they were highly polished but left unpainted.[39]

A small pavement of rough limestone blocks at Uruk is the oldest stone construction in Mesopotamia, and here, too, is found the first ziggurat. The Assyrian-Babylonian word *ziqquratu* comes from the verb *zaqaru* meaning "to be high, or raised up," and hence signifies the top of a mountain, or a staged tower. Such a tower provided a sort of artificial mountain in the flat Mesopotamian plain as a high place for a god whose shrine stood on its summit. From its first appearance here at Uruk, it was ever afterward the most characteristic feature of temple architecture in Mesopotamia, and the locations of more than two dozen such structures are known today.[40]

The Uruk ziggurat was simply a vast mass of clay stamped down hard and strengthened with layers of asphalt and unburnt bricks.

[37] At this point PCAM (p.97) introduces a new terminology and speaks of the Warka and Protoliterate periods, but Albrecht Goetze (in JCS 4 [1950], pp.77f.) favors retention of the scheme already internationally agreed upon of distinguishing the periods subsequent to the 'Ubaid period by the type sites and names of Uruk and Jemdet Nasr, and the latter system is followed here. In *Relative Chronologies in Old World Archeology*, ed. Robert W. Ehrich, 1954, p.46, Miss Perkins employs "Late Prehistoric" as the designation for the period between the 'Ubaid period and the Early Dynastic. For the successive early periods see also the chronological tables of Henri Frankfort, *The Birth of Civilization in the Near East*. 1951, p.112 (using the Warka and Protoliterate terminology), and of Perkins in *Relative Chronologies in Old World Archeology*, pp.52f. (using the sequence Hassuna, Halaf, 'Ubaid, Late Prehistoric, Early Dynastic).

[38] Julius Jordan, *Uruk-Warka nach den Ausgrabungen durch die Deutsche Orient-Gesellschaft*. 1928.

[39] T. J. Meek in Elihu Grant, ed., *The Haverford Symposium on Archaeology and the Bible*. 1938, p.164.

[40] Jean de Mecquenem in *Gazette des Beaux-Arts*. 6e période 18 (1937), pp.201-214; André Parrot, *Ziggurats et Tour de Babel*. 1949, pp.52-54; *The Tower of Babel*. 1955.

Rows of pottery jars were embedded in the upper edges to support them and prevent them from crumbling away. Facing outward, their white rims and dark interiors made a striking ornament. The ziggurat measured some 140 by 150 feet and stood about 30 feet high, its corners being oriented toward the points of the compass. On the summit was the actual shrine, oriented similarly, 65 feet long, 50 feet wide, and built about a long narrow court, 14 feet across, and entered by doors at either end and in the center of the southwest side. The outer walls were ornamented with vertical recesses, and this feature together with the system of orientation remained characteristic of later temples. The original whitewash was still preserved on the mud-brick walls, and hence the German archeologists applied to the shrine the name, *der weisse Tempel*, the White Temple. In similar fashion they named a second temple building, to whose walls a plum-red paint had been applied, the Red Temple. Yet another monumental structure was ornamented beautifully with three-colored mosaic work of clay cones in patterns of zigzags, triangles, and diamonds. This method of ornamentation already had been developed, it will be remembered, at Tell al-'Ubaid, and the use of the hollow clay cones on the Uruk ziggurat was another adaptation of the same principle.

The most notable achievements of the Uruk culture, however, were the introduction of the cylinder seal and of script. In the White Temple mentioned above, two small square tablets of gypsum plaster were found which bore the impressions of cylinder seals. These are the first instances known of the use of cylinder seals, which appear to have been invented by the people of this period. Such a seal was made in the form of a small stone cylinder which left its impression not by being stamped upon a surface but by being rolled across it. The surface of the cylinder was engraved in intaglio, so that when the seal was used it yielded an image in which the design stood out in relief.[41] Such a cylinder seal is shown in Fig. 5 while the impression from the same seal appears in Fig. 6.

The origin of cylinder seals preceded the invention of writing, and at first they were used chiefly to safeguard possessions. A jar or package was sealed with clay, and while this was moist the cylinder was rolled over it. Since each cylinder bore a distinctive design, a permanent proof of personal ownership was left behind. Later, when writing had developed and letters, contracts, and other records were

[41] cf. Job 38:12-14; Albert E. Bailey, *Daily Life in Bible Times*. 1943, p.27.

inscribed upon clay tablets, these documents were conveniently legalized by similar seal impressions.

From their origin here in the fourth millennium B.C., cylinder seals continued in use until finally supplanted by the stamp seal in Persian times, thus having a demonstrable history of more than 3000 years. From Mesopotamia their manufacture and employment spread to peripheral regions as widely distant as India and Egypt. The decoration of the cylinder seals constituted Mesopotamia's most original contribution to art, and the influence of the seals was felt in all the other branches of decorative art as well.

The excellence of the seals upon their first appearance in the Uruk period is amazing. Vivid animal studies, ornamental heraldic compositions, abstract religious symbols, and narrative illustrations of ritual practice all are found. In Fig. 4 is shown the impression of a cylinder belonging to this period which was found at Tell Billa northeast of modern Mosul. The scene represented has not been explained fully but seems to be of a ritual character. At the left appears what may be a shrine, and it is approached by three men who are presumably bringing offerings. At the right is a boat which has plants at either end.

Only an intimation of later developments in the glyptic art may be given here. In the Early Dynastic period a new and distinctive style was achieved. Decoration rather than narration was emphasized. The subject was often reduced to a pattern of lines whose rhythmic recurrence formed a frieze of indefinite extent. The result was a decorative scheme such as a weaver or embroiderer might use, and hence this has been termed the "brocade" style. The long, slender cylinder shown in Fig. 5 comes from this period, and its impression reproduced in Fig. 6 is characteristic of the style just described. In this instance, the basis of the representation is nothing but two goats, one upright and one upside down, with a few additional strokes completing the design. In the time of Sargon and the Old Akkadian period another notable change in style took place, and the art of the seal reached perhaps its highest expression. The continuous frieze was supplanted by the heraldic group and the linear figures gave way to wholly modeled figures whose physical characteristics were emphasized realistically. At the center of the composition there was often a panel containing an inscription. A seal impression displaying these characteristic features of the Sargonid style is illustrated in Fig. 7. The bearded hero appears in various ways in Mesopotamian art but here seems to represent a spirit of water. In this capacity he is watering the buffaloes from a vase out of which flow two streams. The water and rock border at the bottom is in harmony with the same theme. The inscription in the panel names a certain scribe, Ibnisharrum, as the owner of the seal and dedicates it to Shargalisharri, king of Akkad.[42]

Returning now to Uruk and its culture, it may be noted that the introduction of the cylinder seal was soon followed by the emergence of writing, a momentous invention which must have taken place sometime in the middle of the fourth millennium B.C.[43] In the Red Temple at Uruk were found a number of thin, flat clay tablets inscribed in a crude pictographic script. This picture-writing represents the earliest stage of Babylonian writing known and is evidently the direct ancestor of cuneiform. The pictographs were gradually reduced for speed in drawing to arbitrary groups of lines and these developed into the wedge-shaped writing which we call cuneiform. As the tablets show, the writing material which was used in Mesopotamia from the beginning was clay into which the writing signs were pressed with a stylus whose point was formed into a three-sided prism. The clay tablet was held for writing in the left hand, or when larger in size was laid down flat, and the text was written in vertical columns running from left to right. The numerals found on these tablets show that a sexagesimal system of arithmetic, in which the computing was by sixties, was in most common use but that a decimal system was also employed.[44] Since the sexagesimal system was that of the Sumerians, soon to be mentioned, and since the tablets also refer to Sumerian gods such as Enlil, it is believed that the language of these earliest of written records is Sumerian.[45]

JEMDET NASR

Jemdet Nasr, a site in the Mesopotamian Valley not far from

[42] Richard A. Martin, *Ancient Seals of the Near East.* Field Museum of Natural History Anthropology Leaflet 34, 1940, No.5. For the basic discussion of the entire subject of cylinder seals see Henri Frankfort, *Cylinder Seals.* 1939. See also *Corpus of Ancient Near Eastern Seals in North American Collections, Edited for the Committee of Ancient Near Eastern Seals, A Project of the Iranian Institute, The Oriental Institute of the University of Chicago and the Yale Babylonian Collection,* i, *The Collection of the Pierpont Morgan Library,* ed. Edith Porada, Text, Plates (The Bollingen Series, xiv). 1948.

[43] This is the beginning of the Protoliterate period if this terminology is used. For the date around 3500 B.C. see Henri Frankfort, *The Art and Architecture of the Ancient Orient.* 1954, p.1.

[44] A. Falkenstein, *Archaische Texte aus Uruk.* 1940, pp.49,62.

[45] Frankfort, *The Birth of Civilization in the Near East,* p.50 n.1.

1. **Fragments** of Painted Pottery from Tell **Halaf**

2. Pottery from Tell al-'Ubaid

3. Air View of Susa

4. Impression of Cylinder Seal from the Uruk Period

5. Cylinder Seal from the
Early Dynastic Period

6. Impression of Cylinder Seal from the Early Dynastic Period

7. Impression of Cylinder Seal from the Old Akkadian Period

9. Tablet from Nippur with the Story of the Creation and the Flood

8. The Flood Stratum at Kish

11. An Early Sumerian Worshiper

10. Sumerian Statues of the Lord of Fertility and the Mother Goddess

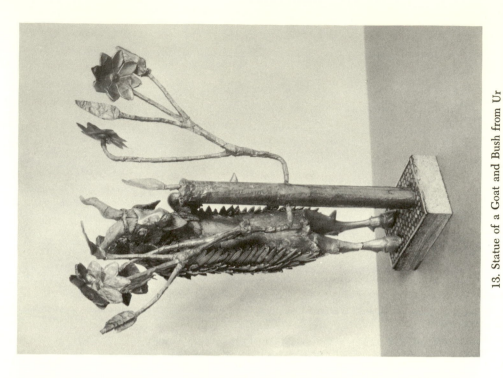

13. Statue of a Goat and Bush from Ur

12. The Headdress of Lady Shub-ad

15. Fluted Gold Bowl from the "Royal" Cemetery at Ur

14. Fluted Gold Tumbler from the "Royal" Cemetery at Ur

17. The Victory Stela of Naram-Sin

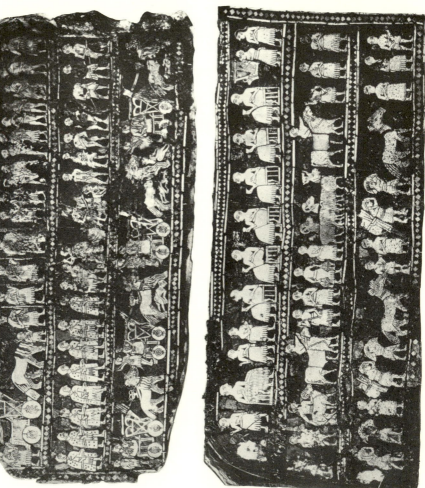

16. The "Standard" of Ur, Showing the "War" Panel (upper) and the "Peace" Panel

18. Statue of Gudea

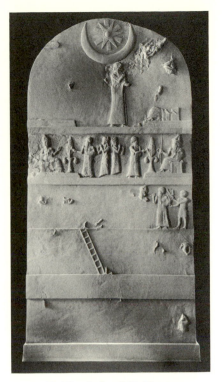

20. The Stela of Ur-Nammu

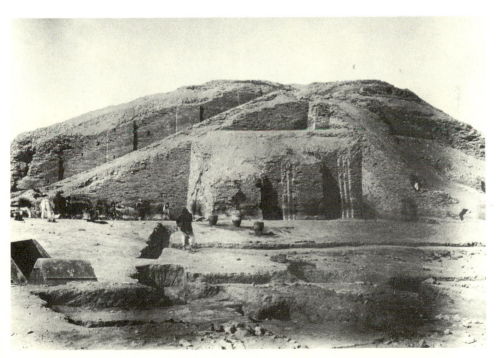

19. The Ziggurat at Ur

22. A Business Contract from the Time of Hammurabi

21. A Worshiper Carrying a Kid for Sacrifice

23. Hammurabi Standing before Shamash

24. The Fourth Tablet of the Epic of Creation

where Babylon was later to stand, may be taken as the type site for the last period in Mesopotamian prehistory.[46] The date of this period is probably around the end of the fourth or beginning of the third millennium B.C. The characteristic pottery at Jemdet Nasr is a painted ware featuring black and yellow on a deep red ground. Metal was employed more freely, and the first use of bronze indicates the beginning of the Bronze Age in Mesopotamia. Tablets were found written in a semipictographic script somewhat more advanced than that of the Uruk period.

Sculpture in stone was a noteworthy achievement of the people of the Jemdet Nasr period. Some of the finest examples come from levels at Uruk and Ur contemporary with Jemdet Nasr. At Uruk a block of basalt was found, carved in bas-relief with a hunting scene in which two bearded men are fighting three lions. At Ur the first example of sculpture in the round was discovered. It was the figure of a crouching boar, carved in steatite or soapstone, and executed in the style of a mature art. The conception is on the whole in terms of an abstract balance of mass, but the character of the animal is suggested realistically by the drawing back of the upper lip over the tusks.

During the Jemdet Nasr period the important cities of Shuruppak (Fara), Eshnunna (Tell Asmar), and Kish were founded. Shuruppak was perhaps eighty-five miles from Jemdet Nasr down the Mesopotamian Valley in the direction of Tell al-'Ubaid, Eshnunna was over fifty miles to the north, while Kish was nearer at hand, some fifteen miles southwest of Jemdet Nasr. All three of these cities will be mentioned again.

THE FLOOD

In a flat river valley such as that of the Tigris and Euphrates and in a region where torrential rains are known, it would be easily possible for great floods to take place. In excavations at a number of Mesopotamian sites, layers of clean clay have been found which could have been deposited by such floods. At the edge of the mound of Ur, C. Leonard Woolley dug down through an early cemetery located in what had once been the rubbish heap of the ancient city. Beneath the level of the graves the diggers continued to find the pottery and other objects of the earlier city, the pottery changing from Jemdet Nasr to Uruk to later 'Ubaid forms. Then they encountered a stratum of perfectly clean silt which the workmen took

---

[46] Ernest Mackay and Stephen Langdon, *Report on Excavations at Jemdet Nasr, Iraq.* 1931.

for the bottom of the original delta. When measurements showed that this was not the case, they dug on down. Beneath some eight to eleven feet of clean clay they came again upon rubbish full of stone implements and bits of hand-painted pottery such as were found in the earliest levels at Tell al-ʿUbaid. This appeared to Woolley to represent a flood of great magnitude which must have inundated the whole valley although Ur itself was high enough that most of the city escaped.[47]

At Shuruppak there was a similar stratum some two feet thick but, whereas the Ur deposit came in the midst of the ʿUbaid period, this was at the end of the Jemdet Nasr period.[48] Likewise at Uruk there was a similar layer five feet in depth which marked the end of the Jemdet Nasr period.[49] Again at Kish there was a layer of sediment one and one-half feet in thickness but this was some distance above the Jemdet Nasr stratification and thus yet somewhat later in date.[50] A picture of this last "flood stratum" is shown in Fig. 8.

It is evident that if the several strata just described are actually flood deposits they still do not represent one and the same inundation since they occur at different points in the stratigraphic sequence. If it was one of these disasters in particular which provided the basis for the later accounts of the flood in Mesopotamian and biblical literature,[51] it might possibly have been that which is attested at Shuruppak and Uruk, or the one at Kish, since in the Sumerian King List, next to be discussed, it is indicated that Shuruppak was the last ruling city before the flood and Kish the seat of the first Sumerian dynasty after the flood.[52]

In the Early Dynastic period of which we shall soon speak the

---

[47] C. L. Woolley, *Ur of the Chaldees*. 1929, pp.22-29; *Excavations at Ur*. Third (corrected) impression 1955, pp.26-36; and in PEQ Jan.-June 1956, pp.17f. For a different interpretation see William A. Irwin in *Church History*. 15 (1946), pp.236f. Concerning this stratum W. F. Albright writes (in BASOR 146 [Apr. 1957], p.35): "Since it brought no change of culture, most archaeologists consider it as a deposit laid down by a river flood which was higher than ordinary, somewhere about the 35th century B.C. or even later."

[48] Erich F. Schmidt in *The Museum Journal*. 22 (1931), pp.200f.

[49] Julius Jordan in *Abhandlungen der preussischen Akademie der Wissenschaften*. 1929, p.20; V. Christian in AO 8 (1932), p.64.

[50] S. Langdon in JRAS 1930, p.603; L. C. Watelin, *Excavations at Kish* IV *1925-1930*. 1934, pp.40-44.

[51] André Parrot, *The Flood and Noah's Ark*. 1955, pp.51f.

[52] Another theory is that the flood stories, which are so widespread in the ancient world, embody a memory of the presumably much more far-reaching inundations which came at the end of the last Ice Age, probably ten thousand years ago. Georges Contenau, *Everyday Life in Babylon and Assyria*. 1954, p.196.

Sumerians were dominant in Lower Mesopotamia. This folk, who called themselves "the black-headed people" and their land Sumer, were neither Semites nor Aryans and their language, in which many texts are now available, was neither Semitic nor Indo-European.[53] Since the pictographic writing found at Uruk, mentioned above, was probably Sumerian, these people must have been in Mesopotamia at least in the later part of the Uruk period. Some think that they were indeed the first settlers in Lower Mesopotamia, but a probably preferable theory supposes that the first civilization was established by Iranians from the East and Semites from the West, upon whom came the Sumerians perhaps early in the fourth millennium B.C.[54] An important cultural center of the Sumerians was Nippur, one hundred miles south of modern Baghdad and about midway between Kish and Shuruppak. Excavated first by the University of Pennsylvania in 1889 to 1900 and again since 1948 by a joint Oriental Institute-University Museum expedition under Donald E. McCown, this site has produced thousands of inscribed tablets and fragments which reveal how extensive was the Sumerian literature which was composed in the third and second millenniums B.C.[55]

The Sumerian King List is an interesting chronological list of early rulers, written not later than the middle of the famous Third Dynasty of Ur and probably in the slightly earlier reign of Utu-hegal of Uruk.[56] It is obvious that the list is not entirely dependable, since it ascribes reigns of the most exaggerated length to the earlier kings. It begins with the statement, "When kingship was lowered from heaven the kingship was in Eridu," and then continues with the names of the sovereigns who reigned before the flood. Eight such antediluvian kings are listed and it is stated that their rule centered in five different cities and lasted for 241,200 years. The last of the eight was Ubar-Tutu who, according to the list, reigned at Shuruppak

[53] Frankfort, *The Art and Architecture of the Ancient Orient*, p.235 n.2; André Parrot, *Discovering Buried Worlds*. 1955, p.72.

[54] Samuel N. Kramer in AJA 52 (1948), pp.156-164; KFTS pp.238-248.

[55] J. P. Peters, *Nippur, or Explorations on the Euphrates*. 2 vols. 1897; H. V. Hilprecht, *The Excavations in Assyria and Babylonia*. 1903, pp.289-568; KFTS p.277.

[56] The Weld-Blundell prism, giving an almost complete text of the King List, was published by S. Langdon, *Oxford Editions of Cuneiform Texts*. II (1923); cf. George A. Barton, *The Royal Inscriptions of Sumer and Akkad*. 1929, pp.346-355. A critical edition of the text, also making use of other tablets now available, is given by Thorkild Jacobsen, *The Sumerian King List*, AS 11, 1939. An excerpt of the King List is translated by A. Leo Oppenheim in ANET pp.265-267.

for 18,600 years. The complete outline of the antediluvian period, according to the cuneiform list, is as follows:

CITY	SOVEREIGN	LENGTH OF RULE
Eridu	Alulim	28,800 years
	Alalgar	36,000 "
Badtibira	Enmenlu-Anna	43,200 "
	Enmengal-Anna	28,800 "
	divine Dumuzi, a shepherd	36,000 "
Larak	Ensipazi-Anna	28,800 "
Sippar	Enmendur-Anna	21,000 "
Shuruppak	Ubar-Tutu	18,600 "

241,200 years

A later form of the same list has long been known from the writings of Berossos, who was a priest of Marduk at Babylon under Antiochus I (281-261 B.C.). Berossos gives the names quite differently, and a further exaggeration of the length of reigns has taken place:

Alorus	36,000 years
Alaparos	10,800 "
Amelon	46,800 "
Ammenon	43,200 "
Megalaros	64,800 "
Daonos or Daos	36,000 "
Euedorachos	64,800 "
Amempsinos	36,000 "
Otiartes	28,800 "
Xisouthros	64,800 "

432,000 years

Amelon and Ammenon may both be corruptions of the name Enmenlu-Anna, while Xisouthros, the hero of the flood, has been added, thus giving ten names in all. There may be some correspondence between this tradition of ten antediluvian kings, and the biblical record of ten patriarchs from Adam to Noah.[57] Then came the flood, apparently wiping out Shuruppak, after which sovereignty again was established from heaven, this time at Kish. The King List states:

> After the flood had swept thereover,
> when the kingship was lowered from heaven
> the kingship was in Kish.

[57] George A. Barton, *Archaeology and the Bible*, 7th ed. 1937, p.320.

After that the King List continues with the First Dynasty of Kish and with other dynasties which we shall mention later.

In addition to the brief allusion in the King List, the Sumerians had an extensive legend concerning a great flood. Like the King List, this legend also, at least in some of its versions, mentions Shuruppak as the particular city upon which the flood came. It is possible, however, that the traditions of other floods such as those at Ur and Kish may have contributed to the development of the story. An early version of this story appears on the fragment of a Sumerian tablet (Fig. 9) found at Nippur and now in the University Museum. It is inscribed on both sides, with three columns to the side.[58]

In the first column some deity is speaking who alludes to an earlier destruction of mankind and then tells how men and animals were created. A portion of this reads as follows:

> After Anu, Enlil, Enki, and Ninhursag[59]
> Had fashioned the black-headed people,
> Vegetation luxuriated from the earth,
> Animals, four-legged creatures of the plain, were
> brought artfully into existence.

The second column relates how some deity founded five cities, these being the same as the five antediluvian cities in the King List, Eridu, Badtibira, Larak, Sippar, and Shuruppak. The deity assigned each city to the special care of a guardian god, and also established irrigation canals.

The third column finds some of the deities weeping over the decision which has evidently been reached to send a deluge upon earth. At that time, it is explained, Ziusudra (the Xisouthros of Berossos' list), whose name means "Life-day prolonged," was king and priest. Other references show that Ziusudra was the son of Ubar-Tutu (the Otiartes of Berossos), and ruled in Shuruppak. In his extremity Ziusudra sought guidance from such divine revelations as might come to him through dreams or the use of incantations. In the fourth column he is told to stand beside a wall where some deity will speak to him. In the revelation which now comes to him the full plan of the gods to destroy mankind by a flood is made known:

> Ziusudra, standing at its side, listened.
> "Stand by the wall at my left side . . .

---

[58] S. N. Kramer in ANET pp.42-44 (ANEA pp.28-30); and Sumerian Mythology. 1944, pp.97f.; S. Langdon, Semitic Mythology. 1931, pp.206-208.
[59] For these deities see below, p.45.

By the wall I will say a word to thee, take my word,
Give ear to my instruction:
By our . . . a flood will sweep over the cult-centers;
To destroy the seed of mankind . . .
Is the decision, the word of the assembly of the gods.

When column five in its broken form again continues the narrative, the terrific deluge has begun, and Ziusudra is riding it out in a great boat.

All the windstorms, exceedingly powerful, attacked as one,
At the same time, the flood sweeps over the cult-centers.
After, for seven days and seven nights,
The flood had swept over the land,
And the huge boat had been tossed about by the windstorms
    on the great waters,
Utu[60] came forth, who sheds light on heaven and earth.
Ziusudra opened a window of the huge boat,
The hero Utu brought his rays into the giant boat.
Ziusudra, the king,
Prostrated himself before Utu,
The king kills an ox, slaughters a sheep.

Thus the terrible storm came to an end, and as column six closes we read how Ziusudra received the gift of immortality and was transferred to live forever in the land of Dilmun.

Ziusudra, the king,
Prostrated himself before Anu and Enlil.
Anu and Enlil cherished Ziusudra,
Life like that of a god they give him,
Breath eternal like that of a god they bring down for him.
Then, Ziusudra the king,
The preserver of the name of vegetation and of the seed of
    mankind,
In the land of crossing, the land of Dilmun, the place where
    the sun rises, they caused to dwell.[61]

Such is the essential outline of the ancient Sumerian story of the flood as preserved in the fragment from Nippur. This story was

[60] The sun-god.

[61] Interpreting the last line as meaning the mountain-land which the sun crosses immediately upon rising in the east, Kramer suggests that the land of Dilmun was in southwestern Iran (BASOR 96 [Dec. 1944], pp.18-28). P. B. Cornwall (BASOR 103 [Oct. 1946], pp.3-11) identifies Dilmun with the island of Bahrein. He believes that the Sumerians came to Mesopotamia by way of the Persian Gulf and stopped on the way at Bahrein, the only place where a sheltered harbor and good fresh water were available. This would help to explain the sacred character which Dilmun assumed in Sumerian tradition.

ultimately incorporated in the famous epic of Gilgamesh and it is here that it is found in most detailed form. Composed in Akkadian, the Semitic language of the non-Sumerian inhabitants of Mesopotamia, probably by the beginning of the second millennium B.C., the Gilgamesh epic is known chiefly from texts preserved in the library of Ashurbanipal at Nineveh in the seventh century B.C. (p. 217), although some fragments have been found elsewhere.[62]

Ziusudra appears now in the Old Babylonian translation of his name as Utnapishtim, "Day of Life." Gilgamesh, a legendary king of Uruk, has a friend named Enkidu who is his faithful companion in adventures and difficulties. Enkidu dies and Gilgamesh expresses his bewilderment in these words:

> Enkidu, my younger friend, thou who chasedst
> The wild ass of the hills, the panther of the steppe!
> We who have conquered all things, scaled the mountains . . .
> What, now, is this sleep that has laid hold on thee?

In sadness and desperation Gilgamesh then undertakes a hazardous pilgrimage across untraversed mountains and the waters of death to find Utnapishtim, the immortal, and seek from him an answer to the question of death.

> For Enkidu, his friend, Gilgamesh
> Weeps bitterly, as he ranges over the steppe:
> "When I die, shall I not be like Enkidu? . . .
> Fearing death, I roam over the steppe.
> To Utnapishtim, Ubar-Tutu's son,
> I have taken the road to proceed in all haste.

On the way he is told by Shamash,

> The life thou pursuest thou shalt not find,

and from the barmaid, Siduri, he receives advice which Ecclesiastes (9:7-9) will echo:

[62] The text of the Assyrian version was published by R. Campbell Thompson, *The Epic of Gilgamish* (1930). The translation quoted here is that by E. A. Speiser in ANET pp.72-99 (ANEA, pp.40f.). Alexander Heidel, *The Gilgamesh Epic and Old Testament Parallels* (2d ed. 1949) gives a translation and full discussion of the relationships of the Gilgamesh epic and the Old Testament. See also Langdon, *Semitic Mythology*, pp.210-223; E. A. Wallis Budge, *The Babylonian Story of the Deluge and the Epic of Gilgamesh.* 1920; R. Campbell Thompson, *The Epic of Gilgamesh, A New Translation from a Collation of the Cuneiform Tablets in the British Museum rendered literally into English Hexameters.* 1928; William E. Leonard, *Gilgamesh, Epic of Old Babylonia, A Rendering in Free Rhythms.* 1934. A cuneiform tablet containing some forty lines of the epic has recently been discovered in the debris of the excavation of Megiddo (BA 18 [1955], p.44; PEQ May-Oct. 1955, p.104).

Gilgamesh, whither rovest thou?
The life thou pursuest thou shalt not find.
When the gods created mankind,
Death for mankind they set aside,
Life in their own hands retaining.
Thou, Gilgamesh, let full be thy belly,
Make thou merry by day and by night.
Of each day make thou a feast of rejoicing,
Day and night dance thou and play!
Let thy garments be sparkling fresh,
Thy head be washed; bathe thou in water.
Pay heed to the little one that holds on to thy hand,
Let thy spouse delight in thy bosom!
For this is the task of mankind![63]

The eternal question still agitates the mind of Gilgamesh, however, and drives him forward upon his quest.

How can I be silent? How can I be still?
My friend, whom I loved, has turned to clay!
Must I too, like him, lay me down,
Not to rise again for ever and ever?

Nevertheless, as Shamash and Siduri have warned him, he is doomed to eventual failure on his mission. Even though at last he reaches and converses with Utnapishtim and at the latter's direction obtains the plant of life, it is stolen from him by a serpent and he returns disconsolate.

It is in the eleventh tablet of this long epic which occupies twelve tablets that Utnapishtim explains his possession of immortality by relating to Gilgamesh the story of the flood. Utnapishtim begins:

Shuruppak—a city which thou knowest,
And which on Euphrates' banks is situate—
That city was ancient, as were the gods within it,
When their heart led the great gods to produce the flood.

The god Ea participates in the assembly of the gods, but reveals their plans to Utnapishtim through the wall of a reed hut.

Ninigiku-Ea[64] was also present with them;
Their words he repeats to the reed-hut:
"Reed-hut, reed-hut! Wall, wall!
Reed-hut, hearken! Wall, reflect!

[63] These two passages are found in an Old Babylonian version of the epic, which may date from around the time of Hammurabi. Bruno Meissner, *Mitteilungen der vorderasiatischen Gesellschaft*. 1902, Heft 1, p.9.
[64] Ea was the same as the Sumerian Enki, god of water and of wisdom.

Man of Shuruppak, son of Ubar-Tutu,
Tear down this house, build a ship!
Give up possessions, seek thou life.
Forswear worldly goods and keep the soul alive!
Aboard the ship take thou the seed of all living things.
The ship that thou shalt build,
Her dimensions shall be to measure.
Equal shall be her width and her length."

The ark which Utnapishtim obediently constructed was a huge cube, 120 cubits or nearly 200 feet on each side. It was divided into seven stories, each containing nine rooms. Onto the ship he loaded all the silver and gold and all the living things which he had, and embarked with his family and relatives. The appointed time came. At evening a frightful storm took place and the next morning a black thunder cloud advanced from the eastern horizon, darkening the entire land. Even the gods were terrified at the deluge and cowered like dogs against the wall of heaven, or sat dejected and weeping. The climax of the flood and the final grounding of the boat on Mount Nisir[65] is described vividly:

Six days and six nights
Blows the flood wind, as the south-storm sweeps the land.
When the seventh day arrived,
    The flood-carrying south-storm subsided in the battle,
Which it had fought like an army.
The sea grew quiet, the tempest was still, the flood ceased.
I looked at the weather: stillness had set in,
And all of mankind had returned to clay.
The landscape was as level as a flat roof.
I opened a hatch, and light fell upon my face.
Bowing low, I sat and wept,
Tears running down on my face.
I looked about for coast lines in the expanse of the sea:
In each of the fourteen regions
    There emerged a region-mountain.
On Mount Nisir the ship came to a halt.
Mount Nisir held the ship fast,
    Allowing no motion.

On the seventh day Utnapishtim sent forth a dove which came back because it could find no resting place. Likewise a swallow returned, but a raven which was sent out saw that the waters were diminishing

---

[65] Mount Nisir was probably in the mountains of Kurdistan east of the Tigris, and may be identified with modern Pir Omar Gudrun (E. A. Speiser in AASOR 8 [1926-27], pp.7, 17f.).

and did not come back. On top of the mountain peak Utnapishtim offered sacrifice to the gods, who smelled the sweet savor and collected about him like flies. Enlil was angry that anyone had escaped destruction in the flood, but Ea urged that it was not right to have endeavored to destroy the righteous together with the sinful. "On the sinner impose his sin," said Ea. Enlil, persuaded, took Utnapishtim by the hand and led him from the boat. With his wife, Utnapishtim knelt before Enlil while the god blessed them:

> Hitherto Utnapishtim has been but human.
> Henceforth Utnapishtim and his wife shall be like unto us gods.
> Utnapishtim shall reside far away, at the mouth of the rivers!

Such is the ancient flood story of Babylonia which, purified of its polytheistic elements, survived among the Israelites in two sources, now woven together into a single moving story in Genesis 6:5 to 9:17.

2. THE EARLY DYNASTIC PERIOD,

c.2800-c.2360 B.C.

AFTER the mention of the flood the Sumerian King List continues with a series of dynasties which may be summarized as follows:

NAME OF DYNASTY	NUMBER OF KINGS	YEARS OF REIGN
First Dynasty of Kish	23	24,510
First Dynasty of Uruk (E-Anna)	12	2,310
First Dynasty of Ur	4	177
Dynasty of Awan	3	356
Second Dynasty of Kish	8	3,195
Dynasty of Hamazi	1?	360?
Second Dynasty of Uruk	1?	60?
Second Dynasty of Ur	4	116
Dynasty of Adab	1	90
Dynasty of Mari	6	136
Third Dynasty of Kish	1 (queen)	100
Dynasty of Akshak	6	99
Fourth Dynasty of Kish	7	491
Third Dynasty of Uruk	1	25

Whereas the King List treats these dynasties as if they succeeded one another in regular order, it is probable that in actuality some of them were contemporary dynasties which ruled at the same time in various cities. Also it may be noted that in the case of the individual cities there is a tendency to start out with reigns of legendary length and work down to reigns of actual historical length. Evidently the compiler of the King List used as sources a collection of local lists from a number of cities, in most of which the earlier periods were treated with legendary exaggeration while the later times were recorded with historical accuracy. By adding all of these lists together in an uncritical fashion the author of our King List has arrived at a total of over 30,000 years, whereas in all probability the entire period covered by these dynasties was not much more than 500 years.

Among the rulers in the First Dynasty of Kish was Etana "a shepherd, the one who to heaven ascended." A very interesting legend came to be told concerning Etana, as is attested by representations on early Sumerian seals and by fragments of Babylonian and Assyrian literature. Seeking "the plant of birth," Etana rode high into the heavens on the back of an eagle but upon reaching such a height that even the sea could no longer be distinguished grew afraid and fell back to earth. This legend was eventually transferred to Alexander the Great, who was said to have ascended by riding in a basket attached to two great and hungry birds that were attracted upward by a piece of meat held upon a spear above their heads.[1] The next dynasty is described as centering at E-Anna, which was the temple precinct of Uruk. Twelve kings are said to have reigned here for 2,310 years. Among these kings was Gilgamesh, the hero of the great epic already described.

The surmise of contemporaneity or overlapping among the dynasties of the King List is confirmed in the case of the First Dynasty of Kish and the First Dynasty of Uruk by an interesting item of evidence outside the King List. This is a Sumerian poem which may be entitled "Gilgamesh and Agga." In the King List, Agga was the last king of the First Dynasty of Kish, and Gilgamesh the fifth ruler of the First Dynasty of Uruk. In the poem, recently translated, the two rulers are contemporaries. Although the tablets containing the poem were probably only written in the first half of the second millennium B.C., and Gilgamesh and Agga probably belong in the first quarter of the third millennium B.C., the events narrated sound authentic and the later author may be believed to have used trustworthy sources.

Most interesting also is the information provided by the "Gilgamesh and Agga" poem about Sumerian political organization. Among

[1] Langdon, *Semitic Mythology*, pp.166-174.

the numerous city-states of Sumer it is evident that Kish and Uruk were strong rivals, and it seems that at this time the former had issued some kind of ultimatum to the latter. Upon receipt of the threat from Agga, Gilgamesh put the matter before the elders of his city and they advised submission to Kish. Not satisfied with this decision, Gilgamesh presented the question to the men of his city, probably meaning the men bearing arms, and they chose to fight for their independence, which pleased Gilgamesh. Since the poem explicitly mentions "the convened assembly of the elders" (line 9), and "the convened assembly of the men" (line 24), there was evidently a sort of primitive democracy in the Sumerian city-state in which the king was advised by a "congress" of two "houses."[2]

TELL ASMAR

Archeologically it is possible to divide the Early Dynastic period into three successive subdivisions. This is largely on the basis of work at Tell Asmar. This site is in the area of the Diyala River fifty miles northeast of Baghdad, and was the ancient city of Eshnunna or Ashnunnak. Beginning in 1930 and continuing for a number of years, excavations were conducted here by Henri Frankfort and others on behalf of the Oriental Institute of the University of Chicago.[3] At the same time, Khafaje, a related site twenty miles east of Baghdad, was also explored with corroborative results. The earliest settlement at Tell Asmar took place in the Jemdet Nasr period and was attested by the typical polychrome pottery of that time. Above that, the subdivision which Frankfort calls Early Dynastic I represents the transition from Jemdet Nasr to later times, and is marked by the erection of the so-called Archaic Temple. In the next subdivision, Early Dynastic II, the culture of Tell Asmar reached the high point marked by the rebuilding of the Archaic Temple into the Square Temple, and by the remarkable hoard of statues found in this temple. The almost perfect preservation of these statues is evidently

---

[2] Thorkild Jacobsen in JNES 2 (1943), pp. 165f.; Samuel N. Kramer in AJA 53 (1949), pp. 1-18; KFTS pp. 26-31; cf. Geoffrey Evans in JAOS 78 (1958), pp. 1-11.

[3] Henri Frankfort, Thorkild Jacobsen, and Conrad Preusser, *Tell Asmar and Khafaje, The First Season's Work in Eshnunna 1930/31*. OIC 13, 1932; Henri Frankfort, *Tell Asmar, Khafaje and Khorsabad, Second Preliminary Report of the Iraq Expedition*. OIC 16, 1933; *Iraq Excavations of the Oriental Institute 1932/33, Third Preliminary Report of the Iraq Expedition*. OIC 17, 1934; *Oriental Institute Discoveries in Iraq, 1933/34, Fourth Preliminary Report of the Iraq Expedition*. OIC 19, 1935; *Progress of the Work of the Oriental Institute in Iraq, 1934/35, Fifth Preliminary Report of the Iraq Expedition*. OIC 20, 1936.

due to the fact that they had been taken out of service and hidden under the floor of the Square Temple. Two of these were idols representing Abu the chief god and lord of fertility, to whom the temple was dedicated, and his wife the mother goddess (Fig. 10). The statue of Abu is about thirty inches high and the god is shown with a full black beard, while his consort wears a one-piece cloak passing under the right arm and fastened together on the shoulder. These figures are of great interest both because they are the first Sumerian cult statues known and because of their fine workmanship, the statue of Abu in particular conveying an impression of extraordinary power. Another statue, shown in Fig. 11, represents a worshiper who is holding a cup, perhaps in connection with his participation in a feast of communion at the temple. Like the others, the figure is made of gypsum, the eyes have disks of black limestone set with bitumen into eyeballs cut from shell, and the dark wavy hair and full beard are reproduced with black pitch. It is indeed interesting to have so striking and naturalistic a representation of one of "the black-headed folk," as we have seen they called themselves, the Sumerians of the early third millennium B.C.[4] The subdivision Early Dynastic III at Tell Asmar corresponds with the time of the First Dynasty of Ur, and we may turn to that site next to study the culminating phase of this entire period.

THE FIRST DYNASTY OF UR

The information in the King List now agrees with contemporary inscriptions surviving until our day. The King List reads: "Uruk was smitten with weapons; its kingship to Ur was carried. In Ur Mes-Anne-pada became king and reigned 80 years; [A-Anne-pada, son of Mes-Anne-pada reigned . . . years;] Meskiag-Nanna, son of Mes-Anne-pada, became king and reigned 36 years; Elulu reigned 25 years; Balulu reigned 36 years. 4 kings reigned its 177 years. Ur was smitten with weapons."

At Tell al-'Ubaid a tablet to the goddess Ninhursag was found, bearing the words "A-Anne-pada king of Ur, son of Mes-Anne-pada king of Ur, has built a temple for Ninhursag." This inscription not only verifies the name of Mes-Anne-pada as a ruler of Ur but also makes it possible to explain the one improbability which appears in the King List at this point, namely the ascription of the extraordi-

[4] Henri Frankfort, *Sculpture of the Third Millennium B.C. from Tell Asmar and Khafajah.* OIP XLIV, 1939.

narily long reign of eighty years to Mes-Anne-pada. It is of course not impossible that a king might inherit a throne in childhood and reign thereafter for eighty years. But Mes-Anne-pada was the founder of his dynasty which was established only by military victory over Uruk. He is not likely, therefore, to have been only a small child at the time, and the more mature a fighting man he was when he came to the throne the less apt he is to have had yet eighty years to reign. Now it appears, however, that in actuality he was followed in the kingship by a son with the very similar name of A-Anne-pada. Due no doubt to this similarity, the son's name dropped out of the King List. At the same time, the length of the son's reign probably was added to that of the father's, so that Mes-Anne-pada emerged with a reign of eighty years. The King List probably preserved correctly, therefore, the total number of years covered by the dynasty, but needs to be corrected by the addition of the name of A-Anne-pada as in brackets in the quotation just given, and by the distribution of the eighty years between the reigns of the two kings. Concerning A-Anne-pada it is of interest to note that another inscription is in existence in which he calls himself "the god A-Anne-pada."

The high culture which was achieved under the First Dynasty of Ur is shown by the famous "royal" cemetery discovered by C. Leonard Woolley at Ur. This is the burial area deep beneath which were found the evidences of the flood. Outside the walls of the primitive town which stood here after the flood, a great rubbish heap accumulated, into which the graves afterward were dug. The date of this cemetery is probably around 2500 B.C.[5]

The largest number of graves were those of common folk who were buried in rectangular pits, with the bodies wrapped in matting or put in coffins of wood, wickerwork, or clay. Often the first sign which showed the excavators that they were coming upon such a grave would be a paper-thin wavy line of white powder remaining from the edge of the reed-mat, or a few small vertical holes left in a line by the decay of the wooden staves which strengthened the sides of the coffin. Personal belongings and other items had been placed in the graves, including bracelets, necklaces, vanity cases, weapons, tools, food, and drink. The body always lay on its side, in the attitude of

[5] Woolley's date of c.3500-c.3200 B.C. (*Ur Excavations*, II, *The Royal Cemetery* [1934] p.223) was criticized by V. Müller in JAOS 55 (1935), pp.206-208; and by H. Frankfort in JRAS 1937, pp.332-341. For the chronological correlations pointing to the date given above see W. F. Albright in BASOR 88 (Dec. 1942), p.32; and in AJA 47 (1943), p.492.

one asleep, and the hands held close to the mouth a cup which probably once contained water. Thus kindly provisions were made for the dead.

The most remarkable graves were those which have become known as the "royal" tombs, although it is now believed by some scholars that they actually belonged not to royal persons but to priests and priestesses sacrificed in fertility rites.[6] The rooms and vaults of these tombs were built of brick and stone—and the stone must have been brought from at least thirty miles away in the higher desert.

In one tomb, which had already been plundered by grave-robbers, a cylinder seal remained to give the name of the deceased, A-bar-gi. Also overlooked against the wall was a silver model of a boat, which was of a type identical with that in use today on the marshes of the lower Euphrates.[7] Above this plundered vault was the untouched grave of a lady, these circumstances suggesting that those who conducted the latter burial were the ones who at the same time contrived to rob the lower tomb. The occupant of the new tomb was identified by a lapis lazuli cylinder as Lady Shub-ad, and her body lay upon the remains of a wooden bier, a gold cup near her hand. Her elaborate headdress was still in good order, and is shown in Fig. 12 upon a head copied from a Sumerian statuette. The headdress contained nine yards of gold band, and was accompanied by huge crescent-shaped earrings and a golden "Spanish comb" whose five points ended in gold flowers with lapis centers.[8]

In a great pit connecting with A-bar-gi's tomb were found the bodies of more than sixty people, while some twenty-five persons had been buried together with Lady Shub-ad. Other such "death-pits" were found, one containing the remains of as many as six men and sixty-eight women. Even chariots were driven down into these death-pits and fine treasures were placed in them. All these people and offerings have the appearance of sacrifices made in honor of the royal or sacred personage who was being buried, yet the indications are that the human victims went willingly to their deaths.

Some magnificent harps or lyres were found in these graves, decorated with heads of animals, including a bearded bull, a cow and a stag, and two statues were recovered each representing a goat

---

6 Sidney Smith in JRAS 1928, pp.862-868; Franz M. Th. Böhl in ZA Neue Folge 5 (39) 1930, pp. 83-98; H. Frankfort in *Iraq*. 1 (1934), p.12 n.3; and in JRAS 1937, pp.341f.; E. A. Speiser in *Antiquity*. 8 (1934), p.451.

7 ANEP Fig. 105.

8 For Woolley's reconstruction see *Ur Excavations*, II, pp.85f., Pl. 128.

standing up in front of a bush from which it is perhaps eating the leaves (Fig. 13).[9]

Another tomb was identified by inscriptions as belonging to "Meskalam-dug, Hero of the Good Land." The body lay in a normal way on its right side, between the hands was a bowl of heavy gold, from a broad silver belt hung a dagger of gold and over the fragments of the skull was a helmet of beaten gold. The helmet was made in the form of a wig with the locks of hair hammered up in relief and the individual hairs engraved as delicate lines. Yet other examples of the work of the goldsmiths of Ur are shown in Figs. 14-15. Their achievement approached perfection.

In the largest of the stone-built tombs was found the so-called "Standard" of Ur. This was a wooden panel twenty-two inches long by nine inches high, with triangular end pieces, inlaid with mosaic work on both sides, and probably carried on a pole in processions. The wooden background had perished entirely but the tiny pieces of inlay kept their relative positions in the soil, and skillful work made possible the accurate restoration of the mosaics.

The two main panels of the Standard (Fig. 16) illustrate War and Peace respectively, there being in each case three rows filled with figures made of shell and set in a background of lapis lazuli. In the first row of the panel depicting War, stands the king, dismounted from his chariot and distinguished by his greater height, while soldiers bring before him naked captives with arms bound behind their backs. In the second row advances the phalanx of the royal army, the men wearing long cloaks and copper helmets, and carrying axes. Ahead of them are the light-armed infantry, without cloaks, and fighting with axes or short spears. In the third row are the chariots of the javelin throwers, drawn by animals which break into an excited gallop as they encounter the corpses strewn on the ground. Thus the ancient Sumerians anticipated the chariotry which other nations adopted later and the phalanx with which Alexander the Great won his victories. On the other side of the panel, Peace is illustrated with the king and royal family sitting at a feast, entertained by musicians, while servants bring food-supplies for the banquet and spoils captured from the enemy. The people wear the old-fashioned sheepskin kilts, with the upper part of the body left bare.

[9] Woolley (Ur Excavations, II, p.266) draws an analogy with Genesis 22:13 but it is difficult to see any actual connection.

LAGASH

Another dynasty which flourished during the last phase of the Early Dynastic period was that founded about 2500 B.C. by Ur-Nanshe at Lagash (Telloh) some fifty miles north of Ur. Telloh has been excavated by French archeologists in twenty campaigns extending from 1877 to 1933.[10] Settled first in the 'Ubaid period, Lagash was only finally deserted in the second century B.C. The inscriptions of Ur-Nanshe make reference to extensive building of temples and digging of canals. His grandson, Eannatum, claims victories over Umma, Uruk, Ur, Akshak, Kish, and Mari, and was evidently, at least for a brief time, ruler of almost all Sumer. The battle of Eannatum against nearby Umma is depicted on the fragmentary Stela[11] of the Vultures, where his soldiers march in a close-packed phalanx with lances protruding from behind huge rectangular shields, and vultures bear heads and limbs away from the field of slaughter.[12]

The eighth ruler after Ur-Nanshe was Urukagina. When he assumed power, probably in the early twenty-fourth century B.C., the citizens of Lagash had fallen prey to the greed of their city officials. In a recently translated text, a contemporary historian of Lagash tells how the government inspectors seized boats, cattle, and fisheries. If a man obtained a divorce he had to pay the *ishakku*, or city governor, five shekels and the vizier one. If a perfumer made an oil preparation he paid the *ishakku* five shekels, the vizier one shekel, and the palace steward one shekel. Although the *ishakku* ruled nominally as the representative of the tutelary god of the city, Ningirsu, he had become so bold as to encroach upon the prerogatives of the priests and to appropriate the properties of the temple. "The oxen of the gods ploughed the *ishakku's* onion-patches; the onion and cucumber patches of the *ishakku* were located in the god's best fields." Even at the cemetery numerous officials extracted large contributions from the bereaved. Throughout the state, writes the historian: "There were the tax collectors." This was the situation which Urukagina undertook to correct. He removed the parasitic officials, eliminated or reduced the exactions upon the people, and stopped the exploitation of the poor by the rich. Now from one end of the land to the other: "There was no tax collector." Thus Uruk-

[10] André Parrot, *Tello, vingt campagnes de fouilles (1877-1933)*. 1948.

[11] Stela or stele is a Greek word (στήλη) meaning an erect stone and is used in archeology for an ancient monument in the form of an upright stone slab.

[12] Parrot, *Tello*, pp. 95-101; ANEP Figs. 298-302.

agina "established the freedom" of the citizens of Lagash. And thus in the oldest known document of social reform the word "freedom" appears for the first time in recorded history.[13]

LUGALZAGGISI

In spite of the commendable reforms of Urukagina, it was only a few years until Lagash fell to its long-time northern rival, the city-state of Umma and to its ambitious ruler, the *ishakku* Lugalzaggisi. A chronicler who may be the same as the author of the reform document just cited, describes the plundering of Lagash and declares that it was not the sin of Urukagina which led to this disaster but the sin of Lugalzaggisi and of his personal deity, Nidaba, goddess of writing and wisdom.[14] In spite of this condemnation, Lugalzaggisi continued his rise in power, ultimately becoming king also of Uruk and Ur, and one of the most important figures in Sumerian history. His twenty-five-year reign constituted, according to the King List, the Third Dynasty of Uruk.

The extent of the dominion which he achieved is indicated in the following triumphal inscription from Nippur, in which Lugalzaggisi prayed Enlil, the wind-god, for the permanence of his reign:

"When Enlil king of the countries had granted to Lugalzaggisi the kingship of the land; had turned the eyes of the land toward him; had prostrated the countries at his feet: then did he make straight his path for him, from the Lower Sea, by Tigris and Euphrates, to the Upper Sea. From East to West Enlil nowhere allowed him a rival. Lugalzaggisi gave the countries to rest in peace; watered the land with water of joy. . . . Then made he Uruk to shine in sheen of countenance; skyward, like a bull's, upraised the head of Ur; Larsa, dear city of the sun-god, watered with waters of joy; nobly exalted Umma, dear city of Shara. . . . May Enlil king of the countries prefer my prayer before his dear father An. May he add life to my life; cause the country to rest at peace with me. Folk as numerous as scented herbs may he bestow on me with open hand; guide for me the flock of An;[15] look benevolently for me upon the land. Let the gods not change the good destiny that they have assigned to me. Shepherd, leader let me be forever!"[16]

The reference to the Upper Sea indicates that the armies of Lugal-

[13] Samuel N. Kramer in IEJ 3 (1953), pp.227-232; in *Archaeology*. 7 (1954), pp.145f.; KFTS pp.40-46. cf. W. v. Soden, *Herrscher im alten Orient*. 1954, pp.8-15.
[14] Kramer in IEJ 3 (1953), p.232 n.45.
[15] i.e. mankind.
[16] Patrick Carleton, *Buried Empires, The Earliest Civilizations of the Middle East*. 1939, p.118.

zaggisi marched as far west as the shores of the Mediterranean. ، great had become the outreach of Sumerian power.

Extensive as it was at this time, the Sumerian kingdom was not permanent, and the more lasting contributions of this ancient people were in their literature and thought. Quotations have already been made from some of this literature which, as it is now known, was very extensive and included myths, epics, legends, law, historiography, hymns, proverbs, and letters. In form the Sumerian poetry, like that of the Old Testament, often exhibits the feature of parallelism, and the proverbs, like those of the Bible, are often couplets characterized by the synonymous or antithetical meaning of the two lines.[17] In its content the literature does not provide a systematic philosophy or theology, but it may be gathered that the Sumerians believed in a flat earth and a vaulted heaven above, this whole heaven-earth being surrounded by a boundless sea. In control of this universe was a pantheon of anthropomorphic but invisible and immortal beings who functioned as an assembly much like the earthly political "congress" we have already mentioned (p. 38). Of the hundreds of deities the most important were An or Anu, the heaven-god, whose main center of worship was Uruk; Enlil, the air-god, a beneficent, fatherly deity with a great temple in Nippur;[18] Enki, the water-god and god of wisdom; and Ninhursag, the mother-goddess. Other members of the pantheon were Nanna or Sin, the moon-god and son of Enlil; Utu, the sun-god, and Inanna, the queen of heaven, both the children of the moon-god. When the creating deities made the universe and ordered its affairs they did so simply by the utterance of their command. Thus the Sumerian thinkers enunciated the doctrine of the creative power of the divine word, a doctrine which was widely accepted thereafter throughout the Middle East.[19]

[17] Samuel N. Kramer in BASOR 122 (Apr. 1951), p.29. For Sumerian proverbs see Edmund I. Gordon, *Sumerian Proverbs, Glimpses of Everyday Life in Ancient Mesopotamia* (to be published); and in JAOS 77 (1957), pp.67-79; JCS 12 (1958), pp.1-21, 43-75.

[18] For the excavation of this temple see Donald McCown in UMB 16 (1951), pp.7-13.

[19] KFTS pp.71-96. On the thought world of the ancient Middle East in general see H. and H. A. Frankfort, John A. Wilson, Thorkild Jacobsen, and William A. Irwin, *The Intellectual Adventure of Ancient Man.* 1946.

3. THE OLD AKKADIAN PERIOD,
c.2360-c.2180 B.C.

strength of the Semitic peoples in Mesopotamia was
were distinguished from the Sumerians by their
_ge which belonged to the great Semitic family of languages.
The Akkadian, Assyrian, and Babylonian dialects constitute the
older East Semitic branch of this family, while Hebrew, Aramaic,
Phoenician, Syriac, Arabic, and Ethiopic are included in the West
Semitic.

Semitic names had been appearing for some time in the King List.
In the First Dynasty of Kish several of the names were definitely
Semitic while the Third Dynasty of Kish consisted of a single ruler
"Ku-Baba, a barmaid," whose own name was Sumerian but who be-
stowed a Semitic name upon her son, Puzur-Sin. The later kings of
the Dynasty of Akshak and all the kings of the Fourth Dynasty of
Kish bore Semitic names, and excavations both at Mari and at Nuzi
show that there were lines of Semitic kings at those places.

In civilization, however, the Old Akkadian period was a continuation of the Sumerian. Indeed on through Babylonian and Assyrian
times it is possible to speak simply of Mesopotamian civilization for,
in spite of differences in language or political control, fundamental
ideas such as those of government and law remain much the same
and provide strongly unifying factors.[1]

SARGON

With Sargon a dynasty of Semitic-speaking kings attained supremacy in all Lower Mesopotamia. This man was of lowly origin.
An inscription makes him say:

> Sargon, the mighty king, king of Agade, am I.
> My mother was a changeling, my father I knew not.
> The brothers of my father loved the hills.
> My city is Azupiranu, which is situated on the banks of the
> Euphrates.
> My changeling mother conceived me, in secret she bore me.
> She set me in a basket of rushes, with bitumen she sealed
> my lid.
> She cast me into the river which rose not over me.

[1] Thorkild Jacobsen in JAOS 59 (1939), pp.485-495; E. A. Speiser in JAOS Supplement 17 (1954), p.14.

The river bore me up and carried me to Akki, the drawer
of water.

Akki, the drawer of water lifted me out as he dipped his
ewer.

Akki, the drawer of water, took me as his son and reared
me.[2]

The story of the baby in the basket of rushes reminds one of the
similar story concerning Moses.

As the text just quoted states, Sargon ruled in the city of Agade or
Akkad. From it the narrow northern plain of Lower Mesopotamia
was also known as Akkad and its Semitic peoples were designated
as Akkadians. Sargon was able to overthrow the powerful Lugalzaggisi and conquer the entire region of Lower Mesopotamia. At
Ur he installed his own daughter as high-priestess of the moon-god
Nannar, the Sumerian Nanna or Sin. A historical inscription of
Sargon describes the victory over Lugalzaggisi in these words: "Sargon, king of Agade . . . defeated Uruk and tore down its wall; in the
battle with the inhabitants of Uruk he was victorious. Lugalzaggisi,
king of Uruk, he captured in this battle, he brought him in a dog
collar to the gate of Enlil."[3]

Eventually the dominion of Sargon was extended on eastward into
Elam and westward as far as Syria and the Mediterranean. An inscription of his gives recognition to "the god Dagan," the chief god
of the Semites of northern Syria, for the Syrian coast lands which
that deity gave him.[4] Thus Sargon became the most powerful monarch who had ever ruled in Mesopotamia.

A small but important city of the Old Akkadian period was Gasur,
the site of which is known now as Yorgan Tepa and is a dozen miles
southwest of modern Kirkuk. Excavations at this place have been
conducted through the cooperation of a number of institutions including the American School of Oriental Research at Baghdad, the
Iraq Museum, Harvard University, and the University Museum of the
University of Pennsylvania.[5] In the time of which we are speaking
the population of Gasur was overwhelmingly Semitic, but later the
city became an important center of the Hurrians at which time it

---

[2] E. A. Speiser in ANET p.119 (ANEA p.85); Hugo Gressmann, *Altorientalische
Texte und Bilder zum Alten Testament.* 1909, I, p.79.

[3] A. Leo Oppenheim in ANET p.267.   [4] ANET p.268.

[5] Richard F. S. Starr, *Nuzi, Report on the Excavations at Yorgan Tepa near Kirkuk,
Iraq, conducted by Harvard University in conjunction with the American Schools of
Oriental Research and the University Museum of Philadelphia 1927-1931.* 2 vols,
1937-39.

was known as Nuzi.[6] Many tablets have been found here which date from the Old Akkadian period and reveal the prosperity and extensive business activity of those days. Among the business records was an inscribed clay map, prepared perhaps to indicate the location of some estate, and ranking now as the oldest map ever discovered.[7] Other tablets show that buying and selling on the installment plan were practiced, and indicate that the commercial dealings of this one community extended over a very considerable portion of the far-flung empire of Sargon.[8]

The development of art in this period was notable and reached its climax under Sargon's grandson, the great ruler Naram-Sin, whose full title was, "The divine Naram-Sin, the mighty, god of Agade, king of the Four Quarters." His Victory Stela (Fig. 17), discovered by de Morgan at Susa and now in the Louvre at Paris, "is the most impressive and beautiful work of early western Asiatic art which we possess."[9] It celebrates his victorious campaign against the mountain-dwelling Lullubians. The scene is the wooded foothills of a mountain whose conical peak rises to the stars. The king's light-armed soldiers advance up the slope, carrying lances and standards. High in the hill above, from which the bodies of the slain are plunging, the king climbs inexorably upward. He is colossal in size, wearing the horned helmet of a god, and carrying war-axe and bow and arrow. His enemies fall beneath his feet, one with throat transfixed by an arrow. Yet another lifts his hands to beg for his life.

4. THE GUTIAN PERIOD, c.2180-c.2070 B.C.

But Naram-Sin's great empire, stretching from central Persia to the Mediterranean and from northeastern Arabia to the Taurus Mountains, lasted only through the reign of his son Shargalisharri. Thereafter the Gutians, a little-known Caucasian people from the eastern mountain country of Gutium overran Lower Mesopotamia.

[6] For the spelling of the name see E. A. Speiser in JAOS 75 (1955), pp.52-55.
[7] For a city map of Nippur made about 1500 B.C. see KFTS pp.271-275.
[8] Starr, *Nuzi*. I (1939), p.23; T. J. Meek, *Old Akkadian, Sumerian, and Cappadocian Texts from Nuzi* (Harvard Semitic Series, 10, 1935), p.xv.
[9] Heinrich Schäfer and Walter Andrae, *Die Kunst des alten Orients*. 1925, p.493.

5. THE NEO-SUMERIAN PERIOD, c.2070-c.1960 B.C.

GUDEA

In the years when the power of the Gutians was declining, a remarkable Sumerian ruled as governor at Lagash and prepared the way for a renaissance of Sumerian power and culture. His name was Gudea and numerous statues have been found of him, one of which is shown in Fig. 18. Gudea is represented as wearing a turban in the fashion which became very popular in those days, and his face is clean-shaven, grave, and kindly.[1]

With true piety Gudea endeavored to be the shepherd of his people and the servant of the gods. Beseeching divine guidance, he prayed in the temple, "I have no mother; my pure mother thou art. I have no father; thou art my pure father." Through a dream it was revealed to him that he should restore Eninnu, "the House of Fifty [gods]," a Lagash temple first mentioned as early as the end of the Jemdet Nasr period.[2] "In the dream a man that shone like the heaven and was joyful like the earth—from the crown of his head he was a god; by his side was the divine black storm-bird as a companion; below and before him was a storm; on his right and left, lions were standing; he commanded to build his house; his meaning I did not understand." There also appeared in this dream a warrior who held a tablet of lapis lazuli in his hand which contained the plan of a temple. Eventually the goddess Nina made it clear to Gudea that the man at whose side was the storm-bird was the god Ningirsu who wished to command Gudea to build his temple Eninnu, and the warrior with the tablet in his hand was the god Nindub who was bringing the plan for the temple.

So Gudea proceeded at once to the task, himself laying the first brick. The work was very extensive, and Gudea's account mentions the bringing of cedar wood all the way from the Amanus Mountains in northern Syria,[3] a part of the same general range as the Lebanon from which Solomon was to cut cedar trees for the temple at Jerusalem (I Kings 5:6). At last the work was finished. "The holy temple rising from earth to heaven . . . shone in the brilliance of heaven with radiant light. . . . It illumined the country."[4]

---

[1] cf. Gaston Cros, *Nouvelles fouilles de Tello.* II (1911), Pl. I; Simon Harcourt-Smith, *Babylonian Art.* 1928, p.19.

[2] Carleton, *Buried Empires*, p.63.

[3] ANET pp.268f.

[4] Barton, *Royal Inscriptions of Sumer and Akkad*, pp.206-235.

THE THIRD DYNASTY OF UR

With the final downfall of the Gutians, the great Third Dynasty of Ur arose in splendor. Its first king was Ur-Nammu who took the new title "King of Sumer and Akkad," and whose mightiest work was the erection of a great ziggurat at Ur. The ziggurat which stood at Babylon in the days of Hammurabi and was known as Etemenanki, "the House of the Terrace-platform of Heaven and Earth,"[5] became more famous and was remembered in biblical tradition as the Tower of Babel, but the ziggurat at Ur is today the best preserved of all monuments of this type and therefore the best fitted to give a vivid impression of their character (Fig. 19).

As long ago as 1854, J. E. Taylor visited Ur (then only a ruined site known by the Arabs as al-Muqayyar, the Mound of Bitumen) and dug down into the corners of the great pile which dominated it. He found cuneiform cylinders of Nabonidus of Babylon (556-539 B.C.), stating that Nabonidus had there restored the ziggurat of Ur, begun by Ur-Nammu. The text reads: "Nabonidus king of Babylon . . . am I. E-lugal-malga-sidi, the ziggurat of E-gish-shir-gal in Ur, which Ur-Nammu, a king before me, had built but not completed, did Shulgi[6] his son finish. On the inscription of Ur-Nammu and of his son Shulgi saw I that Ur-Nammu had built but not completed that ziggurat and that Shulgi his son had finished the work. Now was that ziggurat old. Upon the ancient foundations whereon Ur-Nammu and his son Shulgi had built I made good the structure of that ziggurat, as in old times, with mortar and burnt brick. . . ."[7] Then Nabonidus concluded with a dedication to Nannar, lord of the gods of heaven and earth, and a prayer for the life of himself and of his son Belshazzar.

In 1918 Dr. H. R. Hall cleared part of one end of the mound but the complete excavation requiring the removal of thousands of tons of rubbish was first undertaken by C. L. Woolley in 1922-1923.[8] Ur-Nammu's structure probably was built on top of a smaller ziggurat which may have been as old as the time of Mes-Anne-pada. In its upper part the great artificial mountain clearly was the work of Nabonidus. The bulk of the construction, however, had been carried out by Ur-Nammu himself and his name and title were found

[5] W. F. Albright in AJA 48 (1944), p.305.
[6] The reading of the name, formerly given as Dungi, is uncertain. Thorkild Jacobsen in BASOR 102 (Apr. 1946), pp.16f.
[7] C. L. Woolley, *Abraham, Recent Discoveries and Hebrew Origins.* 1936, p.62.
[8] *Ur Excavations,* V, *The Ziggurat and Its Surroundings.* 1939.

stamped on the bricks. The tower was a solid mass of brickwork, 200 feet long, 150 feet wide, and some 70 feet high. The core was of un-baked brick, with a facing about eight feet thick of baked brick set in bitumen. The whole design was a masterpiece, the lines of the walls all being built on calculated curves to give the appearance of light-ness and strength, a principle used much later by the Greeks. Orig-inally the shrine of Nanna or Nannar, the moon-god, stood on the topmost stage and it is possible that the various terraces were covered with soil and irrigated so that the green of growing plants beautified the whole.[9]

Interestingly enough, we possess a contemporary record of the building of this ziggurat in the Stela of Ur-Nammu, a slab of white limestone nearly five feet across and ten feet high, recovered unfortu-nately only in fragments (Fig. 20). At the top the king stands in the attitude of prayer while from above come flying angels with vases out of which flow the streams of life. An inscription elsewhere enum-erates the canals dug by Ur-Nammu, and here he thanks the gods for the gift of life-bringing water. This is the earliest known represen-tation of an angel in art.[10] At least three panels of the stela are de-voted to the building of the ziggurat. In the first of these Ur-Nammu stands at the left in front of the goddess Ningal and again at the right before the god Nanna, receiving the command to build him a house. In the next panel the king is setting forth, bearing on his shoulder the tools of the architect and builder, compasses, mortar-basket, pick, and trowel, while in the third panel little remains but one of the ladders of the workmen which leaned against the side of the rising structure.

In the course of time other buildings were erected around the ziggurat, so that the entire sacred area was very extensive. One of these was the square temple known as the Gig-par-ku, which was dedicated to Ningal, the moon-goddess and wife of Nanna. The kitchen was an important part of the temple, since worship was by sacrifice and the cooked flesh of the sacrificial animal was shared among the god, the priests, and the worshipers. The temple in the Gig-par-ku was equipped with a well for water, fireplaces for boiling the water, a bitumen-covered brick table on which the carcass of the

[9] cf. Th. A. Busink, *Sumerische en Babylonische Tempelbouw*. 1940, p.69. For the use of bitumen in antiquity see R. J. Forbes, *Studies in Ancient Technology*, I, (1955), pp.1-120.
[10] C. L. Woolley, *The Development of Sumerian Art*. 1935, p.112.

victim was cut up, a flat-topped cooking range, and a domed bread oven.

Much business took place within the sacred area. As sacrifices, tithes and taxes were brought in, a receipt was given to each man. The temple scribe then made a notation for himself on a small clay tablet, and eventually these memoranda were incorporated in weekly, monthly, and yearly reports. Large numbers of such business tablets and ledgers have been found. Factories and workshops also were to be found there. One such establishment at Ur was a weaving factory which produced twelve sorts of woolen cloth. Tablets still give the names of the women weavers, the amount of rations allotted to them, the quantity of wool issued to each, and the amount of cloth manufactured. The temple area was also the home of the law court. Dublal-mah or "Great House of Tablets" was the name of the building at Ur from whose doorway the judges announced their findings and in whose store chambers the clay documents recording their decisions were kept.

In the ruins of Ur at about this time there are some twenty houses per acre. Assuming six to ten persons per house, there were 120 to 200 people per acre, the average figure of 160 being exactly the same as the population density in modern Damascus. Ur covered 150 acres, and it may therefore be estimated that the population was approximately 24,000 inhabitants.[11]

Recently a law code promulgated by Ur-Nammu has been found among the Sumerian texts in the Museum of the Ancient Orient at Istanbul. Dating as it does some three hundred years before Hammurabi, this is at present the oldest code of laws known. The text states that Ur-Nammu was selected by the god Nanna to rule over Ur and Sumer as his earthly representative. It tells how the king removed the dishonest "grabbers" of the livestock of the citizens, and established honest weights and measures. The king was concerned that "the orphan did not fall a prey to the wealthy," "the widow did not fall a prey to the powerful," and "the man of one shekel did not fall a prey to the man of one mina."[12] Of the actual laws which the code contained, only a few can now be restored and read, but they include statements of fines to be imposed upon the man who has caused certain injuries to another.[13]

[11] Henri Frankfort, *Kingship and the Gods, A Study of Ancient Near Eastern Religion as the Integration of Society and Nature.* An Oriental Institute Essay. 1948, p.396 n.23.

[12] 1 mina = 60 shekels.

[13] Samuel N. Kramer in *Archaeology.* 7 (1954), pp.143f.; KFTS pp.48-51. For

Ur-Nammu was succeeded by his son Shulgi, to whom Nabonidus referred as the completer of the ziggurat. Figurines of both Ur-Nammu and Shulgi have recently been discovered in foundation boxes unearthed at Nippur.[14] The latter ruler proclaimed himself "the divine Shulgi, god of his land," and his greatest monument was his own mortuary temple and sepulcher. Extant texts from several sites show that both within his own lifetime and afterward he was honored as a god with temples and offerings.[15] He was succeeded by his son Bur-Sin who was followed in turn by Gimil-Sin and then by Ibi-Sin.

6. THE ISIN-LARSA PERIOD,

c.1960-c.1830 B.C.

It was in the days of Ibi-Sin that disaster came upon the Sumerians. The Elamites stormed down out of the hills, took Ibi-Sin captive and sacked the capital city of Ur. A later poet wrote in lamentation:

> O my city attacked and destroyed, my city attacked without cause,
> Behold the storm ordered in hate—its violence has not abated;
> O my house of Sin in Ur, bitter is thy destruction.[1]

Among the leaders of the invading Amorites were Ishbi-Irra from Mari, and Naplanum. These two settled respectively at Isin and Larsa. An Elamite ruler, Kirikiri, was established at Eshnunna.

Beginning with Ishbi-Irra, a series of sixteen kings held the throne of Isin for 225 years, or until Isin was conquered by Rim-Sin of Larsa in the year after Hammurabi became king of Babylon.[2] As will be shown later, the accession date of Hammurabi was probably about 1728 B.C., and thus the rule of Ishbi-Irra must have begun around 1952 B.C. After a thirty-three year reign, Ishbi-Irra was succeeded by Shu-ilishu who was on the throne for ten years, beginning about 1919 B.C. Contemporary with the latter was an early successor of Kirikiri at Eshnunna, namely Bilalama.

An important code of laws has recently been discovered which

Sumero-Akkadian law see now Adam Falkenstein, *Die neusumerischen Gerichtsurkunden*. 3 vols. 1956-57; cf. Edmond Sollberger in jcs 12 (1958), pp.105-107.

[14] Richard C. Haines in *Sumer*. 11 (1955), pp.107-109.

[15] T. Fish in bjrl 11 (1927).

[1] S. N. Kramer in anet p. 461; *Lamentation Over the Destruction of Ur*. as 12, 1940, p.57.

[2] F. R. Kraus in jcs 3 (1949), pp.13f., 26f.; Francis R. Steele in aja 52 (1948), p.430.

may have been composed by the last-named king.[3] Written in the Akkadian language, the laws are recorded in two copies on two tablets which were excavated at Tell Abu Harmal near Baghdad by the Iraq Directorate of Antiquities and placed in the Iraq Museum. Tell Abu Harmal covers the ruins of a rural town which was a part of the kingdom of Eshnunna, and these are the laws of that kingdom.

The preamble of the code is very badly preserved but contains the statement that Tishpak, the chief god of Eshnunna, bestowed upon some ruler "the kingship over Eshnunna." Upon preliminary study it was thought that the name of king Bilalama was given at this point, but it is now recognized that the name of the king to whom reference is made is lost in a gap in the text, nevertheless it is still held that the code was composed at about the time of Bilalama and perhaps by that very king himself.[4]

The code itself extends through some sixty paragraphs of law, and then breaks off. The subjects on which legislation is enunciated include the price of commodities, the hire of wagons and boats, the wages of laborers, marriage, divorce and adultery, assault and battery, and the matter of responsibility for an ox which gores a man and a mad dog which bites a man. Typical form and sample subject matter of the laws may be seen in these two examples: "If the boatman is negligent and causes the sinking of the boat, he shall pay in full for everything the sinking of which he caused" (§5); "If an ox is known to gore habitually and the ward authorities have had the fact made known to its owner, but he does not have his ox dehorned, it gores a man and causes his death, then the owner of the ox shall pay two-thirds of a mina of silver" (§54).

Returning to Isin, the fifth king at that city was Lipit-Ishtar, who reigned for eleven years beginning about 1868 B.C. A code of laws which he promulgated has also recently become known.[5] Most of the tablets containing this code were excavated at Nippur by the University of Pennsylvania and are now in the University Museum. Although he was king of an Amorite dynasty, Lipit-Ishtar wrote his law code in the Sumerian language and probably derived many of

[3] Albrecht Goetze in *Sumer.* 4 (1948), pp.63-102; ANET pp.161-163 (ANEA pp.133f.); AASOR 31 (1951-52).

[4] Goetze in AASOR 31 (1951-52), p.20 n.18, p.22 n.24.

[5] Francis R. Steele in AJA 52 (1948), pp.425-450; and in *Archiv Orientální, Journal of the Czechoslovak Oriental Institute, Prague.* XVIII, No.1-2 (1950), pp.489-493; S. N. Kramer in ANET pp.159-161.

the laws from a Sumerian heritage running back to Ur-Nammu or earlier.

The laws of Lipit-Ishtar begin with a prologue in which the king states that Anu and Enlil, the leading Sumerian-Akkadian deities, had called him to the princeship of the land, and that in accordance with the word of Enlil he had established justice in Sumer and Akkad. The legal text proper, of which much less than half is preserved, contains some thirty-eight regulations. These deal with such subjects as boat hire, real estate, slaves, tax defaults, inheritance and marriage, and rented oxen. Typical form and sample subject matter of the laws may be seen in these two examples: "If a man cut down a tree in the garden of another man, he shall pay one-half mina of silver" (§10); "If a man rented an ox and damaged its eye, he shall pay one half of its price" (§35). In an epilogue Lipit-Ishtar refers to the fact that he "erected this stela," evidently that on which the code was originally inscribed, and calls down a blessing on those who do not damage it, and a curse on those who do.

The laws of Ur-Nammu, Eshnunna, and Lipit-Ishtar are the earliest such codes now known. Dating well before the famous Code of Hammurabi, they show the sort of materials which were drawn upon in the compilation of that later system of laws.

7. THE OLD BABYLONIAN PERIOD,
c.1830-c.1550 B.C.

No doubt it was the rivalry of the several city-states which now existed in lower Mesopotamia which made it possible for a little-known man with an Amorite name, Sumu-abu, to become master of an unimportant Akkadian city nine miles west of Kish and carve out a small kingdom for himself in that neighborhood. The name of the city was Bab-ilu or Babylon, and Sumu-abu became the founder of the First Dynasty of Babylon.

THE FIRST DYNASTY OF BABYLON

The struggles among the various city-states were long and complex, but eventually Babylon and Larsa faced each other as the two chief powers in lower Mesopotamia. At Larsa an Elamite, Kudur-Mabug, had placed his son Warad-Sin on the throne and he in turn was followed by his younger brother, Rim-Sin. At Babylon Sumu-abu had been followed by Sumu-la-el, Sabum, Apil-Sin, and Sin-muballit. Then Hammurabi came to the throne. When war broke out between Rim-Sin and Hammurabi the outstanding military genius of the latter soon became evident. Rim-Sin and his allies were defeated and Sumer passed into the hands of Hammurabi, Larsa becoming his southern administrative capital. Isin had been captured earlier and Eshnunna soon fell.[1] Mari, the city from which Ishbi-Irra had come, remained as a powerful rival on the northern frontier, athwart the route to the Mediterranean. In the thirty-second year of his reign Hammurabi conquered and partially destroyed this city, too, returning a very few years later to make the destruction complete. Thus was established in full power the Old Babylonian Kingdom.

MARI

Mari is of such importance historically and archeologically that a further word must be said about it at this point. The ancient city was on the Middle Euphrates and is represented today by Tell Hariri six or seven miles north of Abou Kemal. Excavations have been conducted there since 1933 by the *Musée du Louvre* under the leadership of André Parrot.[2] It is revealed that in the third millennium B.C. Mari was one of the most flourishing and brilliant cities of the Mesopotamian world. Among its public edifices were a temple of Ishtar and a ziggurat. Statuettes representing humble worshipers and dedicated to the goddess were found in the temple, and give a vivid picture of the devotion with which Ishtar was regarded. Near the ziggurat another very interesting small statue was found and is shown in Fig. 21. It represents a worshiper carrying in honor in his arms a kid which is doubtless intended for a sacrificial offering.

Most notable of all the buildings in Mari was the palace of the king. This was a tremendous structure covering more than fifteen acres. It contained not only the royal apartments but also admin-

[1] H. Frankfort, T. Jacobsen and Conrad Preusser, *Tell Asmar and Khafaje, The First Season's Work in Eshnunna 1930/31.* OIC 13, 1932, pp.38,41.

[2] A. Parrot in *Syria, Revue d'Art orientale et d'archéologie.* 16 (1935), pp.1-28, 117-140; 17 (1936), pp.1-31; 18 (1937), pp.54-84; 19 (1938), pp.1-29; 20 (1939), pp.1-22; etc.; *Mari, une ville perdu.* 1935; George E. Mendenhall in BA 11 (1948), pp.1-19; A. Parrot, ed., *Studia Mariana.* 1950 (with bibliography to 1949); *Archives royales de Mari*: I, Georges Dossin, *Correspondance de Samši-Addu et de ses fils.* 1950; II, Charles-F. Jean, *Lettres diverses.* 1950; III, J.-R. Kupper, *Correspondance de Kibri-Dagan gouverneur de Tirqa.* 1950; Charles-F. Jean, *Six campagnes de fouilles à Mari, 1933-1939.* 1952; A. Leo Oppenheim in JNES 11 (1952), pp.129-139; A. Parrot, *Mari, documentation photographique de la mission archéologique de Mari.* 1953.

istrative offices and even a school for scribes. Furthermore it was adorned with great mural paintings, portions of which are still preserved. Among these were scenes of sacrifice, and a representation of the king of Mari receiving from Ishtar the staff and ring which were the emblems of his authority.[3] The palace bore the marks of two destructions which had been visited upon it in close succession, evidently corresponding to the two times when Mari fell to Hammurabi.

From the archives of the palace over 20,000 tablets were recovered, constituting a discovery of the greatest importance. A large number of these tablets represent diplomatic correspondence of the last king of Mari, Zimri-Lim, with his ambassadors and agents and with Hammurabi, king of Babylon, himself. Others date from the time of the predecessors of Zimri-Lim. The dynasty of kings ruling at Mari, it is now learned, had been dispossessed temporarily when Shamshi-Adad I of Assyria (p. 200) sent his son Yasmah-Adad to exercise power at Mari. Later Yasmah-Adad had to give way to Zimri-Lim, who was the legitimate heir to the throne. Zimri-Lim then ruled until Mari fell to Hammurabi in the thirty-second year of the latter's reign.[4] The proof given by the Mari documents that Hammurabi was a contemporary of Shamshi-Adad I casts important light on the long-discussed problem of the date of Hammurabi. From the Khorsabad list of Assyrian kings (p. 200 n.5), Shamshi-Adad I can be dated around 1748-1716 B.C. and a detailed examination of the intricate interrelationships leads to fixing the date of Hammurabi at around 1728-1686 B.C.[5]

[3] Parrot in *Syria*. 18 (1937), pp.325-354.
[4] Parrot, *Mari, une ville perdu*, 1935, pp.235f.
[5] François Thureau-Dangin in RAAO 36 (1939), pp.24f.; W. F. Albright in BASOR 88 (Dec. 1942), pp.28-36; and in AJA 47 (1943), p.492. The date given above for Shamshi-Adad I is that proposed by Albright and differs slightly from that at which A. Poebel arrived, namely 1726-1694 B.C. (JNES 1 [1942], p.285). Friedrich Schmidtke (*Der Aufbau der babylonischen Chronologie* [1952], p.46) puts Shamshi-Adad I at 1753-1721 B.C. and Hammurabi at 1730-1688 B.C. See also F. M. Th. Böhl, *King Hammurabi of Babylon in the Setting of His Time (About 1700 B.C.)*. Mededeelingen der Koninklijke Nederlandsche Akademie van Wetenschappen, Afd. Letterkunde, Nieuwe Reeks, Deel 9, No. 10. 1946; M. B. Rowton in JNES 10 (1951), pp.184-204. Further confirmation of the so-called "low" date for Hammurabi has come from the radiocarbon test. In 1950 Donald E. McCown excavated the roof beam of a house at Nippur which, as shown by dated tablets, was built not later than the third year of Ibi-Sin. The radiocarbon date for this beam was 1993 B.C., plus or minus 106 years. Since Ibi-Sin lived about 250 years before Hammurabi, the result is strikingly close to the date given above for Hammurabi. See W. F. Libby in *Science*. 119, No.3083 (Jan. 1954), pp.135f. For arguments for a "high" date around 1900 B.C. see Benno Landsberger in JCS 8 (1954), pp.119f. According to the Mari texts Hammurabi was also a

THE CODE OF HAMMURABI

Hammurabi was not only a great military commander but also an outstanding administrator and law-giver. Relatively little remains today of the Babylon of his time, since the city was reconstructed almost entirely in the sixth century B.C. by Nabopolassar and Nebuchadnezzar, but in one quarter some dwelling houses from Hammurabi's day have been unearthed. The distinctive thing here is the new and planned way in which the streets are laid out in regular straight lines which intersect approximately at right angles. Many letters written by Hammurabi have also been found, revealing his close attention to all the details of his realm and illustrating the terse clarity with which he issued his instructions. But his greatest achievement was represented by his code of laws.[6]

Hammurabi named the second year of his reign the "year when he established justice," and eventually he set forth a compilation and codification of laws which continued in force in Babylonia for a thousand years. In 1901 a copy of this code was found by de Morgan at Susa where it had been carried off by the Elamites. The code was inscribed on a round-topped stela of black diorite, some six feet in height, which now is in the Louvre. At the top is a bas-relief (Fig. 23) showing Hammurabi standing before the enthroned sun-god Shamash, the patron of law and justice. The god wears a pointed headdress with horns, rays are to be seen upon his shoulders, and he holds a ring and staff, the insignia of royalty, in his right hand. Hammurabi, who stands before him to receive his kingly law-giving power,[7] wears a long robe with right arm and shoulder bare, and is shown with beard and clean-shaven upper lip.

---

contemporary of Yarim-Lim of Alalakh. For the excavation of this site and discussion of its chronology see Leonard Woolley, *Alalakh, An Account of the Excavations at Tell Atchana in the Hatay, 1937-1949.* 1955 (for Yarim-Lim see pp.91, 384, 389); see also articles by Albrecht Goetze and W. F. Albright in BASOR 146 (Apr. 1957), pp.20-26, 26-34; and Albrecht Goetze in JCS 11 (1957), pp.53-61, 63-73. The latest stratigraphic correlations by W. F. Albright (in BASOR 144 [Dec. 1956], pp.26-30) reaffirm an accession date for Hammurabi between c.1750 and c.1700. M. B. Rowton, however, distinguishes for the first regnal year of Hammurabi an ultra-high date c.1900, a high date in 1848, a middle date in 1792, and a low date in 1728, and himself now (in JNES 17 [1958], pp.97-111) favors the middle chronology with the reign of Hammurabi assigned to 1792-1750. For the low date see most recently F. Cornelius in JCS 12 (1958), pp.101-104.

[6] Robert F. Harper, *The Code of Hammurabi King of Babylon about 2250 B.C.* 1904; W. W. Davies, *The Codes of Hammurabi and Moses.* 1905; Albrecht Goetze in JAOS 69 (1949), pp.115-120; Theophile J. Meek in ANET pp.163-180 (ANEA pp.138f.); G. R. Driver and John C. Miles, *The Babylonian Laws.* 2 vols. 1952-55.

[7] T. Fish in E. I. J. Rosenthal, ed., *Judaism and Christianity.* III (1938), p.43.

Beneath, were carved fifty-one columns of text, most of which are still preserved, written in the Akkadian language in beautiful cuneiform characters. In a lengthy prologue it is stated that the gods "named me to promote the welfare of the people, me, Hammurabi, the devout, god-fearing prince, to cause justice to prevail in the land, to destroy the wicked and the evil, that the strong might not oppress the weak, to rise like the sun over the black-headed people,[8] and to light up the land." The prologue concludes: "When Marduk[9] commissioned me to guide the people aright, to direct the land, I established law and justice in the language of the land, thereby promoting the welfare of the people." A long epilogue reaffirms Hammurabi's desire "that the strong might not oppress the weak, that justice might be dealt the orphan and the widow," and says: "Let any oppressed man who has a cause come into the presence of the statue of me, the king of justice, and then read carefully my inscribed stela, and give heed to my precious words, and may my stela make the case clear to him; may he understand his cause; may he set his mind at ease! 'Hammurabi, the lord, who is like a real father to the people, bestirred himself for the word of Marduk, his lord . . . and he also ensured prosperity for the people forever, and led the land aright'—let him proclaim this, and let him pray with his whole heart for me!"

The law code itself included nearly three hundred paragraphs of legal provisions touching commercial, social, domestic, and moral life. Procedure in the law courts had to be taken very seriously for false accusation in a capital case was a ground for death (§3). Theft in certain cases, kidnaping, and house-breaking were punishable by death (§§6, 14, 21). In case of stealing at a fire, the thief was to be thrown into the fire (§25). Other laws dealt with the duties of soldiers (§§26-41), and regulated farm rentals (§§42ff.), deposits and debts (§§112ff.). Marriage was legal only when recorded in writing (§128) and the woman as well as the man had the right of divorce (§142). Death for both parties was the penalty in case of adultery between a man and another man's wife (§129), but a woman accused of adultery without proof might clear herself by swearing her innocence, or by the ordeal by water (§§131f.). This latter consisted of leaping into the sacred river where sinking was proof of guilt and floating of innocence. A married woman might hold property

---

[8] In late-Sumerian usage this term refers to men in general.
[9] The god of Babylon, biblical Merodach.

(§150). Inheritance and adoption were regulated (§§162-191). Laws covering assault and battery were based largely on the principle of equal retaliation, but with some complications because of the division of society into three classes, nobles, commoners, and slaves (§§195-214).[10] For example (§§200f.), "If a seignior has knocked out a tooth of a seignior of his own rank, they shall knock out his tooth. If he has knocked out a commoner's tooth, he shall pay one-third mina of silver." One very extreme application of the *lex talionis* was provided for (§§209f.): if under certain circumstances a man caused the death of another man's daughter, his own daughter was to be put to death. The fees of physicians were governed and in the case of an operation under which the patient died the doctor's hand might be cut off (§§215-225)! Likewise if a builder erected an unsafe house which fell upon its owner and killed him, he himself was liable to death (§229). River navigation (§§234-239), rental of cattle (§§242ff.), wages of laborers (§§257f.) and numerous other matters were covered in the code.

That this code was largely based upon earlier systems of Mesopotamian law has long been surmised and may now be demonstrated at least in part by comparison with the earlier codes already mentioned. Concern for the rights of orphan and widow was stated already in the Sumerian code of Ur-Nammu, even as it is also expressed in the epilogue of Hammurabi. Paragraphs 5 and 54 of the Akkadian Laws of Eshnunna, quoted above, correspond to sections 237 and 251 in the Hammurabi corpus: "If a man hire a boatman and a boat and freight it with grain, wool, oil, dates or any other kind of freight, and that boatman be careless and he sink the boat or wreck its cargo, the boatman shall replace the boat which he sank and whatever portion of the cargo he wrecked"; "If a man's bull have been wont to gore and they have made known to him his habit of goring, and he have not protected his horns or have not tied him up, and that bull gore the son of a man and bring about his death, he shall pay one-half mina of silver." Likewise paragraphs 10 and 35 in the Sumerian Code of Lipit-Ishtar, also quoted above, reappear as follows in paragraphs 59 and 247 of the Code of Hammurabi: "If a man cut down a tree in a man's orchard, without the consent of the owner of the orchard, he shall pay one-half mina of silver"; "If a man hire an

---

[10] *Awilum*, a noble or man of the higher class, a seignior; *mushkenum*, a commoner or man of the middle class (the modern Arabic *masqin* is derived from this ancient Babylonian term); and *wardum*, a slave.

ox and destroy its eye, he shall pay silver to the owner of the ox to the extent of one-half its value."

There are also not a few similarities between the Code of Hammurabi and the later laws of Israel which again suggest a relationship or common background. With points which have been mentioned above as included in the Hammurabi code may be compared the following Old Testament laws: According to Deuteronomy 19:18f. a false witness is to be punished with the penalty he had thought to bring upon the other man. Exodus 21:16 makes the stealing and selling of a man a capital offense, and Exodus 22:2 allows the killing of a thief breaking into a house. The biblical law of divorce in Deuteronomy 24:1 permits the man to put away his wife but does not extend the same right to her as the Hammurabi code did. Leviticus 20:10 and Deuteronomy 22:22 agree exactly with Hammurabi's code on the death penalty for both the man and the other man's wife in case of adultery. Exodus 21:23-25 and Deuteronomy 19:21 state vividly the same principle of retaliation upon which a number of Hammurabi's laws were based: "life for life, eye for eye, tooth for tooth, hand for hand, foot for foot, burning for burning, wound for wound, stripe for stripe." Note also how exactly Exodus 21:29 agrees in phrasing with paragraph 54 of the Laws of Eshnunna and paragraph 251 of the Code of Hammurabi, yet how much more severe the imposed penalty is, a fact which can be understood in the light of the higher value set upon human life in Israel than in Babylonia: "But if the ox has been accustomed to gore in the past, and its owner has been warned but has not kept it in, and it kills a man or a woman, the ox shall be stoned, and its owner also shall be put to death."

In addition to Hammurabi's famous code of laws a great many other written documents remain from the Old Babylonian period to attest the intense literary activity of those days. Thousands of letters show that a considerable part of the population was literate.[11] Extant texts indicate that a remarkable knowledge of medicine, botany, chemistry, geology, and mathematics had been attained.[12] A business document from the time of Hammurabi is shown in Fig.

[11] G. R. Driver, *Letters of the First Babylonian Dynasty*. Oxford Editions of Cuneiform Texts, 1942; T. Fish in BJRL 16 (1932), p.508.

[12] R. C. Thompson, *Assyrian Medical Texts*. 1923; *A Dictionary of Assyrian Chemistry and Geology*. 1936; O. Neugebauer, *Mathematische Keilschrift-Texte*. 1-3 (1935-37). For Babylonian and also Egyptian and Hellenistic mathematics and astronomy see O. Neugebauer, *The Exact Sciences in Antiquity*. 1952.

22. The tablet was found in the region of the Diyala River, and contains a contract concerning a loan of grain on which the borrower paid interest. The date formula on the tablet mentions the year when Shamshi-Adad I died. In the Old Babylonian period the story of the flood was reedited, as was the epic of creation.

THE EPIC OF CREATION

Like the legend of the flood so too an account of the creation was at least as ancient as the time of the Sumerians. The fragmentary tablet from Nippur which alluded to the creation as well as narrated the flood has already been mentioned (p. 31), likewise the general nature of the Sumerian conception of the universe has been indicated (p. 45). Here additional reference may be made to other texts, dating probably around 2000 B.C., in which the creation of man is described. As in one of the narratives of creation in the Old Testament man is formed "of dust from the ground" (Genesis 2:7), so in this Sumerian account he is fashioned out of clay. It was Nammu, the goddess of the primeval sea, who besought her son Enki, the water-god and god of wisdom, to "fashion servants of the gods." Thereupon Enki led forth a group of "fashioners," and said to Nammu:

> O my mother, the creature whose name you uttered, it exists,
>   Bind upon it the image of the gods;
> Mix the heart of the clay that is over the abyss,
> The good and princely fashioners will thicken the clay. . . .
> It is man. . . .[13]

But it was in the First Dynasty of Babylon that the account of the creation of the world was given the form in which it was to be told for the next thousand years and the form in which it is most familiar to us. The first tablets containing the Babylonian version of the creation were discovered at Nineveh in the ruins of the seventh century B.C. library of Ashurbanipal (p. 217), and other tablets and fragments of tablets of the epic have been found at Ashur, Kish, and Uruk. Those from Ashur belong to approximately 1000 B.C., while the remaining ones are probably from the sixth century B.C. and later. Despite the relatively late date of the extant tablets, it is almost certain that the epic was composed in substantially its present form in the days of Hammurabi. That was the time when Babylon rose

---

[13] Kramer, *Sumerian Mythology*, pp.37f., 69f.; KFTS pp.142f.

to political supremacy and when Marduk became the national god, and one purpose of the creation epic is to show the preeminence of Babylon over all other cities in the country and especially the supremacy of Marduk over all other Babylonian gods.

The epic, which is written on seven clay tablets and consists in all of about 1,000 lines, was known in Akkadian as *Enuma elish* from its two opening words ("When on high").[14] The account begins with the time when only the two divine principles, the mythical personalities Apsu and Tiamat, were in existence. These two represented the living, uncreated world-matter, Apsu being the primeval sweet-water ocean and Tiamat the primeval salt-water ocean.[15] It has usually been assumed that the Babylonians thought of Tiamat as a dragon or similar monster, but this is uncertain.[16] Tiamat is explicitly called a woman in the myth (Tablet II, line 111) and she and Apsu became the mother and father of the gods. Eventually the doings of these gods became so annoying to their parents that Apsu announced his intention of destroying them. The god Ea, however, perceived the plan and was able to fetter and slay Apsu. Then among the gods the real hero of the myth, Marduk the city-god of Babylon, was born. In the copy of the epic found at Ashur the name of Marduk was replaced by that of the Assyrian god, Ashur. On her side Tiamat created a host of gruesome monsters whose bodies were filled with poison instead of blood. One of her own offspring, Kingu, was exalted to be the supreme director of her forces. So much is related in the first tablet of the myth.

Tiamat now was ready to wage war against the gods and avenge Apsu. The gods were afraid when they learned their danger but

[14] Alexander Heidel, *The Babylonian Genesis, The Story of Creation.* 2d ed. 1951; E. A. Speiser in ANET pp.60-72. (ANEA pp.31f.). For comparison with Genesis 1 see also C. F. Whitley in JNES 17 (1958), pp.32-40.

[15] Jensen in Erich Ebeling and Bruno Meissner, eds., *Reallexikon der Assyriologie.* I (1928), p.123.

[16] A well-known Assyrian relief from Nimrod (E. A. Wallis Budge, *Assyrian Sculptures in the British Museum, Reign of Ashur-nasir-pal,* 885-860 B.C. 1914, Pl. XXXVII) has often been interpreted as representing the combat of Marduk with Tiamat. It shows a winged god striding forward against a fleeing monster which is half lion and half bird. But this relief comes from the temple of Ninurta and bears an inscription beginning with a prayer to Ninurta, and hence must represent this deity rather than Marduk. Moreover, the monster is a masculine creature of land and air, while Tiamat was a feminine water deity. On the other hand it is said in *Enuma elish* that "Tiamat opened her mouth to devour" Marduk, while there are other texts which refer to the tail of Tiamat, and these ways of speech may suggest the idea of a dragon. Heidel (*The Babylonian Genesis,* pp. 83-88) considers the evidence, and concludes with Jensen (in *Reallexikon der Assyriologie,* II, p.85, under "Chaos") that the picture of Tiamat as a dragon is "a pure figment of the imagination."

Marduk volunteered to be their champion. He asked that he should be made the highest god if he should vanquish Tiamat. This is narrated in Tablet II, and Tablet III tells how the gods assembled at a banquet for the council of war. In Tablet IV (Fig. 24) we find Marduk preparing for the struggle. He took bow, arrow, and club, and held lightning before his face. He made a net to enclose the body of Tiamat and raised up the hurricane as his mighty weapon. His chariot was the storm, drawn by four steeds named the Destructive, the Pitiless, the Trampler, and the Fleet. When he came before Tiamat, Marduk uttered his challenge, "Come thou forth alone and let us, me and thee, do single combat!" Then:

> Tiamat and Marduk, the wisest of the gods, advanced against one
>   another;
> They pressed on to single combat, they approached for battle.
> The lord spread out his net and enmeshed her;
> The evil wind, following after, he let loose in her face.
> When Tiamat opened her mouth to devour him,
> He drove in the evil wind, in order that she should not be able
>   to close her lips.
> The raging winds filled her belly;
> Her belly became distended, and she opened wide her mouth.
> He shot off an arrow, and it tore her interior;
> It cut through her inward parts, it split her heart.
> When he had subdued her, he destroyed her life;
> He cast down her carcass and stood upon it.

The helpers of Tiamat now attempted to flee, but were captured and cast into prison. Then Marduk returned to the corpse of Tiamat.

> The lord rested, examining her dead body,
> To divide the abortion and to create ingenious things therewith.
> He split her open like a mussel[17] into two parts;
> Half of her he set in place and formed the sky therewith as a
>   roof.

Next Marduk established the earth, which is represented as a great structure in the shape of a canopy over Apsu, and is poetically called Esharra. Then he determined the residences of the gods, Anu being caused to occupy the sky, Enlil the air, and Ea the waters underneath the earth. Here ends Tablet IV. Only a fragment of Tablet V remains, but it tells how Marduk set up the constellations which mark the days and months of the year, and caused the moon to shine forth, entrusting the night to her.

---

[17] Also translated "like a flat fish" (Barton, *Archaeology and the Bible*, p.288); "like a shellfish" (Speiser in ANET p.67 [ANEA pp.31f.]).

In Tablet VI the creation of man is described. In the assembly of the great gods the guilt for Tiamat's revolt was determined to belong to Kingu, the leader of her hosts. Thereupon, Kingu was slain, and when his arteries were cut open the gods fashioned mankind with his blood. The service of the gods was laid upon mankind, while the gods themselves molded bricks for a year and labored to construct Esagila, the large temple tower of Marduk at Babylon. Then the gods gathered at a festive banquet and joined in singing praises of Marduk. Finally, Marduk's advancement from chief god of Babylon to head of the entire pantheon is signified by the conferring upon him of fifty names which represent the power and attributes of the various Babylonian gods. This is the seventh and last tablet.

Obviously there are some interesting points of comparison between the account of creation given in *Enuma elish* and that in Genesis 1:1-2:3. Both refer to a watery chaos at the beginning of time, and the term *tehom* by which it is designated in Genesis 1:2 may go back to the same Semitic form from which the proper name Tiamat is derived. Genesis 1:7 speaks of a firmament placed to divide the waters beneath it from those above it. The word for firmament means literally "what is spread out" and corresponds in a much more refined way to the crude Babylonian idea of the half of Tiamat used by Marduk to construct the vault of heaven. The sequence of events in the creation also is the same in the two stories, in that the following happenings take place in the same order: the creation of the firmament, the creation of dry land, the creation of the luminaries, and the creation of man. Both accounts begin with the watery chaos and end with the gods or the Lord at rest.

On the whole, however, it must be recognized that the differences between *Enuma elish* and the Old Testament are far more important than the similarities. The Babylonian creation story is mythological and polytheistic while the accounts in Genesis are elevated and strictly monotheistic. Doubtless certain features of the biblical narrative of creation are derived from the Babylonian myth, or at least back of both Israelite and Babylonian thought are certain common sources. But the dignity and exaltation of the words of the Bible are unparalleled.

NUZI

Other materials which have an important relationship to biblical narratives are found in the tablets from Nuzi. In the second millennium B.C. this city (cf. p. 47) was a provincial center of the Hurrians. The latter were a people who seem to have come into Mesopotamia from the north in the second half of the third millennium and who became a dominant ethnic element throughout the Middle East during the second millennium B.C.[18] They were the biblical Horites (Genesis 14:6, etc.), but aside from the few references to them in the Old Testament have become known only through the archeological discoveries of the last decades.[19] At Nuzi thousands of clay tablets were found which had been written by Hurrian scribes in the Babylonian language but with the occasional employment of native Hurrian words. The bulk of these tablets date in the fifteenth century B.C. or just shortly after the Old Babylonian period. Since transactions of all kinds are recorded in them, much information is given concerning the life of the people.[20]

Among the customs and laws which the tablets reveal to have prevailed at Nuzi are many which cast light upon incidents recorded in the Bible and particularly upon events of the patriarchal age.[21] Adoption was frequent at Nuzi, and in particular childless couples often adopted a son who would care for them when they were old, bury them when they died, and be heir to their estate. It was specified however that if, after the adoption, they had a son of their own, the adopted son would have to give way to the real son as the chief heir. This provides a legal explanation for Genesis 15:2-4 where the heir of the childless Abraham is expected to be his slave Eliezer, until the promise is given that a son of his own will be born to become his heir.

Marriage contracts of Nuzi contained a provision obliging a childless wife to provide her husband with a handmaid who would bear children. This explains the action of Sarah in giving Hagar to Abraham (Genesis 16:1f.) and of Rachel in giving Bilhah to Jacob

---

[18] E. A. Speiser in AASOR 13 (1931-32), pp.13-54.

[19] W. F. Albright in L. G. Leary, ed., *From the Pyramids to Paul*. 1935, pp.9-13.

[20] For these texts including related ones from Kirkuk see C. J. Gadd in RAAO 23 (1926), pp.49-161; E. A. Speiser in AASOR 10 (1928-29), pp.1-73; Robert H. Pfeiffer and E. A. Speiser in AASOR 16 (1935-36); Cyrus H. Gordon in *Orientalia*. 5 (1936), pp.305-330; Edward Chiera, *Joint Expedition with the Iraq Museum at Nuzi*. 6 vols. 1927-39; *Harvard Semitic Series*. 5 (1929); 9 (1932); 12 (1942); cf. Cyrus H. Gordon in *Orientalia*. 7 (1938), p. 32 n.1; Francis R. Steele, *Nuzi Real Estate Transactions*. American Oriental Series 25. 1943; Ignace J. Gelb, Pierre M. Purves, and Allan A. MacRae, *Nuzi Personal Names*. OIP 57, 1943. For the seal impressions of Nuzi see Edith Porada in AASOR 24 (1944-45).

[21] Cyrus H. Gordon, *The Living Past*. 1941, pp.156-178; in BA 3 (1940), pp.1-12; and in JNES 13 (1954), pp.56-59.

(Genesis 30:1-3). According to the Nuzi documents the offspring of the handmaid could not be driven out, which shows that there was a legal basis for Abraham's apprehension over the expulsion of Hagar and her child (Genesis 21:11).

Another Nuzi tablet records a relationship between a man named Nashwi and his adopted son called Wullu, which is parallel in some ways to the relationship between Laban and Jacob (Genesis 29-31). Nashwi bestows his daughter upon Wullu, even as Laban promised a daughter to Jacob when he received him into his household. When Nashwi dies, Wullu is to be the heir. If Nashwi begets a son, however, Wullu must share the inheritance with that son, and only the latter shall take Nashwi's gods. Evidently the possession of the household idols implied the leadership of the family. Since Laban had sons of his own when Jacob departed for Canaan, they alone had the right to have their father's gods, and the theft of the teraphim by Rachel (Genesis 31:19, 30-35) was a serious offense.

It will be remembered that Laban searched Jacob's camp in vain for his stolen idols because "Rachel had taken the household gods and put them in the camel's saddle, and sat upon them" (Genesis 31:34). In this connection it is of interest to notice a stone slab sculptured in relief, which was found at Tell Halaf and is shown in Fig. 25. It probably dates from about the ninth century B.C.[22] It shows a camel, with a rider sitting on a saddle which looks very much like a square box, fastened on the animal by crosswise girths. Such a saddle would be exactly the kind in which Rachel could readily have hidden the household idols. Another Tell Halaf sculpture, it may be added, shows a six-winged goddess, the conception of which may have some connection with the description of the seraphim in the Bible (Isaiah 6:2).[23]

HARAN

Other links with patriarchal times appear in northwestern Mesopotamia. The town of Haran (Genesis 11:31f.) is still in existence on the Balikh River sixty miles west of Tell Halaf. Cuneiform sources

[22] E. Douglas Van Buren in OL 50 (1955), cols. 451-455; cf. Joseph P. Free in JNES 3 (1944), p.191. On the camel in ancient Mesopotamian art see also E. Douglas Van Buren, *The Fauna of Ancient Mesopotamia as Represented in Art.* Analecta Orientalia 18. 1939, pp.36f. For some possible early occurrences of the camel in Palestine see B. S. J. Isserlin in PEQ 1950, pp.50-53. For the earliest known reference to horseback riding, in Sumerian literature, see Edmund I. Gordon in JCS 12 (1958), p.19.

[23] Von Oppenheim, *Tell Halaf*, Pl. XXXII B.

make frequent references to Haran, and show that it was a flourishing city in the nineteenth and eighteenth centuries B.C. The city of Nahor, which was Rebekah's home (Genesis 24:10), is mentioned often in the Mari documents as Nakhur, and seems to have been below Haran in the valley of the Balikh. In the time of Hammurabi, both places were ruled by Amorite princes. It may be noted that Haran and Nahor were the names not only of towns but also of members of Abraham's family (Genesis 11:22-27), and the same situation prevails in relation to several other names, including Terah and Serug. Both were among the ancestors of Abraham, and both names appear as designations of towns near Haran.[24] So persistent is tradition in the East that present-day Muslims living in the neighborhood of Haran, particularly at Urfa and at Ain el-Khalil, still relate many legends concerning Abraham, whom they look upon as an Islamic saint. At Urfa, Nimrod is said to have fired glowing charcoal from a catapult against Abraham. Instead of burning the holy man, a pond arose where the charcoal fell, and the glowing bits of charcoal turned into fishes. To this day the fish are holy and not to be eaten. At Ain el-Khalil native Muslim peasants still declare themselves to be direct descendants of Father Abraham.[25] It is certain, therefore, particularly in view of the correspondence between the biblical indications and the archeological evidences, that the region of Haran was an important center in the life of the forefathers of the Israelite people.

THE HABIRU

In the time of the First Dynasty of Babylon, people called Habiru are known in Mesopotamia. A text from Babylon mentions the issue of clothing to Habiru soldiers,[26] a letter to Zimri-Lim of Mari speaks of two thousand Habiru soldiers who have assisted an enemy king in the Middle Euphrates region,[27] and another tablet from Mari refers to thirty Habiru who have come from a district north of Babylonia.[28] Many other texts dating mostly from the eighteenth to the twelfth centuries B.C. and coming from many places largely on the borders of Babylonia and Assyria also mention the Habiru. Although the Habiru are frequently described as foreigners it is also several times indicated that they have fixed places of abode and thus can-

[24] William F. Albright, *From the Stone Age to Christianity.* 2d ed. 1946, pp.179f.
[25] Von Oppenheim, *Tell Halaf,* pp.65f.
[26] Jean Bottéro, ed., *Le problème des Ḥabiru à la 4e rencontre assyriologique internationale.* Cahiers de la Société Asiatique 13. 1954, No.16, p.18.
[27] *ibid.,* No.18, pp.18f.   [28] *ibid.,* No.19, p.19.

not be considered as pure nomads. They find employment not only as soldiers but also as workers of many sorts and, particularly in texts from Nuzi, are found voluntarily entering into labor contracts some of which involve virtual enslavement. Individuals, however, are also found attaining to high positions. The grandfather of a fourteenth century North Syrian king, and himself the possessor of a city, was a Habiru; a man with the Kassite name Harbi-Shihu, active in the twelfth century at the court of Assyria and called by the king of Babylonia the actual ruler of Assyria, and a certain Kudurra, who was in the service of the king of Babylon in the eleventh century, were each designated as "the Habirean," perhaps meaning the descendant of a Habiru.[29]

Habiru are also mentioned frequently in the Tell el-Amarna tablets where they appear as marauding raiders in Syria and Palestine (p. 111). Likewise the name 'Apiru or 'Aperu is found in a number of Egyptian texts (pp. 119f.) and is doubtless to be identified with Habiru.

A form of the name similar to this Egyptian form is also found in cuneiform texts from Ras Shamra.[30] In both Egyptian and Ugaritic it is easy to explain how a foreign b was changed into p, but as far as known an h would have been preserved as such. Contrariwise a cuneiform h could represent a West-Semitic '.[31] Accordingly it is reasoned, the original form of the name may have been 'abiru. Since the root 'br means "to cross a boundary," the name can be explained as meaning "those who have crossed a boundary," that is, "immigrants."

In the Bible the name "Hebrew" is applied first to Abram[32] (Genesis 14:13) and after that to the children of Israel in Egypt (Genesis 39:14, etc., Exodus 1:15, etc.). Phonetically the word Hebrew ('ibri) corresponds very closely with 'Apiru or Habiru,[33] and thus may well have been applied originally to Abraham and to Israel in the sense of "immigrant." The Septuagint agrees with this understanding of the word when it translates it in Genesis 14:13 as ὁ περάτης, meaning "the one who passes through, the wanderer."

[29] ibid., Nos.165, 166, p.131; Julius Lewy in HUCA 14 (1939), pp.618f.

[30] Moshe Greenberg, The Hab/piru. 1955, pp.11, 53, 78.

[31] Battiscombe Gunn and E. A. Speiser in AASOR 13 (1931-32), pp.38f.; J. W. Jack in PEQ 1940 pp. 99f.

[32] Abram (Genesis 11:27, 29, etc.) and Abraham (Genesis 17:5, etc.) are probably only variant spellings of essentially the same name.

[33] Speiser in AASOR 13 (1931-32), p.40.

Ultimately the word "Hebrew" became an ethnic designation for the people of Israel as it is in Judith 10:12, and for their language as it is in Jubilees 12:25-27, both books dating probably in the second century B.C.[34]

ABRAHAM

The migration of Abraham from Mesopotamia, in response to a divine call and promise (Genesis 12:1-3; cf. Hebrews 11:8-10), was regarded as the initial act of faith which made possible the unfolding of all the later history of his descendants. That Abraham's home was originally in Mesopotamia, and specifically at the cities of Ur and Haran, is indicated in several strands of Old Testament narrative. In Joshua 24:2 (E) the people of Israel are reminded of their polytheistic eastern ancestry in these words: "Your fathers lived of old beyond the Euphrates,[35] Terah, the father of Abraham and of Nahor; and they served other gods." Genesis 11:28-30; 12:1-4a, 6-9; cf. 15:7 (J) identifies the birthplace of Abraham with the city of Ur, and this tradition is echoed in a Levitical prayer of praise in Nehemiah 9:7: "Thou art the Lord, the God who didst choose Abram and bring him forth out of Ur of the Chaldees and give him the name Abraham."[36] Genesis 11:10-27, 31f.; 12:4b-5 (P)[37] likewise places the original home in Ur but indicates that the migration was first to Haran and then, after Terah's death at that place, on to Canaan. It has ordinarily been supposed that the Ur referred to in the foregoing citations was the well-known city in lower Mesopotamia already described (pp. 39-42, 50-52). In Genesis 24 (J), however, Abraham speaks of "my country" (v. 4) and "the land of my birth" (v. 7) and then sends his servant "to Mesopotamia, to the city of Nahor" (v. 10). Since Nahor was doubtless in northwestern

[34] For the Habiru see Mary F. Gray, "The Ḫâbirū-Hebrew Problem in the Light of the Source Material Available at Present," in HUCA 29 (1958), pp.135-202.

[35] For "the River" (ASV) as a frequent designation of the Euphrates see HDB IV p.287.

[36] In Genesis 11:28 (J), 31 (P); 15:7 (J), and Nehemiah 9:7 the LXX (ed. Swete, I, pp.18f., 23) reads "the land of the Chaldees" instead of "Ur of the Chaldees," but even so the reference is to the same general area, for the home of the Chaldeans was in lower Babylonia. Strictly speaking, the words "of the Chaldees" are an anachronism. The Chaldeans were a Semitic people who first came into southern Babylonia around 1000 B.C. as far as we can tell, and eventually established the Neo-Babylonian or Chaldean empire. It was, of course, quite natural for the biblical writers to apply to the city or land the appellation customary in their own day.

[37] For the abbreviations, E, J, and P, which are commonly used to distinguish hypothetical source documents in the Old Testament see Robert H. Pfeiffer, *Introduction to the Old Testament*. 5th ed. 1941, pp.139f.

Mesopotamia the question has been raised whether Abraham's original home should not be sought in that region rather than in lower
Mesopotamia. An Akkadian tablet from Ugarit has now become
known in which the Hittite king, Hattusilis III (c.1275-c.1250 B.C.; cf.
below p. 199), writes to the king of Ugarit, Niqmepaʿ by name, about
the status of merchants of Hattusilis who are trading in Ugarit.
These traders are called "merchant men, citizens of the city of Ura."
Since the name Ura could easily become Ur in Hebrew, this may
attest the existence of another city of Ur and one presumably somewhere in the northwest. That this city could be "Ur of the Chaldees"
would require that there had been Chaldeans in the northwest as
well as in lower Mesopotamia (see above p. 70 n. 36), and that this
was the case is attested by Xenophon (c.400 B.C.) who mentions
the Chaldeans as blocking the way to Armenia and as neighbors of
the Armenians.[38].

If we seek for indications in the Bible as to the date of Abraham's
residence in Mesopotamia, we find it necessary to consider a complex
series of chronological notations, most of which are from priestly
sources. In some cases they bear not only on the date of Abraham
but also on the date of the Exodus, a problem to which attention
must be given later.

Priestly notices in Genesis 12:4b; 21:5; 25:26 and 47:9 give a total
of 215 years for the period from Abraham's coming into Canaan to
Jacob's going down into Egypt. As to the length of time the children
of Israel (Jacob) were in the land of Egypt there are two traditions.
The first represents this period as covering 430 years, or in round
numbers 400 years. The precise figure of 430 years is given in the
Hebrew text of Exodus 12:40f. (P), "The time that the people of
Israel dwelt in Egypt was four hundred and thirty years." The round
number, 400 years, is used in Genesis 15:13 in both the Hebrew and
the Septuagint,[39] and is also found in Acts 7:6. Josephus, likewise,
in two passages, represents the Israelites as having been in Egypt
for 400 years.[40] The second tradition as to the length of time the
Israelites were in Egypt appears in the Septuagint version of Exodus

[38] Xenophon, *Anabasis*. IV, iii, 4; cf. V, v, 17; *Cyropaedia*. III, i, 34. The "land of the
Chaldeans" referred to in Isaiah 23:13 may also have been in the northwest. For the
text cited above from Ugarit and for the suggestion that Abraham should be thought
of as a merchant prince like the Hittite merchants of this text, see Cyrus H. Gordon
in JNES 17 (1958), pp.28-31.

[39] Genesis 15 is largely J and E, but v.13 may be by a later hand.

[40] Josephus (A.D. c.37-c.95), *Antiquities*. II, ix, 1; *War* V, ix, 4 (tr. H. St. J. Thack-
eray and Ralph Marcus, LCL [1926-], IV, p.253; III, p.321).

12:40 which reads, "The time that the people of Israel dwelt in Egypt and in the land of Canaan was four hundred and thirty years."[41] Since, as we have seen, the patriarchs were in Canaan for 215 years, this would allow the Israelites only 215 years in Egypt. The statement in Galatians 3:17 evidently was based upon the Septuagint text, for it likewise makes 430 years cover the entire period from the call of Abraham to the Exodus and the giving of the law. Josephus also follows this tradition in one passage where he says of the Israelites, "They left Egypt . . . 430 years after the coming of our forefather Abraham to Canaan, Jacob's migration to Egypt having taken place 215 years later."[42]

It may be held that the standard Hebrew text of Exodus 12:40 is more reliable than the reading in the Septuagint. The affirmation of the following verse 41 that at the end of 430 years, "on that very day," the people went out of Egypt, seems more impressive if it is the anniversary of the beginning of their life in Egypt that is so marked.

On the other hand, Genesis 15:16 (E) says that the Exodus will take place "in the fourth generation," and priestly genealogies in Exodus 6:16-20 and Numbers 26:57-59 make Moses the great-great-grandson of Jacob, and in Joshua 7:1 list Achan, a contemporary of Joshua, as the great-great-great-grandson of Jacob. While the biblical word "generation" is a broad term and may simply mean all the people living at a given time, as in Exodus 1:6, four such groups of contemporaries in general, and a series of four descendants in particular, would surely be much more likely to cover only a span of something like 215 years than of 430.

If, then, we accept the Hebrew text we find that the patriarchs were 215 years in Canaan and the Israelites 430 years in Egypt. Abraham would have entered Canaan, accordingly, 645 years before the Exodus. But if we take the Septuagint text, the entry of Abraham into Canaan would have been only 430 years before the Exodus.

As we shall see in the next chapter the most probable date for the Exodus is either around the middle of the fifteenth century B.C. or toward the middle of the thirteenth century B.C., the latter date appearing definitely preferable. Taking the more probable latter date and adding 645 years we arrive at approximately 1900 B.C. for Abraham's entry into Canaan; adding 430 years we get a date shortly after 1700 B.C.

[41] Some MSS read 435 years (LXX ed. Swete, I, p.128).
[42] *Ant.* II, xv, 2.

The date around 1900 B.C. would mean that Abraham left Mesopotamia in the troubled period of the Elamite and Amorite invasions, which may be judged a likely time for a family to depart from its old home. The date near 1700 B.C., on the other hand, would make Abraham a contemporary of Hammurabi (1728-1686 B.C.) and as far as chronology is concerned would allow an identification of that famous king with "Amraphel king of Shinar" in Genesis 14:1, an identification which while much debated would not be impossible if Am-mu-ra-bi (Hammurabi) were erroneously read as Am-mu-ra-pil (Amraphel).[43]

It is also of interest to find that names very similar to "Abraham" occur at a slightly later time in Babylonia. A clay tablet from the reign of Ammizaduga, tenth king of the First Dynasty of Babylon, deals with the hiring of an ox by a certain Abarama son of Awel-Ishtar. Other similar documents deal with a field leased by Abam-rama.[44] While the reference is of course not to Abraham the son of Terah, the name is essentially the same.

Certainly the patriarchal stories fit with thorough congruity and often with surprising relevance of detail into the historical setting of life in Mesopotamia during the first half of the second millennium B.C. Likewise, as we have seen, other portions of the Old Testament reflect intimate connections with both the mythology and the law of Mesopotamia. It may well have been Abraham himself who carried with him upon his historic migration some of the stories and the laws which his descendants were to raise to so high a level and to pass on to the world. If Abraham did come from Mesopotamia sometime in the early second millennium B.C., it is necessary to revise the picture sometimes painted of him as a primitive nomad accustomed only to the open spaces of the desert, and to recognize that at least to some extent he must have been the heir of a complex and age-old civilization.

[43] *Recueil Édouard Dhorme, études bibliques et orientales.* 1951, pp.262, 265; and see pp.191-272 for Abraham in the setting of history.
[44] Barton, *Archaeology and the Bible,* pp.344f.

II

The Panorama of Egypt

WHEN Hecataeus of Miletus called Egypt "the gift of the river" he characterized the land accurately.[1] Similarly an ancient Egyptian oracle said that all the land watered by the Nile in its course was Egypt, and all who dwelt lower down than the city Elephantine and drank of that river's water were Egyptians.[2] The Nile River upon which Egypt depended for existence was believed by Ptolemy (second century A.D.) to take its rise in farthest Africa at the foot of "the Mountains of the Moon."[3] The ancient geographer was almost correct. In 1888 Henry Stanley for the first time caught sight of a snow-clad mountain towering into the sky at the very Equator. Almost always veiled in mist and clouds and literally invisible, it is small wonder that hitherto it had been known only by rumor. Stanley gave the mountain a new and appropriate name, Ruwenzori, "The Rain-Maker." Early in the twentieth century a mountaineering expedition led by the Duke of the Abruzzi climbed to the 16,791-foot summit of the range and proved that the Nile does rise in the Mountains of the Moon. Their snows and rains drain down to the east and pour into the waters of the lakes, Victoria,

[1] See Arrian (A.D. c.96-c.180), *Anabasis of Alexander.* v, vi, 5. tr. E. Iliff Robson, LCL (1929-33) II, p.23. Hecataeus lived in the sixth or fifth century B.C. The epigram was quoted later by Herodotus (c.484-425 B.C.) II, 5. tr. A. D. Godley, LCL (1020-24) I, p.281, and then repeatedly by Strabo (c.63 B.C.-after A.D. 21), *Geography.* I, ii, 23, 29; XII, ii, 4 (tr. H. L. Jones, LCL [1917-32] I, pp.111,131; v, p.357). cf. William A. Heidel in *American Academy of Arts and Sciences Memoirs.* XVIII, 2 (1935), p.61.

[2] Herodotus II, 18.

[3] *Geography.* IV, 8. ed. Edward L. Stevenson. 1932, p.109.

Albert, and Edward, which in turn are the sources of the famous river of Egypt.[4]

From the Equator to the shores of the Mediterranean is 2,450 miles in a direct line and thither the Nile flows in an estimated 4,000 miles of windings, the "greatest single stream on earth," traversing almost one-tenth of the earth's circumference.[5] At Khartoum the White Nile (Bahr el-Abyad), as the upper part of the main river is known, is joined by a tributary, the Blue Nile (Bahr el-Azraq), which descends from the mountains of Ethiopia. One hundred forty miles farther north the only other tributary, the Atbara, flows in from the east. The almost daily tropical rains of the Equator provide the White Nile with a constant volume of water, sufficient to carry it through the thousand miles of rainless Egypt. Ethiopia, on the other hand, has both a dry and a rainy season. During the latter a great flood of turbid water pours down the "Blue" Nile. This accounts for the annual inundation which from time immemorial irrigated and fertilized the lower Nile Valley. As Herodotus said: "The river rises of itself, waters the fields, and then sinks back again; thereupon each man sows his field . . . and waits for the harvest."[6] Herodotus foresaw that the gradual rise in the level of the land would lessen the effectiveness of this natural irrigation system and expressed anxiety for the future of Egypt when it would be neither inundated by the river nor watered by rain—little dreaming of the enormous dam at Aswan which today is capable of giving Egypt a greater cultivable area than it had in the days of the Pharaohs.

Between Khartoum and Aswan there are six cataracts, where the Nile flows over granite ridges. This region was that of ancient Nubia. From the First Cataract at Aswan, which was ancient Elephantine, on down to Memphis, near modern Cairo, is a distance of 500 miles and was known as the land of Upper Egypt. The last 100 miles from Memphis to the Mediterranean, in which the Nile spreads out into the Delta, constituted Lower Egypt. In Nubia and Upper Egypt the valley of the Nile is but a narrow ribbon of green, rarely more than a dozen miles across and strictly bounded on either side by the cliffs and shelves of the desert. In the Delta, however, the fertile land forms a great triangle, traversed by the various mouths of the Nile, of which the most important are the Rosetta and the Damietta.

[4] James Ramsey Ullman, *High Conquest.* 1941, p.152.
[5] Emil Ludwig, *The Nile.* 1937, p.vii.
[6] II, 14.

The archeological situation in Egypt differs somewhat from that in Mesopotamia. Many of Egypt's monumental structures were built of stone, which was naturally far more enduring than the mud brick of Babylonia. In numerous instances pyramids, obelisks, temples, and other works still stand beneath the sky, relatively well preserved, massive and impressive. Immediately upon the beginning of modern archeological investigations, therefore, extensive materials were at hand, and the publications regarding Egyptian monuments issued by the scholars who accompanied Napoleon (p. 4),[7] by Ippolito Rosellini,[8] Jean François Champollion,[9] Karl Richard Lepsius,[10] Auguste Mariette,[11] and others, made them known to the world at an early date. To the objects already visible above ground in Egypt have now been added, of course, all the many things which have been discovered in actual excavations, which range from bits of prehistoric pottery to the fabulous treasures of Tutankhamun's tomb.

Probably the most important features of many of the temples and other monuments still standing in Egypt were the inscriptions which appeared on their walls and sides. To a remarkable degree these had endured the ravages of time, yet could not but grow dimmer and less legible as the years went on. It was one of the most urgent tasks in Egyptian archeology, therefore, to make a comprehensive survey of all such records as could be found, and to copy and translate them as accurately as possible. To this undertaking indefatigable labors were devoted by James Henry Breasted (1865-1935), America's eminent Egyptologist and founder of the Oriental Institute of the University of Chicago. He traveled throughout Egypt, sailing on the Nile, climbing the cliffs on the edge of the desert, entering temples and tombs, seeking out every place where historical documents might have survived.[12] To copy, translate, and edit the inscriptions which he found was a task of over a decade, but the resultant publication of the *Ancient Records of Egypt* (5 volumes, 1906-1907) made available a standard compilation of historical sources extending from the First Dynasty to the Persian conquest of Egypt.

In the arrangement of these and other Egyptian materials within

[7] *Description de l'Égypte, ou Recueil des observations et des recherches qui ont été faites en Égypte pendant l'expédition de l'armée française, publié par les ordres de sa majesté l'empereur Napoléon le Grand.* 21 vols. 1809-28.

[8] *I Monumenti dell'Egitto e della Nubia.* 9 vols. 1832-44.

[9] *Monuments de l'Égypte et de la Nubie.* 4 vols. 1835-45.

[10] *Denkmäler aus Ägypten und Äthiopien.* 12 vols. 1849-56.

[11] *Voyage dans la Haute-Égypte.* 2 vols. 2d ed. 1893.

[12] Charles Breasted, *Pioneer to the Past.* 1943, p.78.

MEDITERRANEAN SEA

DELTA

Rosetta   Damietta
Alexandria   Buto   Port Said
    Abusir   Damanhur   Pelusium
        Behdet Sais   Avaris
    Karm Abu Mina   LOWER EGYPT   Qantir
        Wadi Natrun   Bubastis
        Nitriäe   Morimdeh   Tell er-Retaba   Tell el-Maskhūta
        Beni-Salamêh   Wadi Tumilat
            Giza   Cairo
        Memphis   Heliopolis
        Saqqara
            Karanis
    FAYUM   Lake Moeris
    Arsinoë   Philadelphia
    Hawara   Medinet el-Fayum
    Tebtunis   Gurob   Herakleopolis

    Oxyrhynchus   Bahr Yusef

ARABIA

    Beni-Hasan
    Akhetaton

    Asyuta   Deir Tasa
    Abutig   Badari

    This   Nile
    Girga
    Abydos
    Diospolis Parva   Ombos
        Naqada   Wadi Hammamat
    Deir el-Bahri
    Medinet Habu   Thebes

UPPER EGYPT

    Hierakonpolis   Nekheb

DESERT

LIBYA

EGYPT

LIBYAN DESERT

GULF OF SUEZ

RED SEA

    1st Cataract   Elephantine

Tropic of Cancer   Jebel el-Arak

MAP 2
EGYPT

0   50   100   150
SCALE OF MILES

    Abu Simbel

2nd Cataract

ANGLO-EGYPTIAN SUDAN   NUBIA

a framework of consecutive dynasties, all modern historians are dependent upon an ancient predecessor. This was an Egyptian priest and writer named Manetho who lived under Ptolemy II Philadelphus (285-246 B.C.). Manetho was born at Sebennytus (now Samannud) in the Delta. Eventually he rose to be high priest in the temple at Heliopolis. Berossos of Babylon (p. 30) was practically a contemporary, and the two priests became rivals in the proclamation of the antiquity and greatness of their respective lands. Manetho's *Egyptian History*,[13] with which we are concerned here, is preserved only in fragments, the text of which is often corrupt. Excerpts from the original work are to be found in Josephus, and Manetho's lists of dynasties together with brief notes on important kings or events are preserved in the *Chronicle* (A.D. c.221) of Sextus Julius Africanus, the *Chronicon* (A.D. 326) of Eusebius, and the history of the world from Adam to Diocletian written by George Syncellus about A.D. 800. With all of these fragments collected and arranged in order[14] it is possible to gain a reasonably good view of Manetho's outline, and the usual division of Egyptian history into thirty dynasties is based directly upon his work.

Throughout the period covered by these thirty successive houses of rulers, life in Egypt manifested a notable continuity which was interrupted but not destroyed by such an event as the Hyksos invasion. While the narrow Nile Valley was by no means isolated from the rest of the ancient world, it offered its inhabitants sufficient protection to render incursions of that sort infrequent. Also, in the character of the people there was a trait of tenacity which may have been exaggerated in the remark that they "could learn but not forget,"[15] but which helps to account for the amazing persistence of many things in Egyptian life. In contrast, therefore, with the changing kingdoms which complicate the scene in Mesopotamia, the drama of Egypt has a linear quality somewhat akin to that of the land itself which, omitting the Delta, may be said to have but one dimension—length.[16]

The immediate availability of a large body of historical documents, the existence of the framework provided by Manetho, and the relative unity of the land and homogeneity of the happenings, have made it possible to reduce archeological findings to the form of actual history more quickly in the case of Egypt than in that of some other

[13] Αἰγυπτιακὰ ὑπομνήματα. [14] *Manetho*, tr. W. G. Waddell. LCL. 1940.
[15] George Foot Moore, *History of Religions*. I (rev. ed. 1920), p.148.
[16] Barton, *Archaeology and the Bible*, p.3.

lands. In telling the archeological story of Egypt, therefore, we can follow an historical outline which has already been formulated with considerable definiteness. Before coming to the First Dynasty, however, it is necessary to mention those earlier vistas in Egyptian life which were too remote to be known even to Manetho but which have reappeared within the horizon of our knowledge, thanks to the investigations of modern archeology.

1. THE NEOLITHIC, CHALCOLITHIC, AND PREDYNASTIC PERIODS, c.5000-c.2900 B.C.[1]

As IN Mesopotamia so too in Egypt, we may note that Neolithic settlements were in existence by probably c.5000 B.C. The culture of this early time is known from discoveries at Deir Tasa opposite Abutig in Middle Egypt,[2] in the Fayum,[3] and at Merimdeh Beni-Salameh[4] west of the Rosetta branch of the Nile.

A Chalcolithic culture of perhaps the middle of the fifth millennium B.C. appears at Badari, twenty miles south of Asyut on the east bank of the Nile, where the people already had knowledge of copper. The Badarians were distinguished for their fine pottery and were accustomed to grind green malachite on slate palettes to use for eye-paint. This is an excellent germicide, still used by Africans, and particularly effective when spread around the eyes as a protection from flies. In their burials the Badarian dead were laid down as if sleeping, and food offerings as well as other objects were placed in the graves with them.[5]

Akin to the Badarians were the succeeding Amratians, who belong perhaps to the beginning of the fourth millennium B.C., and with whom the so-called Predynastic period properly begins. Known first

---

[1] For the dates in Egyptian prehistory see William C. Hayes, *The Scepter of Egypt, A Background for the Study of the Egyptian Antiquities in The Metropolitan Museum of Art,* Part I: *From the Earliest Times to the End of the Middle Kingdom.* 1953, p.8; cf. Helene J. Kantor in Ehrich, ed., *Relative Chronologies in Old World Archeology,* p.16; Robert-P. Charles in JNES 16 (1957), pp.240-253; and for the Egyptian calendar see the Appendix of the present book.

[2] Guy Brunton in *Antiquity, A Quarterly Review of Archaeology.* 3 (1929), pp.456-467.

[3] Gertrude Caton-Thompson and E. W. Gardner, *The Desert Fayum.* 2 vols. 1934.

[4] V. Gordon Childe, *New Light on the Most Ancient East.* 1935, pp.58-61; Hermann Ranke in JAOS 59 (1939) No.4, Supplement p.8.

[5] Guy Brunton and Gertrude Caton-Thompson, *The Badarian Civilization.* 1928, pp.20-42.

from el-Amreh not far from Abydos, their village sites and cemeteries have been found throughout Upper Egypt from Badari to Lower Nubia. The Amratians, it is thought, may have been organized as totemic clans. Copper was used, and boats made out of bundles of papyrus lashed together facilitated travel on the Nile. The dead were buried, doubled up, in shallow oval pits and accompanied by food, ornaments, and weapons. Statuettes of women and of servants bearing water-pots on their heads also were placed in the graves, perhaps as substitutes of magical efficacy for the living wives and attendants who in earlier times were sent to the grave with their master. Representations of men and animals on the pottery in the grave were also probably intended to be of magical help to the deceased.[6]

While the Amratian culture was focused in Upper Egypt, the Gerzean had its center at Gerzeh and other Nile Valley sites in the latitude of the Fayum. From there in Middle Predynastic times, perhaps around the middle of the fourth millennium, the Gerzean culture spread into and came to dominate Upper Egypt as well. Among the characteristic objects of Gerzean times are wavy-handled jars,[7] pear-shaped maces, vessels of clay or stone in the shape of animals, and amulets representing the bull, the cow, the toad, the fly, and the falcon.

The villages were becoming towns and each seems to have recognized an animal or plant as its totem. On decorated pots there are figures of ships which bear totemic standards on their masts. Thus was emerging that structure of society which is known in historic times when the Egyptians lived in independent districts, each designated by a banner or ensign representing an animal or plant. These regional divisions, of which eventually there were twenty-two in Upper Egypt and twenty in the Delta, later were called "nomes" by the Greeks.

Gerzean graves were oblong trenches, on one side of which a ledge accommodated the ever more numerous offerings. Burial places of the rich were lined with mud bricks, and one such has been discovered at the site of Hierakonpolis in which the walls were adorned

[6] Brunton in *Antiquity*. 3 (1929), p.460; Childe, *New Light on the Most Ancient East*, pp.69-74.

[7] It was the progressive degeneration of the wavy-ledges which once served as handholds on these jars into mere decorative marks that provided W. M. Flinders Petrie with his clue for the development of "sequence dating" for the Predynastic period (*Diospolis Parva*. 1901, pp.28-30; *Prehistoric Egypt*. 1920, pp.3f.).

with a mural painting.[8] Thus the vase-paintings of Amratian times now find a place on the walls of the tomb, where Egyptian paintings are so well known and so important in all later years. The comparative splendor of the tomb just mentioned is an indication, also, of the rise of kingship which led at last to the unification of the land.[9]

Two powerful states came into existence first, one in Upper Egypt, the other in Lower Egypt or the Delta. The capital of southern or Upper Egypt was at Ombos on the left bank of the Nile, near the modern town of Naqada. Its king wore a tall white helmet as a crown, and the symbol of the kingdom was a plant not identified botanically but usually called the lotus. The capital of northern or Lower Egypt was at Behdet, near modern Damanhur and Alexandria. The king's crown here was a red wickerwork diadem, and the kingdom's symbol was the papyrus which grew so abundantly in the swamps and marshes of the Delta. These plants which were the symbols of the two lands are represented on two columns still standing at Karnak (Fig. 26), the lotus of Upper Egypt being at the right and the papyrus of Lower Egypt at the left. Although Egypt ultimately became one united land, the remembrance of the two kingdoms always persisted. The ruler of all Egypt bore the title "King of Upper Egypt and Lower Egypt" and wore a crown which combined the tall helmet of Upper Egypt and the wickerwork diadem of Lower Egypt. The symbol of the united land was a device in which the lotus and the papyrus were knotted together (p. 85).[10] Even in the Old Testament the Hebrew name for Egypt remained literally "the two Egypts."[11]

The earliest Egyptian annals begin with the names of kings in this Predynastic period. Herodotus remarked that "the Egyptians . . . who dwell in the cultivated country are the most careful of all men to preserve the memory of the past, and none whom I have questioned have so many chronicles."[12] As early as the Fifth Dynasty historical records were inscribed on slabs of stone, fragments of which still survive and constitute early annals in "the history of history."[13] One of these fragments is the famous Palermo Stone, shown in Fig. 27. It is a small piece of hard black diorite, about 17

---

[8] J. E. Quibell, *Hierakonpolis.* II (1902), pp.20f.
[9] Childe, *New Light on the Most Ancient East,* pp.86-100.
[10] E. A. Wallis Budge, *The Gods of the Egyptians.* 1904, II, pp.42-48.
[11] Genesis 15:18, etc.
[12] II, 77.
[13] James T. Shotwell, *The History of History.* I. 1939, p.79.

inches high, 9½ inches wide, and 2½ inches thick. At the top is a simple row of oblong spaces containing hieroglyphic signs. The clue to their meaning is given by the lower section of each oblong space where a figure wearing a red crown and holding a flail appears. This is the sign for the king of Lower Egypt and consequently each symbol in the space above must be the name of a ruler of the Lower Kingdom. Some nine of these names can still be read, and lost portions of the stone doubtless contained more names for Lower Egypt and a list for Upper Egypt too. As a matter of fact, on a Cairo fragment of the annals some Predynastic kings appear wearing the double crown of Lower and Upper Egypt combined.[14]

This occurrence of the double crown and the domination of Upper Egypt by the Gerzean culture which originated in the Delta, have suggested the hypothesis that a temporary unification of the two lands was accomplished during the Middle Predynastic period. If such a unification did take place it must have been the work of conquerors from the Delta who were able to establish their supremacy also in Upper Egypt. If there was such a union, however, it did not endure, and the Late Predynastic period saw the two lands broken apart again and warring against each other. At this time the capital of Upper Egypt was at Nekheb, a site which later was known as Eileithyiaspolis and is the modern Elkab; and the royal residence was just across the river at Nekhen, which later was called Hierakonpolis. The capital of Lower Egypt was at Buto, with the royal residence in a suburb called Pe. Finally a king of Upper Egypt conquered the Delta and united the two Egypts permanently in a single kingdom under one central rule.[15]

2. THE PROTODYNASTIC PERIOD
(FIRST AND SECOND DYNASTIES), c.2900-c.2700 B.C.[1]

MENES

ACCORDING to Manetho the first king of permanently united Egypt was Menes. The statement of the ancient historian as he introduces

[14] James Henry Breasted, ARE I, §§76-167; and in *Bulletin de l'Institut Français d'Archéologie Orientale.* 30 (1930-31), pp.709-724.

[15] A. Moret, *The Nile and Egyptian Civilization.* 1927, pp.101-113; A. Scharff, *Grundzüge der Ägyptischen Vorgeschichte.* 1927, pp.46-49; Ranke in JAOS 59 (1939) No.4, Supplement, pp.14f.

[1] For the dates see Albright in BASOR 88 (Dec. 1942), p.32, with correlations with Mesopotamian and other Middle Eastern chronologies; cf. Meek in JR 21 (1941),

the First Dynasty runs as follows: "The first royal house numbers eight kings, the first of whom Menes of This reigned for 62 years. He was carried off by a hippopotamus and perished."[2] The native city of Menes was This, not far from the great bend of the Nile below Thebes, near where the modern town of Girga stands. This was the capital of the nome of the same name, and was the seat of both the First and Second Dynasties, which took from it their customary designation as the Thinite dynasties.

Since This was situated far south in Upper Egypt, the new ruler of all the Egyptians also built a fortress three hundred miles to the north, at the apex of the Delta and on the border of the two lands. Herodotus says that the site was gained by building a dam to divert the Nile.[3] In reference to the White Kingdom whose victorious power it represented, the new city was known as "White Wall." From the Sixth Dynasty on it bore the name Men-nefru-Mire or Menfe, from which is derived the familiar Greek name, Memphis.[4]

The cemetery of the Thinite kings was in the desert not far from This and near the site of Abydos. As a result of excavations carried out here in 1899 and following by W. M. Flinders Petrie, the tombs of most of these kings have been discovered.[5] They were in the form of underground pits lined with brick walls, and originally roofed with timber and matting. In the more elaborate examples the burial chamber proper was a wooden hall in the center of the larger pit, surrounded by smaller chambers to hold the offerings. Smaller tombs for the king's servants were ranged about the structure. In the Second Dynasty vaults of brick took the place of the original wooden ceilings for the tombs. In turn a more elaborate superstructure was developed, consisting of a great rectangle of brickwork with slop-

p.404 n.16. See also tables of Egyptian chronology in George Steindorff and Keith C. Seele, *When Egypt Ruled the East*. 2d ed. rev. by Keith C. Seele. 1957, pp.274f.; John A. Wilson, *The Burden of Egypt*. 1951, pp.vii-viii; and Hayes, *The Scepter of Egypt*, I, pp.34, 58, etc. Steindorff and Seele, and Hayes place the beginning of the First Dynasty around 3200 B.C., Wilson around 3100 B.C. A radiocarbon test has given a measure of confirmation to the date c.2900 B.C. in that a piece of wood from a beam in the tomb at Saqqara of Hemaka, a vizier of the First Dynasty, has been dated at 2933 B.C., but there is a possible margin of error of 200 years either way. G. E. Wright in BA 14 (1951), p.31.

2 *Manetho*, tr. Waddell, pp.27-29.

3 II, 99.

4 J. H. Breasted, *A History of Egypt*. 1909, p.37. Memphis is mentioned frequently in the Old Testament (Hosea 9:6; Isaiah 19:13; Jeremiah 2:16; 44:1; 46:14, 19; Ezekiel 30:13, 16), the Hebrew name being Noph, which is perhaps a corruption of the middle part of the ancient Egyptian name.

5 Petrie, *The Royal Tombs of the First Dynasty*. 1900; *The Royal Tombs of the Earliest Dynasties*. 1901.

ing sides, distinctive recesses, and a flat top. To this type of tomb it is customary now to apply the Arabic name *mastaba*, meaning platform or bench.

Like so many of the burial places of ancient Egypt, the royal tombs at Abydos had already been plundered by robbers. Enough of their contents remained, however, to show that with the mummies a profusion of jewelry, stone vases, copper vessels, and other objects had been buried. Also the names of a number of the kings were found, including Narmer, Aha, Zer, and others. These are the "Horus titles" or names of the kings as earthly representatives of the god Horus, rather than their personal names which were used by Manetho. Identifications are not certain, therefore, but it is probable that Narmer is the king who was called Menes by Manetho, and who was founder of the First Dynasty.

The finest monument of Narmer which we possess is a slate palette found at Hierakonpolis and shown in Fig. 28. The palette is like those on which the Egyptians had long ground eye-paint, but is of a very large size as befitted a great king. On the obverse side (right) the king and priests walk in triumphal procession while the long necks of two monsters are curved to form a circular recess where the cosmetics may be ground. On the reverse stands the tall figure of the king who lifts a heavy mace with pear-shaped head of white stone to crush the skull of his enemy whom he grasps by the hair. Upon the king's head is the tall, white, helmet-like crown of Upper Egypt, while a long animal tail hangs from the back of his belt. The latter probably was an ancient North African badge of chieftaincy but it remains henceforth a regular attribute of the Egyptian kingship. Behind the king is his servant, carrying the king's sandals and a water-pot or oil-jar. Around the king's belt and also at the top of the palette are heads of Hathor, the cow-goddess. At one side is a very early example of Egyptian hieroglyphics, or writing in picture form. A falcon, as symbol of the king, holds a length of rope which is attached to a man's head. The head is connected with an area of ground out of which grow six papyrus stalks, representing the marshes of Lower Egypt. Below is a single-barbed harpoon head and a rectangle which is the sign of a lake. The entire pictograph means that the falcon king led captive the people of the Harpoon Lake in Lower Egypt. At the top of the palette, between the heads of Hathor, is the name of the king, Narmer.[6]

[6] Quibell, *Hierakonpolis.* I (1900), p.10.

Other First Dynasty tombs have been excavated recently at Saqqara near Memphis, which are even larger and more elaborate than the ones at Abydos. This discovery has led to the suggestion that the early kings of the then recently united Upper and Lower Egypt may each have had two tombs, one in the south and another in the north. In this case the Abydos tombs could have been their cenotaphs, those at Saqqara their actual burial places. Tomb 3504 at Saqqara is dated to the reign of King Wadjy, fourth monarch of the First Dynasty, and contains a large burial chamber surrounded by magazines for storing the food and other things needed by the deceased in the world beyond. Around three sides of the tomb are also small graves which may have been for retainers sacrificed to accompany the king in death. Striking too is a bench surrounding this tomb structure on which were once probably more than three hundred bulls' heads modeled in clay with real horns attached. Tomb 3505, dating to the reign of King Ka-a, last ruler of the dynasty, was even larger and in general design provides a prototype of the pyramid complex of later times with the funerary temple on the north side of the tomb.[7]

Lines two and three of the Palermo Stone (Fig. 27) give annals from the time of the First Dynasty, although the fragment as we have it does not include the beginning of that dynasty. As compared with the bare list of names of the Predynastic kings the record now is fuller, and an entire oblong is devoted to each year of a king's reign, the dividing lines curling over at the top being the hieroglyphic signs for palms, and signifying years. The name of the king is given in the long horizontal space above the yearly records, as may be seen above rows 3 and 4. The vertical line extending up through the horizontal space near the right end of row 2 marks the termination of a reign. The oblong immediately to the right shows six new moons, a sun, and seven strokes, thus indicating six months and seven days which is some detail as to the time when this reign ceased. Continuing to read from right to left, the next oblong gives the date of the new king's accession, the fourth month and thirteenth day, ten being represented by two strokes joined at the top. When a king came to the throne a feast was celebrated called "Union of the Two Lands," and by it the king's first year was characterized and named. This designation appears in the same oblong in the form of the lotus and papyrus tied together. The measurements in the little rectangles

[7] Walter B. Emery in *Archaeology*. 8 (1955), pp.2-9.

below, giving a number of cubits, palms, and fingers, may have registered the height of the Nile inundation that year.

In the early years and reigns most of the events noted are but names of religious feasts. Lines 4 and 5 are devoted to the Second Dynasty, and here we come upon a mention of the "fourth occurrence of the numbering," a reference to a regular census or inventory of some sort. With line 6 and the Third Dynasty the annal becomes yet more detailed and the yearly sections are necessarily much larger. Here there is reference to the building of ships of some size, and the bringing by sea of cedar wood, probably from Lebanon. A double palace was erected whose double name recalled the old kingdoms of South and North: "Exalted-is-the-White-Crown-of-Snefru-upon-the-Southern-Gate. Exalted-is-the-Red-Crown-of-Snefru-upon-the-Northern-Gate." Most of the record of the Fourth Dynasty is missing, but the lines on the back of the Palermo Stone carry the annals on down into the Fifth Dynasty.

Before continuing the narrative into later eras it should be indicated that already in the late Predynastic and early Protodynastic periods Egypt was in contact with the environing world. Indeed the period of about 3000 B.C. constituted the first great epoch of international commerce. This will be remembered as the Jemdet Nasr period in Mesopotamia, and there are definite evidences of Mesopotamian influence in Egypt at the time. In the painted tomb at Hierakonpolis already mentioned a boat is depicted which is very different from the usual papyrus boats of Egypt but is similar to those represented in Mesopotamia. At Jebel el-Arak a carved ivory knife-handle has been found which not only shows another such foreign-type boat but also reveals a scene whose Mesopotamian character is even more unmistakable. In the latter a hero is shown in combat with two lions which rise against him from either side. Not only is the grouping typically Mesopotamian but the man himself is pictured in Asiatic style with full beard and long robe.[8] Mesopotamian cylinder seals of the Jemdet Nasr period have also been found in Egypt, and the development of Egyptian cylinder seals was a result of original impact from the land of the Two Rivers.[9] Likewise the sudden appearance in Egypt of an advanced technique and style in the erection of recessed brick buildings evidently was

[8] Georges Bénédite in *Académie des inscriptions et belles-lettres, Commission de la fondation Eugène Piot, Monuments et mémoires.* 22 (1916), pp.1-34; René Dussaud in *Syria.* 16 (1935), pp.320-323.

[9] Frankfort, *Cylinder Seals*, pp.292-300.

based upon knowledge of architectural achievements in Mesopotamia which had reached a similar level at this time. These facts show that Mesopotamian influences were a stimulus in Egypt during some of the most formative phases of that land's development.[10]

3. THE OLD KINGDOM (THIRD TO SIXTH DYNASTIES), c.2700-c.2200 B.C.

THE Third to Sixth Dynasties constitute the time of the Old Kingdom or the Pyramid Age, the first great culminating point of Egyptian civilization. Under the rule of Djoser, first king of the Third Dynasty, the remarkable Imhotep attained renown as priest, magician, author of wise proverbs, physician, and architect. For his king, Imhotep undertook the construction of a royal mausoleum of a style more impressive than any hitherto known. Starting with a lofty *mastaba* of stone, and superimposing five successive shells upon it, he built the famous "step pyramid" at Saqqara, a terraced monument 190 feet high, the earliest large structure of stone known in history. From this there developed the great pyramids which have been in all succeeding centuries a wonder of the world.

THE PYRAMIDS

Of all the pyramids[1] the greatest (Fig. 29) was built by Khufu, second king of the Fourth Dynasty. Upon a square base covering some thirteen acres, he heaped up 2,300,000 blocks of yellowish limestone, each weighing on the average two and one-half tons, until the whole pyramid towered originally 481 feet into the sky. According to Herodotus, laborers toiled on the monument in groups of 100,000 men, each group for three months at a time. Ten years were required to make the road whereon the stones were dragged and twenty years more for the pyramid itself. Like a good tourist Herodotus reports that it was written on the pyramid how much was spent on onions and garlic for the workmen and says, "to my sure remembrance the interpreter when he read me the writing said that sixteen hundred talents of silver had been paid."[2] The stonework was done

[10] A. Scharff in ZÄS 71 (1935), pp.89-106; H. Frankfort in AJSL 58 (Jan.-Oct. 1941), pp. 329-358; and *The Birth of Civilization in the Near East*, pp. 100-111; Helene J. Kantor in JNES 3 (1944), pp.110-136; and in Ehrich, ed., *Relative Chronologies in Old World Archeology*, pp.5-8.
[1] I. E. S. Edwards, *The Pyramids of Egypt.* 1947.   [2] II, 124f.

with a precision involving seams of one ten-thousandth of an inch, and the entire exterior was covered with an exquisitely fitted casing of fine white limestone. Such is "the earliest and most impressive witness surviving from the ancient world, to the final emergence of organized society from prehistoric chaos and local conflict, thus coming for the first time completely under the power of a far-reaching and comprehensive centralization effected by one controlling mind."[3]

Khafre, the successor of Khufu, built the even more spectacular Second Pyramid of Giza. Its present height is 447½ feet, only 1½ feet less than the present height of the Great Pyramid, while its base is smaller, each side of the base now measuring 690½ feet as compared with 746 feet on the Great Pyramid. The angle of the sides of the Second Pyramid (52° 20′) is therefore steeper than that of the Great Pyramid (51° 50′) while the upper one-fourth of the slopes still retains the original casing of smooth limestone and granite slabs.[4] Khafre himself is represented in the head of the great Sphinx which stands to the east of the Second Pyramid. The body of the Sphinx is that of a couchant lion, but the head is that of the king, wearing the usual cloth headdress and with the uraeus or deadly cobra coiled on his forehead. This serpent was symbol of the kingship and coiled itself upon the king's brow to destroy his enemies as once it had annihilated the adversaries of the sun-god Re. The Sphinx was carved out of a spur of natural rock and built up with blocks of stone at the same time that the pyramid of Khafre was built or soon after. The monument was gradually half-buried by the ever-drifting sands of the desert but was excavated by Thutmose IV and again by modern Egyptian archeologists in 1926-1927 and 1936-1946.[5]

Kings of the Fifth and Sixth Dynasties built a number of smaller pyramids at Saqqara. On the walls of the inner passages and chambers of these monuments they caused inscriptions to be carved which are known as the Pyramid Texts.[6] Since in some cases they reflect conditions prior even to the union of Upper and Lower Egypt, many of these texts must be much earlier than the time of their

[3] J. H. Breasted, A History of the Ancient Egyptians. 1903, p. 110.
[4] This is the pyramid from which Rand Herron, member of the 1932 mountaineering expedition to Nanga Parbat, fell to his death. Ullman, High Conquest, p.194.
[5] Selim Hassan, The Sphinx, Its History in the Light of Recent Excavations. 1949. See pp.88-91 for the date in the reign of Khafre.
[6] Samuel A. B. Mercer, The Pyramid Texts in Translation and Commentary. 4 vols. 1952; John A. Wilson in ANET pp.32f.

recording in the pyramids and may be supposed to have existed previously, written on papyrus or potsherds. Their theme is the prospect of a glorious hereafter for the deceased king in the presence of the sun-god. Frequently their form is that of couplets which display parallelism in the arrangement of words and thought.

The composing of proverbs was also practiced by the early Egyptians. Imhotep was famous in this regard as we have noted, and so were Kagemni and Hardedef. Of all the sages, however, the best known is Ptahhotep, who was grand vizier under a king of the Fifth Dynasty. His proverbs take the form of instructions to his son and have to do particularly with behavior that is fitting on the part of a state official. "Let not thy heart be puffed-up because of thy knowledge," said the father to the son, "be not confident because thou art a wise man. Take counsel with the ignorant as well as the wise. . . . Good speech is more hidden than the emerald, but it may be found with maidservants at the grindstones." "Wrongdoing has never brought its undertaking into port," he warned, "but the strength of justice is that it lasts." Having given such advice and much more, he admonished gently: "How good it is when a son accepts what his father says!"[7]

4. FIRST INTERMEDIATE PERIOD
(SEVENTH TO ELEVENTH DYNASTIES), c.2200-c.1991 B.C.

As THE glory of the Old Kingdom faded, there ensued a period of disintegration and chaos when weak kings were unable to maintain a strong, central government. Manetho's Seventh and Eighth Dynasties which continued to rule weakly at Memphis, and the Ninth and Tenth Dynasties which arose at Herakleopolis (seventy-seven miles south of Cairo), are included in this Intermediate period. The disturbances and upset conditions which were experienced are reflected in "The Admonitions of Ipuwer."

"Why really, the land spins around as a potter's wheel does. . . . The nomes are destroyed. Barbarians from outside have come to Egypt. . . Laughter has disappeared. . . . It has come to a point where the land is despoiled of kingship by a few irresponsible men. . . . The owners of

[7] John A. Wilson in ANET pp.412-414; cf. T. Eric Peet, *A Comparative Study of the Literatures of Egypt, Palestine, and Mesopotamia.* 1931, pp.101-103; Adolf Erman, *The Literature of the Ancient Egyptians.* 1927, p.60.

robes are now in rags. But he who never wove for himself is now the owner of fine linen."[1]

Ipuwer hoped however for the coming of an ideal king whom he described in the following words: "It shall come that he brings coolness upon the heart. Men shall say: 'He is the herdsman of all men. Evil is not in his heart. Though his herds may be small, still he has spent the day caring for them.' "[2] Such is one of the earliest expressions of the Messianic hope in history.

Another burdened writer of the same period wistfully longed for death itself as a glad release:

> Death is in my eyes today
> As when a sick man becomes whole,
> As the walking abroad after illness.
>
> Death is in my eyes today
> Like the desire of a man to see his home
> When he hath passed many years in captivity.[3]

In the Eleventh Dynasty the Intefs and Mentuhoteps were able at least partially to restore order and to reestablish a centralized state. Their place of rule was at Thebes, a city which was situated on the Nile 440 miles above Memphis, and which was destined later to become Egypt's greatest capital.[4]

5. THE MIDDLE KINGDOM
(TWELFTH DYNASTY), c.1991-c.1786 B.C.[1]

WITH the Twelfth Dynasty which was inaugurated by Amenemhet I, Egypt entered the second great period of its history, the Middle Kingdom. The kings of this dynasty were native Thebans but they

[1] John A. Wilson in ANET pp.441f.; cf. Peet, *A Comparative Study of the Literatures of Egypt, Palestine, and Mesopotamia*, p.118; cf. Josephine Mayer and Tom Prideaux, *Never to Die, the Egyptians in Their Own Words*. 1938, p. 68.

[2] Wilson in ANET p.443; cf. Breasted, *The Dawn of Conscience*, p.198.

[3] Peet, *A Comparative Study of the Literatures of Egypt, Palestine, and Mesopotamia*, pp.116f.; John A. Wilson in ANET p.407; R. O. Faulkner in JEA 42 (1956), pp.21-40.

[4] The Egyptian name for the town was Weset or more briefly Newt, "the city," whence is derived the biblical No (Jeremiah 46:25; Ezekiel 30:14-16) or No-Amon (Nahum 3:8), "city" or "city of Amun." The Greeks called it Thebes (Θῆβαι) and also Diospolis (Διόσπολις), meaning "city of Zeus" (Amun), or Diospolis Magna in distinction from Diospolis Parva or Hou. The modern villages at this site are Luxor and Karnak.

[1] H. E. Winlock, *The Rise and Fall of the Middle Kingdom in Thebes*. 1947, p.91. Hayes (*The Scepter of Egypt*. I, pp.150, 170, 340) treats the Eleventh Dynasty as

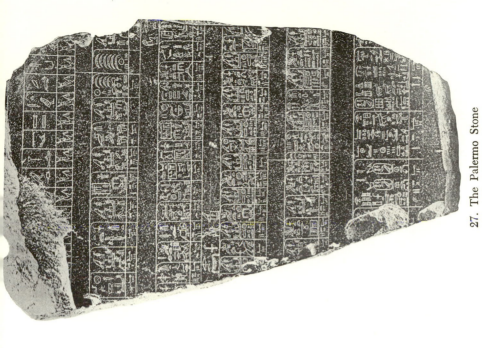

27. The Palermo Stone

26. The Plants that Were the Symbols of Upper and Lower Egypt

28. Cast of the Slate Palette of King Narmer

29. The Great Pyramid at Giza as Seen from the Summit of the Second Pyramid

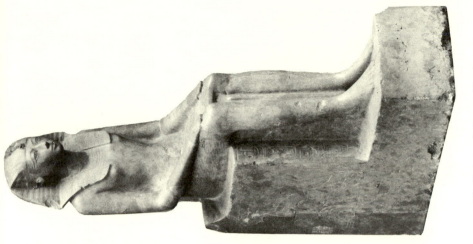

31. Statue of Queen Hatshepsut

30. A Semite with his Donkey, as Painted in the Tomb of Khnumhotep II

32. The Terraced Temple of Hatshepsut at Deir el-Bahri

34. Thutmose III

33. Statue of Senenmut and Nefrure

35. The Obelisk of Thutmose III now in New York City

36. Bricklayers at Work, a Painting in the Tomb of Rekhmire

37. The Judgment Scene in the Papyrus of Ani

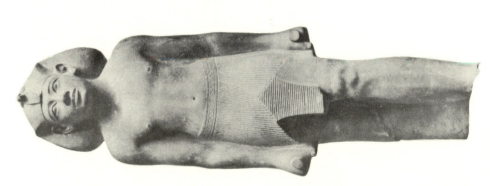

39. Amenhotep II, Standing under the Protection of the Cow-Goddess, Hathor

38. Statue of Amenhotep II

40. Syrians Bringing Tribute

41. Head of Amenhotep III

42. The Colonnade of Amenhotep III at Luxor
(with Pylon of Ramses II in the Background)

43. Fowling in the Marshes

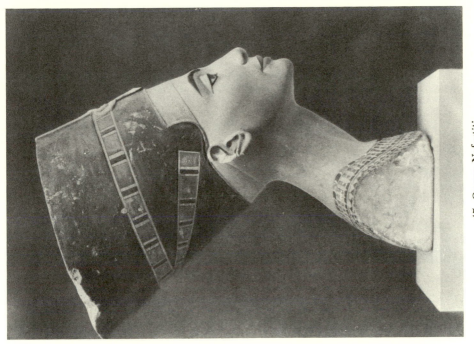

45. Queen Nefertiti

44. Statue of Akhenaton from Karnak

47. Portrait Mask of Tutankhamun

46. Obverse of Tell el-Amarna Tablet with Letter from Rib-Addi to Amenhotep III

49. The Hypostyle Hall in the Temple at Karnak

48. Haremhab as a Royal Scribe, before his
Accession as King

51. The Victory Stela of Merneptah

50. Statue of Ramses II at Abu Simbel

53. Temple Relief of Ramses III at Medinet Habu

52. Philistine Prisoners Being Led into the Presence of Ramses III

55. The Rosetta Stone

54. Israelite Captives of Sheshonk I

ruled chiefly from capitals in Memphis and in the Fayum. Their house endured for over two hundred years, and their accomplishments included the conquest of Nubia to the Second Cataract,[1a] the connecting of the Nile with the Red Sea by canal, and the development of mining in Sinai into a permanent industry. The art and architecture of the age were characterized by refinement. Feminine jewelry was made with unsurpassed beauty of design and microscopic accuracy of execution. A "literature of entertainment" arose for the first time, including such stories as "Baufra's Tale" and "The Eloquent Peasant."[2] In the Fifth and Sixth Dynasties the Pyramid Texts (p. 88) had described a future life to be enjoyed by the king, but now in the Middle Kingdom others besides kings could anticipate the privilege of being buried with texts at hand to guide and protect them in the after-life. These texts were written on the inside of the coffin of the deceased, hence are known as the Coffin Texts.

If Abraham's migration to Palestine and subsequent visit to Egypt[3] (p. 72) fell in the neighborhood of 1900 B.C. then he was in Egypt in the days of the Middle Kingdom; if it was around 1700 B.C. then it was in the Second Intermediate period. Abraham does not figure in Egyptian records of the time, the earliest occurrence of his name being when Pharaoh Sheshonk I (tenth century B.C.) records capturing a place in Palestine called "The Field of Abram" (p. 126).[4] But it is interesting to have such tangible evidence of communication between Egypt and Palestine and Syria in these very days as appears in the following account.

THE TALE OF SINUHE

When Amenemhet I died, his son, Senusert (or Sesostris) I, was campaigning in the western Delta against the Libyans. Word of the

---

marking the beginning of the Middle Kingdom, and the Thirteenth and Fourteenth Dynasties as representing its decline and fall. For the chronology of the Twelfth Dynasty see William F. Edgerton in JNES 1 (1942), pp.307-314, with revisions by PCAE p.69. Several coregencies are involved and the probable dates of the rulers are: Amenemhet I, 1991-1962; Senusert I, 1971-1928; Amenemhet II, 1929-1895; Senusert II, 1897-1879; Senusert III, 1878-1843; Amenemhet III, 1842-1797; Amenemhet IV, 1798-1790; Sebeknefrure, 1789-1786.

[1a] For an Egyptian fortress at Buhen just north of the Second Cataract see *Archaeology*. 11 (1958), pp.215f.

[2] W. M. F. Petrie, *Egyptian Tales*. First Series, 2d ed. 1899, pp.16-22,61-80.

[3] Genesis 12:10-13:1 (J). Genesis 20:1-17 (E) corrects the unfavorable impression created by the story of Sarah in Pharaoh's harem, by transferring the situation to King Abimelech's court at Gerar, and changing many of the details.

[4] ARE IV, §715.

old king's death was dispatched to the son who, upon receiving it, kept the news secret and returned at once to the capital to establish himself firmly as king before any pretender could precede him. This was quite in accord with the spirit of instructions which Amenemhet had given his son earlier. The old king, whose life had been attempted by assassins, had advised:

"Hold thyself apart from those subordinate to thee, lest that should happen to whose terrors no attention has been given. . . . Fill not thy heart with a brother, nor know a friend. Create not for thyself intimates— there is no fulfilment thereby. Even when thou sleepest, guard thy heart thyself, because no man has adherents in the day of distress."[5]

With Senusert I in the field was a noble of high rank, named Sinuhe. Accidentally overhearing the message about Amenemhet's death, he fled the country immediately for political reasons and returned only in his old age and upon the pardon of Senusert. The story of his adventures as he fled overland to Syria is related in "The Tale of Sinuhe." Hiding in the bushes and fields, he passed the Egyptian frontier fort at night. In the desert he grew faint with thirst and his throat was hot with the taste of death but he was rescued at last by an Asiatic sheikh. Eventually he came through Qedem, meaning the East generally, and arrived in Upper Retenu, Retenu being the usual Egyptian name for Syria and Palestine.[6] Here he settled in a "good land," which he describes in language similar to that later applied to Palestine in the Old Testament (Exodus 3:8; Deuteronomy 8:8; etc.):

"Figs were in it, and grapes. It had more wine than water. Plentiful was its honey, abundant its olives. Every kind of fruit was on its trees. Barley was there, and emmer. There was no limit to any kind of cattle."[7]

THE TOMB OF KHNUMHOTEP III

In the days of Senusert II, fourth king of the Twelfth Dynasty, a powerful noble, Khnumhotep III, lived at Beni Hasan, 168 miles above Cairo. In his tomb a famous scene still depicts a visit paid him by a group of thirty-seven Asiatics of the desert, bringing gifts

---

[5] John A. Wilson in ANET p.418; cf. ARE I, §479.

[6] Steindorff and Seele, *When Egypt Ruled the East*, p.47. The same area was also called Khor (Khuru, Kharu), from the Hurrians or Horites, and Palestine was known as Djahi. The region north of the Lebanon was Amor (Amurru), and the land at the upper reaches of the Euphrates was Nahrin (Naharin). On Egyptian influence in Palestine in the time of the Middle Kingdom, see John A. Wilson in AJSL 58 (1941), pp.225-236.

[7] John A. Wilson in ANET p.19 (ANEA p.5); cf. ARE I, §496.

and desiring trade.[8] The men have thick black hair which falls to the neck, and their beards are pointed. They wear long cloaks and carry spears, bows, and throw-sticks. The accompanying inscription reads, "The arrival, bringing eye-paint, which 37 Asiatics brought to him." The leader of the group is labeled "the Ruler of a Foreign Country," and his name is given as Ibsha. A date is appended, the sixth year of Senusert II, or about 1892 B.C.[9] One portion of this very interesting painting is reproduced in Fig. 30. We see a black-bearded nomad walking behind his donkey to the accompaniment of music which he makes upon a lyre. The man carries a water-skin upon his back, while on the donkey's gay saddle-cloth are tied other objects including a spear and throw-stick.

By the end of the Middle Kingdom period, it is clear that the Asiatic peoples had become a threat to Egypt. Numerous broken pottery bowls have been found, dating probably from the reign of Senusert III or later, on which are inscriptions expressing curses against the enemies of the king. It is probable that these were used in magical procedures where the smashing of the inscribed bowl was intended to break the power of the enemy named on it. In these execration texts, as the inscriptions are called, the most prominently named foes are Asiatic rulers. It is very interesting to find that among the places mentioned is Aushamem, which is probably Jerusalem. The names of two rulers of Aushamem are given, Iyqa-'ammu, a Semitic name, and Setj-'anu.[10]

6. SECOND INTERMEDIATE PERIOD
(THIRTEENTH TO SEVENTEENTH DYNASTIES),
c.1786–c.1570 B.C.

IN THE days which followed, native Egyptian power disintegrated more and more and the land fell eventually under rule by foreigners. The Thirteenth and Fourteenth Dynasties were made up of numerous petty kings, some of whom probably ruled contemporaneously. Already in the Thirteenth Dynasty several of the kings bear Semitic names.[1] There is also a papyrus in the Brooklyn Museum, dated in the first and second regnal years of the Thirteenth Dynasty ruler

---

[8] P. E. Newberry, *Beni Hasan*. I (1893), Pl. xxx; ANEP No.3 (ANEA No.2).
[9] ANET p.229; ARE I, p.281, d.
[10] ANEP No.593 (ANEA No.153); ANET p.329.
[1] Hayes, *The Scepter of Egypt*, I, p.351.

Sebek-hotep III, about 1740 B.C., which lists ninety-five slaves, thirty-seven of whom are labeled as "male Asiatic" or "female Asiatic." Nearly thirty of the names are Northwest-Semitic, and one is virtually the same as that of Shiprah, one of the Israelite midwives in Exodus 1:15.[2]

THE HYKSOS

In the Fifteenth and Sixteenth Dynasties the rulers of much of Egypt were the Hyksos. The coming of the Hyksos is described by Manetho in a passage preserved in Josephus. Referring to Tutimaeus, who probably was a king of the Thirteenth Dynasty, Manetho says: "In his reign, for what cause I know not, a blast of God smote us; and unexpectedly, from the regions of the East, invaders of obscure race marched in confidence of victory against our land. By main force they easily seized it without striking a blow; and having overpowered the rulers of the land, they then burned our cities ruthlessly, razed to the ground the temples of the gods, and treated all the natives with a cruel hostility. . . . Finally, they appointed as king one of their number whose name was Salitis."[3] Manetho states further that Salitis ruled from Memphis and that he also rebuilt as a powerful stronghold "a city very favourably situated on the east of the Bubastite branch of the Nile, and called Auaris." The branch of the Nile referred to is the one farthest east, and the city of Auaris or Avaris doubtless is to be identified with Tanis, near the modern fishing village of San el-Hagar. Manetho also explains that the name Hyksos means " 'king-shepherds': for *hyk* in the sacred language means 'king,' and *sos* in common speech is 'shepherd' or 'shepherds': hence the compound word 'Hyksos.' " It is probable, however, that this is only a late popular etymology and that the name actually was derived from Egyptian words meaning "rulers of foreign lands."[4] In the Eighteenth Dynasty Queen Hatshepsut refers to repairs which she made of damage done by the Hyksos:

> I have restored that which was ruins,
> I have raised up that which was unfinished,
> Since the Asiatics were in the midst of Avaris of the Northland,
> And the barbarians were in the midst of them.[5]

[2] W. F. Albright in JAOS 74 (1954), pp.222-233.
[3] *Manetho*, tr. Waddell, pp.79-81; Josephus, *Against Apion.* I, 14.
[4] Adolf Erman and Hermann Grapow, *Wörterbuch der ägyptischen Sprache.* III (1929), p.171, 29.
[5] ARE II, §303.

It is probable that the Hyksos were well established in Egypt by around 1700 B.C. and that they ruled for about a century and a half.[6] The foreigners may have been of mixed stock but the preponderant element among them seems to have been Semitic.[7] As a matter of fact, Josephus identified the Hyksos with the children of Israel. He introduced his quotations from Manetho concerning the Hyksos as statements "about us," that is about the Jewish people, and described "the so-called shepherds" as "our ancestors."[8] His purpose in this identification was that he might adduce the testimony of Manetho as proving the antiquity of the Jews. While it is hardly possible to believe from the biblical records that the Israelites played any such role of conquest and domination in Egypt as did the Hyksos, nevertheless there is probably this much truth in the tradition of Josephus, that the people of Israel were in Egypt at the same time as the Hyksos. This fact could account for the representation found in Josephus, and it is antecedently probable that the Israelites would find a friendly reception in Egypt at a time when the country was under rulers who were themselves of Semitic descent.[9]

While Manetho states that Salitis ruled in Upper as well as Lower Egypt, it is evident that the center of Hyksos power was in the eastern Delta. In Upper Egypt native princes reasserted themselves, and Seventeenth Dynasty kings were rivals of the later Hyksos. At last war broke out between Sekenenre, ruling at Thebes, and Apophis, Hyksos king at Avaris. A folk tale concerning the start of the war, found in a Nineteenth Dynasty papyrus, tells that Sekenenre had a hippopotamus pool in Thebes and the bellowing of the hippopotami was such that King Apophis sent a complaint from Avaris that he could not get any sleep day or night.[10] A more realistic testimony to the outbreak of conflict between the native Egyptians and the

[6] A stela from Tanis commemorates the four hundredth anniversary of that city which was observed probably in the reign of Haremhab (c.1340-c.1303), and thus a time shortly before 1700 B.C. is indicated for the foundation of Tanis. See Kurt Sethe in ZÄS 65 (1930), pp.85-89. Winlock (*The Rise and Fall of the Middle Kingdom in Thebes*, pp. 97-99) follows the Turin Papyrus in assigning 108 years to their reign, and lists the Hyksos kings with approximate dates as follows: (1) Salatis or Salitis (perhaps really a title, "the Sultan"), 1675-1662; (2) Bnon or Beon, 1662-1654; (3) Apachnan, 1654-1644; (4) Khian (also called Iannas or Staan), 1644-1604; (5) Assis or Archles, 1604-1600; (6) Apopi or Apophis, 1600-1567. See also Z. Mayani, *Les Hyksos et le Monde de la Bible*. 1956.
[7] R. M. Engberg, *The Hyksos Reconsidered*. 1939, pp.9,49.
[8] *Against Apion*. I, 14, 16.
[9] cf. J. Leibovitch in IEJ 3 (1953), pp.99-112.
[10] Erman, *The Literature of the Ancient Egyptians*, p.166.

foreigners may be found in the mummy of Sekenenre, which shows three terrible wounds in the head.[11]

The sons of Sekenenre, Kamose and Ahmose, continued the struggle against the Hyksos. It fell to Ahmose to drive out the invaders completely. He took Avaris and then pursued the fleeing Hyksos as far as Palestine. There they made a last stand at Sharuhen (cf. Joshua 19:6) but after a six-year siege Ahmose destroyed this stronghold too. Of these happenings we can read a direct account in the biography of one of Ahmose's naval officers.[12]

Another stronghold in Palestine which was occupied by the Hyksos during the time of their conquest of Egypt was at Tell el-'Ajjul, the "Mound of the Little Calf," four miles southwest of modern Gaza. In excavation at this site, which he identified with ancient Gaza, Flinders Petrie found numerous objects used by the Hyksos including gold jewelry, and bronze daggers, toggle-pins, and horse-bits. There was also evidence which seemed to indicate the practice of horse sacrifice.[13]

Whereas Josephus thought that the expulsion of the Hyksos was identical with the exodus of the children of Israel, it is most probable that the latter still continued to live in Egypt at this time. It is of interest to note that after the expulsion of the Hyksos most of the Egyptian lands and fields, apart from the properties attached to the temples, are found in the possession of the Pharaoh. This is a situation similar to that described in Genesis 47:13-26 as having been instituted by Joseph in time of famine.[14]

7. THE NEW KINGDOM
(EIGHTEENTH TO TWENTIETH DYNASTIES),
c.1570-c.1090 B.C.

THE EIGHTEENTH DYNASTY

AHMOSE is usually regarded as the first king of the Eighteenth Dynasty, which was destined to become probably the most brilliant age in all Egyptian history. The horse and chariot became known to the Egyptians during the Hyksos period, and the use of chariotry now

---

[11] Steindorff and Seele, *When Egypt Ruled the East*, pp.28f., Fig. 7.
[12] ARE II, §§1-16.
[13] Flinders Petrie, *Ancient Gaza, Tell El Ajjul*. 5 vols. 1931-52.
[14] Steindorff and Seele, *When Egypt Ruled the East*, p.88.

facilitated far-flung conquests. An empire soon was to be built which reached from the Fourth Cataract of the Nile to beyond the Euphrates.

HATSHEPSUT

About 1546 B.C. Ahmose was succeeded by his son Amenhotep I, and then (c.1525 B.C.) by his daughter's husband, Thutmose I, who campaigned successfully in Nubia and as far as the Euphrates.[1] The only living child of Thutmose I and his queen was a daughter, the remarkable Hatshepsut (Fig. 31), "the first great woman in history of whom we are informed."[2] Legally, Hatshepsut was the only heir to the throne, yet could not actually reign as "king" but could only convey the crown to her husband by marriage. Thutmose I also had a son who was born by one of his secondary wives. In order to secure the throne for this son, he was married to his half-sister, Hatshepsut, and reigned as Thutmose II. The only son of Thutmose II was born to him by a harem girl and was still a boy when his father died. As Thutmose III (c.1490-c.1436 B.C.) he ruled nominally with Hatshepsut, but actually this powerful and brilliant woman now took full control of the government (c.1486-c.1468 B.C.). She had herself proclaimed "king" and appears in a scene representing this proclamation dressed in king's costume and wearing the double crown of Upper and Lower Egypt.[3] As the court official Ineni remarked in his biography, "The God's Wife, Hatshepsut, settled the affairs of the Two Lands according to her own plans. Egypt was made to labor with bowed head for her."[4]

[1] For the dates see Ludwig Borchardt, *Die Mittel zur zeitlichen Festlegung von Punkten der ägyptischen Geschichte und ihre Anwendung.* 1935, pp.87, 116-128; W. F. Edgerton in AJSL 53 (1936-37), pp.188-197; and now M. B. Rowton in JEA 34 (1948), pp.57-74; and in BASOR 126 (Apr. 1952), p.22. From the data of Manetho, from Assyrian and Hittite synchronisms, and from astronomical calculation of the date of a new moon mentioned in the fifty-second year of Ramses II, Rowton has placed the accession of Ramses II in 1290 B.C. (JEA 34 [1948], p.69; cf. W. F. Albright in BASOR 130 [Apr. 1953], p.7). Other dates in the Eighteenth and Nineteenth Dynasties are reckoned backward and forward from this date. See also W. F. Albright in BASOR 118 (Apr. 1950), p. 19; Albrecht Goetze in BASOR 127 (Oct. 1952), p.24; Richard A. Parker in JNES 16 (1957), pp.39-43.

While in the Old Kingdom the regnal year of a king was considered as coinciding with the civil calendar year, from the New Kingdom to the beginning of the Saite period it was reckoned from the actual accession of the king (see also below p.128 n.24). For the Egyptian calendar see the Appendix.

[2] Breasted, *A History of the Ancient Egyptians*, p.217.

[3] ARE II, §231.

[4] ARE II, §341. For the complicated succession of rulers at this time see W. F. Edgerton, *The Thutmosid Succession.* SAOC 8 (1933), pp.41f.

Part of that labor was directed toward the construction of what remains Hatshepsut's most impressive memorial, her mortuary temple (Fig. 32). This temple rises against the face of an imposing cliff at Deir el-Bahri, near Thebes. It was a beautiful structure of white limestone, built in colonnaded terraces from the plain to the cliff, deep within which the tomb itself was to be found. A major sea expedition to Punt, on the Somali coast, brought back the myrrh trees with which its terraces were planted. Another undertaking on behalf of Hatshepsut was the erection of two great obelisks at Karnak, in a hall built earlier by the queen's father, Thutmose I. The enormous granite shafts were quarried at Aswan and brought down the river on a huge barge drawn by a fleet of galleys. One of these still stands in its place and is the most striking of all known obelisks as well as the largest one now in Egypt. It is 97½ feet high, contains 180 cubic yards of granite, and weighs 700,000 pounds. The obelisks were crowned with pyramidions of polished metal and an inscription said concerning them, "Their height pierces to heaven, illuminating the Two Lands like the sun disk. Never was done the like since the beginning."[5]

These great works were carried out for Hatshepsut by the architect Senenmut, her favorite noble to whom she also entrusted the education of her eldest daughter, Princess Nefrure.[6] Senenmut is represented in the statue shown in Fig. 33 holding the little Nefrure protectingly wrapped in his mantle.

THUTMOSE III

After the great queen Hatshepsut was no more, Thutmose III (Fig. 34) reigned as Pharaoh alone (from c.1468 B.C.). "Pharaoh," it may be explained, is the Hebrew form of the Egyptian title "The Great House," which was pronounced something like per-o. Originally a designation of the palace, it was commonly used as the official title of the king from the Eighteenth Dynasty on. Upon emerging as sole ruler, the long-suppressed energies of Pharaoh Thutmose III burst forth in furious activity. He expressed his resentment at having been kept so long in a minor position by hacking out the figure and the name of Hatshepsut wherever these appeared on monuments throughout Egypt. Then he led his armies into battle in Palestine and Syria. His grandfather, Thutmose I, had begun the subjection

[5] ARE II, §305.   [6] ARE II, §§345-347.

of Asiatic provinces for Egypt but among those peoples there was now general revolt. The inhabitants of Palestine, Coelesyria, and the coastal plain were Semitic tribes called Canaanites, while the Hyksos also remained there after having been driven out of Egypt. A confederation of these peoples was organized against Egypt and the enemies of the Pharaoh were in control of the strong fortress of Megiddo, commanding the road from Egypt to the Euphrates. Thutmose III acted swiftly and surprised his opponents by approaching through a narrow pass in the Carmel ridge. Battle was joined upon the plain of Esdraelon. "His majesty went forth in a chariot of electrum, arrayed in his weapons of war. . . . His majesty prevailed against them at the head of his army, and when they saw his majesty prevailing against them they fled headlong to Megiddo in fear, abandoning their horses and their chariots of gold and silver."[7] Although the Egyptian troops tarried for a time with the spoils, Megiddo soon was besieged and taken.

In sixteen further campaigns during the next eighteen summers, Thutmose the Great[8] established the absolute power of Egypt as far as the Euphrates.[9] "Never before in history had a single brain wielded the resources of so great a nation and wrought them into such centralized, permanent, and at the same time mobile efficiency."[10] In a Hymn of Victory, Amen-Re the god of Thebes was made to address him:

> I have given to thee might and victory against all countries,
> I have set thy fame, even the fear of thee, in all lands,
> Thy terror as far as the four pillars of heaven. . . .
> I have felled thine enemies beneath thy sandals.[11]

Coming home each fall from his campaigns, Thutmose III carried out large-scale building projects. Much work was done in enlargement and beautification of the temple of Amun which had stood at

[7] ARE II, §430.

[8] His full name was "Horus: Mighty Bull, Appearing in Thebes; the Two Ladies: Enduring of Kingship; the Horus of Gold: Splendid of Diadems; the King of Upper and Lower Egypt: Enduring of Form Is Re [Menkheperre]; the Son of Re: Thoth Is Born [Thutmose]." The last of these names was the one given him at birth, the others were adopted upon accession to the throne and indicated that the king was the embodiment of the various gods named, such as the Two Ladies who were the tutelary goddesses of Upper and Lower Egypt. So mighty was the name of Thutmose III that for centuries his praenomen Menkheperre was inscribed on amulets as a good-luck charm.

[9] ARE II, §478.

[10] Breasted, *A History of the Ancient Egyptians*, p.242.

[11] ARE II, §656.

Karnak since the days of the Middle Kingdom[12] and to which many different Pharaohs both before and after Thutmose III made contributions. On the walls of one of the temple's corridors which he built were inscribed the annals of his seventeen military campaigns, from which quotations have just been made. At Karnak and elsewhere he erected great obelisks which have been set up now in places as far distant as Constantinople, the Lateran, London, and New York (Fig. 35).[13] Concluding a list of his building works an inscription of Thutmose III said, "He did more than any king who has been since the beginning."[14]

THE TOMB OF REKHMIRE

Many of the building operations of Thutmose III were supervised by his vizier, Rekhmire. The vizier was a sort of prime minister and grand steward who exercised powers as extensive as those ascribed to Joseph in the Old Testament. All administrative business passed through his hands, and he was also a judge and a superintendent of public works. While there was a time beginning in the Fifth Dynasty when the office was hereditary, later it was bestowed by the king upon a noble of his own choosing. One vizier exercised authority over all Egypt until the time of Thutmose III when two appointments were made, one for Upper and one for Lower Egypt. Rekhmire is well known to us from his tomb near Thebes which is covered with scenes and inscriptions depicting and narrating his career. In one of these pictures Rekhmire leans on his staff and inspects stonecutters, sculptors, brickmakers, and builders who toil before him. A portion of this painting, showing the labor of the bricklayers, is reproduced in Fig. 36. The making of bricks in ancient Egypt was a process which involved breaking up the Nile mud with mattocks, moistening it with water, and then mixing it with sand and chopped straw (cf. Exodus 5:6-19). After that it was formed in molds and taken out and baked in the sun. Among the makers and layers of bricks pictured in Rekhmire's tomb are Asiatic foreigners, and the accompanying inscription refers to the "captives brought by his majesty for the works of the temple of Amun." The bricklayers are quoted as saying, "He supplies us with bread, beer, and every good sort," while the taskmaster says to the builders, "The rod is in my hand; be not idle."[15]

---

[12] ARE I, §§421, 484.

[13] ARE II, §§623-636; cf. George A. Zabriskie in *The New York Historical Society Quarterly Bulletin.* 24 (1940), pp.103-112.

[14] ARE II, §158.

[15] P. E. Newberry, *The Life of Rekhmara.* 1900, p.38; ARE II, §§758f.; Norman de

THE PAPYRUS OF ANI

Some glimpse of Theban religious beliefs in the middle of the Eighteenth Dynasty may be had from the Papyrus of Ani.[16] This papyrus is our finest copy of what is known collectively by the name, "The Egyptian Book of the Dead." The texts which were written in the pyramids of the kings of the Fifth and Sixth Dynasties (p. 88), and the instructions and charms which were inscribed on the interior of coffins in the Middle Kingdom (p. 91), had grown now to be a whole collection of religious compositions relating to the after-life. Written more or less fully on larger or smaller papyrus rolls, everyone might have such a book placed with him in the tomb. The beautiful Papyrus of Ani is no less than seventy-eight feet long and one foot three inches wide. Chapter 125 is the most important and probably the most ancient part. An illustration of this chapter in the Papyrus of Ani (Fig. 37) shows Ani, followed by his wife Tutu, bowing humbly in the great Hall of Judgment. In the middle is the balance, operated by the jackal-headed Anubis. On the left scalepan is Ani's heart, represented by an Egyptian hieroglyph looking much like a tiny vase, while in the other is a feather symbolizing truth or righteousness. The god of Destiny stands beneath the beam of the balance and two goddesses of Birth are between the scale and Ani. The soul of Ani in the shape of a human-headed hawk hovers at the end of the beam. On the other side stands the ibis-headed god Thoth, performing his function as scribe and recording with pen and writing palette the verdict of the weighing. Behind him is Amemit, the Devourer of the Dead, a monster with the head of a crocodile, the body of a lion, and the hindquarters of a hippopotamus. If Ani's heart is proved unjust by the weighing it will be devoured by this monster, and Ani's hope of immortality will be lost. On the left is written Ani's prayer to his heart not to betray him, above is a panel of twelve gods as judges, and at the right is the sentence of acquittal.

In the text of Chapter 125 the deceased recites a great repudiation of sins in which forty-two sins are denied before forty-two judges. Each judge has a specific crime to consider and the deceased addresses him by name and denies ever having committed that crime:

Garis Davies, *Paintings from the Tomb of Rekh-mi-Rēʿ at Thebes* (Publications of the Metropolitan Museum of Art, Egyptian Expedition, x). 1935; *The Tomb of Rekh-mi-Rēʿ at Thebes* (Publications of the Metropolitan Museum of Art, Egyptian Expedition, xi). 2 vols. 1943; ANEP No.115; cf. Charles F. Nims in BA 13 (1950), pp.22-28.

[16] E. A. Wallis Budge, *The Papyrus of Ani.* 1913.

"O Swallower-of-Shadows . . . I have not robbed." "O Dangerous-of-Face . . . I have not killed men." "O Breaker-of-Bones . . . I have not told lies." Other denials of sins include: "I have not added to the weight of the balance; I have not been contentious; I have not committed adultery; I have not been unresponsive to a matter of justice; I have not been quarrelsome; I have not done evil." In a concluding address to the gods the deceased affirms his moral worthiness, here making positive as well as negative statements: "Behold me—I have come to you without sin, without guilt, without evil. . . . I have done that which men said and that with which gods are content. I have satisfied a god with that which he desires. I have given bread to the hungry, water to the thirsty, clothing to the naked, and a ferry-boat to him who was marooned. I have provided divine offerings for the gods and mortuary offerings for the dead. So rescue me, you; protect me, you. Ye will not make report against me in the presence of the great god. I am one pure of mouth and pure of hands. . . ."[17] Having been justified in the hour of judgment, the deceased is led by Horus into the presence of Osiris, where he is welcomed to the joys of paradise. Although the Book of the Dead in most of its parts and in most of its use was a book of magical charms, it reveals a perception of the truth that happiness after death is dependent upon the ethical quality of earthly life.[18]

AMENHOTEP II

Thutmose III died around 1436 B.C. and was followed upon the throne by his son who ruled as Amenhotep II. Since the latter had at least a twenty-six year reign,[19] his dates must be approximately 1436-1410 B.C., although it may be that he was coregent with his father for a year or so. A statue of this king is shown in Fig. 38, and another interesting representation of him appears in Fig. 39, where he stands beneath the protecting head of the cow-goddess Hathor, a deity fervently worshiped by the sovereigns of the Eighteenth Dynasty. Even in his youth Amenhotep II distinguished himself for strength and valor. In rowing, in horsemanship, and in archery he was unsurpassed. A stela recently discovered near the great Sphinx

[17] John A. Wilson in ANET pp.34-36.
[18] H. Frankfort (*Ancient Egyptian Religion*. 1948, pp.118f.) doubts that the protestation of sinlessness in the Book of the Dead has much ethical significance.
[19] Rowton in BASOR 126 (Apr. 1952), p.22 n.9.

at Giza narrates various exploits of the young prince, among them the following:

"And he came also and did the following, which I wish to call to your attention. He entered his northern garden and found set up for him four targets of Asiatic copper of a span [three inches] in their thickness and with twenty cubits [nearly thirty-five feet] between one pole and its fellow. Then his majesty appeared in a chariot like Montu [the god of war] in his power. He seized his bow and grasped four arrows at once. He rode northward, shooting at them [the targets] like Montu in his regalia. His arrows came forth from the back of [one of] them while he attacked another. And that is a thing, indeed, which had never been done nor even heard of in story: that an arrow shot at a target of copper came forth from it and dropped to the earth, excepting [at the hand of] the king, rich of glory, whom Amun has strengthened, . . . Okheprure [Amenhotep II], heroic like Montu."[20]

When the great warrior's mummy was found in 1898 in the Valley of the Kings at Thebes,[21] his famous bow, which he boasted no other man could draw, was still beside him. It bore the inscription, "Smiter of the Cave-dwellers, overthrower of Kush, hacking up their cities— the Great Wall of Egypt, Protector of his soldiers."[22]

Amenhotep II was followed by his son Thutmose IV (c.1410- c.1400). From his time an interesting wall painting survives in the tomb of Sebekhotep at Thebes (Fig. 40). It depicts the arrival of Syrian ambassadors bearing tribute to the Egyptian court. The foremost figures are kneeling and raising their arms in reverence to the sovereign. The faces of the men are bearded, and the shawls which are wound round their bodies from the waist downward are an interesting feature of their costumes.[23]

AMENHOTEP III

The son and successor of Thutmose IV was Amenhotep III who reigned from around 1400 b.c. to around 1364 b.c. Sometimes called "The Magnificent," he was Pharaoh as the empire attained its greatest splendor and Eighteenth Dynasty art reached its zenith. In sculpture, the work of a master is to be seen in the head (Fig. 41) of a gigantic granite statue of the king which once must have stood in

[20] Steindorff and Seele, *When Egypt Ruled the East*, pp.68f.

[21] Thutmose I was the first to have his royal tomb excavated in this secluded valley deep among the western cliffs at Thebes, which became the cemetery of the Eighteenth, Nineteenth, and Twentieth Dynasties.

[22] NGM 43 (Jan.-June 1923), p.488.

[23] cf. James B. Pritchard in BASOR 122 (Apr. 1951), pp.36-41.

his own funerary temple near Thebes. The famous "Colossi of Memnon," each seventy feet high and weighing seven hundred tons, also were statues of Amenhotep III. It was in Roman times that the northern colossus was believed to be a statue of Memnon, who greeted his mother Eos (Aurora), goddess of the dawn, with a sweet and plaintive note when she appeared in the morning. This musical phenomenon is mentioned somewhat skeptically by Strabo[24] and described with complete credulity by Philostratus (A.D. c.170-c.245) in connection with the visit of Apollonius and Damis to the statue: "When the sun's rays fell upon the statue, and this happened exactly at dawn, they could not restrain their admiration; for the lips spoke immediately the sun's ray touched them, and the eyes seemed to stand out and gleam against the light."[25]

In architecture the achievements of the time may be illustrated by the great colonnade of Amenhotep III at Luxor (Fig. 42), while in painting the excellence of the work done may be seen in a superb fowling scene from the Theban tomb of Nebamun (Fig. 43). Nebamun, the "scribe who keeps account of the grain," is depicted "taking recreation, seeing pleasant things, and occupying himself with the craft of the Marsh-goddess," as the accompanying inscription states. Accompanied by his wife and little daughter, Nebamun stands upon his light papyrus skiff which is pressing among the lotuses and water-weeds. Three herons are held as decoys, while Nebamun is about to launch his throw-stick at a covey of pintail ducks, geese, and other fowl rising from a clump of papyrus. A cat, which already has retrieved three birds, sits precariously upon a few papyrus-stems, while delicately drawn butterflies enhance the gaiety of the scene.

AMENHOTEP IV (AKHENATON)

Amenhotep IV (c.1370-c.1353 B.C.) was first coregent with his father, Amenhotep III, who was very ill in his old age, and then successor to him. Even before the father died there were ominous rumblings of revolt and invasion in Palestine, Syria, and the north, but the son's greatness was to lie not in the field of military exploit but in the realm of religious thought. Characterized by his portraits (Fig. 44)[26] as an idealist, an artist, and almost a fanatic, Amenhotep

---

[24] *Geography.* xvii, i, 46.
[25] *The Life of Apollonius of Tyana.* vi, 4. tr. F. C. Conybeare. LCL (1912) ii, p.15.
[26] The statues and the mummy of the king indicate that he suffered from an abdominal deformity. M. A. Murray, *Egyptian Sculpture.* 1930, p.135.

IV allowed the empire of his fathers to break apart while he devoted himself to contemplation. Yet so lofty were the ideals which he cherished and so exalted the philosophy which he developed that he has been called "the first *individual* in human history."[27]

The religion which Amenhotep IV introduced was a solar monotheism. The sun always was a dominant fact in the Nile Valley and already had been frequently identified as a god and even the supreme god. According to one belief, the sun was the eye of Horus, the falcon-god, who represented the sky; according to another idea he was a calf, born each day of the cow-goddess of the sky, Hathor. Again the sun was a scarabaeus, rolling the solar globe across the sky; or a mariner traversing the sky in a boat, and returning in the night to the east by a subterranean river. At Heliopolis, near Memphis, the sun was worshiped under the name of Re. The priests here, who have been called "the first religious thinkers in Egypt,"[28] taught that Re, or Re-Harakhti ("Re-Horus of the Horizon"), was the greatest of all gods. This was the religion of state in the Fifth Dynasty, and was still highly influential. At Thebes, Amun (or Amen), who originally had been a ram-headed god of life or reproduction, was exalted to the position of chief god of the Egyptian world empire. He, too, was connected with the sun, and, united with Re, became the great sun-god Amen-Re, bearing the title, "the father of the gods, the fashioner of men, the creator of cattle, the lord of all being." With Thebes as the capital of the empire, the magnificent temples of Amun at Karnak and Luxor were the center of the state cult and were presided over by a chief priest who claimed to stand at the head of all the priesthoods in the land.

In the exaltation of Re or Amun or Amen-Re to the supreme place in the Egyptian pantheon there was obviously a tendency toward monotheism. Yet the theoretical monotheism of the priests was in most cases accommodated in practice to the practical polytheism of the people. All the other gods were retained in subordinate positions as helpers or as names or forms of the sun-god. Likewise the sun-god himself continued to be represented in all manner of animal and human forms. Amun was connected with the ram, and Re with the falcon, the lion, the cat, and the crocodile. A familiar representation of Re was as a man with a falcon's head, on top of which was the

[27] Breasted, *A History of the Ancient Egyptians*, p.265.
[28] Moore, *History of Religions*. i, p.152.

solar disk. Amen-Re appeared as a man wearing on his head a disk surmounted by tall ostrich plumes.

Amenhotep IV now endeavored to go all the way in establishing an exclusive solar monotheism as Egypt's religion. An ancient but hitherto neglected name of the solar disk was Aton. Under this name the worship of the sun might be set free from its mythological connections and exalted into a purer monotheism. This Amenhotep IV undertook to accomplish. Changing his own name from Amenhotep, "Amun Is Satisfied," to Akhenaton, "He Who Is Beneficial to Aton," the king boldly ousted the powerful priesthood of Amun, suppressed the public worship of Amun, and chiseled the very name of Amun and the other old gods from the monuments throughout the land. Then saying farewell to Thebes, the ancient center of Amun worship, he sailed three hundred miles down the Nile to found on an unoccupied site a completely new center for the worship of Aton. The site chosen was where the cliffs retreat from the east side of the river to enclose a plain some three miles wide and five long. At this place Akhenaton built his holy city, devoted to the service of the one god, and named Akhetaton, "Horizon of Aton."[29] Here the king took up his own residence and established the new capital of Egypt. In the sanctuary of the god no idol represented Aton, but only a sun disk from which long rays issued, each ending in a hand, often holding out the hieroglyphic sign for "life," and thus suggesting the celestial power which reached down into the affairs of men.

In the limestone cliffs surrounding the plain of Tell el-Amarna, as Akhetaton's site is now known, are cut a series of tombs of Akhenaton's nobles. Inscriptions in them contain the hymns of the Aton faith. In the great hymn of praise from the tomb of Eye, which may well have been composed by the king himself, the universal and eternal god is hailed in words echoed centuries later by the 104th Psalm:

> Thou appearest beautifully on the horizon of heaven,
> Thou living Aton, the beginning of life!
> When thou art risen on the eastern horizon,
> Thou hast filled every land with thy beauty.

[29] *The City of Akhenaten, I, Excavations of 1921 and 1922 at el-'Amarneh,* by T. Eric Peet and C. Leonard Woolley. 1923; II, *The North Suburb and the Desert Altars, The Excavations at Tell el-Amarna during the Seasons 1926-1932,* by H. Frankfort and J. D. S. Pendlebury. 1933; III, *The Central City and the Official Quarters, The Excavations at Tell el-Amarna during the Seasons 1926-1927 and 1931-1936,* by J. D. S. Pendlebury. 2 vols. 1951. Memoirs of the Egypt Exploration Society, XXXVIII, XL, XLIV; J. D. S. Pendlebury, *Tell el-Amarna.* 1935.

Thou art gracious, great, glistening, and high over every land;
Thy rays encompass the lands to the limit of all that thou hast made.
Though thou art far away, thy rays are on earth;
Though thou art in their faces, no one knows thy going.

When thou settest in the western horizon,
The land is in darkness, in the manner of death.[30]
They sleep in a room, with heads wrapped up.
Every lion is come forth from his den;[31]
All creeping things, they sting.
Darkness is a shroud, and the earth is in stillness,
For he who made them rests in his horizon.
At daybreak, when thou arisest on the horizon,
When thou shinest as the Aton by day,
Thou drivest away the darkness and givest thy rays.
The Two Lands are in festivity every day,
Awake and standing upon their feet,
For thou hast raised them up.
Washing their bodies, taking their clothing,
Their arms are raised in praise at thy appearance.
All the world, they do their work.[32]

How manifold it is, what thou hast made!
They are hidden from the face of man.
O sole god, like whom there is no other!
Thou didst create the world according to thy desire,
Whilst thou wert alone.[33]

Thou settest every man in his place,
Thou suppliest their necessities:
Everyone has his food, and his time of life is reckoned.[34]
Their tongues are separate in speech,
And their natures as well;
Their skins are distinguished,
As thou distinguishest the foreign peoples.

How effective they are, thy plans, O lord of eternity!
Thou makest the seasons in order to rear all that thou hast made,
The winter to cool them,
And the heat that they may taste thee.
Thou madest millions of forms of thyself alone.
Cities, towns, fields, road, and river—
Every eye beholds thee over against them,
For thou art the Aton of the day over the earth.
Thou art in my heart.[35]

[30] cf. Psalm 104:20.   [31] cf. Psalm 104:21.   [32] cf. Psalm 104:22f.
[33] cf. Psalm 104:24.   [34] cf. Psalm 104:27.
[35] John A. Wilson in ANET pp.369-371; cf. Breasted, *The Dawn of Conscience*,
pp.281-286. Wilson (*ibid.*, and *The Burden of Egypt*, pp.223-229) points out that
while Akhenaton and his family worshiped the sole god Aton, his court still wor-

Thus the king felt that although the darkness fell and men slept, his god was still present in his heart. The life-giving power and fatherly kindness of Aton filled the whole world, he believed. He said, "Thou art the mother and the father of all that thou hast made."[36]

Under the influence of this reformation, art showed an even greater delight than before in lovely natural designs of animals, birds, reeds, and plants, and whereas the Pharaoh had always hitherto been depicted in a conventionalized pose of august immobility, Akhenaton allowed himself to be represented in an entirely informal way, often appearing together with his famously beautiful wife, Queen Nefertiti (Fig. 45), and four little daughters.

It is a pathetic fact that Akhenaton did not combine with his great religious insight any corresponding genius for administration and statesmanship. The days of his concentration upon religious reform were days of disintegration of the Egyptian empire. At home resentment and disorder prevailed, abroad in Asia the possessions of the empire were slipping away.

THE TELL EL-AMARNA TABLETS

The state of affairs abroad is very evident in the Tell el-Amarna letters, a group of clay tablets found accidentally by an Egyptian

---

shiped Akhenaton himself, and most Egyptians remained ignorant of or opposed to the new faith, therefore the significance of this so-called "monotheism" should not be overestimated. He also doubts that the faith of Akhenaton could have been influential in the development of the monotheism of Moses, because it does not appear how it could have been transmitted from the one to the other, and because Atonism lacks the ethical content of Israelite monotheism. See also H. H. Rowley in zaw 69 (1957), pp.9f. On the other hand it is surely the case that Akhenaton desired to convert others to the cult which he cherished (Frankfort, *Ancient Egyptian Religion*, p.3), and that the sun was specially connected with justice in Egypt and elsewhere in the Middle East (Frankfort, *Kingship and the Gods*, pp.157f.). Leslie A. White (in jaos 68 [1948], pp.91-114) has attacked the supposition that Akhenaton was a religious genius at all by endeavoring to show that he originated virtually nothing and that the stirring events of his reign can be accounted for as a part of a general process of cultural change. If the tendencies toward the emergence of such a religion were as widespread as this argument assumes, however, it is difficult to see why the reformation of Akhenaton was as ephemeral as it actually was. W. F. Albright thinks it probable that there was some indirect connection between the cult of Akhenaton and the monotheism of Moses. See his *The Biblical Period* (reprinted from Louis Finkelstein, ed., *The Jews, Their History, Culture and Religion.* 1949). 1950, p.9. On the problem of Akhenaton see also R. Engelbach in *Annales du Service des Antiquités de l'Egypte*. 40 (1940), pp.135-185; Rudolf Anthes in jaos 72 (1952), Supplement 14.

[36] Breasted, *The Dawn of Conscience*, p.288.

peasant woman at Tell el-Amarna. Written in cuneiform, they represent correspondence from vassal princes and governors in Syria and Palestine with Amenhotep III and with Akhenaton. Although many of the details of the letters remain obscure, it is clear that Syria and Palestine were seething with intrigue within and were under attack from without, while adequate help to maintain Egyptian sovereignty was not forthcoming. Rib-Addi, governor at Gubla or Byblus, twenty miles north of Beirut, wrote more than fifty times to Amenhotep III and Akhenaton, the following letter (Fig. 46) probably having been addressed to Amenhotep III:

> Rib-Addi to the king. . . .
> At the feet of my lord, my sun,
> seven times and seven times I fall down. . . .
> The king has let his faithful city
> go out of his hand. . . .
> They have formed a conspiracy with one another,
> and thus have I great fear that there is no man to rescue me
> out of their hand. Like birds that
> lie in a net
> so am I in
> Gubla. Why dost thou hold thyself back in respect to thy land?
> Behold, thus have I written to the palace,
> but thou hast paid no attention to my word. . . .
> May the king care for his land. . . .
> What shall I do in
> my solitude? Behold, thus I ask day
> and night.[37]

The governor of a city in northern Syria wrote in similar appeal to Akhenaton:

> To the king of the land of Egypt, our lord. . . .
> At the feet of the lord we fall down. . . .
> Now for twenty years we have been sending to the king, our
>   lord, . . .
> But now Tunip,
> thy city, weeps,
> and her tears are running,
> and there is no help for us.
> We have been sending to the king, the lord, the king of the land
>   of Egypt,
> for twenty years;

[37] C. Bezold and E. A. W. Budge, *The Tell el-Amarna Tablets in the British Museum.* 1892, No.12; KAT No.74 = MTAT No.74. See also translations of the Amarna Letters by W. F. Albright in ANET pp.483-490 (ANEA pp.262f.).

but not one word
has come to us from our lord.[38]

In Jerusalem, Abdi-Hiba (sometimes Abdi-Heba) was governor,
and he wrote repeatedly to Akhenaton, asking for Egyptian troops
and stating that unless they were sent the entire country would be
lost to Egypt.[39] His letters customarily begin with some salutation of
the greatest deference like this:

> To the king, my lord, say.
> Thus saith Abdi-Hiba, thy servant:
> At the feet of the king, my lord,
> seven times and seven times I fall down. . . .[40]

Then he proceeds, as in the following letter, to protest vehemently
his own loyalty and to beg urgently for help:

> What have I done to the king, my lord?
> They slander me
> to the king, the lord: "Abdi-Heba
> has become faithless to the king, his lord."
> Behold, neither my father
> nor my mother has put me
> in this place.
> The mighty hand of the king
> has led me into the house of my father.
> Why should I practice
> mischief against the king, the lord?
> As long as the king, my lord, lives
> I will say to the deputy of the king, my lord:
> "Why do you love
> the Habiru, and hate
> the regents?" But therefore
> am I slandered before the king, my lord.
> Because I say: "The lands of the king,
> my lord, are lost," therefore
> am I slandered to the king, my lord. . . .
> So let the king, the lord, care for his land. . . .
> Let the king turn his attention to the archers
> so that archers of the king,
> my lord, will go forth. No lands of the king remain.
> The Habiru plunder all lands of the king.
> If archers are here
> this year, then the lands of the king,

[38] KAT No.59 = MTAT No.59.

[39] H. Winckler, *Keilinschriftliches Textbuch zum Alten Testament.* 3d ed. 1909,
pp.4-13.

[40] KAT No.285 = MTAT No.285.

the lord, will remain; but if archers are not here,
then the lands of the king, my lord, are lost.
To the scribe of the king, my lord, thus saith Abdi-Heba,
thy servant: Bring words,
plainly, before the king, my lord: All the lands
of the king, my lord, are going to ruin.[41]

Other letters of Abdi-Hiba include the following passages:

Verily, this land of Urusalim,
neither my father nor my mother has
given it to me; the mighty hand of the king
gave it to me. . . .
Verily, the king has set his name
upon the land of Urusalim for ever.
Therefore he cannot abandon
the lands of Urusalim.[42]

Let the king care for his land.
The land of the king will be lost. All of it
will be taken from me; there is hostility to me. . . .
But now
the Habiru are taking
the cities of the king. . . .
If there are no archers
this year, then let the king
send a deputy that he may take me
to himself together with my brothers and we
die with the king, our lord.[43]

Behold, Milkilim and Tagi
the deed which they have done is this:
After they have taken Rubuda,
they seek now to take Urusalim. . . .
Shall we then let Urusalim go? . . .
I am very humbly thy servant.[44]

The name Habiru, which figures prominently in the letters of
Abdi-Hiba, is the same as that previously discussed (pp. 68f.) in its
occurrence in Mesopotamian texts, and doubtless the same as the
word 'Apiru soon to be mentioned in Egyptian inscriptions. Since it
probably means, "those who have crossed a boundary," and in the
Tell el-Amarna letters describes those who are assaulting Palestinian
cities, it could well be applied to the children of Israel in their
conquest of Palestine. The date of the latter conquest was, however,

[41] KAT No.286 = MTAT No.286. [42] KAT No.287 = MTAT No.287.
[43] KAT No.288 = MTAT No.288. [44] KAT No.289 = MTAT No.289.

probably later than the time of the Tell el-Amarna letters; thus the Israelites were indeed Habiru or "Hebrews," but probably not the same group as these Habiru.

Not even the religious reformation of Akhenaton was permanently successful. Having no son of his own, Akhenaton was followed on the throne, after a period of confusion, by his son-in-law Tutankhaton (c.1353-c.1344). He, abandoning the new religion and the new capital, returned to Thebes and Amun worship. His own name was changed back from "Beautiful in Life Is Aton" to Tutankhamun, "Beautiful in Life Is Amun," and the name of Amun was inscribed again on Egypt's monuments. Tutankhamun's reign was not otherwise of great significance and the young king died at the early age of about eighteen. His prominence in the mind of the modern world is due to the circumstance that of all the royal tombs in the Valley of the Kings, his was the first to be found unplundered and intact. Howard Carter's discovery of the tomb in 1922 revealed that the young Pharaoh had gone to his grave amidst an almost unbelievable splendor of golden coffins, thrones, and jewels.[45]

For a single example out of this wealth of precious objects we show in Fig. 47 the portrait mask from the head of the king's mummy. This is made of beaten and burnished gold, and the headdress and collar are inlaid with opaque glass of many colors in imitation of semi-precious stones. On the forehead are the royal insignia of vulture and serpent. The mask represents Tutankhamun as he appeared at the time of his death, and it was fashioned by the goldsmiths within the relatively brief period before his burial took place. It is a beautiful portrait, and when the actual face of the mummy was exposed it was seen to be a faithful and accurate representation of the young king.[46]

Tutankhamun was followed briefly by Eye (c.1344-c.1340), but soon the government was taken over by a general named Haremhab (c.1340-c.1303), who prepared the way for the Nineteenth Dynasty and another great period of imperial glory.[47] The statue shown in Fig. 48 represents Haremhab as a royal scribe before his accession as king. He sits cross-legged on the floor, holding on his lap a papy-

[45] Howard Carter, *The Tomb of Tut-ankh-Amen.* 2 vols. 1923-27; C. Breasted, *Pioneer to the Past,* pp.327-373.

[46] Edward D. Ross, *The Art of Egypt through the Ages.* 1931, pp.43f.

[47] Haremhab has often been listed as the first king of the Nineteenth Dynasty but may better be considered as the last of the Eighteenth. cf. Keith C. Seele in JNES 4 (1945), pp.234-239.

rus roll which contains a hymn to Thoth, patron god of scribes. Haremhab was a man of real administrative ability and he gave the kingdom an efficient reorganization. His practical legislation for the abolition of abuses survives as one of the important edicts of ancient Egypt. "Behold," said the king, "his majesty spent the whole time seeking the welfare of Egypt."[48] He was also kind to foreigners and a scene in his tomb shows him receiving fugitive Asiatics who come begging a home in Egypt, as they say, "after the manner of your fathers' fathers since the beginning."[49]

THE NINETEENTH DYNASTY

Since he had no son of his own, Haremhab was followed by the son of one of his distinguished army officers. This man, already of an advanced age upon accession to the throne, ruled briefly as Ramses I (c.1303-c.1302), and then was succeeded by his son Seti I (c.1302-c.1290).

Word of the disturbed conditions abroad fell now upon the ear of a man disposed to attempt action. "One came to say to his majesty: . . . 'They have taken to cursing and quarreling, each of them slaying his neighbor, and they disregard the laws of the palace.' The heart of his majesty was glad on account of it. Lo, as for the Good God, he rejoices to begin battle."[50] Henceforth the inscriptions of Seti I speak of campaigns in Palestine and Syria, Pekanan[51] ("the Canaan"),[52] Retenu,[53] and Kadesh[54] being among the places mentioned. One inscription said of his return to Egypt, "His majesty arrived from the countries . . . when he had desolated Retenu and slain their chiefs, causing the Asiatics to say: 'See this! He is like a flame when it goes forth and no water is brought.'"[55]

RAMSES II

Actually "the Asiatics" were not as fearful of Egyptian power as Seti I liked to believe, and his successor, Ramses II (c.1290-c.1224), had to battle throughout the sixty-seven years of his reign against them. Although his only victory in the famous Kadesh-on-the-Orontes battle with the Hittites was that of escaping complete destruction, the personal heroism of Ramses II was depicted proudly in numerous Egyptian scenes. Eventually Ramses II signed a "good

[48] ARE III, §50.   [49] ARE III, §10.   [50] ARE III, §101.
[51] *Pe* is the article.   [52] ARE III, §88.   [53] ARE III, §§103, 111, etc.
[54] ARE III, §141.   [55] ARE III, §139.

treaty of peace and of brotherhood" with the king of the Hittites, which left southern Syria and all of Palestine in the possession of Egypt but relinquished northern Syria and Amurru to the Hittites. This is the earliest extant treaty of international nonaggression. It was sealed by the marriage of Ramses II and a daughter of the Hittite king.

While the military successes of Ramses II in Asia were not as glorious as he might have wished, the magnitude of the king's building enterprises left nothing to be desired. These included the erection of his own mortuary temple at Thebes, known as the Ramesseum, the making of additions to the Luxor temple, and the completion of the enormous hypostyle hall of the Karnak temple (Fig. 49). In the hypostyle hall, 134 tremendous columns, the tallest sixty-nine feet in height, supported the roof of a room which was part of the largest temple ever erected by man, while six acres of painted relief sculpture decorated the interior of the hall.[56] At Abu Simbel, between the First and Second Cataracts of the Nile, Ramses II hewed a complete temple in the sandstone cliff above the Nile and carved four colossal sixty-five-foot statues of himself from the rock before it. The upper part of one of these statues is shown in Fig. 50. An ear on the statue measures over three feet in height, yet, enormous as the statues are, they are fine portraits.

While the old capital of Thebes with its great temple of Amun continued to be esteemed most highly, the political center of gravity shifted somewhat in these times to the Delta which was nearer to the Asiatic portions of the Egyptian empire. Early in the Nineteenth Dynasty the seat of government was actually transferred from Thebes to the Delta. The capital city which was built there was called Per-Ramses, "House of Ramses," or more fully Per-Ramses Meri-Amun, "House of Ramses-beloved-of-Amun," and is mentioned in various Egyptian texts.[57] This is surely the same as the city named Raamses in Exodus 1:11.

This capital may have been at Tanis in the northeastern Delta, near modern San el-Hagar, where the Hyksos had their capital of Avaris. Tanis has been excavated by Pierre Montet.[58] The city was evidently forsaken after the expulsion of the Hyksos, but was re-established by Seti I and enlarged and beautified by Ramses II.

[56] NGM 80 (July-Dec. 1941), p.513.

[57] ANET pp.199, 470f.

[58] P. Montet, *Les nouvelles fouilles de Tanis 1929-1932.* 1933; *Le Drame d'Avaris.* 1941; *Tanis, douze années de fouilles dans une capitale oubliée du delta égyptien.* 1942.

Extensive temple ruins were found there, together with many statues, sphinxes, and stelae, bearing the name of Ramses II and his successors. On the basis of the excavations, Montet maintains strongly that Tanis is the ancient Raamses, an identification proposed by Brugsch as long ago as 1872.[59]

Another possible identification is with Qantir, some twelve miles south of Tanis. This site was excavated by Mahmud Hamza.[60] The ruins of a large palace were found, and also the remains of a factory which made the striking glazed tiles and glazed statues with which the royal residence was adorned. Furthermore there were five ostraca discovered which actually bore the name Per-Ramses. In accordance with these finds, Hamza, believed that this was the ancient Raamses, and has been supported by William C. Hayes and Père Couroyer.[61]

Since there was a palace at Qantir and a temple complex at Tanis, a reconciliation of the alternative identifications may be effected by supposing that the former was essentially the residential site and the latter the place of worship, both being included in fact in a single large area which all together comprised the Delta capital of Ramses II.[62]

Ramses II also built or rebuilt a city the ruins of which have been found at Tell er-Retaba in the Wadi Tumilat, and which was probably known as Pi-Tum, "House of the god Tum," and appears in Exodus 1:11 as Pithom.[63]

THE MERNEPTAH STELA

The great Pharaohs of the past had fought campaigns to extend the empire, but those who followed Ramses II had to struggle to preserve it. Merneptah (c.1224-c.1214), the son and successor of

[59] H. Brugsch in ZÄS 10 (1872), p.18; P. Montet in RB 39 (1930), pp.15-28. This conclusion has also been accepted by Alan H. Gardiner (in JEA 19 [1933], pp.122-128), who previously favored an identification with Pelusium. According to Exodus 12:37; 13:20, Raamses was two days' journey from the edge of the wilderness. This agrees exactly with the location of Tanis, whereas Pelusium is itself on the edge of the wilderness. The possible locations of Etham (Exodus 13:20) and the sites in Exodus 14:2 are discussed by H. Cazelles in RB 62 (1955), pp.321-364.

[60] Hamza in Annales du service des antiquités de l'Égypte. 30 (1930), pp.31-68.

[61] Hamza, op.cit., p.65; William C. Hayes, Glazed Tiles from a Palace of Ramesses II at Kantir. The Metropolitan Museum of Art Papers, 3. 1937; B. Couroyer in RB 53 (1946), pp.75-98.

[62] Albrecht Alt in Festschrift für Friedrich Zucker. 1954, pp.3-13. The distance of twelve miles between the two sites is not greater than the distance between remaining boundary stones marking out the sacred area where Akhenaton built his city of Akhetaton (ibid., p.12 n.19).

[63] The earlier identification of Pithom with Tell el-Maskhuta, a site eight and one-half miles farther east, has been abandoned. Albright, From the Stone Age to Christianity, p.194.

Ramses II, already was advanced in years when he came to the throne. He fought valiantly against Libyans and Mediterranean peoples who were pushing into the western Delta, and also campaigned in Palestine. In the fifth year of his reign (about 1220 B.C.) Merneptah took a large black granite stela set up by Amenhotep III and carved an inscription of victory on it. This stela was found in Merneptah's mortuary temple at Thebes and is shown in Fig. 51. At the top is a double representation of the god Amun and the king. Behind the king on the left stands the goddess Mut, wife of Amun, and behind the king on the right is the moon-god Khonsu, son of Amun and Mut. Below are twenty-eight closely packed lines of inscription, celebrating the triumph over the Libyans and concluding with a strophe in which other defeated foreigners are listed, notably including Israel. This closing portion of the inscription reads as follows:

> The princes are prostrate, saying: "Mercy!"[64]
> Not one raises his head among the Nine Bows.
>
> Desolation is for Tehenu;[65] Hatti[66] is pacified;
> Plundered is the Canaan with every evil;
>
> Carried off is Ashkelon; seized upon is Gezer;
> Yanoam[67] is made as that which does not exist;
>
> Israel is laid waste, his seed is not;
> Hurru[68] is become a widow for Egypt!
>
> All lands together, they are pacified;
> Everyone who was restless, he has been bound
> by the King of Upper and Lower Egypt, Merneptah,
> given life like Re every day.[69]

The foregoing passage is worthy of special attention since it is the only mention in any Egyptian inscription of the name of Israel. In contrast with other names such as Hatti which are written with the determinative indicating a country, Israel is written with the determinative of people, which presumably shows that they were not yet a settled people. The statement that the people Israel "is laid waste, his seed is not," is a conventional way of describing any defeated and plundered foe. The description of Hurru or Syria,

---

[64] The Canaanite word *shalam*, meaning "Peace!" is used.
[65] Libya.   [66] The land of the Hittites.
[67] A town in northern Palestine.   [68] Kharu or Syria.
[69] John A. Wilson in ANET p.378 (ANEA pp.231f.); W. F. Albright in BASOR 74 (Apr. 1939), pp.21f.; ARE III, §617.

doubtless including Palestine, as "a widow for Egypt" means that the land is without a husband, in other words without a protector and helpless against Egypt. Thus Israel is clearly listed among other strong and dangerous peoples in the west of Palestine upon whom Merneptah has inflicted defeat. The stela proves, therefore, that Israel was in western Palestine by around 1220 b.c. and provides a convenient point at which to pause to discuss the Exodus.

THE DATE OF THE EXODUS

There are two chief theories as to when the Exodus of the Israelites from Egypt took place.[70] The first is based upon a perhaps late notation in I Kings 6:1 which states that Solomon began building the temple in the fourth year of his reign and the 480th[71] year after the Exodus from Egypt. The division of the kingdom under Rehoboam and Jeroboam is probably to be dated in 931/930 b.c.,[72] and since Solomon is said to have reigned for forty years (I Kings 11:42) his first year must have been about 970/969 b.c. The fourth year of his reign was accordingly 967/966 b.c., and if this was the 480th year after the departure from Egypt the Exodus must have taken place around 1446 B.C.

The date just mentioned falls within the last few years of the reign of Thutmose III (d. c.1436 b.c.), and if accepted would lead us to consider him as the Pharaoh of the Exodus. The picture of Thutmose III as the oppressor of the Israelites would be quite credible, since we know that he was a great builder and employed Asiatic captives on

[70] cf. W. M. F. Petrie, *Palestine and Israel.* 1934, pp.54-58.

[71] The figure is given as 440 instead of 480 in the lxx (ed. Swete, i, p.684).

[72] Edwin R. Thiele in jnes 3 (1944), pp.147, 184; tmn pp.54f.; and in *Vetus Testamentum.* 4 (1954), pp.187-191. The fixed point from which this reckoning is made is the battle of Qarqar, the date of which is established as 853 b.c. by Assyrian records (see below, p.204). If between the disruption and this point, the reigns of the kings of Judah were recorded in terms of the accession-year system, and those of the kings of Israel according to the nonaccession-year system, the intervening period was 78 years in length, which gives the indicated date for the division of the kingdom. Joachim Begrich (*Die Chronologie der Könige von Israel und Juda und die Quellen des Rahmens der Königsbücher.* 1929, p.155) places the division of the kingdom in 926 b.c. W. F. Albright (in basor 100 [Dec. 1945], pp.16-22; and in *Interpretation.* 6 [1952], pp.101-103) puts it in 922 b.c. The last date, with a correlative of 959 b.c. for the founding of Solomon's temple, has been supported by M. B. Rowton (in basor 119 [Oct. 1950], pp.20-22) from evidence in the king list of Tyre as cited by Josephus from Menander of Ephesus. Dealing with the same materials, however, J. Liver (in iej 3 [1953], pp.113-122) accepts the date of 825 b.c. for the foundation of Carthage as given by Pompeius Trogus (rather than 814 b.c. as stated by Timaeus), puts the beginning of the reign of Hiram of Tyre in 979/978 b.c., and arrives at the date of 968/967 for the commencement of work on the temple, and 931/930 for the separation of the kingdoms.

his construction projects (p. 100). Ahmose who expelled the Hyksos might have been the "new king over Egypt, who did not know Joseph" mentioned in Exodus 1:8, and Hatshepsut might even have been the "Pharaoh's daughter" of Exodus 2:5-10. Allowing the traditional forty years in the wilderness (Exodus 16:35; Numbers 14:33; Deuteronomy 2:7; Joshua 5:6; etc.), the Israelites would have arrived in Palestine shortly before 1400 B.C. and might be identified with the Habiru who were pressing into the land at that time (pp. 111f.).[73] Furthermore we know that there was a city at Jericho around 1400-1350 B.C. which could have been taken by Joshua and, as the excavations at that site now stand, we do not know if there was a city there a century later (p. 159).

Attractive as is the hypothesis just outlined, it must be recognized that there are serious objections to it. The identification of the Habiru of the Amarna letters with the biblical Hebrews is improbable, since the frantic correspondence of Abdi-Hiba indicates that Jerusalem was in imminent danger of serious conquest, and that city does not seem to have been a major objective of Joshua and was only permanently conquered in the time of David (II Samuel 5:6f.). Other evidence, moreover, both in Transjordan (p. 153) and in Palestine (p. 166) requires a date considerably later than around 1400 B.C. for the coming of the Israelites to Canaan. As for the original entry of the Israelites into Egypt, if we reckon backward from an Exodus around 1446 and allow for a sojourn of 430 years in accordance with Exodus 12:40 (pp. 71f) we arrive at a date around 1875 B.C. This is nearly two centuries before the establishment of the Hyksos in Egypt, however, in whose time it seems historically probable that the Israelites first entered that land (p. 95). Furthermore, while Thutmose III carried out large building projects, those activities centered as far as we know in Upper Egypt, and it was not until the Nineteenth Dynasty that the Pharaohs resided in the Delta and directed major attention to building operations there. But it was in the Delta that the Israelites are said to have lived and worked. This brings us to the second and more probable hypothesis as to the date of the Exodus.

The basis of the theory now to be considered is the statement in Exodus 1:11 that the Israelites "built for Pharaoh store-cities, Pithom and Raamses." Raamses can hardly be other than Per-Ramses, the

---

[73] cf. J. W. Jack, *The Date of the Exodus.* 1925.

"House of Ramses [II]," which has been identified with Tanis-Qantir (p. 114). Since Tanis was the Avaris of the Hyksos and was abandoned and allowed to fall into ruins after their expulsion (c.1570 B.C.) and was only reestablished by Seti I (c.1302-c.1290), it is not likely that any large construction activities were being conducted in this vicinity in the years just before 1446 B.C. But in the days of Seti I and Ramses II the Israelites could have toiled in construction work at Raamses and also at Pithom. The only other explanation of Exodus 1:11 would be to say that the Israelites labored at these places at some far earlier time, presumably back in the Hyksos period, and that the use of the name Raamses is an anachronism.

Unless we are to regard Exodus 1:11 as an erroneous or anachronistic statement, we must conclude that Ramses II was the Pharaoh under whom the oppression of the Israelites reached its climax. This is in harmony with our knowledge of his vast building activities and particularly with the fact that he resided in the Delta and devoted the opening years of his reign largely to building operations at Tanis. The general impression given by the book of Exodus is that the Israelites were settled not far from Pharaoh's court, and in Psalm 78:12, 43 they are definitely said to have lived "in the land of Egypt, in the fields of Zoan." Zoan is the Hebrew name for Tanis, as the rendering in the Septuagint shows,[74] and thus we have a picture of the Israelites as living in the vicinity of Tanis at a time when Pharaoh's court was there. This situation is fulfilled in the time of Ramses II but not in the earlier days of Thutmose III.

In connection with the presence of the children of Israel in Egypt it is also of interest to note that a number of Egyptian texts dating from the fifteenth century to the twelfth mention the 'Apiru, a name which we have seen (p. 69) to be phonetically very similar to Hebrew. The oldest are inscriptions accompanying two Theban tomb paintings which identify as 'Apiru men shown at work pressing out grapes.[75] Amenhotep II gives a list of captives which begins with 127 princes of Retenu, that is Syria-Palestine, and includes 3,600 'Apiru.[76] Two papyri of the reign of Ramses II give instructions for the distribution of grain to the 'Apiru as well as the men of the army who were engaged in the transport of stone for a pylon the

[74] LXX, ed. Swete, II, pp.315,317.
[75] Georges Posener in Bottéro, *Le problème des Ḥabiru à la 4e rencontre assyriologique internationale*, Nos.181,182, p.166.
[76] *ibid.*, No.183, p.167; cf. ANET p.247.

Pharaoh was erecting.[77] A papyrus of Ramses III records the gift of over 2,000 persons to be the property of the temple of Re at Heliopolis, among them Asiatic warriors, 'Apiru, and "people settled who are in this place."[78] Again, an inscription from the Wadi Hammamat in Upper Egypt from the time of Ramses IV mentions 8,000 workmen sent to the quarries in that vicinity and lists among them 800 'Apiru.[79] Thus the use of "immigrants" in Egyptian labor forces is attested not only for this period in general but also precisely in the reign of Ramses II.

If we now try to date the Exodus more exactly, we may suppose that the children of Israel were first employed at Tanis by Seti I (c.1302-c.1290) and then had their burdens yet further increased by Ramses II (c.1290-c.1224) to the point of driving them to attempt their escape. During this time Moses was born, grew up, lived in the wilderness, and returned to Egypt, as recounted in Exodus 2-3, thus the reign of Ramses II must have been fairly well advanced by the time of the departure of the enslaved people. Since the Israelites must also have arrived in Palestine and penetrated to the place where Merneptah met them by about 1220 B.C., there is hardly time for them still to have wandered in the wilderness for a full forty years (Exodus 16:35, etc.), but this figure may have been a conventional round number for what was actually a somewhat briefer time.

If, then, the children of Israel made their way from Egypt to Palestine sometime around the middle of the thirteenth century B.C. and had previously dwelt in Egypt for 430 years, their original entry there must have been soon after 1700 B.C. This is not long after the Hyksos established themselves in Egypt, which seems a likely time for another Semitic group to enter there. If the sojourn in Egypt was for only 215 years, then the entry would have been about the middle of the fifteenth century B.C., perhaps in the reign of Thutmose III (c.1490-c.1436 B.C.), which may seem a less likely time, yet withal a time when the presence of Asiatics in the land is otherwise attested (p. 100).

The chief objection to this second theory of an Exodus in the thirteenth century is that it is out of harmony with the 480 years mentioned in I Kings 6:1, an explicit statement which some feel provides the fundamental datum in the entire problem.[80] This is often

[77] ibid., Nos.187,188, p.169f.   [78] ibid., No.189, p.170; cf. ANET p.261.
[79] ibid., No.190, pp.170f.
[80] Merrill F. Unger, Archeology and the Old Testament. 1954, p.141.

regarded, however, as a late addition to the text, and may bear the marks of an artificial reckoning in that it amounts to twelve generations of forty years each. Another suggestion is that the 480 years may refer to the time when an earlier group, perhaps Judah and associated tribes, entered Palestine from the south, this being separate from and prior to the coming of the Joseph tribes under Moses and Joshua, although in tradition the two events were ultimately combined into one.[81] It must be admitted that no single theory as to the date of the Exodus is conclusive, but best justice seems done to the evidence now available if we conclude that the main movement of the Israelites from Egypt to Palestine took place toward the middle of the thirteenth century B.C.

THE TWENTIETH DYNASTY

After the death of Merneptah there ensued a state of confusion in which several kings followed each other in swift succession and even a Syrian prince seized the rule.[82] About 1197 B.C. a certain Setnakht "set in order the entire land, which had been rebellious,"[83] and as the founder of the Twentieth Dynasty left a stable throne for his son, Ramses III.

RAMSES III

Like his predecessors, Ramses III (c.1195-c.1164) had to fight to defend the frontiers of Egypt against invaders who pressed in from the west and the north. Among these enemies were those known as the "peoples of the sea," who included the so-called Peleste. Some of the Peleste settled on the Palestinian coast and became the Philistines of the Bible. In honor of his success in repelling the invaders, Ramses III erected a large temple to Amun at a point on the western plain of Thebes now called Medinet Habu and adorned its walls with a vast record of his achievements. The earliest known representation of a salt-water naval battle is here,[84] and also realistic representations of the Philistines who had been taken captive. Two of these Philistine prisoners are shown in Fig. 52 being led by an Egyptian officer into the presence of the Pharaoh. The unusual manacles which are made in the form of a fish and suspended from

[81] H. H. Rowley, *From Joseph to Joshua* (The Schweich Lectures of the British Academy 1948). 1950, pp.139f.,147f.

[82] ARE IV, §398.

[83] ARE IV, §399.

[84] ARE IV, §69; Harold H. Nelson in JNES 2 (1943), pp.40-55.

the prisoner's neck by a cord are characteristic of this period. In connection with the flight of other enemies, Ramses III expressed himself poetically as the song of Deborah (Judges 5:20) was to do: "The stars of the *seshed*-constellation were frightful in pursuit of them, while the land of Egypt was glad and rejoiced at the sight of his valor: Ramses III."[85] The sovereign himself is depicted (Fig. 53) at Medinet Habu in heroic size, with the falcon sun-god hovering with wings protectingly outspread above his head, reminding us of the figure of speech which the Israelites were to use—"the shadow of thy wings" (Psalms 17:8; 36:7; 57:1; 63:7; cf. Malachi 4:2).

Since Ramses III records the building of a temple of Amun in Pekanan and lists nine towns of Khuru which belonged to the same god,[86] it is evident that Palestine and Syria still belonged to Egypt at this time. After this, however, there is no further record by the Pharaohs of the possession of Asiatic territory, and the days of Egyptian empire were over. A series of kings, still bearing the name of Ramses which had once been so great, ruled weakly at home and enjoyed little prestige abroad. Court documents attest a series of robberies in which most of the royal tombs at Thebes were ransacked,[87] and "The Report of Wenamon" shows the humiliating treatment to which an Egyptian envoy could be subjected in Syria where Egyptian armies once had marched in triumph.[88]

8. THE DECLINE
(TWENTY-FIRST TO THIRTIETH DYNASTIES),
c.1090-332 B.C.

WITH the Twenty-first Dynasty the decline of Egypt had set in fully. The Pharaohs ruled feebly at Tanis in the Delta while the high priest of Amun at Thebes was virtually king of Upper Egypt. The intact tomb of the second king of this dynasty, Psusennes I, was discovered in 1939-1940 at Tanis. The king was buried in a funerary chamber of pink granite and in a series of sarcophagi, the outermost one of which likewise was made of pink granite. The second sarcophagus was sculptured out of black granite in the likeness of the king while the third and fourth were made of silver and of silver overlaid with gold respectively. The other treasures found in the tomb constituted

[85] John A. Wilson in *Medinet Habu Studies 1928/29*. OIC 7, 1930, p.27.
[86] ARE IV, §§219, 384.   [87] ARE IV, §§499-556.   [88] ARE IV, §§557-591.

one of the richest discoveries ever made in Egypt, and included a necklace of lapis lazuli and gold which weighed more than seventy-two pounds.[1]

AMENEMOPET

In these days a certain wise man named Amenemopet was moved to profounder reflections. In a way reminiscent of Ptahhotep (p. 89), he offered sound advice to his son on honesty, integrity, self-control, and kindliness. The dominant ideal which he held up was that of the truly tranquil man whom he contrasted with the hot-headed man in a figure of two trees:

> As for the heated man of a temple,
> He is like a tree growing in the open.
> In the completion of a moment comes its loss of foliage,
> And its end is reached in the shipyards;
> Or it is floated far from its place,
> And the flame is its burial shroud.
>
> But the truly silent man holds himself apart.
> He is like a tree growing in a garden.
> It flourishes and doubles its yield;
> It stands before its lord.
> Its fruit is sweet; its shade is pleasant;
> And its end is reached in the garden.
>
> (vi,1-12)[2]

By reliance on the god, Amenemopet taught that man could attain this tranquility of mind and consequent freedom from overanxiety.

> Do not spend the night fearful of the morrow.
> At daybreak what is the morrow like?
> Man knows not what the morrow is like.
>
> God is always in his success,
> Whereas man is in his failure;
> One thing are the words which men say,
> Another is that which the god does.
>
> There is no success in the hand of the god,
> But there is no failure before him.
> If he[3] pushes himself to seek success,
> In the completion of a moment he damages it.

[1] *The New York Times.* 1940: Feb. 20, p.23; Mar. 6, p.20; May 4, p.6; Montet, *Tanis, douze années de fouilles,* pp.112-123.

[2] John A. Wilson in ANET p.422 (ANEA pp.237f.); cf. F. Ll. Griffith in JEA 12 (1926), p.202.

[3] i.e. a man.

Be steadfast in thy heart, make firm thy breast.
Steer not with thy tongue alone.
If the tongue of a man be the rudder of a boat,
The All-Lord is its pilot.

(xix,11-17,22 - xx,6)[4]

The Wisdom of Amenemopet must have been known to the Israelite people, for it seems to be reflected, or even translated, at a number of points in the Old Testament.[5] Both Jeremiah (17:5-8) and Psalm 1 may reflect Amenemopet's striking picture of the two trees, while freely edited translations from other parts of the Wisdom of Amenemopet are thought to be recognizable in the book of Proverbs. Here are two probable parallels:

AMENEMOPET	PROVERBS
Better is poverty in the hand of the god	Better is a little with the fear of the Lord
Than riches in a storehouse;	than great treasure and trouble with it.
Better is bread, when the heart is happy,	Better is a dinner of herbs where love is
Than riches with sorrow.	than a fatted ox and hatred with it.
(ix,5-8)	(15:16f.)
Better is bread, when the heart is happy,	Better is a dry morsel with quiet than a house full of feasting with
Than riches with sorrow.	strife.
(xvi,13f.)	(17:1)

Especially does Proverbs 22:17-24:22 seem to be based upon the Wisdom of Amenemopet. This may be seen in the following passages.

AMENEMOPET	PROVERBS
Give thy ears, hear what is said,	Incline your ear, and hear the words of the wise,
Give thy heart to understand them.	
To put them in thy heart is worth while,	and apply your mind to my knowledge;
But it is damaging to him who neglects them.	for it will be pleasant if you keep them within you,
	if all of them are ready on your lips.
(iii,9-12)	(22:17f.)
Do not associate to thyself the heated man,	Make no friendship with a man given to anger,
Nor visit him for conversation.	nor go with a wrathful man.
(xi,13f.)	(22:24)

[4] ANET pp.423f. (ANEA p.238); cf. Peet, *A Comparative Study of the Literatures of Egypt, Palestine, and Mesopotamia*, pp.110f.

[5] H. Grimme in OL 28 (1925), cols. 59-62; D. C. Simpson in JEA 12 (1926), pp.232-239.

AMENEMOPET	PROVERBS
As for the scribe who is experienced in his office,	Do you see a man skilful in his work?
He will find himself worthy to be a courtier.	he will stand before kings.
(xxvii,16f.)	(22:29)
Do not strain to seek an excess. . . .	Do not toil to acquire wealth. . . .
If riches are brought to thee by robbery,	
They will not spend the night with thee. . . .	
They have made themselves wings like geese	For suddenly it takes to itself wings,
And are flown away to the heavens.	flying like an eagle toward heaven.
(ix,14-x,5)	(23:4f.)
Do not carry off the landmark at the boundaries of the arable land. . . .	Do not remove an ancient landmark
Nor encroach upon the boundaries of a widow.	or enter the fields of the fatherless.
(vii,12,15)	(23:10)

At one point the phrasing of the wise advice may be traced all the way back to Ptahhotep. He had said: "If thou art one of those sitting at the table of one greater than thyself, take what he may give, when it is set before thy nose. Thou shouldst gaze at what is before thee. Do not pierce him with many stares. . . . Let thy face be cast down until he addresses thee, and thou shouldst speak only when he addresses thee."[6] This counsel from the days of the Fifth Dynasty was echoed by Amenemopet and finally adopted by Proverbs.

AMENEMOPET	PROVERBS
Do not eat bread before a noble,	When you sit down to eat with a ruler,
Nor lay on thy mouth at first.	
If thou art satisfied with false chewings,	observe carefully what is before you;
They are a pastime for thy spittle.	and put a knife to your throat
Look at the cup which is before thee,	if you are a man given to appetite.
And let it serve thy needs.	Do not desire his delicacies
	for they are deceptive food.
(xxiii,13-18)	(23:1-3)[7]

---

[6] ANET p.412 (ANEA p.234).

[7] ANET pp.421-424 (ANEA pp.237f.); cf. Breasted, *The Dawn of Conscience*, pp.372-378.

SHESHONK I

The Twenty-second Dynasty was founded when a soldier from a Libyan family at Herakleopolis seized the royal authority and proclaimed himself Pharaoh. This new king, Sheshonk I (c.945-c.924 B.C.),[8] ruled from a residence at Bubastis (called Pi-beseth in Ezekiel 30:17) in the eastern Delta, and was strong enough to invade Palestine in the fifth year of Rehoboam of Judah (I Kings 14:25, where he is called Shishak). This Palestinian campaign was memorialized in a relief after the style of the earlier Pharaohs on a wall at Karnak. A portion of the relief is shown in Fig. 54 where the god Amun leads forward by cords rows of Asiatic captives, doubtless Israelites. On the entire relief no less than 156 captives are represented, each of whom symbolizes a different Palestinian town which Sheshonk I claims to have taken. In each case the name of the town is enclosed in an oval marked out beneath the head and shoulders of the captive. Of the names which can still be read and identified geographically, many are found in the Old Testament. These include Rabbith, Taanach, Shunem, Beth-shean, Rehob, Hapharaim, Gibeon, Beth-horon, Ajalon, Megiddo, Socoh, and Arad. This is also the list which includes "The Field of Abram" (p. 91).[9] In 1938-1939 the intact burial chamber of Sheshonk I was discovered at Tanis, the body of the king being splendidly arrayed, with a gold mask over his face, and enclosed in a coffin of electrum.[10]

The dynasty founded by Sheshonk I endured for some two centuries, although the country was organized in an essentially feudal way, and Upper Egypt was divided into two principalities dominated respectively by Herakleopolis (called Hanes in Isaiah 30:4)[11] and Thebes. The Twenty-third and Twenty-fourth Dynasties which followed were short and feeble, and Isaiah was quite correct in his description (Chapter 19) of the divided and hopeless state of Egypt at that time.

THE KUSHITE PERIOD

Meanwhile strong native rulers had arisen at Napata near the Fourth Cataract in the region which the Egyptians called Kush.

---

[8] Manetho (tr. Waddell, p.159) gives 21 years for the reign of Sheshonk I. The date given above is that of Breasted (*A History of Egypt*, p.600); Albright (in BASOR 130 [Apr. 1953], p.7) suggests 935-914 B.C. If 931/930 B.C. was the accession year of Rehoboam, the fifth year of Rehoboam, in which Sheshonk I invaded Palestine, would have been 926/925 (TMN p.56; cf. Breasted, *op.cit.*, p.529).

[9] ARE IV, §§712-716.   [10] AJA 44 (1940), p.145.

[11] ARE IV, §790.

One of these, named Kashta, pushed into Thebes, and his successor, Piankhi, conquered all of Egypt as is recorded on a stela of pink granite found at Napata.[12] Piankhi was followed upon the throne by his brother, Shabako, and then by two sons in turn, Shebitko, and Taharqo. The last three are listed by Manetho, who calls them Ethiopians, as comprising the Twenty-fifth Dynasty of Egypt.[13]

The tombs of these Kushite kings have been found in the vicinity of Napata,[14] and a temple built by Taharqo has been excavated among other ruins at Kawa near the Third Cataract.[15] There were several inscriptions of Taharqo in this temple, and they have provided data for a fresh study of the chronology of Taharqo and his predecessors, with the following results established as probable: Piankhi became king in 740 B.C. and invaded Egypt in 720. Shabako began to reign in 708 B.C. Shebitko was associated with Shabako in 699 B.C. and became sole ruler in 697. Taharqo, born in 709 B.C., was associated with Shebitko in 689 and became sole ruler in 684.[16]

In the days of these kings the power of Assyria was being extended more and more threateningly in the direction of Egypt. According to II Kings 19:9 Taharqo, who is there called "Tirhakah king of Ethiopia," went out to fight against Sennacherib when the latter was campaigning against Hezekiah (see below p. 212). In 671 B.C. Esarhaddon invaded Egypt and destroyed Memphis, while Taharqo only escaped by the loss of family and property.[17] Although Esarhaddon claimed the conquest of Egypt, Upper Egypt, and Kush, Taharqo soon asserted himself again, and Ashurbanipal led the Assyrian armies back into Egypt in 667 B.C. The inscriptions of Ashurbanipal tell how Taharqo was driven from Memphis and from Thebes, and how "the night of death overtook him," a decease which probably took place in 664 B.C.[18] Then Tanutamun (664-654/653), whom Ashurbanipal calls Urdamane and describes as a son of Shabako.

[12] ARE IV, §§816-883.

[13] tr. Waddell, pp.167-169.

[14] G. A. Reisner in JEA 9 (1923), pp.34-77; Dows Dunham in AJA 50 (1946), pp.378-388.

[15] M. F. Laming Macadam, *The Temples of Kawa*, II, *History and Archaeology of the Site* (Oxford University Excavations in Nubia), Text. 1955, pp.61-113.

[16] Macadam, *The Temples of Kawa*, I, *The Inscriptions*, Text. 1949, pp.18f.; cf. W. F. Albright in BASOR 130 (Apr. 1953), p.11, who alters Macadam's figures slightly. The names of these kings were formerly read as Shabaka, Shabataka, and Taharka; in Manetho they are Sabacon (Σαβάκων), Sebichos (Σεβιχώς), and Tarcus (Τάρκος); for the spelling used above see Macadam, *op.cit.*, p.124 n.1.

[17] ARAB II, §§580, 710; J. M. A. Janssen in *Biblica*. 34 (1953), pp.37f.

[18] ARAB II, §§901, 906; Janssen, *op.cit.*, pp.38f.

took the throne.[19] He made Thebes his stronghold, and went out to challenge the Assyrians. Ashurbanipal defeated him, pursued him to Thebes and, probably in 663 B.C., "conquered this city completely, smashed it as if by floodstorm."[20] "Thebes that sat by the Nile" with "Ethiopia . . . her strength" (Nahum 3:8f.) was fallen and the Kushite rule of Egypt soon came to its end.

THE SAITE PERIOD

Yet a brief period of restoration was at hand. At Saïs in the Delta native princes had cooperated with the Assyrians and, when the Kushites were eliminated, these rulers had opportunity to rise in influence. According to Manetho there were nine of these kings of Saïs who constituted the Twenty-sixth Dynasty, a dynasty which this authority probably reckoned as extending from the Assyrian invasion in 671 B.C. to the Persian invasion in 525.[21] Stephinates and Nechepsos, the first two in Manetho's list, are otherwise unknown and were probably only insignificant local rulers.[22] The next name is Necho I, and he was probably considered the founder of the dynasty. Beginning with his successor, Psamtik I, the kings are also known from Egyptian inscriptions, the data in which provide material for calculating their probable respective dates.[23] It was Psamtik I (663-610 B.C.)[24] who, evidently by taking advantage of the preoccupation of the Assyrians in their struggles with Babylon and Elam, was able to establish the Saite rule throughout Egypt in freedom from foreign domination.[25] With the renewal of centralized government, peace and prosperity were restored in considerable measure to Egypt. There was a revival of the more ancient Egyptian art and culture; and relations were entered into with the rising country of Greece. Probably at about the end of his reign there was a new

---

[19] The reign of Tanutamun is not included in Manetho's list. Political events of the time are recorded on a stela of Tanutamun which was discovered at Napata (ARE IV, §§919-934).

[20] ANET p.297; ARAB II, §906; Janssen, op.cit., pp.39f.; cf. below pp.215f.

[21] tr. Waddell, pp. 169-173; cf. Rowton in JEA 34 (1948), pp.60-62.

[22] "Ammeris the Ethiopian" heads the list in some versions and may have been Tanutamun.

[23] KPGÄ pp.154-157.

[24] Psamtik I did not actually die until in 609 B.C. but this fraction of a year was counted as a part of the first year of his successor, thus now in the Saite period the years of a king's reign were again (cf. above p.97 n.) considered as coinciding with the years of the civil calendar, that is, the entire calendar year in which a king took the throne was reckoned as the first year of his reign. See ARE IV, §§959, 975, 984. By the Saite period the civil calendar had regressed sufficiently that in 663 B.C. the Egyptian year began on February 5, and in 525 B.C. on January 2. See KPGÄ p.157.

[25] KPGÄ p.16.

threat, however, when the Scythians marched against Egypt. Herodotus describes this, and tells how Psamtik I met them in Palestine and with gifts and prayers persuaded them not to come further.[26]

NECHO II

Psamtik I was succeeded by his son, Necho II (609-595 B.C.). The last king of Assyria, Ashur-uballit II, was now hard pressed by the Babylonians in western Mesopotamia, and Egypt evidently still considered itself on the side of the Assyrians against the so rapidly rising Babylonians. A cuneiform text known as the Babylonian chronicle (B.M. 21901; cf. p. 218) states that in the sixteenth year (610/609 B.C.) of Nabopolassar this king marched against Ashuruballit II, who had established his throne in Haran. In Arahsamnu, the eighth month, or November, 610 B.C., the Babylonians were joined by the Manda-hordes, probably the Scythians, and successfully drove Ashur-uballit II out of Haran. In Addaru, the twelfth month, or February/March, 609 B.C., the Babylonians and Scythians returned to their own countries. Following that, in what (although it is not so specified by the Babylonian chronicle) was obviously the seventeenth year of Nabopolassar, for a period extending from Duzu, the fourth month, to Ululu, the sixth month, that is from June/July to August/September of 609 B.C., Ashur-uballit II and "a large army of Egypt" undertook to reconquer Haran.[27] Since we read in II Kings 23:29 that "Pharaoh Neco king of Egypt went up to the king of Assyria to the river Euphrates," and in the parallel account in II Chronicles 35:21 that he went in "haste," we may conclude that the references in the Babylonian chronicle and in the Old Testament are to the same event, and that Necho II made this expedition with the purpose of giving assistance to Ashur-uballit II. Accordingly, too, the attempt of King Josiah described in the Old Testament (II Kings 23:29f.; II Chronicles 35:20-24) to halt Necho II may be explained as an endeavor to keep this potential aid from reaching Assyria, the power which had been such a terrible enemy of Judah; and the death of Josiah on the plain of Megiddo may be dated shortly before the month Duzu in the seventeenth year of Nabopolassar, that is shortly before June/July 609 B.C.[28]

[26] I, 105.
[27] tr. A. Leo Oppenheim in ANET p.305 (ANEA p.202); cf. C. J. Gadd, *The Fall of Nineveh*. 1923, p.41; ARAB II, §1183. For the principles of Babylonian chronology see the Appendix of the present book.
[28] Hayim Tadmor in JNES 15 (1956), pp.228f. For the previously held theory that it was on a second campaign of Necho II in 608 B.C. that Josiah died, see M. B. Rowton in JNES 10 (1951), pp.128-130.

According to the Babylonian chronicle Ashur-uballit II and his Egyptian supporters did not succeed in taking Haran and afterward "they retired."[29] Perhaps it was then that Necho II captured Gaza, an event mentioned by Herodotus[30] as taking place after the battle of Megiddo, and probably also referred to in Jeremiah 47:1.[31] In spite of failure at Haran the expedition of Necho II had evidently taken all of Syria, and Egyptian forces held the important city of Carchemish for several years. This is shown by two recently published Babylonian texts of the British Museum (B.M. 22047 and B.M. 21946) which constitute a continuation of the Babylonian chronicle. The one text (B.M. 22047) records a successful attack by the army of Egypt upon the Babylonian garrison in the city of Kimuhu on the Euphrates which took place in the twentieth year of Nabopolassar, 606/605 B.C.[32] The other, which will be cited below (pp. 220f.), tells of the final and for the Egyptians disastrous battle which was fought at Carchemish. Here in 605 B.C. the Egyptian army was decisively defeated by the Babylonians under the command of Nebuchadnezzar.

Henceforth Necho II confined his attention to Egypt. II Kings 24:7 states: "And the king of Egypt did not come again out of his land, for the king of Babylon had taken all that belonged to the king of Egypt from the Brook of Egypt[33] to the river Euphrates." Dying in 594 B.C., Necho II was followed by his son, Psamtik II (594-589 B.C.), who continued to avoid military endeavor in Asia and campaigned instead, as Herodotus[34] states, in Ethiopia, perhaps in this case meaning Lower Nubia.[35]

On February 8, 588 B.C.[36] Psamtik II died and was followed on the throne by his son Apries (588-570 B.C.), who is called Hophra in Jeremiah 44:30.[37] Not far from this time Nebuchadnezzar began the

[29] tr. Albright in JBL 51 (1932), p.87 n.33.   [30] II, 159.

[31] If Necho II came down at this time from Haran his invasion of Philistia would have been "out of the north" as Jeremiah 47:2 says. Another interpretation makes Jeremiah 47:2-7 refer to the Scythians. See A. Malamat in IEJ 1 (1950-51), pp.154-159.

[32] WCCK p.67.

[33] This watercourse which marked the border of Egypt was probably the Wadi el-'Arish, between Gaza and Pelusium.

[34] II, 161.   [35] KPGÄ pp.128f.

[36] A stela of Enekhnesneferibre, daughter of Psamtik II, records the death of the Pharaoh: "Year 7, first month of the first season, day 23, went forth this Good God, Lord of the Two Lands, Psamtik II to heaven" (ARE IV, §988E). In 588 B.C. the Egyptian year began on January 17; the twenty-third day of the first month of the first season was February 8.

[37] The name appears as Wahibpre in Egyptian, 'Aπρίηs in Herodotus (II, 161), and Οὔαφρις in Manetho (tr. Waddell, p.170).

final siege of Jerusalem.[38] The predecessors of Apries had abandoned attempts at warfare in Asia, but the new Pharaoh now reversed this policy and boldly undertook to challenge Nebuchadnezzar. According to Herodotus[39] Apries sent the Egyptian fleet against Phoenicia, which would threaten Nebuchadnezzar's line of connection with his homeland, and according to the Old Testament (Jeremiah 37:5, 7, 11) he led the Egyptian army directly into Palestine where Nebuchadnezzar had to lift the siege of Jerusalem temporarily to meet this doubtless unexpected challenge. In Phoenicia Egyptian influence must have been reestablished with some success, since for many years after that the city of Tyre was found holding out against forces of Nebuchadnezzar (Ezekiel 26:1-28:19; 29:18), but in Palestine Apries was evidently unable to accomplish his purpose and must have been driven back into Egypt, since the Babylonian army soon returned to Jerusalem to complete its task of destruction there.

Egypt still offered refuge to those who feared the Babylonians, however, and some time after the fall of Jerusalem the remnant of Judah fled thither, taking with them the prophet Jeremiah (II Kings 25:22-26; Jeremiah 43:4-7). Jeremiah (43:8-13; 46:13-25) and also Ezekiel (29-32) often expressed the expectation that Nebuchadnezzar would invade Egypt, but the opportunity for this action did not come until in the time of the next Egyptian king.

The failure of the policies of Apries must have led to the unrest which marked the end of his reign. In 569 B.C. a rival king, whom Herodotus[40] pictures as a very common man who was backed by the army, challenged Apries and drove him from the throne. This was Amasis,[41] who came from a town called Siuph in the province of Saïs[42] and who reigned from 569 to 527 B.C. Civil war between the new king and the deposed one was probably still in progress and probably provided the favorable occasion at the time when Nebuchadnezzar made some kind of move against Egypt. A fragmentary cuneiform inscription states that in his own thirty-seventh year, that is in 568/567 B.C., Nebuchadnezzar fought against the troops

[38] The final siege of Jerusalem began probably on January 15, 588 B.C., or January 4, 587, either just before or within less than a year after Apries came to the throne. The date is discussed in the Appendix (p.594) where some preference is given to January 4, 587, the date correlative with final destruction of Jerusalem in 586.
[39] II, 161.
[40] II, 162, 172-174.
[41] The name is Ἄμασις in Herodotus, Ἄμωσις in Manetho (tr. Waddell, pp.170-172).
[42] Herodotus II, 172.

of "(Ama)su, of Egypt."[43] The same occasion may be referred to when Josephus relates that Nebuchadnezzar "invaded Egypt in order to subdue it, and, having killed the king who was then reigning and appointed another, he again took captive the Jews who were in the country and carried them to Babylon."[44] It is true that Josephus places this event in the twenty-third year of Nebuchadnezzar, or 582/581 B.C., but that date is in the midst of the reign of Apries and the reference to the elimination of one king and establishment of another looks much more like the time when Apries was being driven from his throne by Amasis.

Whatever the exact action of Nebuchadnezzar at this time, the power of the Babylonians must have been made sufficiently plain to Egypt, for throughout the long reign of Amasis there is no further record of conflict between his kingdom and that of Nebuchadnezzar and his successors. In this period of peace Egypt enjoyed a prosperity which Herodotus, presumably with exaggeration, says was marked by the existence of no less than twenty thousand inhabited cities in the country.[45]

In the latter part of his reign Amasis witnessed the rise of Cyrus the Great of Persia. Even as in his time Necho II took the side of Assyria against the rising power of Chaldea, so now Amasis entered into an alliance which bound Egypt, Lydia, and Babylonia together against the threat which was coming from Persia.[46] This was in vain, however, since in spite of whatever aid Egypt was able to give,[47] both Croesus of Lydia and Nabunaid of Babylon were swiftly overcome by Cyrus (in 546 and 539 B.C.).

Egypt presumably could expect attack soon, but as it transpired Cyrus was occupied with fighting on his northeastern front and died there in the summer of 530 B.C. The son of Cyrus, Cambyses II (529-522 B.C.), was not long in turning toward the Egyptian objective, but by the time his troops reached Egypt, as Herodotus[48] relates, Amasis was no longer alive, having died after a reign of forty-four years and been succeeded by his son Psamtik III. The death of Amasis must have been near the end of 526 B.C. and, since Manetho[49] gives Psamtik III a reign of six months, the defeat of the latter by the

---

[43] ANET p.308 (ANEA p.205); cf. Sidney Smith in CAH III, p.304.
[44] *Ant.* x, 182.   [45] II, 177.   [46] Herodotus I, 77.
[47] Xenophon (c.430-c.355 B.C.), *Cyropaedia.* VI, ii, 10. tr. Walter Miller, LCL (1914) II, p.155, speaks of 120,000 Egyptians coming to fight on the side of Croesus, but Herodotus (I, 77) gives no impression of actualized assistance in such magnitude.
[48] III, 10.   [49] tr. Waddell, p.171.

Persians must have ensued in the spring of 525. The decisive and for Egypt disastrous battle was fought at Pelusium in the eastern Delta and, when it was finished, Egypt belonged to the empire of the Persians.

Cambyses himself appears in the list of Manetho[50] as the first king of the Twenty-seventh Egyptian Dynasty, and the date of his accession to the Egyptian throne is correctly given in the same source as the fifth year of his kingship over the Persians, that is 525 B.C. Henceforward, throughout the Twenty-seventh to Thirtieth Dynasties, Egypt was under Persian rule, although sometimes local kings exercised authority under Persian domination. In 332 B.C. Egypt was conquered by Alexander the Great. After his death (323 B.C.) the land came under the rule of the Ptolemies until the death of Cleopatra (30 B.C.) when it became a Roman province under Octavian.

THE ROSETTA STONE

In 196 B.C. while Alexander's successors were ruling Egypt, the priests at Memphis composed a decree honoring King Ptolemy V Epiphanes (c.203-c.181 B.C.) for numerous benefits which he had conferred upon the temples of Egypt. This decree was ordered engraved on a tablet in three forms, "in the sacred writing, in the native script and in Greek letters." The "sacred writing" was the ancient picture-writing of Egypt which only the priests then understood, and which the Greeks called *hieroglyphics,* literally "sacred carvings."[51] The "native script" was what the Greeks called *demotic* meaning "common," or "popular," and was a new and simplified form of the Egyptian language and writing that had come into use some hundreds of years before. It was the Greek language which was to provide the clue for the decipherment of the inscription.

A stone inscribed with this decree (Fig. 55) was found in 1798 by an officer of Napoleon's expedition at Rosetta (Rashid) near the westernmost mouth of the Nile. The Greek text at the bottom of the Rosetta Stone was read easily and scholars at once took up the challenge to solve the problem of the two Egyptian scripts above. Silvestre de Sacy of France and J. D. Akerblad of Sweden successfully studied the demotic text on the monument, identifying the Greek personal names which it contains—Ptolemy, Berenike, and Arsinoë.

[50] tr. Waddell, p.175.
[51] When hieroglyphics were written on papyrus with a brush-pen, a bolder and more cursive form of writing developed, to which the Greek name *hieratic,* or "priestly," was applied.

Thomas Young of England was then able to identify the name of Ptolemy in the hieroglyphic portion, where groups of signs enclosed in oval frames (called "cartouches") had already been thought to be kings' names. Finally the young French scholar Jean François Champollion (1790-1832) was able to demonstrate the true nature of the hieroglyphic system of writing, to formulate an Egyptian grammar and dictionary, and to read numerous Egyptian texts. Thus the key was found which unlocked the doors to a knowledge of ancient Egypt.[52]

MOSES AND THE CHILDREN OF ISRAEL

In conclusion we may say that Egypt has afforded us no direct evidence of the sojourn of the Israelites, but it has revealed much which makes that sojourn and the Exodus which followed entirely credible. There are many connections between life in Egypt as known from archeology and the details of the biblical narrative at this point.[53] It was not uncommon for Asiatic people to find refuge in Egypt nor for them to be set at heavy labor on the great building projects of the Pharaohs. Without doubt the children of Israel were in Egypt in the days of the Hyksos, and their oppression and Exodus probably fell under Ramses II. The very name of Moses is clearly Egyptian, being the Egyptian word *mose* meaning "is born." Names like Amenmose ("Amun Is Born") and Thutmose ("Thoth Is Born") were familiar, and it may be presumed that Moses originally bore some fuller name of which only the "Mose" continued in current usage.[54]

In Egypt it has also been possible to trace ideas of the overshadowing care of God, and of ethical demands on earthly life. Actual passages from the wisdom literature of Egypt appear to have been taken over by Israelite writers. Thus the psalms, wisdom books, and prophetic works of Israel exhibit connections with Egyptian literature just as the mythology and law of the Old Testament are related to that of Babylonia.[55]

[52] E. A. Wallis Budge, *The Rosetta Stone in the British Museum.* 1929; H. Hartleben, *Champollion, sein Leben und sein Werk.* 2 vols. 1906.

[53] G. Ernest Wright, *Biblical Archaeology.* 1957, pp.53f.; Jozef M. A. Janssen in *Jaarbericht No.14 van het Vooroaziatisch-Egyptisch Genootschap Ex Oriente Lux.* 1955-56, pp.63-72. Greta Hort in zaw 69 (1957), pp.84-103; 70 (1958), pp.48-59.

[54] cf. J. Gwyn Griffiths in jnes 12 (1953), pp.225-231.

[55] cf. J. M. P. Smith in ajsl 49 (1933), pp.172-184; William S. Smith in jbr 19 (1951), pp.12-15.

III

Penetrating the Past in Palestine

THE land of Palestine derives its name from the Philistines (Peleste) who settled along the southern coast in the twelfth century B.C. (p. 121). The area where they settled became known as Philistia (Joel 3:4, etc.) and from that in turn came the Greek name Palestine.[1] Josephus refers to the territory which extends from Gaza to Egypt and says that the Greeks call that area Palestine.[2] Herodotus even uses the name to include Phoenicia as well. Referring to the northern part of the coast where the Phoenicians settled, he says, "that part of Syria and as much of it as reaches to Egypt, is all called Palestine."[3] Elsewhere he speaks of "the part of Syria called Palestine,"[4] and "the Palestine part of Syria."[5] The Romans in their turn called the land *Palaestina* and from that came the English name Palestine.

The older name of the land was Canaan. This name is found frequently in the Bible (Genesis 11:31, etc.), in Egyptian texts of the Nineteenth Dynasty and later,[6] and in the Amarna letters.[7] According to Genesis 10:19 Canaanite territory extended from Gaza to Sidon. In the Amarna letters, for example in a letter of Abimilki of Tyre, the name Canaan applies to the Phoenician coast as far north as Ugarit.[8]

In the Akkadian of the Amarna letters and also in Hurrian[9] the form of the name is Kinahhi. Since there is also a common noun *kinahhu* in Hurrian which means "purple," it seems probable that the original meaning was "land of the purple," probably referring to the purple dye made from the murex shellfish found on the coast. Since the name Phoenicia comes from Greek φοῖνιξ, also meaning

---

[1] ἡ Παλαιστίνη.   [2] *Ant.* i, vi, 2.   [3] vii, 89.
[4] i, 105.   [5] ii, 106.
[6] ANET pp.258,261,264,378,478; and cf. above pp.113,116.
[7] KAT No.8 = MTAT No.8, lines 15, 17, 25; etc.
[8] KAT No.151 = MTAT No.151, line 50.   [9] ANET p.352.

"purple," the original reference of the name to that region is substantiated. From Phoenicia then the name was evidently extended to include the whole region between the Jordan and the Mediterranean.[10]

The land east of the Jordan was simply called "beyond the Jordan," or "the other side of the Jordan" (Genesis 50:10; Numbers 32:19, etc.), even as it is still known as Transjordan.

Syria, of which as Herodotus said Palestine is a part, includes the entire area of fertile land, bounded by the desert on the east and south, the sea on the west, and extending to the Taurus Mountains on the north. The name Syria was derived by the Greeks from Assyria, but whereas it was at first applicable to the entire Assyrian Empire from the Caucasus to the Levant, it shrank finally to the limits just stated.

Palestine proper, meaning the country west of the Jordan and running from Dan in the north to Beersheba in the south (cf. Judges 20:1, etc.), is 150 miles in length and averages something like 40 miles in breadth. In comparison with the 6,000 square miles of Palestine proper, Transjordan, running east to the desert, comprises some 4,000 square miles.

Between the sea and the desert the land of Palestine and Transjordan may be conceived as lying in four parallel strips running north and south.[11] First, along the coast is the maritime plain, of which the most famous portion is the Plain of Sharon between Mount Carmel and Joppa. Secondly, a rugged series of hills runs through the interior and may be known as the central range. This line of hills descends from the mountains of Lebanon far to the north. Between Galilee and Samaria a spur of the range runs out to the Mediterranean and terminates in 1,810-foot Mount Carmel, to the north of which lies the Plain of Esdraelon. In Judea the range attains an average elevation of 2,400 feet, a high point a few miles north of Jerusalem being 3,317 feet in elevation, Jerusalem itself 2,593 feet, and Bethlehem 2,550 feet. On the western border between Judea and Philistia the high central range drops toward the maritime plain in a region of low hills

[10] Sabatino Moscati, *I predecessori d'Israele*. 1956, pp.42-74; and in JBR 24 (1956), pp.247-249.

[11] For Bible geography see George Adam Smith, *The Historical Geography of the Holy Land*. 25th ed. 1931; Félix Marie Abel, *Géographie de la Palestine*. 2 vols. 1933-38; Denis Baly, *The Geography of the Bible*. 1957. For Bible atlases see G. Ernest Wright and Floyd V. Filson, *The Westminster Historical Atlas to the Bible*. rev. ed. 1956; L. H. Grollenberg, *Atlas of the Bible*, tr. Joyce M. H. Reid and H. H. Rowley. 1956; Emil G. Kraeling, *Rand McNally Bible Atlas*. 1956.

called the Shephelah or "lowland" (Joshua 15:33, etc.). On the southern frontier of Judea the range breaks down and spreads out in the area known as the Negeb, sometimes translated "the South" (ASV), but literally meaning the Dry or Parched Land (Genesis 13:1, etc.).

On its eastern side the central range drops quickly to the Jordan Valley, whose great depression constitutes the third of the four parallel bands in which the country may be seen to lie. The Jordan River has sources at Banias and elsewhere in the north in the neighborhood of 9,100-foot-high Mount Hermon, where snow and rain provide ample water. Soon it flows through Lake Huleh, where the valley is about 230 feet above sea level. Next, the river flows through the Sea of Galilee, about 695 feet below the level of the sea, and then follows an ever-deepening valley until it terminates in the Dead Sea about 1,290 feet below sea level. As will be explained more fully in Chapter v, this profound depression represents a geological rift which runs on down along the Wadi el-Arabah to the Gulf of Aqabah and through the Red Sea into Africa. Beyond the Jordan and towering some 4,400 feet above the Dead Sea is an eastern range of barren hills which constitutes the fourth of the parallel bands and beyond which is the desert.

The lower valley of the Jordan is subtropical, but the greater part of Palestine lies one or two thousand feet above the level of the sea and enjoys a temperate climate. The year is divided into a dry season and a rainy season, the rains coming from the end of October to the middle of April. During the rainy or winter season, snow is not uncommon in the hills.

Of all the geographical facts that may be adduced about Palestine, the most significant is that it constitutes a "bridge" connecting Mesopotamia and Egypt. With the sea on the one hand and the desert on the other, Palestine was the natural and only highroad between those two great homes of empire, the valley of the Tigris and Euphrates, and the valley of the Nile. Palestine's history was connected intimately, therefore, with that of its powerful neighbors, and it was the fate of the land at most times to be a dependency, a buffer state, or a battleground.

A land as often invaded as Palestine, and as perennially dominated by various foreign powers, cannot display an historical development of such homogeneity and directness as was manifest in Egypt. Nor do we find in Palestine, at such ancient periods as in both Egypt and

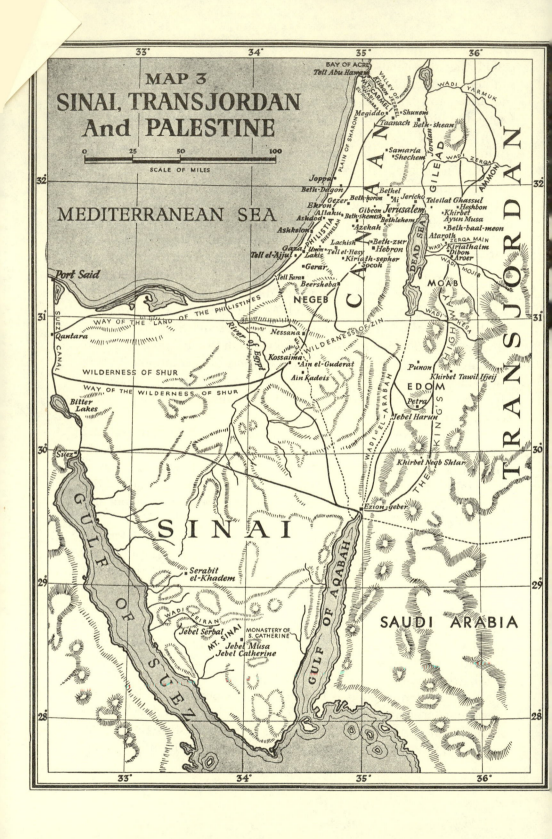

MAP 3
SINAI, TRANSJORDAN
And PALESTINE

0   25   50   100
SCALE OF MILES

MEDITERRANEAN SEA

BAY OF ACRE
Tell Abu Hawam
VALLEY OF JEZREEL
MT. CARMEL
KISHON R.
EL-MUGHAR
WADI YARMUK

Megiddo
Shunem
Taanach Beth-shean

Samaria
Shechem

GILEAD
Jordan R.
WADI ZERQA

AMMON

Joppa
Beth-Dagon
PLAIN OF SHARON
Bethel
Ai Jericho
Teleilat Ghassul
Heshbon
Gezer Beth-horon
Khirbet
Ayun Musa
Ekron Gibeon Jerusalem
Altaku Bethlehem
Ashdod Beth-shemesh
Beth-baal-meon
Askelon Azekah
Ataroth
ZERQA MAIN
PHILISTIA Kiriathaim
SHEMELAH Lachish Beth-zur
WADI MOJIB
Gaza Tell el-Hesy Hebron Dibon
Umm Lakis
Tell el-Ajjul Kiriath-sepher Aroer
Socoh
Gerar MOAB

Tell Fara
WADI MOJIB
Beersheba
WADI EL-HESA

NEGEB

Port Said

CANAAN

DEAD SEA

WAY OF THE LAND OF THE PHILISTINES
SUEZ CANAL
Qantara River of Egypt
Nessana WILDERNESS OF ZIN
Kossaima THE KING'S HIGHWAY
WILDERNESS OF SHUR Ain el-Guderat Punon
Ain Kadeis Khirbet Tawil Ifjeij
WAY OF THE WILDERNESS OF SHUR EDOM
Bitter WADI EL-ARABAH Petra
Lakes Jebel Harun
Suez
Khirbet Neqb Shtar

Ezion-geber

SINAI

GULF OF SUEZ

Serabit
el-Khadem

WADI FEIRAN
Jebel Serbal
MT. SINAI
MONASTERY OF
S. CATHERINE
Jebel Musa
Jebel Catherine

GULF OF AQABAH

SAUDI ARABIA

TRANSJORDAN

56. Jericho

57. Tell el-Mutesellim, the Site of Megiddo (Armageddon)

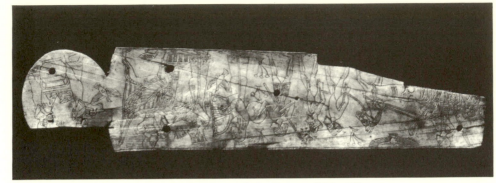

58. Ivory Plaque of the Prince of Megiddo

59. Standing Stones at Gezer

60. Ras Shamra Stela with the God El

61. Ras Shamra Stela with the God Baal

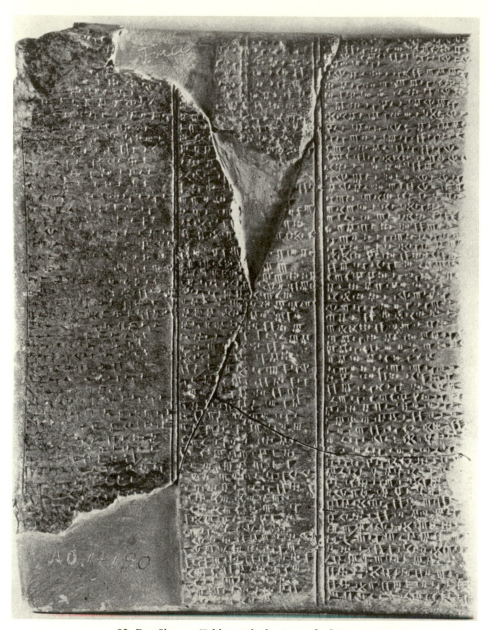

62. Ras Shamra Tablet with the Legend of Keret

64. The Sacred Rock beneath the Dome of the Rock

63. The Dome of the Rock

65. The Great Stables at Megiddo

66. Ivory Medallion with the Child Horus

68. The Siloam Tunnel

67. Cast of the Moabite Stone

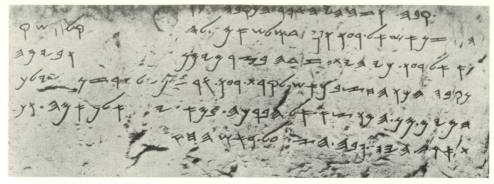

69. The Siloam Inscription

70. One of the Lachish Letters

Mesopotamia, powerful rulers and well established dynasties whose records survive to show the course of events. It is only in the time of the Israelite kings, and then chiefly because of the records preserved in the Bible, that a relatively precise historical framework can be established.

For the earlier Palestinian times we can speak only in terms of broad archeological periods, and it is customary to refer to the Stone, Chalcolithic, Bronze, and Iron Ages and their respective subdivisions. It will be desirable, therefore, first to sketch briefly the salient characteristics of these successive periods, and then to deal more fully with the archeological discoveries which relate particularly to biblical times and happenings.

1. THE ARCHEOLOGICAL PERIODS IN PALESTINE

THE STONE AGE, UP TO c.4500 B.C.

THE traces of the presence of man in Palestine go back into the earliest periods of human life. The famous "Galilee skull" which was found by F. Turville-Petre in 1925 in the "robbers' cave" near the Sea of Galilee, and the fossil human remains which were excavated by Theodore D. McCown in 1932 in the Wadi el-Mughara or "valley of the cave" at Mount Carmel, belong to the Paleolithic or Early Stone Age and represent a primitive type of humanity akin to the Neanderthal, which is commonly dated from 50,000 to 100,000 years ago.[1]

Other discoveries in the Wadi el-Mughara reveal a Mesolithic or Middle Stone Age culture whose people had learned to grow wheat and to carve statuettes and were in the habit of burying their dead, laying the body on its side with legs drawn up and sometimes leaving ornaments with it. To this culture the name Natufian is given, and its date is supposed to have been around 8000 B.C.[2]

In the Neolithic or Late Stone Age man had learned to shape and polish his stone implements, and during the period pottery was made for the first time in Palestine. Mugharet Abu Usba, a cave on Mount

[1] Arthur Keith, *New Discoveries relating to the Antiquity of Man.* 1931, pp.173-198; Theodore D. McCown and Arthur Keith, *The Stone Age of Mount Carmel,* II, *The Fossil Human Remains from the Levalloiso-Mousterian.* 1939; J. Philip Hyatt in JBR 12 (1944), pp.232-236.
[2] Dorothy A. E. Garrod and D. M. A. Bate, *The Stone Age of Mount Carmel,* I, *Excavations at the Wady el-Mughara.* 1937; W. F. Albright, *The Archaeology of Palestine.* 1949, pp.59-61.

Carmel, has preserved the sickle blades and pottery fragments of a people whose culture may have been derived from the Natufian but was definitely in advance of it and clearly belongs to the Neolithic period. This may be called the Usbian culture, and a date around 7500 B.C. has been suggested for it.[3]

At a prehistoric village close to Sha‘ar ha-Golan and near where the Yarmuk River flows into the Jordan, over three thousand flint implements were unearthed, including arrowheads, axes, and other tools for hunting and for agriculture. The accompanying pottery was coarse, but decorated with triangular and zigzag lines and short parallel strokes. To this culture the name Yarmukian is given, and a date around 7000 B.C. has been suggested.[4]

At Jericho in the excavations conducted in 1930-1936 by John Garstang of the University of Liverpool, levels of the Neolithic period were reached and it was discovered that there had been a phase here with pottery and an earlier phase without pottery.[5] When the excavation of Jericho was resumed in 1952 and following years under Kathleen M. Kenyon of the British School of Archaeology in Jerusalem, one of the chief aims was to explore further in the Neolithic levels and it is in fact in the pre-pottery Neolithic that the most important discoveries have thus far been made.[6]

It has been found that the pre-pottery Neolithic town extended over an area of more than seven acres, and that its debris is more than forty feet in depth, indicating a very long occupation in this period. As a matter of fact it is now known that there were at least two distinct phases in the pre-pottery period. In the earlier of these two phases dwellings were built of elongated oval bricks which most characteristically have a pointed section on account of which the excavators describe them as "hog-backed." The rooms were generally circular and sunk somewhat beneath the surrounding level, with sloping entrance passages leading to them. The walls incline inwards which may indicate that the rooms were domed, and there are traces of timber or wattling which suggest that the roofs were made of

[3] M. Stekelis and G. Haas in IEJ 2 (1952), pp.15-47.
[4] M. Stekelis in IEJ 1 (1950-51), pp.1-19.
[5] Immanuel Ben-Dor in Annals of Archaeology and Anthropology, issued by the Institute of Archaeology, University of Liverpool. 23 (1936), pp.77-90.
[6] Kathleen M. Kenyon in PEQ 1952, pp.72f.; 1953, pp.83-88; 1954, pp.47-55; 1955, pp.109-112; 1956, pp.69-77; 1957, pp.101-107; and in Scientific American. 190 (1954), pp.76-82; Kathleen M. Kenyon and A. Douglas Tushingham in NGM 104 (1953), pp.853-870; A. Douglas Tushingham in BA 16 (1953), pp.50-55; 17 (1954), pp.98-102; Kathleen M. Kenyon, Digging Up Jericho. 1957.

plastered branches. It would not be difficult to think, therefore, that here were settlers only recently removed from nomadism who were endeavoring to reproduce in more permanent material the round tents to which they had been accustomed. Already in this earlier phase the town was defended by a strong stone wall with a ditch cut out of the solid rock in front of it and, at least at one point, an imposing tower behind it.[7]

In the later phase of the pre-pottery Neolithic, which is separated from the earlier by a distinct break in the stratigraphy, bricks of a different kind are used which the excavators describe as thumb-impressed and of a flattened-cigar shape. The houses now have rectangular rooms with wide entrances and, most characteristically, the walls and floors are covered with highly burnished plaster. In some of the houses rush mats had also been used on the floors, and these survived as a thin white film which showed the grain of the rushes and the curve of the coils. Most remarkable of all were a number of portrait skulls. These were actual human skulls on which the features of the face had been modeled in plaster. The eyes were inset with shell, with slits to represent the pupils. It is surmised that these may have been the heads of important leaders or venerated ancestors.[8]

Radiocarbon tests have been made of material from both the "plastered-floor" and the "hog-backed brick" phases of pre-pottery Neolithic Jericho, and have given dates around 5850 and around 6800 B.C. respectively, hence the beginnings of settlement at Jericho must have been as early as the beginning of the seventh millennium B.C.[9]

Even as the two phases of the pre-pottery Neolithic were separated by a clear stratigraphic break, so too there was a plain demarcation between the pre-pottery and the pottery levels at Jericho. There was a period of erosion and quarrying and then after that the first debris containing pottery is found. The pottery includes both coarse ware mixed with straw and finer vessels decorated with geometric designs, and both sorts appear together from the first. The architecture is also again different in this time, and the bricks have a distinctive bun-shaped or plano-convex form.[10]

Since the finest decorated pottery appears from the first at Jericho,

[7] Kenyon in PEQ 1956, pp.69-72.
[8] Kenyon in PEQ 1953, pp.86f.; 1954, pp.48f.; 1955, pp.110f.; 1956, pp.72-74.
[9] Kenyon in PEQ 1956, pp.74-76; 1957, p.105.
[10] Kenyon in PEQ 1953, pp.84f.

the making of pottery must have begun at other places and been introduced at Jericho by those who were already familiar with it, and we have already noted that at Mugharet Abu Usba and Sha'ar ha-Golan pottery was made at what seem to be very early times. Also at Abu Ghosh, ten miles west of Jerusalem, finely polished axes, hatchets, sickles, and other stone objects attest the existence of a small community whose chief occupations were tilling and harvesting, and there pottery was found which is very similar to that found at Jericho.[11]

While Jericho shows the existence of relatively excellent accommodations for human life, it is probable that during the Stone Age many people still lived in caves even as some inhabitants of Palestine have done until modern times. At Gezer a number of caves in which people of the Stone Age dwelt were explored by R. A. S. Macalister.[12] Some of these were natural, some had been enlarged, and others had been cut out of the soft limestone. In size they varied from eighteen to forty feet in diameter and the roofs were usually very low, the entrance in most cases being through a hole in the roof. Rude drawings on the walls show an animal among reeds, shot by an arrow, and a man plowing with a pair of oxen or buffaloes. At Jerusalem under ancient Zion there is a large natural cave which originally was entered through a sort of rock funnel. Those who dwelt in it lived at one end and buried their dead at the other, while a rough pit in the floor served as the place where pottery was made.[13]

Across in Transjordan we find prehistoric rock-drawings, including representations of the ox and the ibex, which probably come from the Middle Stone Age,[14] and also menhirs and dolmens, which quite likely date from the Late Stone Age. The latter are megalithic monuments in which huge stones are placed in an upright position as monoliths or arranged to form a chamber covered by a flat capstone. These are believed to have been burial monuments in most cases and to have belonged to pastoral peoples who ranged across these regions.[15]

[11] Jean Perrot in *Syria*. 29 (1952), pp.119-145; cf. in IEJ 2 (1952), pp.73-81.
[12] Macalister, *The Excavation of Gezer*. I (1912), pp.72-152.
[13] J. Garrow Duncan, *Digging Up Biblical History*. 1931, I, pp.14-17.
[14] Nelson Glueck, *The Other Side of the Jordan*. 1940, pp.45-49. For Stone Age exploration in Jordan see also F. E. Zeuner in PEQ 1957, pp.17-54.
[15] Albright, *From the Stone Age to Christianity*, pp.95f.; Edwin C. Broome, Jr., in JBL 59 (1940), pp.479-497.

THE CHALCOLITHIC AGE, c.4500-c.3000 B.C.

As in the countries hitherto studied, so also in Palestine the Stone Age was followed by a period in which flint still was used extensively but in which copper also was employed. This was the Chalcolithic period to which it will be remembered the cultures of Tell Halaf in Mesopotamia (p. 16) and Badari in Egypt (p. 79) belonged. As in the neighboring lands, the first appearance of copper in Palestine was probably about 4500 B.C.

At Jericho Level VIII in the Garstang excavations is considered to belong to the Early Chalcolithic period, perhaps toward the end of the fifth millennium.[16]

In recent investigation at Tell Abu Matar near Beersheba many copper objects were found along with flint implements, handmade pottery, and human and animal figurines. Four levels of occupation were recognized, the first two of which were remarkable for the subterranean dwellings which were used. These were dug around the summit of a hill, connected in groups by tunnels, and entered by shafts or galleries. In Level IV there were rectangular houses built of brick or earth on foundations of stone. In this last stage the culture of Tell Abu Matar was similar to the Ghassulian, next to be mentioned.[17]

The Ghassulian culture takes its name from the site of its first discovery, Teleilat Ghassul, just north of the Dead Sea and not far from Jericho. The pottery of this period was improved in technique and more varied in form, simple painted designs being common. At Teleilat Ghassul the houses were made of mud brick and the plastered inner surfaces of some were adorned with amazing mural paintings. Among the frescoes which survive are intricate and elaborate geometric patterns, figures now almost destroyed but apparently representing a seated god and goddess, and a well-preserved painting of a bird executed in a most naturalistic and lifelike way.[18] In date the Ghassulian culture is considered to represent the Middle Chalcolithic period and to fall in the first half of the fourth millennium, corresponding approximately to the time of the Amratian culture in Egypt and that of 'Ubaid in Mesopotamia.[19]

[16] Albright, *The Archaeology of Palestine*, pp.65f.
[17] J. Perrot in IEJ 5 (1955), pp.17-40, 73-84, 167-189; and in *Syria*. 34 (1957), pp.1-38.
[18] *Teleilât Ghassûl, compte rendu des fouilles de l'Institut Biblique Pontifical*. I, 1929-1932, by Alexis Mallon, Robert Koeppel, and René Neuville. 1934; II, 1932-1936, by Robert Koeppel. 1940; cf. Nelson Glueck in BASOR 97 (Feb. 1945), pp.10f.
[19] Albright, *The Archaeology of Palestine*, p.66.

Probably a little later than the latest level at Teleilat Ghassul are the remains, including stone buildings and good pottery, found at Khirbet el-Bitar near Beersheba. A Carbon 14 analysis of charcoal from a sealed pit, probably a granary, at Khirbet el-Bitar yielded a date of 3325 B.C. with a margin of error of 150 years in either direction.[20] At Jericho, also, there are tombs which belong to about this time, that is to the Late Chalcolithic period. A piece of burned wood from one of these has given a date, by the radiocarbon method, of 3260 B.C. plus or minus 110 years.[21]

The first clay lamps in Palestine also belong to the fourth millennium B.C. and are simply small bowls with the wick laid over the edge. Later, by the Hyksos period, the rim is pinched together at one place to make a groove to hold the wick.

THE EARLY BRONZE AGE, c.3000-c.2000 B.C.

By somewhere around 3000 B.C. metal had displaced stone as the dominant material for tools and weapons in Palestine and the Bronze Age was ushered in. It is customary to divide this era into three periods of which the Early Bronze Age is dated from around 3000 to around 2000 B.C. This corresponds approximately to the Early Dynastic period in Sumer and the succeeding empire of Sargon in Akkad and to the time of the first half-dozen or more dynasties in Egypt. As far as material culture is concerned, Palestine at this time was but an outlying and destitute part of Syria, and nothing like the magnificence of the First Dynasty of Ur or of the Pyramid Age is to be found. The cities were often on low hills and fortified with strong walls, but their buildings were usually constructed rather crudely as compared with the architecture of Mesopotamia and Egypt. The pottery likewise is poorer than that of the neighboring lands, although made in some cases with considerable excellence. No writing has been found as yet in the Early Bronze Age in Palestine proper, but at Byblus on the Syrian coast a number of syllabic inscriptions on copper have been discovered which date probably from the late third millennium B.C.[22]

The earliest sanctuaries which have been discovered in Palestine belong to this age and include examples at Megiddo, Jericho, and Ai. In the case of the temple at Ai there were two main rooms, the first

[20] M. Dothan in IEJ 3 (1953), pp.262f.; 6 (1956), pp.112-114.
[21] Kenyon in PEQ 1954, p.67; 1955, p.113.
[22] W. F. Albright in *The Haverford Symposium on Archaeology and the Bible*, p.13.

of which was approached by a ramp, and contained ledges perhaps for the purpose of holding offerings. Through a narrow door access was gained to the inner room, where behind a partition stood the altar. Bones of birds, fowls, and lambs were found in the ashes on the ground.[23]

Since a number of the cities known to have been founded in the Early Bronze Age, such as Ai and Beth-shemesh, have names which are probably or certainly Semitic, it is indicated that there were Semitic-speaking peoples in Palestine in this period.[24]

In Transjordan an important civilization flourished between the twenty-third and twentieth centuries B.C. A long line of settlements existed along the main north-south track through central Transjordan and the fertile plateau lands of the country were employed for agriculture.[25]

THE MIDDLE BRONZE AGE, c.2000-c.1500 B.C.

The Middle Bronze Age is dated in Palestine from around 2000 to around 1500 B.C. and includes, according to our reckoning, the time of Abraham's migration as well as the period of Hammurabi and his predecessors and successors in Mesopotamia and the time of the Hyksos invasion of Egypt. The Hyksos must have moved through Palestine and Transjordan on their way into Egypt, and after their expulsion from that land they remained in Palestine at least until the time of Thutmose III. Their presence in Palestine is indicated by the appearance of a new type of fortification, namely great rectangular camps surrounded by massive sloping ramparts of packed earth, and doubtless used to shelter the horses and chariots which were introduced into Palestine as well as Egypt at this time.

According to the Old Testament Amorites were already in Palestine when Abraham came (Genesis 14:13) as well as later when the children of Israel invaded the land (Amos 2:9). The word Amorite is evidently related to Sumerian Martu and Akkadian Amurru which, in the first place, simply meant "West." Thus in the same passage in which Gudea tells of bringing cedar wood from Mount Amanus which was in northern Syria (cf. above p. 49), he also speaks of

---

[23] Millar Burrows, *What Mean These Stones?* 1941, p.200.

[24] Moscati, *I predecessori d'Israele*, pp.28-40; and in JBR 24 (1956), pp.246f.

[25] Nelson Glueck, *The Other Side of the Jordan*, pp.114-125; and in BASOR 122 (Apr. 1951), pp.14-18. See AASOR XIV, pp.1-113, XV, XVIII-XIX, XXV-XXVIII, for Glueck's *Explorations in Eastern Palestine*. I (1934), II (1935), III (1939), IV, Part I, Text, Part II, Pottery Notes and Plates (1951).

obtaining great blocks of alabaster from the mountains of Martu,[26] doubtless meaning the West and referring to some region not far from that of Amanus. In the Amarna letters Amurru is definitely a geographical district in Syria and also a political state, ruled at the time by Abdi-Ashirta.[27] Thus it seems probable that a term which at first simply meant the West in general, later became the designation of a specific political region in the West, and from that came to be applied in the form Amorite to the peoples of Syria and Palestine.[28]

There must also have been Hittites in Palestine during the Middle Bronze Age. In Genesis 23, Hebron is described as in possession of the Hittites at the time when Abraham purchased the cave of Machpelah there as a burial place. The traditional site of this famous cave is in a large enclosure at Hebron known as the Haram el-Khalil, Arabic *khalil* meaning "friend" and referring to Abraham under this designation which is familiar in the Bible and the Qur'an.[29] From the nature of its stonework the wall of this enclosure was probably built by Herod the Great. Within is a church, probably originally of Byzantine date, rebuilt by the Crusaders, and finally remade into a mosque. Since the entrance to the cave is within the mosque, it is quite inaccessible to research.[30] The legal code of the ancient Hittites has been found at Boghazköy in Asia Minor, capital of the Hittite Empire from 1800 to 1200 B.C., and a comparison of its regulations about real estate with Genesis 23 shows that the biblical account corresponds accurately with Hittite law and custom.[31]

In Ezekiel 16:3,45 Jerusalem is described as a Canaanite city founded and built by a combination of the Amorites and Hittites: "Your origin and your birth are of the land of the Canaanites; your father was an Amorite, and your mother a Hittite."

An important city of the time of the patriarchs was Gerar (Genesis 20-21, 26). The Valley of Gerar is probably the present Wadi esh-Shari'ah, between Beersheba and Gaza, and Gerar may be identified with Tell Abu Hureira, a site on the edge of that wadi where abundant sherds of the Middle Bronze Age have been found.[32]

[26] ANET p.269.   [27] KAT No.60 = MTAT No.60, line 8.

[28] Moscati, *I predecessori d'Israele*, pp.79f.,104f.,125f.; and in JBR 24 (1956), pp.249-252.

[29] II Chronicles 20:7; Isaiah 41:8; James 2:23; Qur'an 4:125.

[30] L. H. Vincent and E. J. H. Mackay, *Hébron, le Ḥaram el-Khalil, sépulture des patriarches.* 2 vols. 1923; Eric F. F. Bishop in JBR 16 (1948), pp.94-99; C. F. Arden-Close in PEQ 1951, pp.69-77.

[31] Manfred R. Lehmann in BASOR 129 (Feb. 1953), pp.15-18.

[32] Y. Aharoni in IEJ 6 (1956), pp.26-32.

In general the cities of the Middle Bronze Age were powerfully fortified—walls, towers, and moats being employed. Some of the walls were constructed in a type of masonry known as Cyclopean which employed huge irregularly shaped blocks of stone and filled the spaces between them with small stones. The potter's wheel, which had been introduced in the Early Bronze Age, was in general use, and good pottery is characteristic of the time.

We know a Canaanite shrine of this period which stood on the slope of Mount Gerizim above Shechem, and consisted of a small central court surrounded on all four sides by chambers. Also three buildings were found at Megiddo which are to be dated around 1900 B.C. and probably were used for sacred purposes. In each of these a porch with end walls gave access to a single large room, off which in at least two instances a smaller room opened. The three buildings stood in connection with a circular structure ascended by a flight of steps, which evidently was a sacrificial altar of unique form.[33]

It must also have been in the Middle Bronze Age that the catastrophic destruction of Sodom and Gomorrah (Genesis 19:24-28) took place. A careful survey of the literary, geological, and archeological evidence points to the conclusion that the infamous "cities of the valley" (Genesis 19:29) were in the area which now is submerged beneath the slowly rising waters of the southern part of the Dead Sea, and that their ruin was accomplished by a great earthquake, probably accompanied by explosions, lightning, ignition of natural gas, and general conflagration.[34]

In the Negeb in cultivable valleys and along routes of travel there were many settlements in the first part of the Middle Bronze Age, as has been shown by recent archeological exploration.[35] Here, however, as also in Transjordan, about 1900 B.C. there was a break in sedentary occupation as the people for some reason ceased living in towns and returned to nomadic life. Not until the Iron Age, about 1200 B.C., was there again extensive settlement in the Negeb and Transjordan.[36]

The city of Dothan figures in this period in the story of Joseph (Genesis 37:17) and is also listed by Thutmose III among places

[33] Gordon Loud in *The Illustrated London News.* Nov. 25, 1939, p.794.
[34] J. Penrose Harland in BA 5 (1942), pp.17-32; 6 (1943), pp.41-54.
[35] Nelson Glueck in BASOR 131 (Oct. 1953), pp.6-15; 137 (Feb. 1955), pp.10-22; 138 (Apr. 1955), pp.7-29; 142 (Apr. 1956), pp. 17-35; and in BA 18 (1955), pp.2-9.
[36] Glueck in BA 18 (1955), p.9; BASOR 142 (Apr. 1956), p.21.

he captured.[37] It is identified with Tell Dotha sixty miles north of Jerusalem. Excavations conducted there since 1953 by Professor Joseph P. Free of Wheaton College have revealed eleven levels of successive occupation from Early Bronze to Iron II. Middle Bronze Age pottery attests the existence of the city in the patriarchal period and the time of Joseph. The skeleton of a child, accompanied by Middle Bronze pottery, was found under the corner of a stone wall and raises the question whether this was a foundation sacrifice.[38]

Toward the end of the Middle Bronze Age pottery was being decorated much more frequently with geometric designs and with pictures of birds, fishes, and animals. Particularly notable was the work of an unknown vase-painter of about the sixteenth century whose products were found by Flinders Petrie at Tell el-'Ajjul a few miles from Gaza, and whose animal paintings were executed in a sensitive and beautiful way.[39]

Down in the peninsula of Sinai a number of inscriptions have been found which are probably to be dated at the end of the Middle or beginning of the Late Bronze Age, about 1500 B.C. These are written on monuments and rocks at Serabit el-Khadem, only about fifty miles from the traditional site of Mount Sinai. They were discovered in 1904-1905 by Flinders Petrie, have been published by Alan H. Gardiner and T. Eric Peet, and were restudied in 1948 by W. F. Albright as a member of the University of California African Expedition.[40]

In distinction from the properly so-called Sinaitic inscriptions which consist of a large number of Nabatean inscriptions dating from the first several centuries A.D. these are known as the proto-Sinaitic inscriptions. The script seems to be founded upon Egyptian hieroglyphic, but is actually alphabetic in character. There are ancient turquoise mines in this region which were worked by the Egyptians, and the inscriptions are thought to have been written by Semitic people whose home was in Egypt, perhaps around Tanis, who were laborers in the Egyptian mines. The inscriptions contain appeals to deities and overseers to provide offerings on behalf of

[37] ANET p.242.
[38] Joseph P. Free in BASOR 131 (Oct. 1953), pp.16-20; 135 (Oct. 1954), pp.14-20; 139 (Oct. 1955), pp.3-9; BA 19 (1956), pp.43-48.
[39] W. F. Albright in AJSL 55 (1938), pp.337-359; W. A. Heurtley in QDAP 8 (1939), pp.21-37.
[40] Petrie, *Researches in Sinai*. 1906, pp.129-132; Gardiner and Peet, *The Inscriptions of Sinai*, 2d ed. rev. by Jaroslav Černý. 2 vols. 1952-55; Albright in BASOR 109 (Feb. 1948), pp.5-20; 110 (Apr. 1948), pp.6-22.

deceased persons. The script is now considered to be "normal alphabetic Canaanite" of this period,[41] containing most of the letters later found in Hebrew and Phoenician, out of which ultimately grew the Greek, Latin, and English alphabets.[42]

THE LATE BRONZE AGE, c.1500-c.1200 B.C.

The Late Bronze Age in Palestine covers the years from around 1500 to around 1200 B.C. and corresponds to the days of the Kassites in Babylonia and the Hittites at Boghazköy and the time of Thutmose III, Amenhotep IV, and Ramses II in Egypt. One of the interesting discoveries belonging to this period is that of an actual potter's workshop, which was found in a cave at Lachish (Tell ed-Duweir). The workshop still contained the stone seat on which the potter sat, a limestone pivot on which no doubt the potter's wheel turned, and sherds, pebbles, shells, and a bone point, all of which had been used for smoothing, burnishing, and incising the vessels.[43]

Mycenaean pottery also was imported into Palestine by sea at this time. Excavations in 1932-1933 at Tell Abu Hawam, near modern Haifa, have shown that between 1400 and 1200 B.C. this place probably was an important port for the reception of such wares.[44]

IRON I, c.1200-c.900 B.C.

The beginning of the Iron Age in Palestine is dated around 1200 B.C. Iron was known before this, as is shown by a steel battle-axe of about 1400 B.C. found at Ras Shamra, but it took the place of bronze only gradually.[45] As far as the Israelites were concerned, the Philistines managed to maintain a monopoly of the importing and forging of iron until the reign of Saul (I Samuel 13:19-22).[46] It is interesting to note that in stating the charge made by the Philistines for sharpening plowshares and mattocks I Samuel 13:21 uses the word pim (RSV). At one time quite unknown, this word has been found on small stone weights in Palestine. The name of the weight was evidently the expression of a price, as was the case also with the shekel.[47]

---

[41] Albright in BASOR 110 (Apr. 1948), pp.13,22.

[42] Martin Sprengling, *The Alphabet, Its Rise and Development from the Sinai Inscriptions.* OIC 12, 1931; John W. Flight in *The Haverford Symposium on Archaeology and the Bible*, pp.115-118; David Diringer, *The Alphabet.* 1948, pp.199-202; G. R. Driver, *Semitic Writing.* rev. ed. 1954, pp.94-98,140-144,194f.

[43] Burrows, *What Mean These Stones?* p.163.

[44] R. W. Hamilton in QDAP 3 (1934), pp.74-80; 4 (1935), pp.1-69.

[45] Burrows, *What Mean These Stones?* p.158.

[46] W. F. Albright in AASOR 4 (1922-23), p.17.

[47] E. J. Pilcher in PEFQS 1914, p.99.

It is customary to divide the Iron Age into three periods of which the first is from around 1200 to around 900 B.C. This is known as Iron I. This period includes the time when Tiglath-pileser I was beginning to raise Assyria toward world power and when the kings of the Twentieth and Twenty-first Dynasties were allowing Egypt to slip into decline.

IRON II, c.900-c.600 B.C.

The second period is Iron II around 900 to around 600 B.C. In these years the world trembled before the power of Assyria, and Palestine felt the tramp of the armies of Shalmaneser III, Sargon II, and Sennacherib, while the continuing decline of Egyptian power was only slightly relieved by the exploits of such kings as Sheshonk I and Taharqo.

IRON III, c.600-c.300 B.C.

The third period is Iron III and is dated from around 600 to around 300 B.C. During these centuries the New Babylonian and Persian Empires followed each other swiftly on the stage of world history, while Egypt enjoyed a brief renaissance under Psamtik I and his successors and then bowed to Persian power. But before the close of the period all the world was ruled by Alexander the Great.[48]

2. EXCAVATIONS AND DISCOVERIES RELATING TO ISRAELITE TIMES

THE COMING OF THE ISRAELITES

IF OUR earlier reckoning (p. 120) was correct it was not far from the middle of the thirteenth century B.C. or near the beginning of the Iron Age that the children of Israel came into the promised land. Is any light cast upon their coming by archeological evidences in Transjordan and Palestine?

To some extent we can trace the probable course of the Israelites in their journey from Egypt to Palestine. The name of the wilderness and the mount where the law was given was Sinai according to J (Exodus 19:18, 20, etc.) and P (Exodus 19:1, etc.; Numbers 10:12;

[48] The later archeological periods in Palestine are the Hellenistic (c.300-63 B.C.), Roman (63 B.C.-A.D. 323), Byzantine (323-636), Arabic (636-1517), and Turkish (1517-1918). For tables of archeological periods in Palestine with more detailed subdivisions and, in some cases, slightly varying dates, see Glueck, *Explorations in Eastern Palestine*, IV, i, p. XIX; G. E. Wright in BA 15 (1952), p. 18 n.1. For new subdivisions in the Iron Age see Y. Aharoni and Ruth Amiran in IEJ 8 (1958), pp.171-184.

33:16) although in other sources (Exodus 3:1; 33:6 [E]; Deuteronomy 1:2, 6, 19; 4:10, etc.) "the mountain of God" is called Horeb. At least since Byzantine times Christian tradition has placed the giving of the law somewhere in the lofty granite range of Sinai in the south central part of the peninsula of Sinai (cf. p. 434), and this tradition may well be correct. The range of Sinai is an impressive mass of mountains, dominated by three peaks, all of which might be enclosed within a circle twenty-five miles in diameter. The three peaks are known today as Jebel Serbal (6,759 feet), Jebel Musa or "Mountain of Moses" (7,519 feet) and Jebel Catherine (Katerina) (8,551 feet), the latter two being side by side and the first named farther distant. Geologically speaking, the crystalline masses of these mountains appear to have loomed up here practically unchanged since the oldest times. Encircled by the desert, their towering cliffs, stupendous precipices, and magnificent summits form a wild and imposing scene.[1]

From the wilderness of Sinai the Israelites journeyed by many stages to Ezion-geber (Numbers 33:16-35 [P]). Ezion-geber probably is to be identified with Tell Kheleifeh at the head of the Gulf of Aqabah, which is the site where Solomon later built a port city and factory town (p. 181). As far as is known from excavations there, no city existed at Tell Kheleifeh at the time of the Exodus, but what is meant is that the Israelites stopped at the place where the city later was established.[2]

From Ezion-geber the Israelites came to Kadesh or Kadesh-barnea in the wilderness of Zin (Numbers 20:1; 33:36f.; Deuteronomy 1:19) and apparently made their headquarters there for some considerable time.[3] Miriam died and was buried there (Numbers 20:1b) and from there the spies were sent to view the promised land (Numbers 13:21-26; Deuteronomy 1:19-25). The wilderness of Zin has been explored by C. Leonard Woolley and T. E. Lawrence and the probable location of Kadesh-barnea discussed in the light of their ex-

[1] F. E. Hoskins in NGM 20 (1909), pp.1021f.; Karl Baedeker, *Palestine and Syria.* 5th ed. 1912, pp.196,206,208.

[2] Ezion-geber is connected with Elath in Deuteronomy 2:8 and is said to be beside Eloth in I Kings 9:26. The exact connection between the two is obscure but perhaps in its later history Ezion-geber was called Elath or Eloth.

[3] According to Numbers 20:14 (JE) they still were encamped at Kadesh in their fortieth year, just previous to making the circuit of Edom. Deuteronomy 1:46 says that they "abode in Kadesh many days" but seems to imply that they spent the last thirty-eight years of their wanderings in compassing Mount Seir and coming to the brook Zered (Deuteronomy 2:1, 14). The total of forty years may, however, be a conventional figure.

periences. Largely because of the similarity of names, Kadesh-barnea has been traditionally identified with Ain Kadeis. But Woolley and Lawrence found Ain Kadeis only an obscure water-hole, "too small to water the flocks of other than the few poor families who live near it, and . . . too remote from all roads to come to the notice of such Arab guides as live at any distance." They think, however, that the Israelites may have come upon the valley of Kadeis first and have extended its name to the whole district as far as Kossaima. This larger area would have been a very likely place for the Israelites to abide. The Kossaima Plain is relatively extensive and fertile, and enjoys the proximity of a strong though not easily found spring known as Ain el-Guderat, "The Spring of the Earthenware Kettles." Strategically, this district agrees well with what is known of Kadesh-barnea, for roads run out to north, south, east, and west. The road to the south runs to Elath or Ezion-geber. The Darb el-Shur or "Way of the Wilderness of Shur" runs westward directly to Egypt and may have accentuated the longings for a return thither (cf. Numbers 14:4). Northward the same road runs to Hebron, whither the men went to spy out the land. Eastward other roads lead into the Wadi el-Arabah, the great valley which runs from the Gulf of Aqabah to the Dead Sea, and to Jebel Harun, the traditional Mount Hor, "by the border of the land of Edom," where Aaron died (Numbers 20: 22-29; 33:38f.).[4] In the Wadi el-Arabah it has been possible to identify one of the points mentioned in the route of the Exodus, namely Punon (Numbers 33:42f.). The Arabs, who cannot pronounce the letter "P" and change it into either "B" or "F," still call the place Feinan.[5]

From Kadesh, Moses sent messengers to the king of Edom requesting permission for the Israelites to pass through the land: "Thus says your brother Israel . . . here we are in Kadesh, a city on the edge of your territory. Now let us pass through your land. . . . We will go along the King's Highway, we will not turn aside to the right hand or to the left, until we have passed through your territory" (Numbers 20:14, 16f.). These words presuppose that at that time a strong kingdom existed in Edom and that the land was traversed by the "king's highway." As we have noted (p. 145) there was a flourishing civilization in Transjordan in the Early Bronze Age. A main central highway ran from north to south through the land at that time

[4] Woolley and Lawrence, *The Wilderness of Zin*. 1936, pp.70-88.
[5] Glueck, *The Other Side of the Jordan*, p.27.

and is clearly traceable by the ruins of sites dated from the twenty-third to the twentieth centuries B.C. This was probably the line along which the eastern kings of Genesis 14 moved when they pushed the length of Transjordan and as far as El-paran, which may have been on the north shore of the Gulf of Aqabah. The same route was followed by the famous Trajan highway built by the Romans in the first part of the second century A.D. The Roman road was paved all the way from Aqabah to Bosrah and many sections of it still are comparatively intact. It was divided into two lanes with the middle line and the sides marked by raised stones. The modern highway constructed by the Government of Transjordan follows the old Roman road almost exactly. Thus the "king's highway" has a history from before the twentieth century B.C. to the twentieth century A.D.

But the Early Bronze Age civilization of Transjordan disappeared about 1900 B.C. (p. 147) and from then until upon the eve of the Iron Age there is a gap in the history of permanent sedentary occupation in that land. Not until the beginning of the thirteenth century did a new agricultural civilization appear belonging to the Edomites, Moabites, Ammonites, and Amorites.[6] Therefore the situation presupposed in Numbers 20:14-17 did not exist before the thirteenth century B.C. but did prevail from that time on exactly as reflected in the Bible. If the Israelites had come through southern Transjordan at any time within the preceding 600 years they would have found neither the Edomite nor the Moabite kingdoms in existence and only scattered nomads would have disputed their passage. But coming sometime in the thirteenth century as we have reason for believing they did, they found their way blocked at the outset by the well organized and well fortified kingdom of Edom. The high, comparatively fertile, and well watered plateau of Edom drops off precipitously on the south. At Khirbet Neqb Shtar on the southwestern corner of the plateau, at Khirbet Tawil Ifjeij on the eastern side, and at a series of other strategic points, the frontiers were guarded by fortresses whose ruins still are impressive. Many of them were so well located that their sites serve as major triangulation points for modern government surveys.

Thus when the ruler of Edom refused permission for the Israelites to traverse the land by the "king's highway" it became necessary for

---

[6] *ibid.*, pp.125-147; and in BA 10 (1947), pp.77-84. Discovery of a Middle Bronze Age tomb at Amman (G. Lankester Harding in PEFA 6 [1953], pp. 14-26) may, however, require modification of the theory of the long interval in permanent settlement in Transjordan. See Olga Tufnell in PEQ 1958, p.150.

them to make their weary way around through the wilderness. It is written that when "they journeyed . . . to compass the land of Edom, . . . the soul of the people was much discouraged because of the way" (Numbers 21:4, asv).

North of Edom was Moab. The boundary between the two countries was the Wadi Hesa, which runs into the lower corner of the Dead Sea. It is known in the Bible as the valley of Zered or the brook Zered, and the arrival of the Israelites at it is mentioned in Numbers 21:12. Moab stretched eastward from the Dead Sea to the desert and extended northward to the Wadi Mojib which is the biblical river Arnon. Like Edom, Moab was strongly fortified at strategic sites on the borders and in the interior. Therefore the Israelites had to continue to march "in the wilderness which is opposite Moab, toward the sunrise" (Numbers 21:11) until they reached "the other side of the Arnon" (Numbers 21:13). Beyond the Arnon (Wadi Mojib) lay the land of Gilead which was the territory of the Amorites. The king of the Amorites was Sihon, who had taken or retaken land from Moab and made Heshbon his capital city. From the River Arnon his land extended north to the River Jabbok (Judges 11:22) which is now the Wadi Zerqa. This wadi runs east from the Jordan and then turns south. The latter portion of the Wadi Zerqa, running approximately north and south, constituted the eastern border of Sihon's territory, beyond which was the kingdom of Ammon. North of the east-west stretch of the River Jabbok was the territory of King Og, which extended to the Wadi Yarmuk, not far below the Sea of Galilee. While the Israelites had laboriously to make the circuit of Edom and Moab they were able successfully to challenge Sihon and Og in battle and so to arrive at the Jordan Valley opposite Jericho (Numbers 21:21-35; 22:1; Deuteronomy 2:26-3:11).[7] Incidentally, Balaam who figures in the story at this point (Numbers 22:2-24:25) seems to have been a typical Babylonian diviner, and has been shown from parallels in Mesopotamian ritual to have proceeded with what was at the time quite an approved ceremony of divination.[8]

[7] In view of our date for these events at the end of the Late Bronze Age and near the beginning of the Iron Age it is interesting to note that King Og is reported to have had a bedstead of iron (Deuteronomy 3:11). The term is believed by some, however, to refer instead to a sarcophagus made of black basalt which has an iron content of about 20 per cent. S. R. Driver in icc, *Deuteronomy*. 1895, pp.53f.

[8] Samuel Daiches in *Hilprecht Anniversary Volume*. 1909, pp.60-70; cf. W. F. Albright in jbl 63 (1944), p.231 n.141.

From the top of Pisgah (Deuteronomy 3:27), which was presumably a part of Mount Nebo (Deuteronomy 34:1), Moses looked upon the promised land and then died and was buried in the valley in the land of Moab (Deuteronomy 34:6). Mount Nebo is probably the present Jebel Neba, and Pisgah may be a lower and western summit of the same mountain now called Ras es-Siaghah. From these heights a very fine view is obtained of western Palestine. A steep trail leads down from the mount to the Ayun Musa or "Springs of Moses," overlooking which are the ruins of a fortress, the Khirbet Ayun Musa, that may have been in existence in the time of Moses.[9] There are also ruins not far away now known as Khirbet el-Mekhayyat which may be identified with the town of Nebo (Numbers 32:3, etc.),[10] while on the mountain itself are the remains of a Byzantine church.[11]

The Jordan River was crossed by the children of Israel at a point which is described in Joshua 3:16 as "opposite Jericho," which has traditionally been identified with the present ford known as el-Maghtas or el-Hajleh,[12] some two miles south of the Allenby Bridge. The crossing seems to have been made in the spring when the river was out of its banks (Joshua 3:15), but it is stated that at this particular time "the waters coming down from above stood and rose up in a heap far off, at Adam" (Joshua 3:16), and so the people went over on dry ground. The city of Adam may be identified with Tell ed-Damiyeh, some fifteen miles up the river. There are limestone cliffs there which could have been shaken into the river by an earthquake to dam it for a time completely. Such an event is reported to have shut off the flow of the Jordan for more than twenty hours as recently as 1927.[13]

GILGAL

After the crossing of the Jordan the Israelites camped in Gilgal (Joshua 5:9f.). The location of Gilgal has been difficult to establish although it was clearly in the vicinity of Jericho which has long

[9] Glueck, *The Other Side of the Jordan*, pp.143f.

[10] Sylvester J. Saller and Bellarmino Bagatti, *The Town of Nebo (Khirbet el-Mekhayyat)*, *With a Brief Survey of Other Ancient Christian Monuments in Transjordan*. 1949.

[11] Sylvester J. Saller, *The Memorial of Moses on Mount Nebo*. 2 vols. 1941.

[12] Kraeling, *Rand McNally Bible Atlas*, p.134. This is also the traditional place of the baptism of Jesus (cf. below p.301).

[13] John Garstang, *Joshua Judges, The Foundations of Bible History*. 1931, pp.136f.; Kraeling, *Rand McNally Bible Atlas*, p.133.

been identified with Tell es-Sultan. The site has been sought both at en-Nitleh, three miles south of Tell es-Sultan, and at Khirbet el-Mefjir, one and one-quarter miles northeast of the same tell. Josephus states that the Israelites, after crossing the Jordan, went on fifty stadia and then pitched camp ten stadia from Jericho.[14] The location of en-Nitleh, twenty-six stadia from Tell es-Sultan, is not in harmony with these data, but the place of Khirbet el-Mefjir agrees almost exactly. Reckoning a Roman stadium at 607 feet, Khirbet el-Mefjir is 10.87 stadia from Tell es-Sultan, and fifty stadia from the el-Maghtas ford. In excavation at en-Nitleh in 1950 by James L. Kelso no remains earlier than the fourth century A.D. were found, but in soundings in one of several small tells at Khirbet el-Mefjir in 1955 by James Muilenburg many sherds were found indicating settlement there in the Iron I and Iron II periods. Therefore it seems probable that Gilgal was at or near Khirbet el-Mefjir.[15]

JERICHO

The chief city of strategic importance commanding the entrance to Canaan from the east was Jericho. As already indicated, the mound which represents the Old Testament site is now known as Tell es-Sultan. It rises above an oasis and a spring called Ain es-Sultan, which is the most abundant water supply in the vicinity. In the background the hills of the western highlands rise very sharply, and only a mile away the bold, 1,500-foot-high ridge called Jebel Kuruntul casts its shadow upon the city in the early afternoon. These were "the hills" to which Joshua's spies fled from Rahab's house (Joshua 2:22). Forbidding as the western barrier appears, it is actually cut by gorges which give access to the interior plateau of Palestine. Jericho's strategic significance lay in the fact that it guarded these passes.

The excavation of Jericho was first attempted by Professor Ernst Sellin and the Deutsche Orientgesellschaft in 1907-1909,[16] and was continued by Professor John Garstang in 1930-1936.[17] A portion of the mound as it appeared in the latter excavations is shown in the

---

[14] *Ant.* v, i, 4.

[15] Muilenburg in BASOR 140 (Dec. 1955), pp.11-27.

[16] Ernst Sellin and Carl Watzinger, *Jericho.* 1913.

[17] J. Garstang in *Annals of Archaeology and Anthropology, issued by the Institute of Archaeology, University of Liverpool.* 19 (1932), pp.3-22; 20 (1933), pp.3-42; 21 (1934), pp.99-136; 22 (1935), pp.143-168; 23 (1936), pp.67-76; J. and J. B. E. Garstang, *The Story of Jericho.* 1940.

foreground of Fig. 56, while in the background is the nearby oasis. Again, beginning in 1952, further excavations have been conducted by Kathleen M. Kenyon of the British School of Archaeology in Jerusalem.[18]

The remarkable discoveries in the Neolithic period have already been noted (pp. 140f.), and the existence of the city in Chalcolithic times as well (p. 143). In the Early Bronze Age Jericho was an important walled city which must have been attacked often by nomads trying to force their way into Palestine from the desert. The wall which defended the city was built of flat mud bricks on a foundation of rough stones, and Miss Kenyon found that it had been broken down and rebuilt no less than seventeen times. The tumbled bricks of its first collapse probably indicate destruction by an earthquake. On the last occasion it was still being reconstructed with marks of haste when it was burned in a great conflagration. This destruction may have been at the hands of invading Amorites at about 2100 B.C.[19]

Above the burned wall was a layer of silt with pottery of a new kind, and then scanty architectural remains. This suggests that the newcomers were nomads who at first did little more than camp on the site, and only later began to build poor houses for themselves. Tombs of this intermediate period were surprisingly large, however, and contained pots, daggers, and javelins. On a rock face in the shaft of one of these were several graffiti or rudely scratched drawings. Several show horned animals, probably goats, some of which seem to be browsing on trees, while two drawings represent men who hold square shields in their left hands and long shafts, evidently javelins, in the right. Presumably these picture the very nomads who brought the Early Bronze Age civilization of Jericho to an end.[20]

By probably about 1900 B.C. well-built houses and strong city walls are found again at Jericho. Not only the architecture but also the pottery, weapons, and burial customs indicate the arrival of a new people of a more advanced culture. In this period, which occupied most of the Middle Bronze Age, Jericho grew to the greatest size it ever attained. The defensive system was of a new sort with a

[18] Kenyon in PEQ 1952, pp.62-82; 1953, pp.81-95; 1954; pp.45-63; 1955, pp.108-117; 1956, pp.67-82; and in *Scientific American*. 190 (1954), pp.76-82; Kenyon and A. Douglas Tushingham in NGM 104 (1953), pp.853-870; A. Douglas Tushingham in BA 16 (1953), pp.46-67; 17 (1954), pp.98-104.

[19] PEQ 1952, pp.64-70; 1953, pp.88-90; 1954, pp.55f.; 1955, pp.114f.; 1956, p.77. For the destruction of the first wall by earthquake see PEQ 1952, pp.64,68.

[20] PEQ 1954, pp.56-58; 1956, p.78.

sloping ramp, commonly called a glacis, at the base of the city wall, presumably for defense against the chariotry which the Hyksos introduced at this time. Three phases of construction are distinguished: in the first two the steep ramp was covered with plaster; in the third there was also a stone revetment with mud-brick parapet at the foot of the slope.[21]

In the cemetery area at Jericho a number of Middle Bronze Age tombs have been explored, among them one group in particular, dating probably in the seventeenth century B.C., in which the objects placed with the deceased were in an amazing state of preservation. Almost perfectly intact although very fragile were wooden tables and stools, bowls and boxes, many with bone inlay, and baskets with toilet articles such as wooden combs and little boxes. There were also fragments of textiles, remains of rush mats, and many pottery vessels. Pomegranates and raisins were still recognizable, roast meat was preserved, and within some of the human skulls the desiccated brain was found, its convolutions plainly to be seen. In an endeavor to account for such remarkable preservation of organic material, F. E. Zeuner sampled the air in one tomb and found the concentration of carbon dioxide to be ten times as great as in the atmosphere outside. Since Jericho lies on a series of faults on the western side of the Jordan Valley and must have experienced a great many earthquakes, it is possible that natural gas came up through the faults and collected in the tombs to produce the result noted.[22]

Middle Bronze Age houses and storerooms, many of the latter containing jars full of corn, were found on the east side of the tell by both Professor Garstang and Miss Kenyon. The latest of these structures were destroyed by fire, and it is supposed that this was at a date shortly before the middle of the sixteenth century B.C. when the Egyptians expelled the Hyksos and reasserted their authority in Palestine.[23]

After this destruction at the end of the Middle Bronze Age, Jericho must have been rebuilt and again occupied during the Late Bronze Age, but according to the present understanding of the tell very little now remains there from this latter period. Just under the surface of the tell on the east side were the foundations of a wall together with a small patch of floor. On the floor was a small oven,

[21] PEQ 1952, pp.70f.; 1954, pp.58-60; 1956, pp.79f.
[22] Kenyon in PEQ 1952, p.74; 1953, pp.93f.; 1954, pp.62f.; 1955, p.116; 1956, p.81; Zeuner in PEQ 1955, pp.118-128.
[23] Kenyon in PEQ 1954, p.61; 1955, p.116; 1956, p.81.

and beside it a juglet of fourteenth century date.[24] Some other Late Bronze Age pottery was found by Garstang, and Kenyon dates it between 1400 and somewhat after 1350 B.C.[25] Otherwise whatever city stood at Jericho in the Late Bronze Age has, as far as present knowledge goes, simply disappeared in what Miss Kenyon calls the "tremendous denudation" of the upper strata of the tell.[26] In the areas excavated there is a gap in the remains until in the Iron Age when some materials, probably of the seventh century B.C., are found.[27] There is now, therefore, virtually no evidence at the site by which to try to determine at what date Joshua might have taken Jericho. There was a city there in the fourteenth century but since almost all of it has disappeared there could also have been a thirteenth century city which is completely lost.[28] If the walls of such a city did collapse before Joshua's forces it remains possible that an earthquake was the agency[29] since the geological situation of the city is conducive to such occurrences and, as we have noted, the first wall of the Early Bronze Age appears to have fallen by that very cause.

While much-to-be-desired evidence is therefore lacking at Jericho, in the case of the cities of Bethel, Lachish, Debir, and Hazor, we have evidence of their destruction within the thirteenth century B.C., which is in agreement with the hypothesis that the Israelite conquest was in progress at that time. These cities will be among those next to be considered.

AI AND BETHEL

The capture of Ai is described in Joshua chapters 7-8. Ai is identified with et-Tell, a site thirteen miles west and somewhat north of Jericho, and 3,200 feet higher in the hill country. The place was excavated between 1933 and 1935 by Mme. Judith Marquet-Krause and the remains of an important city of the Early Bronze Age were uncovered. This city was completely destroyed and abandoned about 2200 B.C., and the site was not occupied again except by a brief village settlement sometime between 1200 and 1000 B.C.[30] At the

[24] PEQ 1954, p.61.   [25] PEQ 1951, pp.120,133.   [26] PEQ 1952, p.71.
[27] PEQ 1952, p.71; 1953, p.91.
[28] PEQ 1954, p.61; cf. ADAJ 3 (1956), p.75. Although she points to this possibility, Kathleen Kenyon thinks it more probable that the latest Bronze Age occupation was in the third quarter of the fourteenth century and that it was at this time that Jericho fell to Joshua (Digging Up Jericho, pp.262f.).
[29] Garstang, Joshua Judges, The Foundations of Bible History, pp.144f., 404.
[30] Marquet-Krause, Les fouilles de 'Ay (et-Tell) 1933-1935. 2 vols. 1949. W. F. Albright in AJA 40 (1936), p.158; and in BASOR 118 (Apr. 1950), p.31.

time of the Israelite conquest, therefore, no city existed at this place. As a matter of fact, the Hebrew name Ai means "the Ruin."

The most probable explanation of the difficulty at this point lies in a confusion between Ai and Bethel. The site of the latter city is less than one and one-half miles distant from Ai, and is known now as Beitin. Excavations were conducted here by joint expeditions of the American School of Oriental Research in Jerusalem and the Pittsburgh-Xenia Theological Seminary under W. F. Albright in 1934 and under James L. Kelso in 1954 and following.[31] Bethel was found to have been occupied first after the destruction of the Early Bronze Age city of Ai and to have existed as a well-built town in the Middle and Late Bronze Ages. Sometime in the thirteenth century B.C. the city was consumed by a tremendous conflagration which left behind a solid mass of burned brick, ashes, and charred debris. There can be little doubt but that this destruction represents the conquest of the city by the children of Israel. In the Iron I period the town was rebuilt, presumably by the Israelites, and in a rude fashion as compared with the earlier city. In the sixth century B.C. Bethel was again destroyed by fire, probably by the Chaldeans, and afterward reoccupied in the Persian and Hellenistic periods.

It may be noted that in the book of Joshua no account is given of the capture of Bethel while, on the other hand, in the probably older account of Judges 1 the taking of Bethel by the house of Joseph is narrated (vv. 22-25) but nothing is said of Ai. Therefore it may be supposed that at a later date the tradition of the sack of Bethel was attached, erroneously but naturally, to the nearby and impressive ruins of Ai.[32]

GIBEON

Through the well-known stratagem of its emissaries related in Joshua 9, the city of Gibeon made peace with Israel. The location of this "great city," as it is called in Joshua 10:2, was at a place eight miles northwest of Jerusalem still known as el-Jib. Excavations were begun here in 1956 by the University Museum of the University of Pennsylvania, the Church Divinity School of the Pacific, and the American Schools of Oriental Research, under the direction of

---

[31] W. F. Albright in BASOR 56 (Dec. 1934), pp.2-15; James L. Kelso in BA 19 (1956), pp.36-43; BASOR 137 (Feb. 1955), pp.5-10; 151 (Oct. 1958), pp.3-8.

[32] W. F. Albright in BASOR 74 (Apr. 1939), pp.15-17; G. E. Wright in BA 3 (1940), p.36. For the valley of Achor (Joshua 7:24, etc.) see Frank M. Cross, Jr., and J. T. Milik in BASOR 142 (Apr. 1956), pp.5-17.

Professor James B. Pritchard of the Church Divinity School of the Pacific.

In the portions first explored of the large tell evidences were found of occupation in the Early and Middle Bronze Ages and again in Iron I and II. Some walls of the Iron I period were found together with three grain pits, and the great city wall of Iron II was partially traced. A sloping rock tunnel was cleared which probably belonged to the Iron II period. This led down ninety-six steps to a pool, into which through another tunnel the waters of a spring were led, thus providing safe access for the inhabitants of the city to their water supply. Elsewhere on the tell there was an enormous pool, thirty-six feet in diameter, and more than thirty feet deep, with a spiral staircase around the side. This, built perhaps around 1200 B.C., may have been the "pool of Gibeon" of II Samuel 2:13. In the debris which filled the pool were three jar handles bearing the name Gibeon in Hebrew characters of the eighth century B.C.; thus the identification of the site seems positive.[33]

LACHISH

One of the next cities to fall to the Israelites was Lachish as is told in Joshua 10:31f. The site of Lachish was sought first at Umm Lakis and then at Tell el-Hesy,[34] but finally was identified at Tell ed-Duweir.[35] Excavations were begun here by the Wellcome-Marston Archaeological Expedition in 1933, the work being directed by J. L. Starkey until his murder by brigands January 10, 1938, and continued thereafter by Charles H. Inge and Lankester Harding. It was found that the site had been occupied by a cave dwellers' settlement in the Early Bronze Age and thereafter by a whole series of cities. The city with which we are concerned at this point is the Lachish of the Late Bronze Age which was standing when the Israelites came.

One of the important features of Lachish at this time was the temple, which probably was constructed in its earliest form in the first part of the fifteenth century B.C. and was rebuilt at least twice thereafter.[36] The temple had walls of stone plastered with lime,

[33] James B. Pritchard in BA 19 (1956), pp.65-75; UMB 21 (1957), pp.3-26; 22 (1958), pp.12-24. The identification is questioned by Karl Elliger in ZDPV 73 (1957), pp.125-132.
[34] W. M. F. Petrie, Tell el-Hesy (Lachish). 1891; F. J. Bliss, A Mound of Many Cities. 1894.
[35] W. F. Albright in ZAW 6 (1929), p.3.
[36] Olga Tufnell, C. H. Inge, and L. Harding, Lachish II (Tell ed Duweir), The Fosse Temple. 1940.

the floor was of hard clay, and the roof was supported by wooden columns. A small vestibule gave access to the sanctuary proper, where there was a raised shrine on top of which presumably the cult statue or statues stood. At the base of the shrine was a small hearth, beside it was a pottery stand to hold a bowl for libation, and nearby was a niche for lamps. Benches running around three sides of the room provided a place for the laying of offerings, for the storage of which there were also a large bin and a back storeroom. Around the shrine and in the rubbish pits connected with the building were large quantities of bones of sheep, oxen, and other animals. Most of the bones were from the right foreleg, which corresponds to the prescription for sacrifice in Leviticus 7:32.[37]

One of the lion-hunt scarabs of Amenhotep III, commemorating his feat of killing 102 lions with his own hand during the first ten years of his reign, was found at Lachish and the continuation of Egyptian dominance until in the thirteenth century was indicated by the presence of a scarab of Ramses II. But the most important discovery for the fixing of the date when the Late Bronze Age city was destroyed, was that of a broken bowl on which had been written in Egyptian and apparently by an Egyptian tax collector a record of certain wheat deliveries. All of these were dated in the "year four" of a certain Pharaoh. The character of the script points to the time of Merneptah, and it is believed almost certain that he is the Pharaoh in question. The "year four," therefore, is to be referred to his reign and is equivalent to about 1221 B.C. Since the fragments of the bowl were found, all together, in the debris of the burned city, the bowl was doubtless broken at the very time when the city fell. The destruction of Lachish thus must have taken place just about 1221 B.C. and doubtless was the work of the Israelites just as it is stated in the Old Testament.[38]

There must also be mentioned the discovery, in the Late Bronze Age temple at Lachish, of a bowl and a jar on which were inscriptions written in an early type of Canaanite script. This script is identical with that of the proto-Sinaitic inscriptions found at Serabit

[37] G. Ernest Wright points out that such similarity between early Canaanite ritual and late priestly legislation in the Old Testament tends to support the claim that the substance of much of the ritual contained in the priestly document is very old and reflects practices of the Solomonic temple perhaps ultimately borrowed from the Canaanites (AJA 45 [1941], p.634).

[38] W. F. Albright in BASOR 68 (Dec. 1937), pp.23f.; 74 (Apr. 1939), pp.20-22; 132 (Dec. 1953), p.46; Raymond S. Haupert in BA 1 (1938), p.26.

el-Khadem (pp. 148f.). Other specimens of similar script also have come to light in Middle and Late Bronze Age levels at such Palestinian sites as Shechem (see below), Gezer, Tell el-Hesy, and Beth-shemesh. The Lachish inscriptions together with these others constitute very important connecting links between the proto-Sinaitic and the earliest known Phoenician forms of the alphabet.[39]

DEBIR

Debir, earlier known as Kiriath-sepher, was another city taken by the Israelites (Joshua 10:38f.; 15:15-17; Judges 1:11-13). Kiriath-sepher is believed to be the mound now called Tell Beit Mirsim, thirteen miles southwest of Hebron. The excavation of Tell Beit Mirsim was carried out in 1926 and following years by a joint expedition of the Pittsburgh-Xenia Theological Seminary and the American School of Oriental Research at Jerusalem under the leadership of Melvin G. Kyle and William F. Albright.[40] A beautiful royal scarab of Amenhotep III was found which doubtless was used by the Egyptian official at Kiriath-sepher. This is clear evidence that in the reign of Amenhotep III Egypt was still in power here and the Israelites had not yet taken possession of the land. At the end of the Late Bronze Age there is a great burned layer and above it are Israelite remains. Thus the evidences here, too, point to the arrival of the Israelites and the destruction of the Canaanite city shortly before 1200 B.C.[41]

Among the interesting discoveries made at Tell Beit Mirsim was a household stela showing a Canaanite serpent goddess. She appears as a woman clad in a long robe and with a large snake coiling around her. Exactly the same kind of representation was found on a small limestone plaque at Shechem (Balatah) in 1934 by Dr. H. Steckeweh. This plaque also carried an inscription written in the early alphabetic script of Canaan.[42]

[39] Tufnell, Inge, and Harding, Lachish II (Tell ed Duweir), The Fosse Temple, pp.47-57; W. F. Albright in BASOR 58 (Apr. 1935), pp.28f.; 63 (Oct. 1936), pp.8-12; S. Yeivin in PEQ 1937, pp.180-193; Chester C. McCown, The Ladder of Progress in Palestine. 1943, pp.100-117.

[40] Albright in ZAW 6 (1929), pp.1-17; and in AASOR 12 (1930-31); 13 (1931-32), pp.55-128; 17 (1936-37); 21-22 (1941-43); M. G. Kyle, Excavating Kirjath-Sepher's Ten Cities. 1934.

[41] Kyle, Excavating Kirjath-Sepher's Ten Cities, p.192; Albright in AASOR 17 (1936-37), p.79.

[42] Albright in AASOR 17 (1936-37), Pls. 21a, 22; pp.42f.

In Joshua 11 a great victory of Joshua over a coalition of kings at the waters of Merom is described, after which it is stated (11:10-13) that he turned back and took the city of Hazor, the head of all those kingdoms, and burned it with fire. The prominence of Hazor is confirmed by its appearance in other ancient sources including the Egyptian execration texts of the nineteenth century[43] and the Amarna letters of the fourteenth century B.C.[44] The ancient city has been identified with Tell el-Qedah in the plain of Huleh, some five miles southwest of Lake Huleh and nine miles north of the Sea of Galilee. The site comprises a more-or-less oval-shaped tell nearly 2,000 feet in length and, north of this mound, a very large rectangular plateau about 2,300 feet wide and 3,300 feet long. On the west side this plateau was fortified by a wall of beaten earth which still stands over forty-five feet high, and on the other naturally steep sides there was also a protective glacis. The latter area was called a "camp enclosure" by John Garstang, who made soundings there in 1928. Because he found no Mycenaean pottery which otherwise occurs in northern Palestine about 1400-1200 B.C.,[45] Garstang concluded that Hazor must have been destroyed about 1400 B.C., the same date he gave for the fall of Jericho.[46]

Beginning in 1955 excavations have been conducted at Hazor by the Hebrew University—James A. de Rothschild Expedition under the direction of Yigael Yadin.[47] Several areas have been excavated on the tell and on the rectangular plateau. Area A on the tell was penetrated through four levels of occupation of the Iron II period. Uppermost were the remains of a small town of the end of the eighth and beginning of the seventh centuries B.C.; beneath that a city destroyed by fire in the second half of the eighth century, probably by Tiglath-pileser III in 732 B.C.; then a city with pottery of the ninth and eighth centuries; and a town constructed perhaps in the time of Ahab in the third quarter of the ninth century. Area B on

[43] ANET p.329 n.8.

[44] KAT Nos.148,227,228 = MTAT Nos.148,227,228; MTAT No.256a.

[45] cf. above p.149; Hamilton in QDAP 4 (1935), p.11.

[46] Garstang, *Joshua Judges, The Foundations of Bible History*, pp.184f., 382f., cf. 146.

[47] Yadin in BA 19 (1956), pp.2-11; IEJ 6 (1956), pp.120-125; 7 (1957), pp.118-123; *Archaeology*. 10 (1957), pp.83-92; BA 20 (1957), pp.34-47; 21 (1958), pp.30-47; *The James A. de Rothschild Expedition at Hazor, Hazor I, An Account of the First Season of Excavations. 1955.* 1958; cf. W. F. Albright in BASOR 150 (Apr. 1958), pp.21-25; Yadin in IEJ 8 (1958), pp.1-14.

the highest point of the tell at the west was defended with a series of citadels which were traced down from the Hellenistic period to about the ninth century B.C.

The areas explored on the rectangular plateau showed that, at least at these points, this was not just a camp enclosure but a city with well-constructed houses and drainage systems. In Area C four strata were explored. Stratum I, completely uncovered, had dwellings with rooms opening onto a cobbled courtyard, and on the floors was Mycenaean as well as locally-made pottery. The stratum, in which two phases were recognized, was dated by the Mycenaean pottery to the Late Bronze Age and the thirteenth century B.C. Strata II, III, and IV, explored by trench, revealed earlier settlements of the Late and Middle Bronze Ages, as far back as the Hyksos period. Nearby, at the foot of the beaten-earth wall, were two temples, one above the other, of the Late Bronze Age, the upper of the same date as the lower phase of the dwellings. In Areas D and E there were also dwellings, cisterns, and tombs, which confirmed the picture of the rectangular plateau as containing a series of cities dating back to the Hyksos period and coming to an end in the thirteenth century B.C. A small jar fragment of the thirteenth century from Area D has two letters of the proto-Sinaitic alphabet; the script is like that on the Lachish bowl of about the same date (p. 162).

Hazor was thus in existence at the time which seems most probable for the Israelite invasion, the middle of the thirteenth century B.C. With its very large area, justifying an estimate of 40,000 inhabitants, it must have been a place of great prominence exactly as represented in the book of Joshua. Since the last city on the rectangular plateau was probably destroyed in the second half of the thirteenth century, it may well be that it was at the hands of Joshua that it fell, although of that specific fact there is, at least as yet, no actual proof.

Yet another city occupied by the Israelites was Beth-zur, according to Joshua 15:58, although no description of its capture is given. Excavation was inaugurated at this site in 1931 and resumed in 1957.[48] The city was formidably fortified in the Middle Bronze Age but was evidently abandoned during the fourteenth and thirteenth centuries and only reoccupied at the beginning of the Iron Age, or around 1200 B.C. Also mentioned in Joshua 15:27 is the city of Beth-

[48] O. R. Sellers, *The Citadel of Beth-zur.* 1933; and in BA 21 (1958), pp.71-76; Robert W. Funk in BASOR 150 (Apr. 1958), pp.8-20.

pelet. Petrie believed that he found Beth-pelet at Tell Fara, south-east of Gaza,[49] but Albright thinks that this is more probably ancient Sharuhen.[50]

In the case, therefore, of at least some cities which the Israelites are said in the Bible to have captured, notably including Bethel, Lachish, Debir, and Hazor, there is evidence upon the site of destruction of the city at the end of the Late Bronze Age or shortly before 1200 B.C. The identification of this event with the conquest by the children of Israel seems very probable.

It is significant, also, to note that at the beginning of the Iron Age the houses and fortifications of Palestine are considerably poorer than before. Likewise the pottery shows in general a great deterioration in quality, and is little ornamental. This sudden drop in the cultural level fits well with the invasion of the Israelites from the desert, any cultivation of the arts among whom would have suffered during the long years in the wilderness. The characteristic city walls as built by the Israelites were only five, six, or seven feet in width. Perhaps because with their looser patriarchal form of society there was no systematic coercion of the individual and it was not possible to make the people submit to the prolonged and difficult labor of constructing a massive city wall.[51] It is also of interest to note how, as may be seen very clearly at Bethel for example, in the earlier city levels there are many Canaanite cult objects, but at the point believed to represent the Israelite conquest these suddenly disappear, presumably in accordance with the avoidance of idols enjoined upon the children of Israel.[52]

Viewed in its entirety the work of Joshua was evidently very successful and it could be said in Joshua 11:23 that he "took the whole land"; yet the conquest was neither easy nor swift, and it is stated that "Joshua made war a long time with all those kings" (Joshua 11:18). Even after the death of Joshua the individual tribes doubtless had to make many more conquests as they settled down in the land, as is described in Judges 1. In some cases places once overcome may have had to be retaken as, for example, Debir which was smitten by Joshua and all Israel according to Joshua 10:38f. and then captured for the tribe of Judah by Othniel according to Joshua 15:15-17 and Judges 1:11-13. Likewise additional places may have been taken at

---

[49] W. M. F. Petrie, *Beth-pelet I* (*Tell Fara*). 1930.
[50] W. F. Albright, *The Archaeology of Palestine and the Bible.* 2d ed. 1933, p.53.
[51] *ibid.,* p.102.
[52] Kelso in BA 19 (1956), p.40.

this time and then again lost as, for example, Jerusalem which was burned by the men of Judah according to Judges 1:8 but only finally taken for permanent control by the Israelites in the time of David (p. 177).[53]

There may also have been yet other cities which were too strong to be taken at all at this time, or where at any rate the native inhabitants were not dispossessed. Listed in Judges 1 among cities where the inhabitants were not driven out are a number of well-known and powerfully fortified places including Beth-shean, Taanach, Megiddo (Judges 1:27), Gezer (Judges 1:29), and Beth-shemesh (Judges 1:33). From discoveries at these sites we may learn more of the culture of the land into the midst of which the Israelites had come.

BETH-SHEAN

Beth-shean, also known as Beth-shan or Beisan, and later the Hellenistic city of Scythopolis, is identified with the imposing mound Tell el-Husn above the Jordan in the Valley of Jezreel. Excavations have been conducted on the site by the University Museum of the University of Pennsylvania under the leadership of Clarence S. Fisher, Alan Rowe, and G. M. Fitzgerald.[54] The Canaanite city here was found to have been fortified with double walls, and the inner and outer walls were connected with cross walls which formed small rooms. The fortifications included a strong tower, built with large unbaked bricks on a foundation of basalt blocks. Beth-shean was occupied by Egyptian garrisons down at least to the time of Ramses III. An Egyptian stela of Seti I (c.1302-c.1290 B.C.) was found there which refers to the 'Apiru of some mountain district with a Semitic name.[55]

No less than four Canaanite temples have been excavated at Beth-shean: one, of the seventh city level which is ascribed to the thirteenth century B.C.; another, of the sixth level which dates in the twelfth and early eleventh centuries; and two of the fifth level belonging to the eleventh and tenth centuries. Since the last two temples continued in use until approximately the tenth century it has been suggested that the Southern Temple may have been the Temple of Dagon of I Chronicles 10:10, and the Northern Temple may have been the House of Ashtaroth of I Samuel 31:10.

[53] G. Ernest Wright in JNES 5 (1946), pp.105-114.
[54] Alan Rowe, *The Topography and History of Beth-shan*. 1930.
[55] W. F. Albright in BASOR 125 (Feb. 1952), pp.24-32.

Serpents played an important part in the cult here too (cf. p. 163) and plaques with serpents and shrine-houses with serpents on them were found in the temples.[56]

TAANACH

Taanach still bears the name Tell Taanak and attracted the attention of Professor Ernst Sellin of Vienna on a visit to Palestine as early as 1899. His excavations there in 1902 and 1903 were the first to be carried out in northern Palestine.[57] Taanach was found to have been fortified with stone walls built in the so-called Cyclopean style of masonry (p. 147), and the remains of a fourteenth century B.C. palace of a local king were uncovered. Tablets unearthed at Taanach contain the interesting expression, "If the finger of Ashirat points," which is interpreted as meaning that oracles were given in the name of a goddess Ashirat, who probably is the same as the goddess Asherat known from Ras Shamra (p. 173). The Asherim mentioned in the Old Testament may have been wooden symbols, perhaps trees or poles, of this goddess (Exodus 34:13; Deuteronomy 16:21; I Kings 14:23; II Kings 17:10; 18:4; 23:14), while she herself probably is referred to in other passages (Judges 3:7; I Kings 15:13; 18:19; II Kings 21:7; 23:4, 6, 7).[58] Later brick houses whose ruins were found at Taanach may represent the eventual Israelite settlement there.[59] In a building which may have been a private house of Israelite times was found a terra-cotta incense altar possibly used by some of the Israelites in worship.[60]

MEGIDDO

Commanding the best pass from the Mediterranean coastal plain to the Valley of Esdraelon and on north to Galilee and Damascus, Megiddo always has been a point of great strategic importance. This was where Thutmose III met the Asiatics (p. 99) and where Josiah was slain by Necho (p. 129). It was through the same pass

---

[56] Alan Rowe, *The Four Canaanite Temples of Beth-shan.* I (1940); G. E. Wright in AJA 45 (1941), pp.483-485.

[57] E. Sellin, *Tell Ta 'annek.* 1904.

[58] Burrows, *What Mean These Stones?* p.231. Numerous nude female figurines have been found in most Palestinian excavations of the second and first millenniums B.C., and it is probable that they are representations of Asherah or of other similar Canaanite goddesses such as Ashtart or Anat. See James B. Pritchard, *Palestinian Figurines in Relation to Certain Goddesses Known through Literature.* 1943; G. E. Wright in JBL 63 (1944), pp.426-430; P. J. Riis in *Berytus.* 9 (1949), pp.69-90.

[59] Duncan, *Digging Up Biblical History.* I, p.181.

[60] Barton, *Archaeology and the Bible,* p.221.

that Allenby's cavalry surprised the Turkish armies in 1918,[61] and it is here that the book of Revelation expects the climactic battle "on the great day of God the Almighty" (16:14, 16).

The modern name of the site of Megiddo is Tell el-Mutesellim (Fig. 57), and Dr. G. Schumacher of the Deutsche Orientgesellschaft first drove an exploratory trench into it in 1903-1905.[62] Large-scale systematic horizontal clearance of the site was begun by the Oriental Institute of the University of Chicago under the direction of Clarence S. Fisher in 1925 and continued in succeeding years by P. L. O. Guy and by Gordon Loud.[63] It appears that in the Early Bronze Age, Megiddo was surrounded by a massive city wall, originally some thirteen feet thick and later strengthened to twice that thickness. A mud brick wall and gate of about 1800 B.C. are known, and the present indications are that the Canaanite city was destroyed near the end of the twelfth century, while the Israelite occupation, represented for example by the mud brick wall of Level V, began about a half century later.

In 1937 Gordon Loud explored the palace of the princes who ruled at Megiddo as vassals of the Pharaohs of Egypt. The palace showed five building periods, running from the sixteenth into the twelfth century B.C., and the fifth palace had a subterranean treasury in which a wonderful find of more than two hundred carved and incised ivories was made. One of these was an ivory pen case belonging to an Egyptian who bore the title, "Royal Envoy to every Foreign Country." It is to be dated just after 1200 B.C. since it carries the cartouche of Ramses III. Another is an ivory plaque which shows the prince of Megiddo probably celebrating a victory (Fig. 58). At the right he drives naked captives before his chariot. At the left he sits upon his sphinx-sided throne and drinks from a bowl while a musician, "a David of his court," plays upon the harp. At the extreme left is a large jar, with animal heads.[64]

[61] It is a well-known fact that Allenby depended chiefly upon the Bible and upon *The Historical Geography of the Holy Land* by George Adam Smith for information concerning the topography of Palestine. cf. David S. Cairns in *Religion in Life*. 11 (1942), pp.532f.

[62] G. Schumacher and C. Steuernagel, *Tell El-Mutesellim*. 1908.

[63] Robert S. Lamon and Geoffrey M. Shipton, *Megiddo I, Seasons of 1925-34*. OIP XLII, 1939; Gordon Loud, ed., *Megiddo II, Seasons of 1935-39*. OIP LXII, 2 vols. 1948; Robert M. Engberg in BA 3 (1940), pp.41-51; 4 (1941), pp.11-16; G. E. Wright in BA 13 (1950), pp.28-46.

[64] Loud, *The Megiddo Ivories*. 1939; C. de Mertzenfeld in *Syria*. 19 (1938), pp.345-354. On the ivory trade, in which the Phoenicians were active, see Richard D. Barnett in *Archaeology*. 9 (1956), pp.87-97.

GEZER

The site of Gezer was identified at Tell Jezer by Professor Clermont-Ganneau in the nineteenth century, and the city was excavated for the Palestine Exploration Fund by Professor R. A. S. Macalister in 1902-1908.[65] Gezer is well situated on the lower slope of hills above the maritime plain to guard the western frontier. Cave dwellers lived here at an early time in natural rock caverns, and apparently practiced the cremation of their dead. In the Early Bronze Age several of the caves were used for interments as the inhabitants gradually shifted to homes on the rock surface above.[66] Later the city was fortified with a brick wall, and still later with a thirteen-foot-thick stone wall. After the destruction of the latter, its materials were employed in the construction of what is now known as the outer wall, fourteen feet thick and enclosing an area of twenty-seven acres. One hundred and twenty feet below the present surface of the ground and ninety-four feet below the surface of the rock is a spring in a cave to which a tunnel was cut to enable the people of the city to obtain water in time of siege.

In the northern part of the city and above one of the caves in which early burials were made is a row of standing stones (Fig. 59) which have elicited much interest. Originally the series consisted of ten rough stone pillars varying in height from five to ten feet, and standing in a slightly curved line from north to south. At the time of discovery one was fallen and two were broken off at the bottom, but the remainder still stood upright. At a point near the middle of the row and just to one side was a stone base with a rectangular depression in which doubtless yet another stela once stood. The area containing these standing stones has been regarded as of cultic significance and interpreted as a Canaanite "high place,"[67] but it now appears more probable that the pillars were simply memorial stones of the kings of the city.[68]

BETH-SHEMESH

Beth-shemesh, now known as Ain Shems or Tell er-Rumeileh, and lying southeast of Gezer in the Shephelah, was the next site after Gezer whose excavation was undertaken by the Palestine Explora-

---

[65] Macalister, *The Excavation of Gezer.* 3 vols. 1912.

[66] G. E. Wright in PEQ 1937, pp.67-78.

[67] R. A. S. Macalister, *Bible Side-Lights from the Mound of Gezer.* 1906, pp.57-65.

[68] Carl Watzinger, *Denkmäler Palästinas.* I (1933), pp.63f. On the search for "high places" of Israelite times, see C. C. McCown in JBL 69 (1950), pp.205-219.

tion Fund. The work was directed by Dr. Duncan Mackenzie during the years 1911-1912 and was the last Palestinian excavation just before the First World War.[69] Further excavations were carried out in 1928 and following by Professor Elihu Grant of Haverford College.[70] It appears that the site was occupied by a series of cities between 2000 and 600 B.C., final destruction having probably come from the army of Nebuchadnezzar II of Babylon. Fine pottery, weapons, jewelry and scarabs were uncovered from the late Canaanite and early Israelite periods and further illustration of Canaanite religion appeared in a plaque with a serpent goddess.

RAS SHAMRA

The insights which Palestinian archeology has been giving as to Canaanitish culture and religion have been greatly supplemented by recent discoveries in Syria, particularly at Ras Shamra. This is a site on the northern coast of Syria, opposite the island of Cyprus, which was discovered almost by chance in 1929 and studied since that date in a series of campaigns conducted by C. F. A. Schaeffer.[71] The site was already occupied in the Neolithic Age, to which time the plain pottery of the lowest level belongs.[72] As early as the second millennium B.C. the city is called by the name Ugarit and it is mentioned in Egyptian inscriptions, in the Tell el-Amarna letters, and in Hittite documents. In the days of the Twelfth Dynasty, Egyptian influence was strong, as is shown by the finding of a statue of the wife of Senusert II and two sphinxes sent by Amenemhet III. In the fifteenth and fourteenth centuries Ugarit flourished greatly but was overwhelmed by an earthquake about the middle of the fourteenth century (c.1360 B.C.). After the earthquake the city again prospered, being first under the dominance of the Hittites but coming again

---

[69] R. A. S. Macalister, A Century of Excavation in Palestine. 1930, p.69.

[70] E. Grant, Beth Shemesh (1929); Ain Shems Excavations. 5 vols. 1931-39.

[71] C. F. A. Schaeffer in Syria. 10 (1929), pp.285-297; 12 (1931), pp.1-14; 13 (1932), pp.1-27; 14 (1933), pp.93-127; 15 (1934), pp.105-131; 16 (1935), pp.141-176; 17 (1936), pp.105-149; 18 (1937), pp.125-154; 19 (1938), pp.193-255,313-334; 20 (1939), pp.277-292; 28 (1951), pp.1-21; etc.; The Cuneiform Texts of Ras Shamra-Ugarit. 1939; Ugaritica, études relatives aux découvertes de Ras Shamra. Première série, 1939; Ugaritica II, nouvelles études relatives aux découvertes de Ras Shamra. 1949; Stratigraphie comparée et chronologie de l'Asie occidentale (IIIᵉ et IIᵉ millénaires). 1948, pp.8-39; Johannes Friedrich, Ras Schamra, Ein Überblick über Funde und Forschungen. Der Alte Orient 33, 1/2, 1933; W. F. Albright in AJA 54 (1950), p.164. And see now the publications of the Mission de Ras Shamra, ed. by C. F. A. Schaeffer, including VI, Le palais royal d'Ugarit, III, Textes accadiens et hourrites des archives est, ouest et centrales. 2 vols. 1955.

[72] Schaeffer, Ugaritica, Première série, pp.3-8; T. H. Gaster in Antiquity. 13 (1939), p.306.

under Egyptian authority with Ramses II. Toward the close of the thirteenth or beginning of the twelfth century the city suffered invasion from the peoples of the north and from the sea, and after the twelfth century Ugarit ceased to exist.

The discovery of greatest importance at Ras Shamra was that of documents in a library which had been housed in a building situated between the city's two great temples, one dedicated to Baal and the other to Dagon. Hundreds of clay tablets were uncovered, dating from the fifteenth and early fourteenth centuries, and bearing texts in a cuneiform alphabet which is the earliest known alphabet written with wedge-shaped signs. The language was recognized by Professor H. Bauer of the University of Halle to be of Semitic origin and its decipherment was finally accomplished by Bauer and the French scholars É. Dhorme and C. Virolleaud. Known as Ugaritic, this language is closely related both to biblical Hebrew and to Phoenician. Most of the Ras Shamra texts are poetic in form, and the Ugaritic poetry exhibits exactly the same characteristic feature of parallelism as does Hebrew poetry. This may be seen in an example such as the following:

> The heavens rain oil
> The wadies run with honey.[73]

The majority of the documents under consideration are in the nature of mythological poems concerning Canaanite gods and heroes, but some of the texts deal with other subjects including even the treatment of sick and infirm horses. Incidentally, one of the remedies mentioned in this "veterinary manual" is a sort of pressed fig-cake which is similar to what Isaiah ordered for Hezekiah's boil (II Kings 20:1-8). The early Canaanitish beliefs which are reflected in the religious and mythological texts are of the greatest interest, and the discussion of them and their evident relationship with many of the religious beliefs and practices reflected in the Old Testament has already elicited an extensive literature.[74] The supreme god is known

[73] Cyrus H. Gordon, *The Loves and Wars of Baal and Anat and Other Poems from Ugarit*. 1943, pp.xi,10.
[74] Charles Virolleaud in *Antiquity*. 5 (1931), pp.405-414; William C. Graham in JR 14 (1934), pp.306-329; Walter G. Williams in AJSL 51 (1934-35), pp.233-246; J. W. Jack, *The Ras Shamra Tablets, Their Bearing on the Old Testament*. 1935; Ditlef Nielsen, *Ras Šamra Mythologie und biblische Theologie*. Abhandlungen für die Kunde des Morgenlandes, Deutsche morgenländische Gesellschaft. 21 (1936), No.4; René Dussaud, *Les découvertes de Ras Shamra (Ugarit) et l'Ancien Testament*. 2d ed. 1941; Samuel H. Hooke, *The Origins of Early Semitic Ritual*. 1938, pp.28-38; J. Philip Hyatt in BA 2 (1939), pp.2-8; John H. Patton, *Canaanite Parallels in the Book*

as El, a name by which God is called in the Old Testament.[75] On a stela found at Ras Shamra the god El is shown seated upon a throne with the king of Ugarit presenting an offering before him (Fig. 60). The god is represented as mature in age and paternal and majestic in appearance. The wife of El is Asherat-of-the-Sea, the counselor of the gods, and their son is the god Baal. Baal is a god of the rain and storm and is represented on a Ras Shamra stela brandishing a mace in his right hand and holding in his left hand a stylized thunderbolt ending in a spear-head (Fig. 61). One of his titles is "Zabul [Prince], Lord of the Earth," and this doubtless has survived in the name of the god Baal-zebub in II Kings (1:2, etc.) and of Beelzebub in the New Testament (Mark 3:22, etc.). Asherat probably is to be identified with Asherah in the Old Testament (p. 168), and Baal of course figures prominently there. Asherat is mentioned regularly after Baal in the Ras Shamra texts and the similar and close connection of the two is likewise reflected in I Kings 18:19 and II Kings 23:4.[76] Among the adventures related of Baal in the Ras Shamra tablets is a conflict with Lotan, "the nimble serpent . . . the sinuous serpent, the mighty one with seven heads." Lotan is the same as the Hebrew Leviathan that is described in similar terms in Isaiah 27:1 (cf. Job 26:12f.).

Baal or Aliyan Baal figures prominently in the mythology made known by the Ras Shamra tablets. Aliyan represents the growth of plants, and fights against Mot, the god of the dried-up summer soil, but is slain by him. Thereupon the goddess Anat, the sister and lover of Aliyan, goes in search of him, recovers his body and slays his enemy, Mot. Aliyan is then brought back to life and placed on Mot's throne so that he may ensure the revival of vegetation in another season.[77]

An interesting legend is written on four large tablets found at Ras Shamra, one of which is shown in Fig. 62. This is the Legend of

---

of Psalms. 1944; H. L. Ginsberg in BA 8 (1945), pp.41-58; Robert de Langhe, Les textes de Ras Shamra-Ugarit et leurs rapports avec le milieu biblique de l'Ancien Testament. 2 vols. 1945; Julian Obermann, Ugaritic Mythology, A Study of Its Leading Motifs. 1948; Cyrus H. Gordon, Ugaritic Literature. 1949; Theodor H. Gaster, Thespis, Ritual, Myth and Drama in the Ancient Near East. 1950, pp.113-313; Arvid S. Kapelrud, Baal in the Ras Shamra Texts. 1952; Marvin H. Pope, El in the Ugaritic Texts. 1955.

[75] Genesis 33:20, and frequently in the plural of majesty, Elohim.

[76] H. Bauer in ZAW 10 (1933), p.89. For a seventeenth century B.C. temple at Nahariyah, twelve miles north of Haifa, probably dedicated to Asherat, see M. Dothan in IEJ 6 (1956), pp.14-25.

[77] W. F. Albright, Archaeology and the Religion of Israel. 1942, pp.84-90.

Keret and tells of the time when El entrusted Keret with the command of "the army of the Negeb."

One rite is mentioned in the Ras Shamra texts in which the seething of a kid in milk is prescribed as an item in the magical technique for producing the early rains. This procedure is practically what the Israelites are forbidden to carry out, in Exodus 23:19; 34:26. A wise hero Daniel is mentioned who is identified by some with the Daniel spoken of in Ezekiel 14:14. Such biblical words occur as "anoint" from which "Messiah" is derived, and also the expression for "bring good tidings." The *rpem* or *rpum* are mentioned frequently, these probably being the same as the Old Testment *rephaim*, the "shades" or inhabitants of the world of the dead (Job 26:5, etc.).

Such are a few of the glimpses given us by the Ras Shamra tablets of the religion which prevailed among the Canaanites of Ugarit at a time only shortly before the period when the Israelites entered Palestine. This religion was polytheistic, mythological, and ritualistic, and was centered to a large degree in interest in the fertility of the soil. When the children of Israel came in contact with this environment they evidently adopted some of the customs and beliefs of their neighbors, but through the leadership of the prophets were able to rise superior to the grosser features of the Canaanite fertility religion.

SHILOH

According to Joshua 18:1 the Israelites under Joshua set up their tent of meeting at Shiloh, and in the days of the judges this place remained the central sanctuary of Israel where an annual festival was held (Judges 21:19). In the time of Eli and during the early years of Samuel the tabernacle and ark were still at Shiloh (I Samuel 1:9; 2:22; 3:3), but when the Philistines defeated the Israelites and took the ark they probably destroyed Shiloh too. This is suggested by the fact that when the ark was returned it was not brought back to Shiloh but taken to Beth-shemesh (I Samuel 6:12) and afterward to Kiriath-jearim (I Samuel 7:1f.). Furthermore in the time of Jeremiah, although Shiloh was again inhabited (Jeremiah 41:5), it is evident that the memory and the marks of a great destruction of that place were still vivid. The prophet stated the Lord's message in these words: "Go now to my place that was in Shiloh, where I made my name dwell at first, and see what I did to it for the wickedness of my people Israel" (Jeremiah 7:12; cf. 26:6).

Shiloh has been identified with Tell Seilun, about ten miles north of Bethel (cf. Judges 21:19), and this site was studied and partially excavated in 1926 and 1929 by a Danish expedition under the leadership of Hans Kjaer. It is clear that the city was inhabited and flourishing in the twelfth and early eleventh centuries B.C., and also that it was destroyed by conflagration at a time around 1050 B.C., after which it remained deserted for several centuries. That this destruction was that visited upon Shiloh by the Philistines seems beyond doubt.[78]

TELL EN-NASBEH

A town which was probably settled by the Israelites in the time of the judges, and which is of the greater interest because it has been so thoroughly excavated and studied, was at Tell en-Nasbeh, eight miles north of Jerusalem. The excavations were conducted by Professor William F. Badè of Pacific School of Religion in a series of five expeditions from 1926 to 1935, and after the death of Dr. Badè the publication of the results was carried out by Professor Chester C. McCown of the same institution with the assistance of several others.[79]

The first occupation of Tell en-Nasbeh was at least as early as the Early Bronze Age in the third millennium B.C. A number of caves and tombs in the limestone rock of the hill contained the pottery, implements, ornaments, and skeletons of some of the inhabitants of this time. Then in Iron i, probably in the twelfth century B.C., a small town was founded on the same hill, the settlers presumably being the Israelites. The wall which first protected this settlement was a comparatively thin one, perhaps a yard thick, built of rubble. By the end of Iron i, around 900 B.C., a new and very powerful city wall was built. It was half a mile in circumference and enclosed an area of eight acres. Made of large, roughly-shaped stones laid in clay mortar, it had an average thickness of over thirteen feet. Still standing in places to a height of twenty-five feet, it was probably at one time thirty-five or forty feet high, and was strengthened with nine

---

[78] Hans Kjaer in JPOS 10 (1930), pp.87-174; *The Excavation of Shiloh 1929.* 1930; Albright, *Archaeology and the Religion of Israel*, pp.103f.

[79] *Tell en-Nasbeh, Excavated under the Direction of the Late William Frederic Badè*, i, *Archaeological and Historical Results*, by C. C. McCown, with contributions by James Muilenburg, J. C. Wampler, Dietrich von Bothmer, and Margaret Harrison; ii, *The Pottery*, by J. C. Wampler, with a chapter by C. C. McCown. 1947. See also C. C. McCown, *The Ladder of Progress in Palestine.* 1943, pp.209-214; W. F. Albright in JPOS 3 (1923), pp.110-121; and in AASOR 4 (1922-23), pp.90-111; G. E. Wright in BA 10 (1947), pp.69-77; James Muilenburg in *Studia Theologica.* 8 (1955), pp.25-42.

or ten rectangular towers. At the northeast side of the city the ends of the wall were caused to overlap, and in the thirty-foot space between them the great city gate was set. Inside the gate were guard rooms, and on the outside the court was lined with stone benches. This was the place where many of the business and legal transactions of an ancient Middle Eastern city were conducted, as the Old Testament indicates with its frequent references to events which transpired "in the gate" (Deuteronomy 22:15; Ruth 4:11; II Samuel 19:8; etc.).

Occupation continued at Tell en-Nasbeh down to Hellenistic times, although from the fifth century on the population was greatly reduced and the once powerfully fortified city became only a small, defenceless village. Dating probably from the later pre-exilic period, over eighty stamp impressions on jar handles were found at Tell en-Nasbeh with the inscription *lemelekh*, meaning "belonging to the king," which suggests that it designated royal property. Perhaps the contents of the jars were to go to the king as taxes. Such *lemelekh* stamps have also been found at other sites in the southern kingdom and were doubtless used widely there before the exile. Since no such stamps were found at Bethel, three miles to the north, this is taken as evidence that at this time Tell en-Nasbeh belonged to the southern kingdom, with the boundary line running between this city and Bethel. Twenty-eight stamps were found, probably postexilic in date, with an inscription the three Hebrew letters of which have been read as either $m \ s \ h$ or $m \ s \ p$. A bronze fragment, with part of a cuneiform inscription, dating perhaps around the seventh century B.C., indicates some contact with the East. Most interesting of all, for the possible Old Testament relationship which will be indicated in the next paragraph, is the seal found in a tomb at Tell en-Nasbeh with a Hebrew inscription reading, "Ya'azanyahu, servant of the king."

The foregoing archeological history of Tell en-Nasbeh has many points which support an identification of this site with the ancient Mizpah, a city which was prominent in the time of Samuel (I Samuel 7:5, etc.), and after the destruction of Jerusalem was the residence of Gedaliah, whom Nebuchadnezzar made governor of Judah. The powerful wall which was such a conspicuous feature of the city may have been built by King Asa of Judah, who is known to have fortified Mizpah against the northern tribes (I Kings 15:22; II Chronicles 16:6). If the stamp impressions mentioned above are read *m ṣ p*, the vocalization could be Miṣpah and would support the identification. The Ya'azanyahu of the seal inscription could be the Jaazaniah mentioned in II Kings 25:23 and Jeremiah 40:8, who was a captain of forces and who came to Mizpah to pay his respects to Gedaliah. Perhaps he died at Tell en-Nasbeh and was buried in the tomb where his seal was found.

There are, however, possible objections to the identification of Tell en-Nasbeh with Mizpah. It may be said that if Asa built these walls as a military measure against the north it is strange that the gate was placed to face the north. It is not certain that the stamp inscriptions should be read *m ṣ p*; if the letters are really *m ṣ h* no connection with Mizpah is apparent. At all events one example of the same inscription was also known from Jericho, and three more have now been discovered at Gibeon.[80] It has also been proposed to identify Tell en-Nasbeh with some ancient place other than Mizpah, possibly Ataroth-addar or Beeroth. The Arabic place name, Khirbet 'Attarah, doubtless derived from Ataroth, is attached to a site not far south of Tell en-Nasbeh. The ruins at this site are not older than the Roman period, and it could be supposed that after Tell en-Nasbeh was abandoned its name was transferred to this new town which arose not far away. Also it has been suggested that Mizpah itself could have been at Nebi Samwil, a site about four miles southwest of Tell en-Nasbeh with a commanding view appropriate to a place called Mizpah or "watchtower." Named for the "prophet Samuel," Nebi Samwil is held in Arab tradition as the burial place of Samuel. Although excavation has not been possible, potsherds have been collected on the surface showing that a village of Israelite date did once exist here. In view of these facts, identification of Tell en-Nasbeh with Mizpah is not positive although it may be regarded as probable.

JERUSALEM

Jerusalem was captured by the Israelites under David and made the capital of the kingdom (II Samuel 5:6-10; I Chronicles 11:4-9). The city has a strategic location of exceptional strength. Its site is a rocky plateau with two promontories running south from it. Between these two rocky ridges is the valley el-Wad, which in Roman times was known as the Tyropeon. On the east is the valley of the

---

[80] Pritchard in UMB 21 (1957), p.21. N. Avigad (in IEJ 8 [1958], pp.113-119) reads the inscription as *moṣah* and thinks it refers to the Mozah of Joshua 18:26, from which town products might have come to Tell en-Nasbeh.

Kidron, and on the south and west the valley of Hinnom. Two springs provide water. One, an intermittent spring known as Gihon (now Ain Sitti Maryam or "Fountain of the Virgin"), is at the foot of the eastern hill in the Kidron Valley. The other, known as En-rogel (now Bir Aiyub or "Job's Well") is farther distant, at the point where the valleys of Kidron and Hinnom join, and beneath the hill where the modern village of Silwan (Siloah) stands.[81] An interesting discovery in connection with the Gihon spring was made by Charles Warren in the earliest explorations at Jerusalem by the Palestine Exploration Fund. He found that the early inhabitants of Jerusalem had made a rock-cut passage, similar to the ones we have mentioned at Gibeon and Gezer (pp. 161, 170), to enable them to secure water from the spring without going outside the city walls. From the cave in which the Gihon spring empties,[82] a horizontal tunnel was driven back into the hill, some thirty-six feet west and twenty-five feet north. This led the spring waters back into an old cave, which thus served as a reservoir. Running up from this was a vertical shaft perhaps forty feet high, at the top of which was a platform on which the women could stand to lower and lift their water vessels. From this a sloping passage ran on up to open within the city walls. This probably constituted the water system which was in use by the Jebusites who occupied Jerusalem through the period of the Judges (Judges 19:10f.) and in the time of David. The account of David's capture of the city includes the words (II Samuel 5:8), "Whoever would smite the Jebusites, let him get up the water shaft," which makes it seem likely that access to the city was first gained when Joab (I Chronicles 11:6) penetrated this tunnel.[83]

Thus "the stronghold of Zion," as the city of the Jebusites was called, became "the city of David" (II Samuel 5:7, 9), and the capital of the Israelite nation. It is quite certain that Zion was the lower eastern hill at Jerusalem and that David's city was situated on the portion of the hill known as Ophel or "hump" (II Chronicles

[81] Baedeker, *Palestine and Syria*, pp.83f.

[82] Actually its source is a great crack in the rock at the bottom of the valley, at the eastern end of which a wall was built by some of the earliest inhabitants of the place which compels the water to flow into the cave rather than emptying into the valley.

[83] Macalister, *A Century of Excavation in Palestine*, pp.173-178; and in CAH III, p.343. The meaning of the Hebrew word translated "water course" or "water shaft" in II Samuel 5:8 is debatable. Duncan (*Digging Up Biblical History*, I, p.15) thinks it refers to the funnel entrance from within the city to a large cave which also has an eastern exit in the hill above the Gihon spring. For another explanation of the matter see Hans J. Stoebe in ZDPV 73 (1957), pp.73-99.

27:3, etc.) above the Virgin's Spring.[84] Excavations at Zion have revealed a strong stone wall which was broken through violently, and it may be that this is the breach made by David in his assault on the city. Behind the breach a lighter wall was built which perhaps was put there by David as a temporary barricade, and may have been the work referred to in II Samuel 5:9. Above the breach a fortress tower was finally built, which filled the gap in the wall and used the fallen stones of the breach as a foundation. This may have been the "Millo" which was built by Solomon (I Kings 9:15, 24; 11:27).[85]

Solomon may also have included the western hill inside "the wall around Jerusalem" which he constructed (I Kings 3:1; cf. 9:15). In early excavations on the western hill, walls were found which may have been the work of Solomon. The most famous building of Solomon, of course, was the temple, which he began to construct in the fourth year of his reign (I Kings 6:1). According to II Chronicles 3:1 this was on Mount Moriah at a place where Ornan (or Araunah) the Jebusite had had a threshing floor. The threshing floor had been purchased earlier by David for the erection of an altar at the time of pestilence (II Samuel 24:15-25). Moriah is also named in Genesis 22:2 as the place where Abraham went to offer Isaac.

The site lies today within the sacred enclosure of the Muslims known as the Haram esh-Sherif, "the Noble Sanctuary." The most striking natural feature is a great outcropping of rock some fifty-eight feet long, fifty-one feet broad, and four to six and one-half feet high. This is known as es-Sakhra or the Sacred Rock, and today is covered by a structure called the Qubbet es-Sakhra ("Dome of the Rock"). The Dome of the Rock is shown in Fig. 63 and in Fig. 64 we look down from within the balcony of the Dome upon the sacred rock enclosed as it now is by a wooden screen. Evidently the rock was used as an altar in very ancient times, since channels can still be traced on it; they may have conducted the blood of the sacrificial

[84] George Adam Smith, *Jerusalem*. 1908, i, pp.134f.,161f.; ii, p.39. Josephus (*War.* v, iv, 1; *Ant.* vii, iii, 2) and later tradition erroneously located the city of David on the western hill and this error is preserved in modern names like that of "David's Tower" near the Jaffa Gate which probably actually stands on the base of Herod's Tower of Phasael.

[85] If Millo was built first by Solomon, its mention in II Samuel 5:9 must be regarded as meaning that David built from the point where later Millo stood. On the other hand, Solomon's work might have been that of rebuilding an earlier structure, known already in David's time as Millo.

animals to an opening and on down to a cavity below. The rock itself most likely served as Araunah's threshing floor, since presumably the strongest breeze for the threshing was found on it. Therefore David's altar probably was erected on the very rock.[86] On the other hand, it is possible to suppose that the relatively large and level area directly east of the rock provided a better surface for the work of threshing, and became the site of the altar. In the latter and somewhat less probable case it was the Holy of Holies which eventually arose over the sacred rock itself.[87]

The building of the temple required seven years, while thirteen years were spent by Solomon in the building of his own palace (I Kings 6:38; 7:1). Phoenician craftsmen and workers were supplied for these enterprises by Hiram of Tyre (I Kings 5:1-12) and doubtless the work was of a character unusually imposing in Palestine. The buildings are described in detail in the Old Testament[88] but, save for the great ancient rock, almost everything connected with them has been lost to us. Nevertheless it is possible to draw upon archeological knowledge of the architecture of the time at other places and, combining this with the biblical data, to make a reconstruction of Solomon's temple which has at least good grounds for a claim to authenticity.[89]

THE STABLES AT MEGIDDO

Solomon is also known to have rebuilt the city of Megiddo (I Kings 9:15). In view of the king's well-known interest in horses and chariots (I Kings 10:26-29; II Chronicles 1:14-17) it was a matter of great interest to discover extensive stables in the excavation of Megiddo.

[86] A. T. Olmstead, *Jesus in the Light of History.* 1942, p.85; G. Dalman, *Neue Petra-Forschungen und Der heilige Felsen von Jerusalem.* 1912, pp.133-145; Floyd V. Filson in BA 7 (1944), p.81.

[87] F. J. Hollis, *The Archaeology of Herod's Temple, with a Commentary on the Tractate "Middoth."* 1934, pp.84-86,99; Hans Schmidt, *Der Heilige Fels in Jerusalem.* 1933, pp.26,55. The supposition encounters the difficulty that the rock was larger (58 by 51 feet) than the Holy of Holies (20 cubits long and 20 cubits wide, according to I Kings 6:20), and at any rate could not have been enclosed within the room. cf. below p.326.

[88] I Kings 6:1-7:51; II Chronicles 3:1-5:1. Ezekiel's vision of the future temple (40:1-44:3) probably was based on his memories of the first temple before its destruction in 586 B.C. cf. Watzinger, *Denkmäler Palästinas.* I, pp.88-95. A description of Solomon's temple, in which the biblical account is amplified somewhat, is given by Josephus, *Ant.* VIII, iii.

[89] G. Ernest Wright in BA 4 (1941), pp.17-31; 7 (1944), pp.73-77; Paul L. Garber in BA 14 (1951), pp.1-24; and in *Archaeology.* 5 (1952), pp.165-172. For the entire history of the temple see now André Parrot, *The Temple of Jerusalem.* 1955. On Old Testament Jerusalem in general see J. Simons, *Jerusalem in the Old Testament.* 1952; L.-H. Vincent and M.-A. Steve, *Jérusalem de l'Ancien Testament.* 2 vols. 1954.

A photograph of them is shown in Fig. 65. It is evident that they were composed of units built on a standard plan. Stone pillars, with holes in their corners, separated the horses and served as hitching-posts. Stone mangers were provided, and the ground on which the horses stood was paved with rough stones to prevent hoofs from slipping.

The date of these stables has not been determined with certainty, and it is believed by some that they were the work of the warrior king Ahab (cf. p. 205) rather than of Solomon.[90] The most authoritative study of the chronology of Megiddo, however, places Stratum IV in which the stables were found, at least partly within the reign of Solomon, and it remains probable that these famous structures really belonged to that king.[91]

EZION-GEBER

In I Kings 9:26 (cf. 9:27f.; 10:11, 22) it is recorded that Solomon furthermore built a fleet of ships at Ezion-geber, beside Eloth, on the shore of the Red Sea. This seaport city of the king has been discovered and excavated at Tell Kheleifeh at the head of the Gulf of Aqabah (cf. p. 151).[92] The city was built on a carefully chosen and hitherto unoccupied site, according to plans which had been worked out in advance. The site selected was between the hills of Edom on the east and the hills of Palestine on the west, where the north winds blow most steadily and strongly down the center of the Wadi el-Arabah. This was because Ezion-geber was to be not only a seaport but also an important industrial city. An elaborate complex of industrial plants, devoted to the smelting and refining of copper and iron and the manufacturing of metal articles for markets at home and abroad, was uncovered there. The furnace rooms were set at an angle carefully calculated to get the full benefit of the winds from the north and to utilize these to furnish the draft for the fires. Ezion-geber was able to draw upon the important mineral deposits which are found in the Wadi el-Arabah all the way from the Gulf of Aqabah to the Dead Sea, and a series of mining centers of Solomon's time is known where these ores were dug and subjected to an initial smelting process. The mines of the Wadi el-Arabah were probably used first

[90] J. W. Crowfoot in PEQ 1940, pp. 143-147.
[91] W. F. Albright in AJA 44 (1940), pp.546-550; and in AASOR 21-22 (1941-43), p.2 n.1; Robert M. Engberg in BA 4 (1941), pp.12f.; G. E. Wright in BA 13 (1950), p.44.
[92] Glueck, *The Other Side of the Jordan*, pp.50-113; and in NGM 85 (Jan.-June 1944), pp.233-256.

by the Kenites, whose name means "smiths,"[93] and the related Kenizzites, from whom in turn the Edomites learned mining and metallurgy. When David subjugated the Edomites (II Samuel 8:13f.; I Kings 11:15f.; I Chronicles 18:11f.) he may well have continued to exploit these mines, but it was Solomon who had the ability and power to put the mining industry in the Wadi el-Arabah on a truly national scale. Ezion-geber still belonged to the domain of Judah in the days of King Jotham, and a signet seal ring inscribed with the name of the latter was found there in the stratum belonging to the eighth century B.C.[94] In connection with the statement in I Kings 9:28 that Solomon's fleet went to Ophir and brought gold from there, much interest attaches to a potsherd of the eighth century B.C. recently discovered at Tell Qasile near Jaffa on which is the inscription: "Gold of Ophir for Beth-horon: 30 shekels."[95] Ophir, it is now suggested, may have been (S)uppara, near Bombay, India, since in some Indian dialects the initial "S" disappears.[96]

THE GEZER CALENDAR

In Canaan itself agriculture, of course, always remained far more important than industry. A side light on Palestinian agriculture comes from the Gezer calendar. This is a small limestone tablet, about four inches long and three inches wide, which was found at Gezer and comes probably from a time around 925 B.C. It seems to be simply a schoolboy's exercise, but it contains a list of the various months and the agricultural work done in them. Written in good biblical Hebrew, it reads:

> His two months are (olive) harvest,
> His two months are planting (grain),
> His two months are late planting;
> His month is hoeing up of flax,
> His month is harvest of barley,
> His month is harvest and feasting;
> His two months are vine-tending,
> His month is summer fruit.[97]

[93] A. H. Sayce in HDB II, p.834.   [94] AJA 45 (1941), p.117.
[95] B. Maisler in IEJ 1 (1950-51), pp.209f.
[96] R. D. Barnett in *The Manchester Guardian Weekly*. Vol. 71, No.19, Nov. 4, 1954, p.15; and in *Archaeology*. 9 (1956), p.92. The Greeks credited Hippalus in the first century B.C. with the discovery of the seasonal monsoons and the opening of a direct sea route to India, but even if it was unknown to the Greeks there must have been commerce by others on the Indian Ocean and even utilization of the monsoon winds long before that. See Gus W. Van Beek in JAOS 78 (1958), p.147.
[55] W. F. Albright in BASOR 125 (Feb. 1952), pp.24-32.
pp.16-20; Sabatino Moscati, *L'epigrafia ebraica antica 1935-1950*. 1951, pp.8-26.

In view of the oppression which the peasantry endured at the hands of Solomon and which contributed to the division of the kingdom after his death, some interest attaches to an inscription on an Aramean stela of King Kilamuwa which reads: "Before the former kings the Muskabim [peasant farmers] crawled like dogs, but I [Kilamuwa] was a father to one, a mother to another."[98]

Unfortunately Rehoboam was not as wise as this Kilamuwa and, about 931/930 B.C.,[99] the great kingdom of Solomon broke into two parts (I Kings 12:1-20). Jeroboam, a political exile in Egypt in Solomon's time (I Kings 12:2), returned to lead the revolt of the northern tribes. Egypt itself, which had entered into an alliance with Solomon (I Kings 3:1), now took advantage of the divided and weakened kingdom, and invaded Palestine. Shishak (Sheshonk I), founder of the Twenty-second Dynasty, plundered Jerusalem in the fifth year of King Rehoboam (I Kings 14:25f.) and also conquered other cities both in Judah and Israel, a record of which exploits was duly inscribed at Karnak (p. 126). Among the cities mentioned in the Karnak inscription was Megiddo, and in the excavation of Megiddo a fragment of a stela of Shishak was found.[100]

SHECHEM

Jeroboam I made his residence first at Shechem (I Kings 12:25), which is probably the same as Tell Balatah east of modern Nablus. German expeditions under E. Sellin, G. Welter, and H. Steckeweh worked here between 1913 and 1934, but did not obtain clear results chronologically. Excavations were begun here in 1956 and 1957 by Drew University, McCormick Theological Seminary, and the American Schools of Oriental Research, under the direction of G. Ernest Wright.[101] The site was evidently settled as early as the Chalcolithic period and again in the Bronze Age. The city probably reached its height in the Middle Bronze Age and the time of the Hyksos, and there is evidence of its destruction about the middle of the sixteenth century B.C., perhaps when the Egyptians took the place from the Hyksos. After that it was again an important site in the Late Bronze

[98] Duncan, *Digging Up Biblical History*. II, p.132.

[99] For the date of the division of the kingdom see above p.117 n.72, and for the dates of the kings of Israel and Judah see TMN p.283.

[100] R. S. Lamon and G. M. Shipton, *Megiddo I, Seasons of 1925-34, Strata I-V*. 1939, p.61.

[101] Eduard Nielsen, *Shechem, A Traditio-Historical Investigation*. 1955; G. Ernest Wright in BASOR 144 (Dec. 1956), pp.9-20; Walter Harrelson, Bernhard W. Anderson, and G. Ernest Wright in BA 20 (1957), pp.1-32; G. Ernest Wright in BASOR 148 (Dec. 1957), pp.11-28; H. C. Kee and L. E. Toombs in BA 20 (1957), pp.82-105.

Age and in the Iron Age down to the eighth century. As far as presently known evidence goes, the place was then uninhabited for several centuries but was again a large city in the Hellenistic period from the end of the fourth to the end of the second century B.C. Features of the city were the powerful wall of the Middle Bronze Age, with its large East Gate, and an extensive temple of the Late Bronze Age which may have been the "house of Baal-berith" of Judges 9:4.

TIRZAH

After Shechem Jeroboam I resided at Tirzah, as we learn almost incidentally from I Kings 14:17, and this place remained the capital of northern Israel until the time of Omri. In the Song of Solomon 6:4 Tirzah ranks with Jerusalem as a standard of beauty, a reference which would seem to belong to a time when Tirzah was a flourishing place. When Omri, formerly commander of the army, was made king of Israel he besieged and took Tirzah and reigned there for six years until he transferred the capital to Samaria (I Kings 16:17, 23). Tirzah has been tentatively identified with Tell el-Far'ah, a large mound some seven miles northeast of Nablus, and excavations have been made here since 1946 by the Dominican Biblical School at Jerusalem under the direction of R. de Vaux.[102]

Tell el-Far'ah was occupied in the Chalcolithic, Bronze, and Iron Ages. In the Iron Age the excavators distinguish four periods which correspond very well with the biblical history of Tirzah. Period 1, that of Level III in the tell, is marked by well-built houses and abundant pottery. This period probably extended from the end of the eleventh to the beginning of the ninth century B.C., and the end of the period could very well coincide with the taking of Tirzah by Omri at the beginning of his reign in 885/884 B.C.[103] Periods 2 and 3 belong to an intermediate level in the tell. In Period 2 building work of considerable magnitude was begun but left unfinished. This could be work Omri started at Tirzah before moving to Samaria. Period 3 has only poor and limited remains, which could reflect a virtual transfer of the population to Samaria when Omri made the move thither. Period 4, that of Level II in the tell, has excellent buildings again, and could correspond to the time of Israel's prosperity in the eighth century under Jehoash and Jeroboam II. Finally Level

---

[102] R. de Vaux and A.-M. Steve in RB 54 (1947), pp.394-433,573-589; 55 (1948), pp.544-580; 56 (1949), pp.102-138; R. de Vaux in RB 58 (1951), pp.393-430,566-590; 59 (1952), pp.551-583; 62 (1955), pp.541-589; 64 (1957), pp.552-580.
[103] TMN p.60.

II comes to an end at a time which is probably that of the Assyrian invasion of 725/724-723/722,[104] and in Level I above this it is Assyrian pottery which is prominent.[105]

SAMARIA

It was evidently in his sixth year (880/879 B.C.) that Omri moved the capital of northern Israel from Tirzah to Samaria (I Kings 16:24). The hill of Samaria, probably meaning "Watch-Mountain," rises three or four hundred feet above the valley and provided a strong strategic site for the fortified city which Omri built. Excavations were carried out at Samaria in 1908-1910 by Harvard University under the leadership of G. A. Reisner, C. S. Fisher, and D. G. Lyon,[106] and this work was continued in 1931-1933 under the direction of J. W. Crowfoot in a joint expedition in which Harvard University, the Hebrew University in Jerusalem, the Palestine Exploration Fund, the British Academy, and the British School of Archaeology in Jerusalem participated. In 1935 further work was done by the three last-named institutions.[107]

The stratigraphy of Israelite times was clarified by the last excavations, and the following sequence of levels and dates is now recognized:[108] Levels I and II, 880-850 B.C., the time of the Omri-Ahab Dynasty; Level III, 850-800 B.C., including the time of Jehu who made a great slaughter there (II Kings 10:17); Levels IV-VI, 800-722 B.C., the period of the city's greatest prosperity; and Level VII, after the Assyrian conquest in 722 B.C. The correlation between this sequence and that which was arrived at for Tell el-Far'ah is extremely interesting. At Tell el-Far'ah Period 1 and Level III came to an end prior to the first Israelite occupation of Samaria, and Period 2 with its incompleted buildings probably immediately preceded Level I at Samaria. Levels I, II, and III at Samaria correspond to Period 3 or

[104] TMN p.128.

[105] de Vaux in RB 62 (1955), pp.587f.; and in PEQ 1956, pp.125-140; cf. W. F. Albright in JPOS 11 (1931), pp.241-251; and see also *Asiatische Studien.* 1/2 (1947), p.78; BA 12 (1949), pp.66-68.

[106] Reisner, Fisher, and Lyon, *Harvard Excavations at Samaria 1908-1910.* 2 vols. 1924.

[107] J. W. Crowfoot, Kathleen M. Kenyon, and E. L. Sukenik, *The Buildings at Samaria.* 1942; *Samaria-Sebaste, Reports of the Work of the Joint Expedition in 1931-1933 and of the British Expedition in 1935;* cf. W. F. Albright in BASOR 150 (Apr. 1958), pp.21-25.

[108] Kathleen M. Kenyon as cited by de Vaux in RB 62 (1955), p. 587. Note that these strata are numbered from the lower toward the upper, while at Tell el-Far'ah the numbering of levels was from the upper toward the lower.

the rest of the intermediate period at Tell el-Far'ah. Levels iv-vi at Samaria agree in their signs of prosperity with Period 4, Level ii, at Tell el-Far'ah, while at the end of this period both cities share a common ruin, doubtless that of the Assyrian invasion. Thus the findings at the two sites agree well with the biblical history of Tirzah and Samaria.

In their work at Samaria Omri and Ahab evidently leveled the top of the hill, banked its sides, and built inner and outer walls with geometrical precision around the summit. Later walls were built on the middle terraces and also on the lower slopes of the hill, thus rendering the city exceedingly well fortified. These walls constitute a graphic commentary on the two sieges which Samaria underwent, the first when the city held out against the Syrians to the terrible lengths described in II Kings 6:24-30, and the second when Samaria withstood the mighty Assyrians for so long before succumbing (II Kings 17:5). The city has also been found to have been provided with a number of large cisterns which were very important in time of siege since there was no natural water supply.

The Israelite kings built their palaces within the walls on the western brow of the hill. The first palace was relatively simple but served as a core for later and more splendid structures. The palace which first was ascribed to Ahab, but perhaps belonged to Jeroboam II instead, was built from large blocks of limestone, and boasted a strong rectangular tower and an extensive outer court. At the north end of the palace courtyard was a cemented water pool, which may even have been the "pool of Samaria" in which the bloodstained chariot of Ahab was washed (I Kings 22:38).

It is probably from the time of the reign of Jeroboam II in the first part of the eighth century that the famous Samaritan ostraca come.[109] These are potsherds with writing on them, which were found in a storehouse in one of the palaces. They contain notes or accounts of oil and wine received as royal revenue for the king. A typical one reads:

> In the tenth year.
> To Gaddiyau.
> From Azah.
> Abi-ba'al 2
> Ahaz   2
> Sheba   1
> Meriba'al 1

[109] J. W. Jack, *Samaria in Ahab's Time.* 1929, pp.37-105; McCown, *The Ladder of Progress in Palestine*, p.199; W. F. Albright in ANET p.321 (ANEA p.211).

In this case Gaddiyau was the steward of the treasury to whom the wine was sent, Azah the name of the village or district, and the other names those of the peasant farmers who paid their taxes in the form of so many jars of wine. The stewards frequently have names which are used also in the Bible, such as Ahinoam, Gamar (Gomer), and Nimshi. Too, the senders of contributions often have biblical names, as do Ahaz, Sheba, and Meribaal in the ostracon quoted above. The name Meribaal and many other names compounded with Baal testify to the prevalence of Baal-worship. It will be remembered that Meribbaal is the name borne by Jonathan's son, for which Mephibosheth (*bosheth* meaning "shame") later was substituted when it came to be felt wrong to use the title Baal (lord) in connection with the God of Israel.[110] On the other hand many of the names have *Yahu* as an element, thus suggesting that the divine name Yahweh was often used in personal names at this time. The ostraca also mention over twenty place-names in the northern kingdom, six of which—Abiezer, Helek, Shechem, Shemida, Noah, and Hoglah—appear as names of clans in the Old Testament (Joshua 17:2; Numbers 26:30-33). Two more of the ostraca may be quoted since they provide a commentary on Amos 6:6:

> In the tenth year.
> From Abiezer to Shemariyo.
> A jar of old wine.
> To Ish-Ba'al [?].
> A jar of old wine.
> From Tetel.
>
> In the tenth year. From Azzah.
> To Gaddiyo. A jar of fine
> oil.

The old wine or "pure clarified wine," and the fine oil used probably for anointing the body, which are specified here, are exactly the things whose use by the luxurious and selfish rich people of Samaria is mentioned and condemned by the prophet.[111]

In view of the similar denunciation by Amos (6:4, 3:15) of the "beds of ivory" and "houses of ivory" of the rich people of Samaria and the mention in I Kings 22:39 of the "ivory house" which Ahab (874/873-853 B.C.) built, it is of much interest that numerous ivories were found in the excavation of Samaria. These are mostly in the

---

[110] I Chronicles 8:34; 9:40; II Samuel 4:4; 9:6, 10, etc.; cf. HDB II, pp.501f.
[111] René Dussaud in *Syria*. 7 (1926), pp.9-29.

form of plaques or small panels in relief and presumably were once attached to furniture and inlaid in wall paneling. The subjects depicted in the ivories include lotus, lilies, papyrus, palmettes, lions, bulls, deer, winged figures in human form, sphinxes, and figures of Egyptian gods such as Isis and Horus. A richly decorated ivory medallion in relief showing the infant Horus sitting upon a lotus, holding a flail in the right hand and raising the forefinger of the left hand to his lips in typical gesture, is shown in Fig. 66. This and other subjects as well as the technique of execution of the ivories indicate that Egyptian influence was strong in Palestine at this time.[112]

THE MOABITE STONE

In the days of Ahab the kingdom of Moab was tributary to Israel and sent annual payments of "a hundred thousand lambs, and the wool of a hundred thousand rams," but "when Ahab died . . . the king of Moab rebelled against the king of Israel" (II Kings 3:4f.). Ahab's immediate successor Ahaziah reigned but briefly and it was Jehoram who went out to do battle with Mesha king of Moab. In the midst of the battle Mesha offered his oldest son as a burnt offering upon the wall and "there came great wrath upon Israel" (II Kings 3:27).

A contemporary record of the relations between Israel and Moab exists in the famous Moabite Stone (Fig. 67). It was erected, with a long inscription by King Mesha at the Moabite capital of Dibon (the present Dhiban), north of the Arnon. Reports of its existence came to the French scholar Clermont-Ganneau in Jerusalem, and a Prussian traveler, the Reverend F. A. Klein, saw it for the first time in 1868. A squeeze[113] was taken of it, but before the stone itself could be obtained it was broken into pieces by the Arabs. Finally two large fragments and eighteen small pieces were recovered and a restoration and reconstruction was made and the monument placed in the Louvre.[114] In the inscription Mesha says in part:

"I am Mesha, son of Chemosh. . . , king of Moab, the Dibonite—my father had reigned over Moab thirty years, and I reigned after my father,—who made this high place for Chemosh in Qarhoh . . . because he saved me from all the kings and caused me to triumph over all my adversaries. As for Omri, king of Israel, he humbled Moab many years, for

[112] J. W. and Grace M. Crowfoot, *Early Ivories from Samaria.* 1938.
[113] A squeeze is a facsimile impression made by forcing a plastic substance into the depressions.
[114] C. S. Clermont-Ganneau, *La Stèle de Mésa.* 1887.

Chemosh was angry at his land. And his son followed him and he also said, 'I will humble Moab.' In my time he spoke thus, but I have triumphed over him and over his house, while Israel hath perished for ever! Now Omri had occupied the land of Medeba, and Israel had dwelt there in his time and half the time of his son, forty years; but Chemosh dwelt there in my time."[115]

Obviously there are differences between this and II Kings 3:4-27 and it is not certain whether the two accounts relate to the same or different campaigns. According to the Bible the total reigns of Omri and his son Ahab amounted to only thirty-four years,[116] but Mesha's "forty years" could be a round number. Also he claims that "Israel perished for ever" in the days of Ahab, while it was under Jehoram that Israel suffered the defeat which is probably referred to in the cryptic statement of II Kings 3:27. In general it is evident that on each side the writers selected that part of the history of the two lands to record which was most pleasing to them. Also it is noteworthy that Israel ascribed its victory to the Lord (II Kings 3:18) while Mesha thanked his god Chemosh for his. In the entire inscription the following places are mentioned which are also named in the Bible: the Arnon (Numbers 21:13, etc.; Deuteronomy 2:24; 3:16, etc.), Aroer (Joshua 13:16), Ataroth (Numbers 32:34), Baal-meon or Beth-baal-meon (Joshua 13:17; Numbers 32:38), Beth-bamoth (Bamoth-baal, Joshua 13:17), Beth-diblathaim (Jeremiah 48:22), Bezer (Joshua 20:8), Dibon (Numbers 32:34; Joshua 13:17; Isaiah 15:2), Horonaim (Isaiah 15:5), Jahaz (Joshua 13:18; Isaiah 15:4), Kerioth (Jeremiah 48:24), Kiriathaim (Joshua 13:19; Jeremiah 48:23), Medeba (Madeba, Joshua 13:9, 16; Isaiah 15:2), and Nebo (Numbers 32:38; Deuteronomy 34:1; Isaiah 15:2).

DIBON

Excavations have been conducted at Dhiban since 1950-1951 by the American School of Oriental Research in Jerusalem. The remains of four or five city walls have been brought to light, together with a square tower, and a number of buildings. Pottery ranges from Early Bronze to Early Arabic, but there is almost none of Middle and Late Bronze Age date, thus confirming to that extent the conclusion that Transjordan largely reverted to nomadism during those periods. In the Moabite Stone Mesha states that he said to all the

[115] W. F. Albright in ANET pp.320f. (ANEA p.209f.); G. A. Cooke, *A Text-Book of North-Semitic Inscriptions.* 1903, pp.1-14.
[116] I Kings 16:23—Omri, 12 years; 16:29—Ahab, 22 years.

people of Qarhoh (which may have been the name of Dibon for a time), "Let each of you make a cistern for himself in his house!" and it is therefore of interest that at Dhiban nearly one hundred cisterns have already been catalogued. A small fragment of another inscribed stela has also been found there, probably, like the Moabite Stone, dating from the ninth century B.C.[117]

THE SILOAM TUNNEL

In 722 B.C. Samaria fell to Assyria. In 701 B.C. Sennacherib of Assyria invaded Palestine and besieged Jerusalem itself. Hezekiah was king of Judah at this time, and he seems to have taken a far-sighted measure to strengthen the city against siege. II Kings 20:20 states that "he made the pool, and the conduit and brought water into the city." The same achievement is narrated in II Chronicles 32:30: "This same Hezekiah closed the upper outlet of the waters of Gihon and directed them down to the west side of the city of David." Thus the attackers were deprived of water at the same time that the besieged city was assured of an unfailing supply. "Why should the kings of Assyria come and find much water?" they asked as they stopped the waters that were outside the city (II Chronicles 32:2-4).

It will be remembered (p. 178) that Jerusalem's main source of fresh water was the Gihon spring, outside the city wall on the edge of the Kidron Valley, and that the Jebusites had somewhat difficult access to these waters through a vertical shaft and connecting tunnel. The entire system of tunnels related to the Gihon spring was cleared by Captain Parker in 1909-1911 and studied, measured, and photographed by Father Vincent at that time.[118] The Jebusite water system was found to have been walled off near the cave at the foot of the vertical shaft, and from this point a new rock tunnel was cut west and southwest for around 1,777 feet to empty into the Pool of Siloam (Ain Silwan). The ancient wall of Jerusalem used to cross the Tyropeon Valley just below this point, so at that time this pool was within the walls and safe from attackers in time of siege. It is natural to conclude that the cutting of this tunnel was the work of Hezekiah as referred to in II Kings 20:20 and II Chronicles 32:30.

Another tunnel also remains which runs south from the spring of Gihon near the outside edge of the rock and probably emptied into

---

[117] F. V. Winnett in BASOR 125 (Feb. 1952), pp.7-20; Roland E. Murphy in BASOR 125 (Feb. 1952), pp.20-23; A. Douglas Tushingham in BASOR 133 (Feb. 1954), pp.6-26.
[118] H. Vincent, *Jerusalem sous terre*. 1911.

the old Pool of Siloam or a similar reservoir within the city. It may be that this tunnel was cut by one of the earlier kings, perhaps David or Solomon, and afterward repaired by Hezekiah. This would provide a possible explanation of the difficult passage in which Isaiah (22:11) reproaches Hezekiah: "You made a reservoir between the two walls for the water of the old pool. But you did not look to him who did it, or have regard for him who planned it long ago." This would mean that Hezekiah took the entire credit for the conduit to himself, and also failed to follow David's example in faithfulness to God. Even if this is the correct explanation of its character, this tunnel must have proved insufficient, for ultimately it was supplanted by the more efficient tunnel cut right back through the heart of the rock and identified with Hezekiah's work as described in II Kings and II Chronicles.[119]

The great tunnel of Hezekiah was excavated in the solid rock with wedge, hammer, and pick, and the marks of the expertly wielded pickaxes are still to be seen on the walls. The excavators worked from both ends, and after many windings and turnings met in the middle. The average height of the tunnel is about six feet, but later cutting has made it much higher at the Siloam end. A photograph of the tunnel at the point where the workers met is shown in Fig. 68. On the right wall of the tunnel, about nineteen feet in from the Siloam entrance, an inscription was discovered in 1880 by a boy who had been wading in the pool. This inscription (Fig. 69) was later cut out and placed in the Museum of the Ancient Orient at Istanbul. It is translated as follows:

". . . when the tunnel was driven through. And this was the way in which it was cut through:—While . . . were still . . . axes, each man toward his fellow, and while there were still three cubits to be cut through, there was heard the voice of a man calling to his fellow, for there was an overlap in the rock on the right and on the left. And when the tunnel was driven through, the quarrymen hewed the rock, each man toward his fellow, axe against axe; and the water flowed from the spring toward the reservoir for 1,200 cubits, and the height of the rock above the heads of the quarrymen was 100 cubits."[120]

Such was the conclusion of a truly notable engineering feat.

[119] Duncan, *Digging Up Biblical History.* II, pp.126f., 201-215.

[120] W. F. Albright in ANET p.321 (ANEA p.212); A. H. Sayce, *Records of the Past.* New Series, I, pp.168-175; Gesenius-Kautzsch, *Hebrew Grammar.* ed. Collins and Cowley, 1898, p. xix; Cooke, *A Text-Book of North-Semitic Inscriptions,* pp.15-17; David Diringer, *Le iscrizioni antico-ebraiche palestinesi.* 1934, pp.81-102; Hans J. Stoebe in ZDPV 71 (1955), pp.124-140. The Hebrew cubit was probably about seventeen and one-half inches, and for simplicity may be taken as one and a half feet.

THE LACHISH LETTERS

Although Jerusalem was wonderfully delivered from Sennacherib as Isaiah promised (Isaiah 36-37; II Kings 19:20, 32-36; II Chronicles 32:20-22), its downfall came at last. In succession to the Assyrians, the Neo-Babylonian Empire dominated western Asia. When King Jehoiakim of Judah ventured to rebel, he and his son Jehoiachin who succeeded him were punished speedily by the invasion of Judah and the taking of Jerusalem in 597 B.C. (II Kings 24:1-17). Zedekiah was installed at Jerusalem as puppet king and when he, too, broke faith with his Babylonian master the city's final doom was sealed, Nebuchadnezzar II advanced for the last time upon Judah, and after an eighteen-month siege Jerusalem fell (586 B.C.), its walls were broken down, its houses and great temple burned with fire, and its people, save for the very poorest of the land, carried into exile (II Kings 25:1-12).

Jeremiah the prophet lived through these terrible events and in the introduction to one of the prophecies which he addressed to Zedekiah there is a striking reference to the time "when the army of the king of Babylon was fighting against Jerusalem and against all the cities of Judah that were left, Lachish and Azekah; for these were the only fortified cities of Judah that remained" (Jeremiah 34:7). Both of these cities have been excavated. Azekah is identified with Tell Zakariya in the Shephelah. It was excavated in 1898 by Dr. Frederick J. Bliss of the Palestine Exploration Fund and revealed a strong inner citadel fortified with eight large towers. This may have been built by Rehoboam, who is reported to have fortified this city, as well as Lachish (II Chronicles 11:9).[121]

The identification of Lachish with Tell ed-Duweir and the excavations at this site have already been mentioned (pp. 161f.) with particular reference to the city of the Late Bronze Age and its destruction presumably by the incoming Israelites. This devastation marked the end of Level VI as the strata are counted downward from the top by the excavators. In the succeeding Iron Age[122] Lachish was fortified with a great brick wall twenty feet thick around the summit of the mound and a revetment of stone and brick about fifty feet below on the slope of the mound. The initial building of these defenses may reasonably be attributed to Rehoboam after the division of the kingdom (II Chronicles 11:9). In his time Sennacherib

[121] Macalister, *A Century of Excavation in Palestine*, pp.55f.
[122] Olga Tufnell, *Lachish III (Tell ed-Duweir), The Iron Age.* 2 vols. 1953.

(704-681 B.C.) captured Lachish and took booty from it, as is mentioned in an inscription and pictured in a relief of the Assyrian king (p. 214). A large pit tomb at Tell ed-Duweir with the jumbled remains of 1,500 human bodies may represent the clearance of the city after this conquest, since the pottery which is mingled with the bones is probably of the eighth or early seventh century B.C.[123] Levels V, IV, and III are not yet clearly distinguishable for lack of sufficiently extensive excavation, but it is plain that Level III came to an end with the burning of the city and the overthrow of its walls. Amidst the debris of this destruction the city of Level II arose. The wall was repaired hastily with whatever material was available, the palace was not yet rebuilt. Then Level II also experienced a violent end. So intense was the fire in which the city perished that masonry was melted into a liquid stream of white and red which flowed down over the lower wall where charred heaps of burned timber still remain. While some think that a greater time must have intervened between the end of Level III and of Level II, it seems very probable that the two destructions mark the coming of Nebuchadnezzar in 597 and again in 588 B.C.[124]

Of great interest was a discovery made by J. L. Starkey in 1935. In a small room, believed to be the guard room, adjoining the outer gate of the city of Lachish and lying buried in the burned layer of charcoal and ashes which represented the last destruction of the city mentioned just above, were eighteen ostraca with Hebrew writing in the ancient Phoenician script.[125] Almost all of them were dispatches or letters which had been written by a certain Hoshaiah, who was at some military outpost, to a man named Yaosh, who must have been a high commanding officer at Lachish. At the time of writing the final siege of Jerusalem and Lachish was probably beginning, and Azekah may even have fallen already, since one of the letters (No. IV) says, "We are watching for the fire-signals of Lachish according to all the signs which my lord arranged, for we no longer can see the signals of Azekah."[126] Lachish itself appears to have

---

[123] G. Ernest Wright in BA 18 (1955), p.13 n.1.

[124] W. F. Albright in BASOR 132 (Dec. 1953), p.46; Briggs W. Buchanan in AJA 58 (1954), pp.335f.; G. Ernest Wright in BA 18 (1955), pp.14f.; Herbert G. May in JBL 75 (1956), p.343.

[125] Harry Torczyner, *Lachish I (Tell ed Duweir), The Lachish Letters*. 1938; W. F. Albright in BASOR 70 (Apr. 1938), pp. 11-17; and in ANET pp.321f. Three additional ostraca, bringing the total number up to twenty-one, were found in the last campaign at Lachish in 1938 (BASOR 80 [Dec. 1940], pp. 11-13; 82 [Apr. 1941], p.24).

[126] Frank M. Cross, Jr., in BASOR 144 (Dec. 1956), p. 25; cf. W. F. Albright in ANET p.322.

held out at least until after the autumn olive harvest since many carbonized olive stones were found in the embers of the burned city.

One of the letters (No. III) reads as follows:

"Thy servant Hoshaiah hath sent to inform my lord Yaosh: May Yahweh cause my lord to hear tidings of peace! And now thou hast sent a letter, but my lord did not enlighten thy servant concerning the letter which thou didst send to thy servant yesterday evening, though the heart of thy servant hath been sick since thou didst write to thy servant. And as for what my lord said, 'Dost thou not understand?—call a scribe!', as Yahweh liveth no one hath ever undertaken to call a scribe for me; and as for any scribe who might have come to me, truly I did not call him nor would I give anything at all for him!

"And it hath been reported to thy servant, saying, 'The commander of the host, Coniah son of Elnathan, hath come down in order to go into Egypt; and unto Hodaviah son of Ahijah and his men hath he sent to obtain . . . from him.'

"And as for the letter of Tobiah, servant of the king, which came to Shallum son of Jaddua through the prophet, saying, 'Beware!', thy servant hath sent it to my lord."[127]

Hoshaiah is a biblical name and appears in Jeremiah 42:1 and Nehemiah 12:32. God is referred to by the four letters *Yhwh*, which are the consonants of the name Yahweh and in this and other of the letters many of the men's names have Yahweh endings. The prophet who is mentioned in this letter has been believed by some to be Jeremiah himself,[128] but this is not necessarily or even probably true.[129]

Another of the Lachish letters (No. VI) is illustrated in Fig. 70 and translated as follows:

"To my lord Yaosh: May Yahweh cause my lord to see this season in good health! Who is thy servant but a dog that my lord hath sent the letter of the king and the letters of the princes, saying, 'Pray, read them!' And behold the words of the princes are not good, but to weaken our hands and to slacken the hands of the men who are informed about them. . . . And now my lord, wilt thou not write to them saying, 'Why do ye thus even in Jerusalem? Behold unto the king and unto his house are ye doing this thing!' And, as Yahweh thy God liveth, truly since thy servant read the letters there hath been no peace for thy servant. . . ."[130]

The mention in this letter of words which are weakening the hands of the people, reminds us again of Jeremiah against whom it

[127] W. F. Albright in ANET p.322; cf. in BASOR 82 (Apr. 1941), pp.20f.
[128] J. W. Jack in PEQ 1938, pp.165-187.
[129] Gordon, *The Living Past*, p.189.
[130] W. F. Albright in ANET p.322; and in BASOR 82 (Apr. 1941), pp.22f.

was charged: "he is weakening the hands of the soldiers who are left in this city, and the hands of all the people, by speaking such words to them" (Jeremiah 38:4). In the letter, however, the discouraging words appear to have come from princes rather than from a prophet, and so Jeremiah is probably not referred to here either. Nevertheless, despite the enigmatical language of the letters we can discern conditions very comparable to those which are known from the biblical records to have prevailed at this time.

It was also of interest to find at Lachish a clay seal, the back of which still showed the mark of the fibers of the papyrus document to which it had been affixed, and on which was the inscription, "The property of Gedaliah who is over the house." This is the same name as that of the man who was made governor of Judah by Nebuchadnezzar after 586 B.C. (II Kings 25:22; Jeremiah 40:5f.; 41:2) and his title "who is over the house" is elsewhere known in the Old Testament (Isaiah 22:15; 36:3).[131]

The ravages of the conquest of Palestine by Nebuchadnezzar were very terrible. The land was devastated and laid waste, and the best of the population was carried off into captivity. From this awful time Judah did not recover for two or three hundred years. The exiles were allowed to return to their homeland at last but the population remained small and poor, while the temple which Zerubbabel rebuilt was as nothing in the eyes of those who had seen it in its former glory (Haggai 2:3). This pitiful state of affairs is reflected only too clearly in the archeological realm by the paucity of important materials. We know that the small Jewish state stamped official jar handles and also silver coins with the legend Yehud, that is "Judah,"[132] but it is not until in the Hellenistic period (c.300-63 B.C.) that solidly constructed buildings and abundant pottery again appear. Even then the archeological monuments thus far discovered in Palestine are relatively scant.[133]

[131] PEFQS 1935, pp.195f.
[132] E. L. Sukenik in JPOS 14 (1934), pp.178-184.
[133] For daily life in Old Testament Palestine see E. W. Heaton, *Everyday Life in Old Testament Times.* 1956.

IV

Empires of Western Asia: Assyria, Chaldea and Persia

I N ITS later Old Testament days the fate of the Israelite people was connected closely, as we have just seen, with the great powers to the north and east.

1. THE KASSITES, c.1650-c.1175 B.C.

THE beginnings of civilization in the valley of the Tigris and Euphrates have already been traced and Mesopotamia has been described as it was in the time of Abraham and of Hammurabi (Chapter I). In the days that followed, the entire northern boundary of the Fertile Crescent felt the pressure of advancing Indo-European hordes[1] and the kings who came after Hammurabi on the throne of Babylon had to struggle against Kassites from the eastern mountains and Hittites from the west. Samsuiluna, Hammurabi's immediate successor, repelled a wholesale invasion of Kassites but the latter continued to make a peaceful penetration of the country, and for almost 150 years Kassite names appear in Babylonian business documents as laborers, harvesters, and hostlers. Finally the Kassites attained power and established a dynasty which ruled in Babylon for half a millennium. On the whole the Kassite period is obscure historically but it is thought that the main outlines of the social order as established by Hammurabi continued to exist. It is known that the horse, which was a divine symbol to the Kassites, became common in Babylonia only after their entry.[2]

[1] Albrecht Götze, *Hethiter, Churriter und Assyrer.* 1936, p.27.
[2] George G. Cameron, *History of Early Iran.* 1936, pp.89-95.

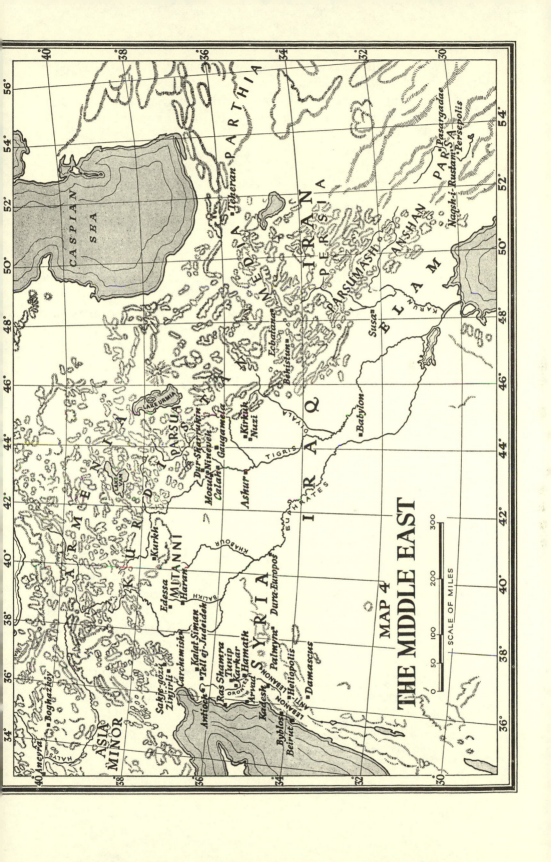

CASPIAN SEA

PARTHIA

ARMENIA

ASIA MINOR

HALYS

Ancyra
Boghazköi

Saktje-gözi
Zinjirli
Carchemish

LAKE VAN

Kurkh

KURDISTAN

PARSUA

LAKE URMIA

Der-Sharrukin
Mosul
Nineveh
Calah
Gaugamela

Kirkuk
Nuzi

Ashur

TIGRIS

DIYALA

MEDIA

Ecbatana

Teheran

Behistun

IRAN

PERSIA

PARSUMASH

ANSHAN

KARUN

Susa

ELAM

PARS

Pasargadae
Naqsh-i-Rustam
Persepolis

Babylon

IRAQ

EUPHRATES

MITANNI

Edessa
Harran

BALIKH

KHABOUR

Kalat Siman
Tell el-Judeideh

Antioch
Ras Shamra
Turuip
Karkar
ORONTES
Hamath
Arvad
Kadesh
LEBANON
Palmyra
Dura-Europos

Byblos
Beirut
ANTI-LEBANON
Heliopolis
Damascus

SYRIA

MAP 4

THE MIDDLE EAST

SCALE OF MILES

0   50   100   200   300

Eventually the Kassite Dynasty gave way to the Pashe Dynasty which ruled Babylonia for perhaps a century and a quarter. The greatest king was Nebuchadnezzar I who reigned probably around the middle of the twelfth century B.C. In the middle of the next century the country was overrun by Elamites, and for the next 450 years Babylonia was of little importance politically.

2. THE HITTITES, c.1900-c.1200 B.C.[1]

THE center of the Hittites' power was in Asia Minor, where an empire that was once great but had been long forgotten was rediscovered by modern archeology. William Wright, a missionary at Damascus, and Professor A. H. Sayce were among the first to reconstruct from scattered monuments the picture of this empire.[2] Then in 1906 excavations were begun by Professor Hugo Winckler at Boghazköy (Boghaz-keui), a site which lies ninety miles east of Ankara in a great bend of the Halys River.[3] It was found in this and long-continued later work that Boghazköy had been an important Hittite capital, and many clay tablets were unearthed containing texts in a half-dozen different languages. Among these were a large number written with cuneiform characters in the Hittite language. Through the labors of many men and particularly of the Czech scholar Friedrich Hrozný this language was eventually deciphered.[4]

There are two chief periods of Hittite power, the first that of the Old Kingdom which goes back into the time of the First Dynasty of Babylon, and the second that of the Empire which flourished in the years around 1460 to 1200 B.C.[5] One of the greatest rulers of the Empire was Suppiluliumas who was on the throne at Boghazköy about 1375-1335 B.C. Suppiluliumas conquered and incorporated in his realm the Mesopotamian kingdoms of Mitanni and the Hurri and also sent his armies southward into Syria and to the confines of Palestine. The ruler of Mitanni whom he conquered was Tushratta, who is known to us from his correspondence with Amenhotep III and Amenhotep IV of Egypt.[6] Tushratta gave his daughter Taduhepa

---

[1] Götze, *Hethiter, Churriter und Assyrer*, p.80.

[2] Wright, *The Empire of the Hittites*. 1884; Sayce, *The Hittites, The Story of a Forgotten Empire*. rev. ed. 1925. See now O. R. Gurney, *The Hittites*. 1952; C. W. Ceram, *The Secret of the Hittites*. 1956.

[3] Winckler, *Die im Sommer 1906 in Kleinasien ausgeführten Ausgrabungen*. Sonderabzug aus der OL, Dec. 15, 1906.

[4] Hrozný, *Die Sprache der Hethiter*. 1917.

[5] cf. Kurt Bittel, *Die Ruinen von Boğazköy, der Hauptstadt des Hethiterreiches*. 1937, table following p.102.

[6] KAT Nos.17-25, 27-29 = MTAT Nos.17-25, 27-29.

to be the wife of Amenhotep III. Suppiluliumas also corresponded with Amenhotep IV, whom he called Huria, and the following is one of the letters which has been preserved:

> Thus hath Suppiluliumas, the great king,
> king of Hatti-land, to Huria,
> king of Egypt, my brother, spoken:
> I am well. With thee may it be well.
> With thy wives, thy sons, thy house, thy warriors, thy chariots,
> and in thy land, may it be very well.
>
> Now, thou, my brother, hast ascended the throne of thy father,
> and, just as thy father and I
> mutually requested presents,
> so wilt also thou and I now be mutually
> good friends.[7]

So great, indeed, was the influence of Suppiluliumas that a queen of Egypt, probably Ankhesenamun, daughter of Akhenaton and widow of Tutankhamun, wrote and asked for one of his sons to be her husband. The son was actually sent but was killed in Egypt, probably at the instigation of Eye who became the next Pharaoh.[8]

Suppiluliumas was succeeded by his son, Arnuwandas III, and then by the latter's brother, Mursilis II. His son and successor was Muwatallis who reigned about 1306-1282 b.c. The rivalry with Egypt now reached its climax in the famous battle of Kadesh on the Orontes. Here in the fifth year of Ramses II (1286 b.c.) Muwatallis routed the Egyptian forces, although the fact that the Pharaoh himself managed to escape with his life enabled him afterward to boast of the encounter. The brother of Muwatallis and second king after him was Hattusilis III (c.1275-c.1250 b.c.), who signed a nonaggression pact with Ramses II in the twenty-first year of the latter's reign. The agreement was confirmed by the marriage of a daughter of Hattusilis to Ramses II (p. 114).

By this time, however, both the Hittites and the Egyptians were greatly weakened and around 1200 b.c. the Hittite Empire reached its end.[9] The "Hittite City," as Boghazköy was called, fell, and such Hittite kingdoms as continued to exist at Carchemish, Zinjirli (Senjirli), Sakje-gözü (Sakjegeuzi), Hamath, and other places were relatively small and impotent, although Hittite cultural influence is

---

[7] KAT No.41 = MTAT No.41.
[8] Gurney, *The Hittites*, p.31.
[9] K. Bittel and R. Naumann, *Boğazköy*. 1938, p.5.

traced until in the first century A.D. in the Kingdom of Commagene.[10] Thus the old balance of power was destroyed and Assyria's opportunity had come to emerge in international affairs as the dominant world power.

3. ASSYRIAN BEGINNINGS, c.3000-c.1700 B.C.

THE homeland of Assyria was in the northeast corner of the Fertile Crescent where the Tigris River flows southward across the plains, and the mountains of Kurdistan loom up in the background. The country has a length of about 350 miles and a width of from 200 to 300 miles, with a total area of some 75,000 square miles or somewhat smaller, for example, than the state of Nebraska. In contrast with stoneless Babylonia, Assyria was supplied abundantly with limestone, alabaster, and, in the Kurdistan hills, marble.[1]

The city which gave its name to the country and empire, even as it took its own name from the national god, was Ashur.[2] It was located strategically on a low bluff on the right bank of the Tigris at a place now called Qalat Sharqat. After some earlier digging done there by Layard, Rassam, and Place, Ashur was excavated in 1903-1914 by a German expedition under the direction of Walter Andrae.[3] It appears that the site was occcupied from the early part of the third millennium B.C., while the earliest literary references to the city of Ashur occur in texts which were found at Nuzi and which date from the Old Akkadian period.[4]

Under Shamshi-Adad I (c.1748-c.1716 B.C.)[5] Assyria enjoyed a

---

[10] Ceram, *The Secret of the Hittites*, pp.213, 260. For the excavation of the temple-tomb of Antiochus I of Commagene (c.69-34 B.C.) at Nemrud Dagh see Theresa Goell in BASOR 147 (Oct. 1957), pp.4-22.

[1] Morris Jastrow, *The Civilization of Babylonia and Assyria*. 1915, p.6.

[2] A. T. Olmstead, *History of Assyria*. 1923, p.1.

[3] Andrae, *Das wiedererstandene Assur*. 1938.

[4] Meek, *Old Akkadian, Sumerian and Cappadocian Texts from Nuzi*, p.xi.

[5] The dates of the kings are based now upon a list of Assyrian rulers discovered in the palace of Sargon III at Khorsabad by the Oriental Institute of the University of Chicago in 1932-33 and published by A. Poebel in JNES 1 (1942), pp.247-306,460-492; 2 (1943), pp.56-90. From the thirty-third king on, not only the names but also the lengths of reign are given. Albright's revision of Poebel's date for Shamshi-Adad I is that which is given here (cf. p.57 n.5). In contrast with the Sumerians and early Babylonians, who designated individual years by naming them after important events which had just transpired, the Assyrians selected a high official each year, often even the king himself, to be known as the *limmu* and to give his name to the year. Lists of these limmus or eponyms were kept (see for example ARAB II, §§1194-1198), and provide important materials for chronology along with the king lists. Since in connection with Bur-Sagale, eponym in the tenth year of Ashur-dan III, an eclipse of the sun is mentioned, and since this has been identified with an astronomically computed eclipse which took place on June 15, 763 B.C., a fixed point is won from which other chronological calculations are made (TMN pp.44f.).

period of independence and Ashur began to be a great city, well fortified and with a fine temple to house its god.[6]

4. THE ASSYRIAN KINGDOM, c.1700-c.1100 B.C.

As THE First Dynasty of Babylon declined the power of Assyria increased. Doubtless there was also stimulus at this time from the present of the Hurrians, whose important city of Nuzi has already been mentioned (p. 66).

Some light is cast on the life of this period by the Assyrian laws which were discovered at Ashur. The Babylonian code, or a body of laws of closely related character, was still the law of the land. However, in cases where the Babylonian code was inadequate to Assyrian requirements and customs or in need of amendment to suit Assyrian conditions, further regulations were necessary and these are represented by the laws just mentioned.[1] Of interest also is an Assyrian text of this time found at Susa which contains a collection of dream-omens, showing how dreams were interpreted as indications of events to come.[2]

In the days of Suppiluliumas of the Hittites and Amenhotep IV of Egypt, Ashur-uballit I, "Ashur-has-given-life" (c.1362-c.1327) was king of Assyria. Among the Tell el-Amarna tablets are letters which he addressed to Amenhotep IV. In one he wrote:

> To the king of Egypt,
> say.
> Thus saith Ashur-uballit, king of Assyria:
> With thee, thy house, thy wives,
> thy chariots, and thy chief men
> may it be well!

In another he told of the gifts he was sending:

> A beautiful royal chariot, with my span,
> and two white horses, with my span, also
> one chariot without a span, and one seal of beautiful lapis lazuli.

But he expected gifts in return:

> If thou art very friendly disposed,
> then send much gold.[3]

---

[6] ARAB I, §43A.

[1] G. R. Driver and J. C. Miles, *The Assyrian Laws*. 1935, pp.14f.

[2] A. Leo Oppenheim, *The Interpretation of Dreams in the Ancient Near East, With a Translation of an Assyrian Dream-Book*. Transactions of the American Philosophical Society. New Series, Vol. 46, Pt. 3, 1956.

[3] KAT Nos.15f. = MTAT Nos.15f.

His proud assumption of equality with the Egyptian Pharaoh was not entirely unjustified, for Ashur-uballit I was one of the men who by conquest and political strategy began to make the kingdom of Assyria into the great Assyrian Empire.

5. THE ASSYRIAN EMPIRE, c.1100-633 B.C.

WITH Tukulti-apil-Esharra I, better known as Tiglath-pileser I (c.1114-c.1076), we enter the period that may properly be called that of the Assyrian Empire. This was the time described above (pp. 199f.) when the stage was clearly set for the emergence of Assyria as the greatest power in the Middle East. Amidst the confusion of small, hostile states which had taken the place of the old balance of power, Tiglath-pileser I was able to extend the conquests of Assyria westward to the Mediterranean Sea and northward to the region of Lake Van. Now, too, for the first time in Assyrian history, detailed annals are available describing many of the campaigns in which Tiglath-pileser I strove for the mastery of the world.[1] He said: "Ashur and the great gods, who have made my kingdom great, and who have bestowed might and power as a gift, commanded that I should extend the boundary of their land, and they entrusted to my hand their mighty weapons, the storm of battle. Lands, mountains, cities, and princes, the enemies of Ashur, I have brought under my sway, and have subdued their territories. . . . Unto Assyria I added land, unto her peoples, peoples. I enlarged the frontier of my land, and all of their lands I brought under my sway."[2]

ASHUR-NASIR-PAL II

The next two centuries, however, were ones of relative darkness for Assyria, and it remained for Ashur-nasir-pal II (883-859)[3] to make Assyria the ruthless fighting machine whose calculated frightfulness was the terror of its enemies. The merciless cruelty of his campaigns is the constant boast of Ashur-nasir-pal II:

"I stormed the mountain peaks and took them. In the midst of the mighty mountain I slaughtered them, with their blood I dyed the mountain red like wool. With the rest of them I darkened the gullies and preci-

---

[1] A. T. Olmstead, *Assyrian Historiography*. The University of Missouri Studies, Social Science Series, III, 1. 1916, p. 10.

[2] ARAB I, §219.

[3] The dates are cited now according to the accession-year system which is explained in the Appendix. Thus 859 B.C. is the last year of Ashur-nasir-pal II and the accession year of Shalmaneser III, while 858 is the first regnal year of Shalmaneser III.

pices of the mountains. I carried off their spoil and their possessions. The heads of their warriors I cut off, and I formed them into a pillar over against their city, their young men and their maidens I burned in the fire."

"I built a pillar over against the city gate, and I flayed all the chief men who had revolted, and I covered the pillar with their skins; some I walled up within the pillar, some I impaled upon the pillar on stakes, and others I bound to stakes round about the pillar; many within the border of my own land I flayed, and I spread their skins upon the walls; and I cut off the limbs of the officers, of the royal officers who had rebelled."[4]

The quotations just given are typical of many more which can be read in the annals of this king. The final edition of these annals was inscribed on the pavement slabs of the entrance to the temple of Ninurta at Calah. It was characteristic of some of the most energetic rulers of Assyria to move the royal residence to a new center, and the already ancient and ruined city of Calah (cf. Genesis 10:11) was that chosen by Ashur-nasir-pal II for his new capital. Calah is now represented by the mound of Nimrod and that is where the young Englishman, Austen Henry Layard, began his Assyrian excavations in 1845. At the very outset the palace of Ashur-nasir-pal II was uncovered. When the first colossal winged man-headed lion (Fig. 71) which guarded the palace entrance came into view the Arab chief cried, "This is not the work of men's hands, but of those infidel giants of whom the prophet (peace be with him!) has said that they were higher than the tallest date-tree. This is one of the idols which Noah (peace be with him!) cursed before the Flood."[5] In a small temple near by, a statue of Ashur-nasir-pal II, about half life-size, was found which is the only perfect statue in the round of an Assyrian king that is extant. This statue is shown in Fig. 72. The king holds in each hand a symbol of sovereignty, that in the right hand resembling an Egyptian scepter and that in the left is a mace. On the breast are eight lines of inscription, giving the king's name and titles and stating that he had conquered the whole region from the Tigris to Mount Lebanon and the Great Sea, meaning the Mediterranean.

A century after Layard terminated his work at Nimrod, the British School of Archaeology in Iraq undertook further excavations at the same site. These were conducted in 1949 and 1950 by M. E. L. Mallowan. Work centered again to a considerable extent on the great

---

[4] ARAB I, §§447, 443.
[5] Frederic Kenyon, *The Bible and Archaeology*. 1940, p.38; Seton Lloyd, *Foundations in the Dust*. 1947, pp.94-143.

palace of Ashur-nasir-pal II. Some of the sculptured wall reliefs which had been exposed and then reburied by Layard were again uncovered and recorded by photography. Also a new southeastern wing of the palace was found and excavated. Inscriptions with dates in the reign of Sargon II were found here, and also fine carved ivory pieces which had probably once adorned the royal furniture. Another palace was found too, bricks in which were inscribed with the name and titles of Shalmaneser III. In two rooms of this palace, over one hundred clay tablets were found, dating for the most part from the reign of Tiglath-pileser III. These suggest that this building was an administrative headquarters, for they contain government and military archives, records of loans and contracts, lists of individual possessions, and lists of personal names. In one contract it is stated that if either party infringes the agreement, "his eldest son he shall burn before Sin and his eldest daughter before. . . ."[6]

SHALMANESER III

The ruthless Assyrian fighting machine which Ashur-nasir-pal II had developed was directed by his son Shulmanu-ashared III or Shalmaneser III (858-824) in repeated campaigns against Syria and Palestine. "In my first year of reign," states Shalmaneser III, "I crossed the Euphrates at its flood. To the shore of the sea of the setting sun I advanced. I washed my weapons in the sea."[7] A few years later a great battle was fought at Qarqar (Karkar) on the Orontes River against a formidable Syrian coalition of twelve kings. The "Monolith Inscription" of Shalmaneser III, which came to the British Museum from Kurkh, records the military activities of the king up to his sixth year, and in the annals of the sixth year includes a description of this battle. The date of the battle of Qarqar is therefore 853 b.c.[8] Among the allied leaders who opposed Shalmaneser III, Hadadezer of Damascus is named first. Then Irhuleni of Hamath is mentioned, and in third place stands "Ahab, the Israelite."[9] While the Bible does not mention this incident, the Assyrian inscription

[6] M. E. L. Mallowan in *Sumer.* 6 (1950), pp.101f.; 7 (1951), pp.49-54; Donald J. Wiseman in *Sumer.* 6 (1950), p.103; 7 (1951), pp.55-57.

[7] ARAB I, §558.

[8] Military campaigns were usually launched in the spring, after the winter rains, and since the record in the Monolith Inscription (ARAB I, §610; ANET p.278 [ANEA p.188]) states that Shalmaneser III left Nineveh on the fourteenth day of Aiaru and crossed the Euphrates at its flood, it is probable that the battle of Qarqar took place in the summer of 853 b.c.

[9] ARAB I, §611; ANET p.279 (ANEA p.188).

testifies to the prominence of Ahab among the rulers of the time. The inscription gives statistics on the fighting forces involved and describes Ahab as commanding 2,000 chariots and 10,000 soldiers. In chariotry, Ahab's forces were much larger than those of any other king, Hadadezer being credited with 1,200 and Irhuleni with 700. The mention of Ahab is of importance also in giving an entirely independent confirmation of the fact that this king was on the throne of Israel just before the middle of the ninth century B.C. In this battle Shalmaneser III claimed an overwhelming triumph in which he made the blood of his enemies flow down the valleys and scattered their corpses far and wide, yet the fact that he avoided Syria thereafter for several years may mean that the victory was not as decisive as his boasts would indicate.

On one of the later campaigns of Shalmaneser III, Jehu of Israel paid heavy tribute to him. This is known to us from the famous Black Obelisk which Layard found in 1846 in the palace of Shalmaneser at Nimrod.[10] This is a four-sided pillar of black limestone six and one-half feet in height with five rows of roughly executed bas-reliefs extending around it and with texts between and below them. The inscriptions record the military achievements of Shalmaneser III from the first thirty-one years of his reign and the reliefs illustrate the payment of tribute from five different regions. A reproduction of the Black Obelisk is seen in Fig. 73 where, on the front of the monument in the second row of reliefs, Jehu is actually pictured kneeling before Shalmaneser III. The Assyrian king accompanied by two attendants, one of whom holds a sun-shade above him, stands proudly, with the symbols of Ashur and Ishtar in the field above. At his feet kneels Jehu in all humility. The Israelite king is shown with a short, rounded beard and wears a soft cap on his head. He is clothed in a sleeveless jacket and long fringed skirt with girdle. Following him come Israelites in long robes, carrying precious metals and other tribute. The inscription reads: "The tribute of Jehu, son of Omri; I received from him silver, gold, a golden bowl, a golden vase with pointed bottom, golden tumblers, golden buckets, tin, a staff for a king, and wooden [word unknown]."[11] Another inscription preserves a fragment of the annals of Shalmaneser III, in which he also refers to the taking

[10] A. H. Layard, Nineveh and Its Remains. 1849, I, p.282. The Black Obelisk was nearly lost at sea when the sailing ship on which it was being transported to England came close to foundering in a great storm in the Indian Ocean. C. J. Gadd, The Stones of Assyria. 1936, p.48.

[11] ANET p.281 (ANEA p.192); ARAB I, §590.

of tribute from Jehu, son of Omri, and dates this event in the eighteenth year of his reign. The date was, therefore, 841 B.C.[12]

Shalmaneser III liked to call himself "the mighty king, king of the universe, the king without a rival, the autocrat, the powerful one of the four regions of the world, who shatters the might of the princes of the whole world, who has smashed all of his foes like pots,"[13] but despite his boasts, he died amidst revolts with which his son Shamshi-Adad V (823-811) had to contend. Shamshi-Adad V, Sammuramat or Semiramis the famous queen, and her son Adad-nirari III (810-783), were fairly successful in maintaining the power of Assyria but under Shalmaneser IV (782-773), Ashur-dan III (772-755), and Ashur-nirari V (754-745) came decline.

TIGLATH-PILESER III

Then the throne was usurped by a great warrior and statesman who took the famous name of Tiglath-pileser (p. 202). Tiglath-pileser III (744-727), a sculptured representation of whose head is shown in Fig. 74, brought the moribund Assyrian Empire back to vigorous life. He carried out conquests to the east and west and in Babylon itself was recognized as king. There they called him Pulu, and it is by a form of this name, Pul, that he is referred to in II Kings 15:19 and I Chronicles 5:26.[14] In one of his inscriptions Tiglath-pileser III mentions receiving tribute from a number of kings, among whom he names Azriau from Iuda, probably meaning King Azariah of Judah.[15] In another he speaks of taking tribute from Menahem of Samaria,[16] doubtless the event mentioned in the Old

---

[12] ANET p.280 (ANEA p.192); ARAB I, §672. Ahab fought against Shalmaneser III at Qarqar in 853 B.C., and Jehu paid tribute to the same king in 841 B.C. Between Ahab and Jehu the rulers of Israel were Ahaziah and Joram, who are credited with reigns of two years and twelve years respectively in I Kings 22:51 and II Kings 3:1. By the nonaccession-year system these two reigns would actually total twelve years, which is the time between Qarqar and the paying of tribute by Jehu. Therefore the death of Ahab at Ramoth-gilead (I Kings 22:3, 35) must have taken place in 853 B.C. soon after Qarqar, and the accession of Jehu have been in 841 B.C. TMN pp.48-53,62.

[13] ARAB I, §674.

[14] I Chronicles 5:26 should probably be translated: "So the God of Israel stirred up the spirit of Pul king of Assyria, even the spirit of Tiglath-pilneser king of Assyria" (TMN p.77).

[15] ANET p.282 (ANEA p.193); ARAB I, §770. This reference belongs to the third year of the reign of Tiglath-pileser III; since he departed from the traditional system of counting regnal years and included his accession year (745 B.C.), his third year was 743 B.C. A. Poebel in JNES 2 (1943), p.89 n.23.

[16] ANET p.283 (ANEA p.194); ARAB I, §772. The year is unknown. W. F. Albright (in BASOR 100 [Dec. 1945], pp.18,21) puts it in 738 B.C.; Thiele (TMN pp.75-98) in 743 B.C.

Testament (II Kings 15:19). Another text which probably refers to the same Israelite king reads: "[As for Menahem I] overwhelmed him . . . and he . . . fled like a bird, alone. . . . I returned him to his place . . . gold, silver, linen garments with multicolored trimmings . . . I received from him."[17]

A few years later, as is related in II Kings 16:5-9, Pekah of Israel and Rezin of Damascus allied themselves against Assyria and also attacked Ahaz of Judah, evidently to try to force him to join the coalition too. Ahaz appealed to Tiglath-pileser III for help, and the Assyrian king moved again into the west. In Israel he took captive many of the people and deported them to Assyria, while Pekah was slain by conspiracy and Hoshea made ruler in his place. This is told in II Kings 15:29f. and I Chronicles 5:26, and there is a corresponding record in the inscriptions of Tiglath-pileser III: "Bit Humria [Israel] . . . all its inhabitants and their possessions I led to Assyria. They overthrew their king Paqaha [Pekah] and I placed Ausi' [Hoshea] as king over them. I received from them 10 talents of gold, 1,000 talents of silver as their tribute and brought them to Assyria."[18] Bit Humria or House of Omri had been the usual Assyrian designation for the land of Israel since the days of King Omri more than one hundred years before. That such a ruthless deportation of peoples, doubtless in order to prevent future rebellions, was a usual feature of Tiglath-pileser's policy we know from other of his inscriptions. Elsewhere he says, for example: "[I deported] 30,300 inhabitants from their cities and settled them in the province of the town. . . . 1,223 inhabitants I settled in the province of the Ullaba country."[19]

In Syria Tiglath-pileser III attacked Damascus and killed Rezin (II Kings 16:9). This event is probably referred to in another inscription of Tiglath-pileser III where he speaks of the defeat inflicted upon Rezon (Rezin) in a campaign which may be dated according to the eponym lists in 732 B.C.[20] This was, accordingly, also the date of the deportation in Northern Israel and of the change in rule from Pekah to Hoshea.

In Damascus Ahaz also presented himself before Tiglath-pileser

[17] ANET pp.283f. (ANEA pp.194f.); ARAB I, §815. The year to which this text refers is also unknown.

[18] ANET p.284 (ANEA p.194); ARAB I, §816.

[19] ANET p.283 (ANEA p.193); ARAB I, §770.

[20] ANET p.283 (ANEA p.194); ARAB I, §779; cf. TMN pp.90,106,121; Albright in BASOR 100 (Dec. 1945), p.22 n.26.

III (II Kings 16:10), and this event is no doubt referred to in another text of Tiglath-pileser III where he lists "Iauhazi of Judah" among those from whom he received tribute.[21] The fact that he calls the king by this name shows that Ahaz was probably an abbreviated form of Jehoahaz.

SHALMANESER V

The son and successor of Tiglath-pileser III was Shalmaneser V (726-722). In his time, Hoshea ventured to rebel against Assyria, whereupon Shalmaneser V laid siege to the Israelite capital. According to II Kings 18:9f., Samaria was thus besieged for three years, beginning with the seventh year of King Hoshea and ending with the fall of the city in the ninth year of Hoshea. If the accession of Hoshea was in the summer or later in 732 b.c., as the records of Tiglath-pileser III mentioned above make probable, his first full year of reign began in Nisan 731 b.c. The seventh regnal year of Hoshea was then that from Nisan 725 to Nisan 724 b.c., and his ninth year that from Nisan 723 to Nisan 722 b.c. If the fall of Samaria is placed at the latest possible point allowed by these data it was in the spring of 722 b.c., and this was still within the reign of Shalmaneser V. A Babylonian chronicle written in the twenty-second year of King Darius, 500 b.c., and covering Assyrian and Babylonian history from Tiglath-pileser III to Ashurbanipal, states that the death of Shalmaneser V was in the month Tebetu and the accession of his successor, Sargon, on the twelfth day of the same month, this being late in December, 722 b.c. This Babylonian chronicle also records as the noteworthy event of Shalmaneser's reign that he destroyed the city of Shamarain, which may be identified with Samaria. This evidence, therefore, suggests that the fall of Samaria should be attributed to Shalamaneser V and placed in the fighting season of 722 b.c.,[22] that is sometime between spring and autumn of that year.

SARGON II

Sharrukin II or Sargon II came to the throne at the time described in the preceding paragraph and enjoyed a reign of seventeen years (721-705). He bore a name which appears once before in the Khorsa-

---

[21] ANET p.282 (ANEA p.193); ARAB I, §801.
[22] *Babylonian Chronicle* I, 27-31; Hugo Winckler, *Keilinschriftliches Textbuch zum Alten Testament.* 2d ed. 1903, p.61; cf. A. T. Olmstead, *Western Asia in the Days of Sargon of Assyria, 722-705 B.C.* 1908, p.45 n.9; *History of Assyria,* p. 205; TMN pp.122-128. It should be noted that some wish to read the word in question in the Babylonian chronicle as Shabarain instead of Shamarain and to identify it with

bad King List[23] somewhat earlier than Shamshi-Adad I, a name which was also famous from the exploits of the yet earlier Sargon of Agade (p. 46). According to one record he was a brother of Shalmaneser V.[24] Sargon is mentioned in Isaiah 20:1 in connection with his capture of Ashdod,[25] and for a long time this was the only place in extant literature where his name was known. In 1843 the French consular agent at Mosul, Paul Émile Botta, began to dig at Khorsabad (Dur-Sharrukin) and discovered the palace of Sargon II. Sargon had made his capital successively at Ashur, Calah, and Nineveh, and then finally here at this place. He called the new capital after himself, Dur-Sharrukin or Sargonsburg, but eventually the ruin was ascribed to a Sasanid hero, Khosroes, and called Khorsabad, "town of Khosroes." The large palace which Botta discovered and which has been reexplored more intensively in recent years by the Oriental Institute of the University of Chicago, was built by Sargon II in the closing years of his reign and was adorned on the walls with texts describing the events of his kingship.[26]

In his Khorsabad inscriptions known as Annals, Sargon II claims the taking of Samaria as his own accomplishment. The text is fragmentary at this point but is reconstructed and translated as follows: "At the begi[nning of my royal rule, I . . . the town of the Sama]rians [I besieged, conquered] . . . [for the god . . . who le]t me achieve this my triumph. . . . I led away as prisoners [27,290 inhabitants of it] and [equipped] from among [them soldiers to man] 50 chariots for my royal corps. . . . [The town I] re[built] better than it was before and [settled] therein people from countries which [I] myself [had con]quered. I placed an officer of mine as governor over them and imposed upon them tribute as is customary for Assyrian citizens."[27] Again in Sargon's so-called Display Inscriptions at Khorsabad there is this record which presumably, like the foregoing, refers to the beginning of his reign: "I besieged and conquered Samaria, led away as booty 27,290 inhabitants of it. I formed from among them a contingent of 50 chariots and made remaining inhabitants assume

---

some other city than Samaria, but this is little probable (A. T. Olmstead in AJSL 21 [1904-5], pp.180f.). For the conclusion that Samaria was taken by Shalmaneser V see now Hayim Tadmor in JCS 12 (1958), pp.22-40.

[23] Poebel in JNES 2 (1943), p.86.   [24] ibid., p.89 n.26.

[25] cf. ANET p.286 (ANEA p.197); ARAB II, §30; Tadmor in JCS 12 (1958), pp.83f.

[26] Gordon Loud, Khorsabad I, Excavations in the Palace and at a City Gate. OIP XXXVIII, 1936; G. Loud and Charles B. Altman, Khorsabad II, The Citadel and the Town. OIP XL, 1938.

[27] ANET p.284 (ANEA p.195); ARAB II, §4; cf. A. G. Lie, The Inscriptions of Sargon II, Part I, The Annals. 1929, p.5.

their social positions. I installed over them an officer of mine and imposed upon them the tribute of the former king."[28]

If these statements comprise the authentic record of the fall of Samaria, then that city must have been captured at the earliest in the accession year of Sargon II, that is sometime after late December, 722 B.C., hence probably in 721 B.C. This is, however, in conflict with the data which indicate that Samaria was taken by Shalmaneser V. If Samaria fell in the summer or fall of 722 B.C. it was only a few months until the death of Shalmaneser V in December of that year, and this may have made it easy for Sargon II, in inscriptions written late in his reign, to claim for his own glory the conquest which was actually accomplished by his predecessor. Furthermore, in the few months before his death Shalmaneser V may have but barely begun the deportation of the people of Samaria and the actual carrying out of this deportation may have actually been the work of Sargon II, as the latter says.[29]

An alabaster relief from Khorsabad gives us an impressive picture of the kind of fighting man Sargon II could send into action (Fig. 75). Carrying bow and arrow, short sword and short club, this powerfully muscled warrior stands in calm confidence, a symbol of the overwhelming military might of Assyria. Yet sometimes even the Assyrians faced enemies against which the bowsman could not avail and terrible plagues of locusts devastated the land as they did in Judah in the days of Joel. An enameled tile painting (Fig. 76) from the time of Sargon II shows some great man of Assyria standing in front of the all-seeing sun-god Shamash to ask for deliverance from a plague of locusts, or possibly to give thanks for the deliverance which has already taken place. The theme of his prayer is made unmistakable by the representation of the locust above his head.

SENNACHERIB

Sargon II fell in battle and was succeeded by his son, Sin-ahhe-eriba or Sennacherib (704-681). The capital of Sennacherib was the famous city of Nineveh on the east bank of the Tigris, across

[28] ANET pp.284f. (ANEA pp.195f.); ARAB II, §55; cf. A. T. Olmstead in AJSL 47 (1930-31), pp.262f.

[29] Tadmor in JCS 12 (1958), pp.37f. It has also been thought that Sargon II might have participated in the taking of Samaria along with his brother, Shalmaneser V, but prior to his own accession to the kingship, and in this connection it is pointed out that II Kings 18:9f. says that Shalmaneser besieged Samaria but that "they" (ASV) took it. The use of the word "they" could allow for the association of Sargon with Shalmaneser at the end of the siege; on the other hand it may be simply a reference to the Assyrian army in the plural. See TMN p.124.

from where the modern city of Mosul now stands. Sennacherib planned the fortifications of this city, gave it a system of water-works, restored its temples and built its most magnificent palaces. The ancient city is represented by two large mounds known as Kuyunjik and Nebi Yunus, the latter being so named because it is the site of the reputed tomb of the prophet Jonah. In 1820 Claudius James Rich, the British resident at Baghdad, visited Mosul. Although he died of cholera the next year, the posthumous publication in 1836 of his *Narrative of a Residence in Koordistan* awakened much interest in the possibilities of archeological work in Assyria. In 1842 Paul Émile Botta was sent to Mosul by the French government as con-sular agent. He made brief and unsuccessful attempts to dig at Nebi Yunus and Kuyunjik before transferring his efforts to Khorsabad where he made the brilliant discovery mentioned above (p. 209). He was followed in work both at Khorsabad and at Kuyunjik by Victor Place. Austen Henry Layard, the English archeologist, con-cerned himself first with Nimrod, as we have seen (p. 203), but also did some digging at Kuyunjik and in 1847 discovered there the great palace of Sennacherib. During Layard's second expedition, which lasted from 1849 to 1851, this palace was largely unearthed. No less than seventy-one rooms were found, and it was computed that the palace had contained approximately 9,880 feet of walls lined with sculptured slabs.[30]

Early in the reign of Sennacherib, Hezekiah of Judah revolted against Assyria and in 701 B.C. the Assyrian king moved west and south. The campaign is described in the annals of Sennacherib which were recorded on clay cylinders or "prisms." The final edition of these annals appears on the Taylor Prism of the British Museum and in an even better copy on a prism now in the Oriental Institute of the University of Chicago (Fig. 77). The prism is hexagonal in form, and the middle column in the photograph contains the reference to Hezekiah quoted below.

Sennacherib names Sidon, Beth-Dagon, Joppa, and other cities as having fallen before him and tells of his victory in a great battle fought in the neighborhood of the city of Altaku or Eltekeh[31] in which the Palestinian forces were assisted by Egyptian bowmen and chariotry. Then Sennacherib continues:

---

[30] Layard, *Nineveh and Its Remains.* 1849; *Discoveries among the Ruins of Nineveh and Babylon.* 1875; *The Monuments of Nineveh.* 1853; *A Second Series of the Monu-ments of Nineveh.* 1853; André Parrot, *Nineveh and the Old Testament.* 1955.
[31] Probably the same city mentioned in Joshua 19:44; 21:23 (HDB I, p.698).

"As to Hezekiah, the Jew, he did not submit to my yoke, I laid siege to 46 of his strong cities, walled forts and to the countless small villages in their vicinity, and conquered them by means of well-stamped earth-ramps, and battering-rams brought thus near to the walls combined with the attack by foot soldiers, using mines, breeches as well as sapper work. I drove out of them 200,150 people, young and old, male and female, horses, mules, donkeys, camels, big and small cattle beyond counting, and considered them booty. Himself I made a prisoner in Jerusalem, his royal residence, like a bird in a cage. I surrounded him with earthwork in order to molest those who were leaving his city's gate. His towns which I had plundered, I took away from his country and gave them over to Mitinti, king of Ashdod, Padi, king of Ekron, and Sillibel, king of Gaza. Thus I reduced his country, but I still increased the tribute and the presents due to me as his overlord which I imposed later upon him beyond the former tribute, to be delivered annually. Hezekiah himself, whom the terror-inspiring splendor of my lordship had overwhelmed and whose irregular and elite troops which he had brought into Jerusalem, his royal residence, in order to strengthen it, had deserted him, did send me, later, to Nineveh, my lordly city, together with 30 talents of gold, 800 talents of silver, precious stones, antimony, large cuts of red stone, couches inlaid with ivory, chairs inlaid with ivory, elephant-hides, ebony-wood, box-wood and all kinds of valuable treasures, his own daughters, concubines, male and female musicians. In order to deliver the tribute and to do obeisance as a slave he sent his personal messenger."[32]

Presumably this inscription refers to the same invasion that is described in II Kings 18:13-19:37; II Chronicles 32:1-22; Isaiah 36:1-37:38. In comparing the Old Testament account with Sennacherib's record we note that Hezekiah's tribute is placed at 30 talents of gold in both sources but at only 300 talents of silver in II Kings 18:14 as compared with 800 talents of silver which the Assyrian king claims to have received.

In II Kings 19:9 = Isaiah 37:9 it is stated that "Tirhakah king of Ethiopia" came out to fight against Sennacherib. In 701 B.C. a Kushite dynasty, commonly called "Ethiopian," was indeed ruling Egypt, but according to the chronology given above (p. 127) King Taharqo, who is the biblical Tirhakah, was first associated with his predecessor Shebitko in 689 B.C. and was sole ruler only from 684 on. To account for this discrepancy it has previously been suggested that while Taharqo was not yet king in 701 B.C. he might have been a military commander under his uncle Shabako and as such have fought

---

[32] ANET p.288; ARAB II, §240. Like other Assyrian campaigns, this one was no doubt launched in the spring and the date of the siege of Jerusalem was summer, 701 B.C. According to II Kings 18:13; Isaiah 36:1 this was the fourteenth year of Hezekiah. cf. TMN pp.101,110; Albright in BASOR 100 (Dec. 1945), p.22 n.28.

against Sennacherib.[33] According to the present chronology, however, not even this would have been possible, since Taharqo was probably only born in 709 B.C. and was yet much too young. Therefore strength is given to the alternative hypothesis which had also already been advanced, namely that Sennacherib made a second invasion of Palestine after Taharqo was actually ruling as king, that is after 689 or 684, and before his own death in 681 B.C. In this case we might consider II Kings 18:13-19:8 as describing Sennacherib's first invasion when Hezekiah paid heavy tribute, and II Kings 19:9-37 with its mention of Tirhakah as king as referring to Sennacherib's second campaign. Some support is gained for this view if II Kings 19:37 is interpreted as giving the impression that Sennacherib's death ensued shortly after his return from the disaster at Jerusalem. It is true that such a second and later Palestinian campaign on the part of Sennacherib cannot be verified in his own annals but inscriptions referring to the last eight years of his reign are lacking.

At all events we must acknowledge that Sennacherib says nothing of the disaster which overwhelmed his armies at Jerusalem according to II Kings 19:35f. = Isaiah 37:36f. In view of the general note of boasting which pervades the inscriptions of the Assyrian kings, however, it is hardly to be expected that Sennacherib would record such a defeat. Perhaps the fact that he claims to have shut up Hezekiah in Jerusalem "like a bird in a cage," but does not claim to have taken the city, is evidence that he did suffer discomfiture there. Incidentally, the Old Testament account finds support in a somewhat enigmatic story recorded by Herodotus and running as follows:

"The next king was the priest of Hephaestus, whose name was Sethos. He despised and took no account of the warrior Egyptians, thinking he would never need them; besides otherwise dishonouring them, he took away the chosen lands which had been given to them, twelve fields to each man, in the reign of former kings. So presently came king Sanacharib against Egypt, with a great host of Arabians and Assyrians; and the warrior Egyptians would not march against him. The priest, in this quandary, went into the temple shrine and there bewailed to the god's image the peril which threatened him. In his lamentation he fell asleep, and dreamt that he saw the god standing over him and bidding him take courage, for he should suffer no ill by encountering the host of Arabia: 'Myself,' said the god, 'will send you champions.' So he trusted the vision, and encamped at Pelusium with such Egyptians as would follow him, for here is the road into Egypt; and none of the warriors would go with him,

---

[33] ARE IV, §892; L. L. Honor, *Sennacherib's Invasion of Palestine.* 1926, p.34 n.112.

but only hucksters and artificers and traders. Their enemies too came thither, and one night a multitude of field-mice swarmed over the Assyrian camp and devoured their quivers and their bows and the handles of their shields likewise, insomuch that they fled the next day unarmed and many fell. And at this day a stone statue of the Egyptian king stands in Hephaestus' temple, with a mouse in his hand and an inscription to this effect: 'Look on me, and fear the gods.' "[34]

The mention of mice may well indicate that it was plague which struck Sennacherib's army, since mice are a Greek symbol of pestilence and since rats are carriers of the plague. Perhaps this is the real explanation of the disaster referred to in II Kings 19:35 as a smiting of the army by an angel of the Lord, for plague and disease elsewhere in the Bible are regarded as a smiting by an angel of God (II Samuel 24:15-17; Acts 12:23).[35]

In Fig. 78 we see a portion of a frieze illustrating one of Sennacherib's wars in the west. His soldiers are advancing to the attack in relentless procession. At the left are auxiliaries in crested helmets, carrying round shields and long spears, and wearing knee-coverings. In the center are spearsmen of a different type and in front are slingers. Another sculpture (Fig. 79) shows Sennacherib seated upon his throne before the captured city of Lachish (cf. II Kings 18:14, 17; 19:8, etc.) and receiving the spoils of the city to the accompaniment of the torture of hapless prisoners.[36] The inscription states: "Sennacherib, king of the world, king of Assyria, sat upon a throne and passed in review the booty taken from Lachish."[37]

ESARHADDON

Sennacherib was assassinated in 681 B.C. He had named his favorite son Ashur-aha-iddina or Esarhaddon to be his successor, although the latter was not the eldest son. The other sons, hoping to gain the kingship, slew Sennacherib their father, but Esarhaddon swiftly attacked the rebels and secured the crown.[38] The most important achievements of Esarhaddon's reign (680-669) were the restoration of the city of Babylon, which had been destroyed by his father, and

[34] II, 141.

[35] Samuel I. Feigin has pointed out that Assyrian omen texts speak of the outbreak of the *shibu* fever in an army as foreshadowing victory for the enemy. See William A. Irwin in JNES 9 (1950), p.123.

[36] Layard, *Discoveries among the Ruins of Nineveh and Babylon*, pp.126-128; R. D. Barnett in IEJ 8 (1958), pp.161-164.

[37] ANET p.288; ARAB II, §489.

[38] ANET pp.288f.; ARAB II, §§500-506.

the defeat of Taharqo, now upon the throne of Egypt, at whose border Sennacherib had been turned back.

The victory over Taharqo was commemorated with a victory stela (Fig. 80) set up at Zinjirli in northern Syria, and discovered in 1888 by a German expedition. It shows the king with a mace in his left hand, and in his right a cup from which he has poured a libation to the gods symbolized at the top of the stela. From the left hand extend ropes which pass through the lips of the two figures at his feet. The kneeling figure is doubtless Taharqo, represented with strongly marked Negroid features. His hands are lifted in supplication, and both hands and feet are shackled. The other figure, standing, may be Ba'alu of Tyre, although the inscription does not claim his surrender. The inscription says concerning the conquest of Egypt: "I fought daily, without interruption, very bloody battles against Tirhakah, king of Egypt and Ethiopia, the one accursed by all the great gods. Five times I hit him with the point of my arrows inflicting wounds from which he should not recover, and then I laid siege to Memphis, his royal residence, and conquered it in half a day by means of mines, breaches and assault ladders; I destroyed it, tore down its walls and burnt it down.[39] Proudly Esarhaddon says of himself, "I am powerful, I am all powerful, I am a hero, I am gigantic, I am colossal," and for the first time an Assyrian ruler takes the new title, "King of the kings of Egypt."[40]

ASHURBANIPAL

Taharqo may have been wounded grievously, but he survived to fight again, while Esarhaddon died on his next march toward Egypt. Esarhaddon was succeeded by his son Ashurbanipal (668-633), the great king who was called Osnappar in the Old Testament (Ezra 4:10) and Sardanapalus by the Greeks. Ashurbanipal campaigned in Egypt, defeating both Taharqo and Tanutamun and taking both Memphis and Thebes (pp. 127f.). Concerning the triumphs in Egypt, the defeat of Taharqo and of Tanutamun, whom he calls Urdamane, and the plundering of Thebes, Ashurbanipal wrote:

"In my first campaign I marched against Egypt and Ethiopia. . . . Tirhakah, king of Egypt and Nubia, heard in Memphis of the coming of my expedition and he called up his warriors for a decisive battle against me. . . . I defeated the battle-experienced soldiers of his army in a great open battle. . . . He left Memphis and fled, to save his life, into the town

---

[39] ANET p.293; ARAB II, §580.   [40] ARAB II, §§577, 583.

of Thebes. This town too I seized and led my army into it to repose there. . . . The terror of the sacred weapon of Ashur, my lord, overcame Tirhakah where he had taken refuge and he was never heard of again. Afterwards Urdamane, son of Shabako, sat down on the throne of his kingdom. He made Thebes and Heliopolis his fortresses and assembled his armed might. He called up his battle-experienced soldiers to attack my troops, and the Assyrians stationed in Memphis. . . .

"In my second campaign I marched directly against Egypt and Nubia. Urdamane . . . left Memphis and fled into Thebes to save his life. . . . I followed Urdamane and went as far as Thebes, his fortress. He saw my mighty battle array approaching, left Thebes and fled to Kipkipi. . . . I, myself, conquered this town completely. From Thebes I carried away booty, heavy and beyond counting: silver, gold, precious stones, his entire personal possessions, linen garments with multicolored trimmings, fine horses, certain inhabitants, male and female. I pulled two high obelisks, cast of shining bronze, the weight of which was 2,500 talents, standing at the door of the temple, out of their bases and took them to Assyria. Thus I carried off from Thebes heavy booty, beyond counting. I made Egypt and Nubia feel my weapons bitterly and celebrated my triumph. With full hands and safely, I returned to Nineveh, the city where I exercise my rule."[41]

Ashurbanipal's wars were numerous and his conduct often ruthlessly cruel, yet he is remembered most of all for his culture. The paradox of his culture and his cruelty is well represented in the relief which shows him at a banquet in the royal pleasure garden with his queen Ashur-sharrat (Fig. 81). The scene is one of peaceful beauty until it is noted that the head of the leader of the Elamites, whom Ashurbanipal has just conquered, hangs like ghastly fruit from the coniferous tree at the left.

In his inscriptions Ashurbanipal refers frequently to the education which he received in the days of his youth and to his intellectual as well as military and sporting achievements.

"I, Ashurbanipal, learned the wisdom of Nabu,[42] the entire art of writing on clay tablets. . . . I learned to shoot the bow, to ride, to drive and to seize the reins.

"I received the revelation of the wise Adapa, the hidden treasure of the art of writing. . . . I considered the heavens with the learned masters. . . . I read the beautiful clay tablets from Sumer and the obscure Akkadian writing which is hard to master. I had my joy in the reading of inscriptions

---

[41] ANET pp.294f.; ARAB II, §§770-778; Arthur C. Piepkorn, *Historical Prism Inscriptions of Ashurbanipal*. I (AS 5), 1933, pp.39-41.

[42] The patron god of the art of writing. (A. H. Sayce in HDB III, pp.501f.).

on stone from the time before the flood. . . . The following were my daily activities: I mounted my horse, I rode joyfully . . . I held the bow . . . I drove my chariot, holding the reins like a charioteer. I made the wheels go round. . . . At the same time I learned royal decorum and walked in kingly ways."[43]

The interest of Ashurbanipal in education resulted ultimately in the establishment of a great royal library. In the Temple of Nabu at Nineveh one library had already been in existence at least since the time of Sargon II, but the collection of Ashurbanipal was to surpass all others in size and importance. He sent scribes throughout Assyria and Babylonia with authority to copy and translate the writings they found, and tens of thousands of clay tablets were brought together, containing historical, scientific, and religious literature, official dispatches and archives, business documents and letters. Ashurbanipal's royal palace containing this library was discovered in 1853 by Hormuzd Rassam, the brother of the British vice-consul at Mosul, who was continuing Layard's work at Kuyunjik.

Among the tablets which Rassam unearthed and sent to the British Museum were the ones which were later found to contain Assyrian copies of the Babylonian flood and creation stories (pp. 33, 62). The identification and decipherment of these particular tablets was the work of George Smith, then a young assistant in the British Museum. In 1872, while engaged in the sorting and classification of the Kuyunjik tablets, he noticed pieces containing portions of mythical stories. "Commencing a steady search among these fragments," Smith afterward related, "I soon found half of a curious tablet which had evidently contained originally six columns. . . . On looking down the third column, my eye caught the statement that the ship rested on the mountains of Nizir, followed by the account of the sending forth of the dove, and its finding no resting-place and returning. I saw at once that I had here discovered a portion at least of the Chaldean account of the Deluge."[44]

In the royal palace were also found the magnificent reliefs of the lion hunts of Ashurbanipal, one section of which is reproduced in Fig. 82. With their close attention to animal forms, their thrilling realism and unmistakable atmosphere of the excitement of the chase, these sculptures represent the climax of Assyrian art.

[43] Maximilian Streck, *Assurbanipal und die letzten assyrischen Könige bis zum Untergang Ninevehs.* 1916, ii, pp.5,255,257.
[44] R. C. Thompson, *A Century of Exploration at Nineveh.* 1929, p.49. Quoted by permission of the publishers, Luzac and Co., London.

6. THE DECLINE AND FALL OF ASSYRIA,

633-612 B.C.

FOLLOWING Ashurbanipal with Assyria at the height of its glory, three undistinguished rulers, Ashur-etil-ilani, Sin-shum-lishir, and Sin-shar-ishkun occupied the throne, and then the end came with startling suddenness and Assyrian civilization was snuffed out.

For the story of Nineveh's fall and the end of the Assyrian Empire, we can now turn to a contemporary record of events. Assyrian records are largely lacking during the last twenty-five years before the end, perhaps because the kings were reluctant to record their reverses, but a Babylonian clay tablet which chronicles the fall of Nineveh has been discovered and is in the British Museum.[1] This Babylonian chronicle, known as B.M. 21901, is inscribed with a summary of the chief events in years ten to seventeen of the reign of Nabopolassar, king of Babylon. Nabu-apal-usur, or Nabopolassar in the Greek form of the name, was a Chaldean. The Chaldeans, whom Jeremiah (5:15) called "an ancient nation," were a Semitic people who entered Babylonia around 1000 B.C.[2] They stirred up disaffection against Assyrian rule of Babylonia, and in the days of Sargon II one of their chiefs, Merodach-baladan (II Kings 20:12; Isaiah 39:1), was able to rule Babylon for a time. The persistent rebelliousness of Babylon was finally punished by Sennacherib, who destroyed the city completely. Esarhaddon restored Babylon, hoping to gain the support of the south, and when he died left Ashurbanipal's younger brother, Shamash-shum-ukin, as king of Babylon. After the rebellion and death of Shamash-shum-ukin, Ashurbanipal was himself king of Babylon. But when he died, Nabopolassar, a Chaldean and a descendant of Merodach-baladan, seized the kingship of Babylon and established an independent Chaldean or New Babylonian empire.

Another British Museum tablet from Babylon recently published (B.M. 25127), gives the date of the accession of Nabopolassar to the throne of Babylon: "On the twenty-sixth day of the month of Arahsamnu, Nabopolassar sat upon the throne in Babylon. This was the 'beginning of reign' of Nabopolassar."[3] The reference is to the

---

[1] C. J. Gadd, *The Fall of Nineveh*. 1923; ARAB II, §§1166-1186; ANET pp.303-305 (ANEA p.202).

[2] Olmstead, *History of Assyria*, p.250.

[3] WCCK pp.50f.

71. Man-headed Lion from the Palace of Ashur-nasir-pal II

72. Ashur-nasir-pal II

74. Head of Tiglath-pileser III

73. Cast of the Black Obelisk of Shalmaneser III

77. The Prism of Sennacherib

76. An Assyrian Prays to Shamash Concerning a Plague of Locusts

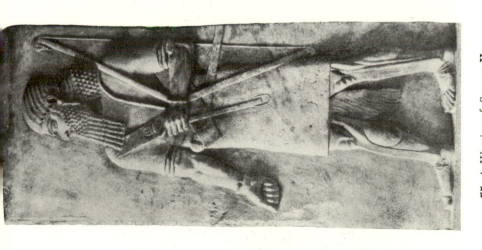

75. A Warrior of Sargon II

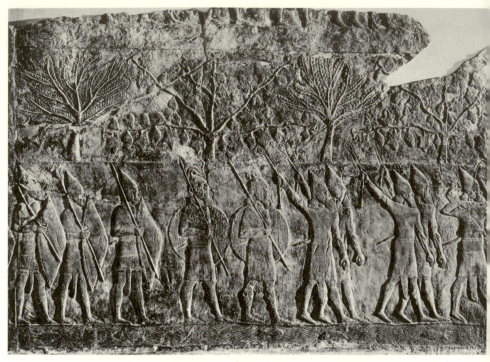

78. The Army of Sennacherib Advances to the Attack

79. Sennacherib at Lachish

80. The Zinjirli Stela of Esarhaddon

81. Victory Banquet of Ashurbanipal and his Queen

82. Ashurbanipal on the Lion Hunt

83. The Ruins of Babylon

84. Enameled Lion from the Processional Street in Babylon

85. Enameled Bricks from the Throne Room of Nebuchadnezzar II

86. The Cyrus Cylinder

87. Relief from the Palace of Cyrus at Pasargadae

88. The Tomb of Cyrus the Great

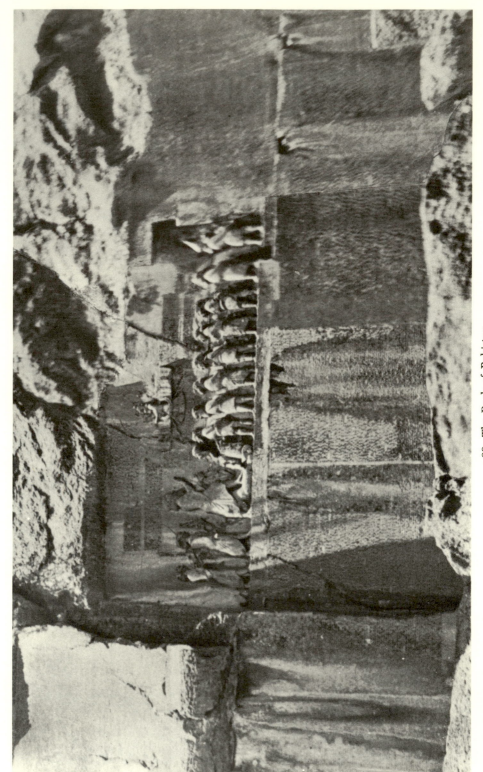

89. The Rock of Behistun

90. Darius Triumphs over the Rebels

91. The Rock-hewn Tomb of Darius I the Great

92. The Palace of Darius (Tachara) at Persepolis

94. Standing Columns of the Hall of Xerxes (Apadana) at Persepolis

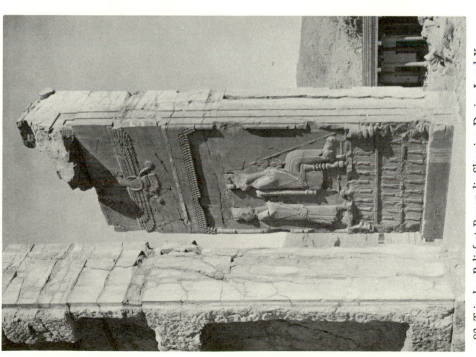

93. Tripylon Relief at Persepolis Showing Darius I and Xerxes

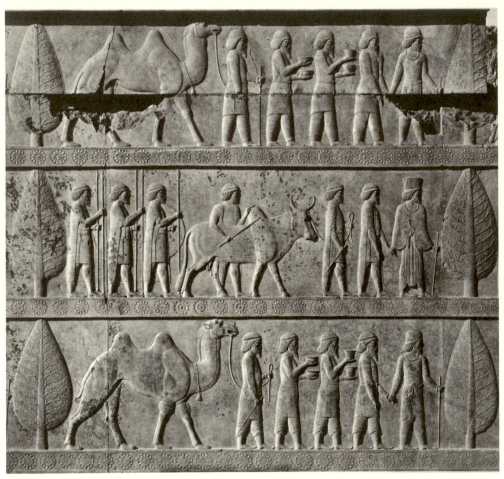

95. Relief from the Apadana Stairway at Persepolis

96. Eastern Portal of the Gate of Xerxes at Persepolis

97. Enameled Brick Panels from Susa Showing Spearmen of the Achaemenid Period

year 626 B.C. and the date would be November 23;[4] his ensuing twenty-one years of reign were 625-605 B.C.[5]

It was in the fourteenth year of Nabopolassar, according to the Babylonian chronicle first mentioned above (B.M. 21901),[6] that Nineveh fell, and this date was accordingly 612 B.C. In the destruction of Nineveh Nabopolassar of Babylon was joined by Cyaxares the Mede (p. 231) and by the king of the Scythians. As a matter of fact, the Median king was the most important figure in the enterprise. He had begun operations against Nineveh a few years earlier, and although he did not take the capital at that time he did capture the city of Ashur. In 613 B.C. the siege of Nineveh seems to have been lifted, and this may have been due to a Scythian attack upon the Medes, which is mentioned by Herodotus.[7] But in 612 B.C. the Babylonians, Medes, and Scythians all combined for the final and successful attack upon the Assyrian capital. The siege lasted from Simanu to Abu, that is from May/June to July/August, but eventually Nineveh fell and its last king, Sin-shar-ishkun, died. Yet one more man, a certain Ashur-uballit II (611-608), reigned for a few years as king of Assyria in the western city of Haran, but this last capital of a great empire soon was also taken by its enemies. Nineveh the Great had fallen. The destruction predicted by Zephaniah (2:13-15) had taken place. As he saw the end come Nahum cried (3:1-3):

> Woe to the city, bloody throughout,
> Full of lies and booty!
> Prey ceases not.
> The crack of the whip, and the noise of the rumbling wheel,
> And the galloping horse, and the jolting chariot;
> The charging horseman, and the flashing sword,
> And the glittering spear, and a multitude of slain,
> And a mass of bodies, and no end to the corpses!
> They stumble over the corpses![8]

The spoils were divided equally, the Medes taking the regions east and north of the Tigris, and the king of Babylon taking those to the

---

[4] PDBC p.27. A temple record at Sippar recognizes Nabopolassar as king two months earlier, this city evidently having become independent of Assyria before Babylon (WCCK pp.7,93).

[5] For most of the dates in the remainder of this chapter see PDBC; and cf. Dubberstein in JNES 3 (1944), pp.38-42. See also the Appendix of the present book.

[6] ANET p.304 (ANEA p.202); ARAB II, §§1177f.

[7] I,103-106.

[8] *An American Translation.*

west and south of that natural dividing line.[9] The agreement was sealed by the marriage of Amytis, daughter of Cyaxares's son Astyages, to Nebuchadnezzar II, son of Nabopolassar.

7. THE NEW BABYLONIAN EMPIRE, 612-539 B.C.

NEBUCHADNEZZAR II

IT HAS already been noted (p. 129) that Pharaoh Necho II made an attempt to assist the Assyrians and resist the rising power of the New Babylonian Empire, but that the Egyptians were finally defeated by Nebuchadnezzar at Carchemish in 605 B.C. This decisive battle is mentioned in Jeremiah 46:2 where it is stated that Pharaoh Necho was defeated at Carchemish by Nebuchadrezzar[1] king of Babylon in the fourth year of Jehoiakim king of Judah. Berossos as quoted by Josephus[2] also narrates the event and provides the further details that Nebuchadnezzar was sent as commander of the Babylonian army by his father King Nabopolassar, and after the victory learned that his father had just died and so hastened home to ascend the throne himself.

This information is now confirmed by a newly published text from Babylon in the British Museum (B.M. 21946), which covers events from the twenty-first year of Nabopolassar to the eleventh year of Nebuchadnezzar, that is from 605 to 594 B.C. It begins as follows, the king of Akkad mentioned at the outset being Nabopolassar:

"In the twenty-first year the king of Akkad stayed in his own land, Nebuchadrezzar his eldest son, the crown-prince, mustered the Babylonian army and took command of his troops; he marched to Carchemish which is on the bank of the Euphrates, and crossed the river to go against the Egyptian army which lay in Carchemish. . . . He accomplished their defeat and to non-existence beat them. As for the rest of the Egyptian army which had escaped from the defeat so quickly that no weapon had reached them, in the district of Hamath the Babylonian troops overtook and defeated them so that not a single man escaped to his own country. At that time Nebuchadrezzar conquered the whole area of the Hatti-

[9] George Stephen Goodspeed, *A History of the Babylonians and Assyrians.* 1902, p.333.
[1] In Babylonian the king's name is Nabu-kudurri-usur and means "Nabu protect the border." Jeremiah (21:2, etc.) and Ezekiel (26:7, etc.), both contemporary prophets, render the name Nebuchadrezzar; it is given as Nebuchadnezzar in part of Jeremiah (27:6, etc.), and in II Kings (24:1, etc.), Chronicles (I 6:15; II 36:6, etc.), Ezra (1:7, etc.), Nehemiah (7:6), Esther (2:6), and Daniel (1:1, etc.). The former rendering is closer to the original, the latter more familiar.
[2] *Against Apion.* I, 19; *Ant.* x, xi, 1.

country. For twenty-one years Nabopolassar had been king of Babylon. On the 8th of the month of Abu he died; in the month of Ululu Nebuchadrezzar returned to Babylon and on the first day of the month of Ululu he sat on the royal throne in Babylon."[3]

It is certain, therefore, that the battle of Carchemish took place in 605 B.C. The exact month is not given but it had to be between Nisanu when the twenty-first year of Nabopolassar began and Abu when the king died; perhaps Simanu (May/June) is a reasonable guess.[4] Precise dates are stated for the death of Nabopolassar and the accession of Nebuchadnezzar; they are equivalent respectively to August 15 and September 7, 605 B.C.

After the battle of Carchemish, according to the same Babylonian text, Nebuchadnezzar took all of "the Hatti-country." In the record of the seventh year, which will be quoted below, "the Hatti-land" includes "the city of Judah," therefore this term must be used as a general designation for Syria-Palestine.[5] As our text continues with the record of Nebuchadnezzar's reign it states that in his first year (604/603 B.C.) he returned to the West:

"In the first year of Nebuchadrezzar in the month of Simanu he mustered his army and went to the Hatti-territory, he marched about unopposed in the Hatti-territory until the month of Kislimu. All the kings of the Hatti-land came before him and he received their heavy tribute."[6]

Jehoiakim king of Judah had been put on the throne by Necho II (II Kings 23:34), but after the defeat of the Pharaoh at Carchemish fell necessarily under the power of Nebuchadnezzar. His submission is recorded in II Kings 24:1, and if he was one of "the kings of the Hatti-land" just mentioned in the Babylonian text, this was in 604/603 B.C.

In his second and in his third years Nebuchadnezzar went back to the Hatti-land, and in his fourth year (601/600 B.C.) he marched to Egypt. An open battle was fought with the Egyptians and the Babylonian chronicle honestly reports that each side inflicted great havoc on the other, and that Nebuchadnezzar and his troops "turned back and returned to Babylon."[7] This virtual defeat, as it appears to have been, of the Babylonians may well have been what encouraged Jehoiakim to the act of rebellion against Nebuchadnezzar which is recorded in II Kings 24:1. It is there stated that this was

---

[3] wcck pp.67-69.   [4] wcck p.25.
[5] cf. J. Philip Hyatt in jbl 75 (1956), p.280.
[6] wcck p.69.   [7] wcck p.71.

after Jehoiakim had been servant to the Babylonian king for three years, which would probably indicate this very year of 601/600 B.C.[8]

"In the fifth year the king of Akkad stayed in his own land and gathered together his chariots and horses in great numbers," the Babylonian text continues.[9] In the sixth and seventh years he marched again to the Hatti-land. The purpose of Nebuchadnezzar now undoubtedly included punishment of the defection of Judah and re-establishment of his control there, and in the record of the seventh year we are told explicitly of attack upon "the city of Judah" which must mean Jerusalem:

"In the seventh year, the month of Kislimu, the king of Akkad mustered his troops, marched to the Hatti-land, and encamped against [i.e. besieged] the city of Judah and on the second day of the month of Addaru he seized the city and captured the king. He appointed there a king of his own choice, received its heavy tribute and sent them to Babylon."[10]

The seventh year of Nebuchadnezzar began on the first day of Nisanu, 598 B.C. The month of Kislimu when he marched to Hatti-land and besieged Jerusalem began on December 18, 598 B.C. The second day of Addaru when he seized the city and captured the king was March 16, 597 B.C. Thus the Babylonian record has provided the exact date of the first fall of Jerusalem. The name of the king of Judah captured by Nebuchadnezzar is not given in the Babylonian source but from the biblical record it is evident that it was Jehoiachin (II Kings 24:12). The "king of his own choice," whom Nebuchadnezzar then put on the throne at Jerusalem is also not named in the Babylonian chronicle but must have been Jehoiachin's uncle, Mattaniah, whose name was changed to Zedekiah according to II Kings 24:17 and II Chronicles 36:10.[11]

Even though Zedekiah was installed in the kingship of Judah as vassal of Nebuchadnezzar, the time came when he too ventured to rebel against his Babylonian master. Thereupon Nebuchadnezzar came back again to besiege Jerusalem. While the Babylonian tablet (B.M. 21946) which has supplied such valuable information about the first fall of Jerusalem reports several succeeding expeditions of Nebuchadnezzar to the Hatti-land it terminates with the eleventh year (594/593 B.C.) of the Babylonian king and does not extend far enough to chronicle the final fall of Jerusalem. According to II Kings

---

[8] The three years of submission were 604/603, 603/602, 602/601.
[9] WCCK p.71.   [10] WCCK p.73.
[11] He is called the brother of Jehoiachin in the passage in II Chronicles.

25:2, 8 and Jeremiah 52:5, 12 the final destruction of the city was in the eleventh year of King Zedekiah and the nineteenth year of King Nebuchadnezzar. If this date is given in terms of the accession-year system and the regnal year beginning in Nisan, it indicates 586 B.C. According to II Kings 25:8 it was on the seventh day of the fifth month that the city was destroyed; according to Jeremiah 52:12 it was on the tenth day of the same month. In 586 B.C. these days corresponded to August 14 and 17.[12]

The Babylonian tablets just discussed, which have added so much to our knowledge of the relations of Nabopolassar and Nebuchadnezzar with Syria, Palestine, and Egypt, show that the kings of the New Babylonian Empire were much engaged in military activities. According to the record they provide for the twenty-three years from 616 to 594 B.C., the Babylonian army was called out twenty-one times in seventeen different years.[13] We also know from Josephus[14] that Nebuchadnezzar conducted a thirteen-year siege of Tyre; and another inscription has already been cited (pp. 131f.) which tells of a battle against King Amasis of Egypt as late as the thirty-seventh year of Nebuchadnezzar. Another inscription describes his conquests in general terms: "In exalted trust in him [Marduk] distant countries, remote mountains from the upper sea [Mediterranean] to the lower sea [Persian Gulf], steep paths, blockaded roads, where the step is impeded, where was no footing, difficult roads, desert paths, I traversed, and the disobedient I destroyed; I captured the enemies, established justice in the lands; the people I exalted; the bad and evil I separated from the people."[15]

Concerning Babylon itself and its splendor under Nebuchadnezzar II much is known. Many of the king's inscriptions deal with his

---

[12] That two different days are given might possibly correspond with the beginning and the completion of the final destruction. For the rabbinic tradition to this effect see below p.328 n.4. For the chronology in the light of the Babylonian chronicles see David N. Freedman in BA 19 (1956), pp.56f.; W. F. Albright in BASOR 143 (1956), pp.31f.; Edwin R. Thiele in BASOR 143 (Oct. 1956), pp.22-27; Hayim Tadmor in JNES 15 (1956), pp.226-230; A. Malamat in IEJ 6 (1956), pp.246-256; J. Philip Hyatt in JBL 75 (1956), pp.275-284; and see also the Appendix in this book.

[13] WCCK p.95.

[14] Against Apion. I, 21 (quoting "the Phoenician record"); Ant. x, xi, 1 (citing a certain Philostratus, author of a History of Phoenicia). The statement in Against Apion puts the beginning of the siege in the seventh year of Nebuchadnezzar (598 B.C.), but it has been surmised that this is a corruption from the seventeenth year (588 B.C.). Ezekiel's prophecy (chapters 26-28) against Tyre, which is probably connected with Nebuchadnezzar's siege, is dated (26:1) in the eleventh year, doubtless meaning the eleventh year of the exile of Jehoiachin.

[15] Barton, Archaeology and the Bible, p.478.

extensive building operations, and his capital city was excavated thoroughly by the Deutsche Orientgesellschaft under the direction of Robert Koldewey from 1899 onward.[16] Nebuchadnezzar's work included the design and construction of a vast system of fortifications, and the building of streets, canals, temples, and palaces. The king could well have uttered the words which are put in his mouth in Daniel 4:30, "Is not this great Babylon, which I have built by my mighty power as a royal residence and for the glory of my majesty?"

A general view of the tremendous complex of ruins that is Babylon today is shown in Fig. 83. Most prominent is the Ishtar Gate, a double gate leading through the double wall of fortifications and adorned with rows of bulls and dragons in enameled, colored brick.[17] The gate gave access to the city's processional street whose walls were lined with enameled lions like the one shown in Fig. 84. The throne room in the palace of Nebuchadnezzar II likewise was adorned with enameled bricks in patterns such as are shown in Fig. 85. In the temple area the most conspicuous structure was the ziggurat which Nebuchadnezzar rebuilt (cf. p. 50). Only the ground plan now remains but Herodotus says that it rose to a height of eight stages, with an ascent to the top running spirally around the successive towers.[18] Not far away was Esagila ("House whose Top is Lofty"), the temple of Marduk or Bel, which the king also restored, a tremendous pile, built with step-backs like a skyscraper in a modern city. Most famous of all Nebuchadnezzar's works at Babylon were the hanging gardens which the king built in terraces to compensate his Median queen for the absence of her beloved mountains, and which were known to the Greeks as constituting one of the seven wonders of the world. The gardens can no longer be identified with any certainty. The ruins of a series of vaulted rooms found near the Ishtar Gate were believed by the excavators to represent their substructure, but now appear more probably to have been a part of some other important public building, perhaps a distribution depot for the royal storehouses.

Thus Nebuchadnezzar II was interested in construction as well as destruction, and under his rule the arts of civilization flourished.

[16] Koldewey, *Das wieder erstehende Babylon.* 4th ed. 1925; Oscar Reuther, *Die Innenstadt von Babylon* (*Merkes*). 2 vols. 1926.

[17] R. Koldewey, *Das Ischtar-Tor in Babylon.* 1918.

[18] I, 181. For a reconstruction of the Tower of Babel according to a description on a cuneiform tablet of the third century B.C. see E. Unger, *Assyrische und babylonische Kunst.* 1927, Fig. 104. See also Parrot, *The Tower of Babel.*

The typical Babylonian gentleman, as described by Herodotus little
more than a century later, was obviously a man of culture: "For
clothing, they wear a linen tunic, reaching to the feet; over this the
Babylonian puts on another tunic, of wool, and wraps himself in a
white mantle; he wears the shoes of his country, which are like
Boeotian sandals. Their hair is worn long, and covered by caps; the
whole body is perfumed. Every man has a seal and a carven staff,
and on every staff is some image, such as that of an apple or a rose
or a lily or an eagle: no one carries a staff without a device."[19]

The inscriptions of Nebuchadnezzar also express lofty sentiments
in religion:

> O eternal prince! Lord of all being!
> As for the king whom thou lovest, and
> Whose name thou hast proclaimed
> As was pleasing to thee,
> Do thou lead aright his life,
> Guide him in a straight path.
> I am the prince, obedient to thee,
> The creature of thy hand;
> Thou hast created me, and
> With dominion over all people
> Thou hast entrusted me.
> According to thy grace, O Lord,
> Which thou dost bestow on
> All people,
> Cause me to love thy supreme dominion,
> And create in my heart
> The worship of thy god-head,
> And grant whatever is pleasing to thee,
> Because thou hast fashioned my life.[20]

THE CAPTIVITY OF JEHOIACHIN

Amidst the splendors of Babylon, however, our greatest interest lies
in the inquiry as to whether any traces of the Jewish exiles remain.
A discovery of much importance to the biblical archeologist makes
it possible to give an affirmative answer to this question.[21] In the
ruins of the vaulted building near the Ishtar Gate which was mentioned just above, some three hundred cuneiform tablets were un-

[19] i, 195; cf. Ezekiel 23:14f. For the daily life in general of the period 700-530
B.C. see Georges Contenau, *Everyday Life in Babylon and Assyria*. 1954.
[20] Goodspeed, *A History of the Babylonians and Assyrians*, p.348.
[21] Ernst F. Weidner in *Mélanges Syriens offerts a Monsieur René Dussaud*. ii,
1939, pp.923-927; W. F. Albright in BA 5 (1942), pp.49-55; Oppenheim in ANET
p.308; D. Winton Thomas in PEQ 1950, pp.5-8.

earthed. Upon study these have been found to date from between 595 and 570 B.C., and to contain lists of rations such as barley and oil paid to craftsmen and captives who lived in and near Babylon at that time. Among the recipients of these rations are persons from Egypt, Philistia, Phoenicia, Asia Minor, Elam, Media, Persia, and Judah. The Jews who are mentioned include some with such biblical names as Gaddiel, Semachiah, and Shelemiah, the last named being called a "gardener." But the name of most sigificance to us is none other than that of Yaukin, king of Judah, with whom also five royal princes are listed.

The name of this king is written in several ways on the tablets, but clearly was pronounced something like "Yow-keen." The same name had already been found stamped on some jar handles in Palestine and had been recognized as an abbreviated form of Jehoiachin. On the tablets from Babylon, Yaukin is explicitly called "king of the land of Yahud." Yahud is simply a shortened form of the name of Judah such as is perfectly familiar in the time after the exile (cf. p. 195). Since the date of the tablets in general corresponds to the time when the first Jewish exiles were in Babylon, and since one of the documents which mentions Yaukin is specifically dated in 592 B.C., there can be little doubt that the reference is to the biblical Jehoiachin himself, who at that time was residing with his family in the land of his banishment.

Immediately after the name of Yaukin, the tablets three times refer to his five sons who are described as in the hands of an attendant with the Jewish name of Kenaiah. Doubtless several or all of these young sons lived to be included in the list of seven sons of Jehoiachin (Jeconiah) given in I Chronicles 3:17f., where Shealtiel is named as the oldest (cf. Matthew 1:12; Luke 3:27).

It is evident from these tablets that the Babylonians themselves continued to regard Jehoiachin as the legitimate claimant to the throne of Judah, although they did not see fit to restore him to actual rule. At this time he seems to have been free, moreover, to move about in the city, as is suggested by the distribution of rations to him. Presumably it was only at a later date, therefore, that he was cast into the prison out of which in the thirty-seventh year of his captivity we find him being lifted up and restored to favorable and even preferential treatment (II Kings 25:27-30).

In view of this understanding of Jehoiachin's position in Babylon, the dating of events by Jewish writers according to the years of his captivity is thoroughly understandable. He was the lawful but exiled king of Judah. Since his actual rulership had been terminated by the Babylonians, events could hardly be dated by the years of his reign but they could be stated in terms of the years of his exile. Such a mention of his thirty-seventh year is found in II Kings 25:27 and Jeremiah 52:31, while in Ezekiel there is a series of such dates (1:2; 8:1; etc.) which evidently have the same reference and run from the fifth to the twenty-seventh year.[22]

In connection with the exile Ezekiel mentions the river Chebar a number of times (1:1, etc.). This was probably a large canal called Kabaru which came out of the Euphrates above Babylon and flowed past Nippur before it entered the Euphrates again. There are references to it in business documents found at Nippur, written in the time of Artaxerxes I.[23]

NABUNAID AND BELSHAZZAR

The New Babylonian empire was also destined to fall, and the decline came rapidly. Nebuchadnezzar II was followed on the throne by his son Amel-Marduk (561-560), the Evil-merodach of II Kings 25:27. This man was soon slain by his brother-in-law, Nergal-shar-usur (Neriglisar). The latter ruled but four years (559-556) and his son, Labashi-Marduk (Laborosoardoch), was on the throne only a few months (556) when conspirators made away with him. One of the conspirators, a Babylonian noble named Nabunaid (Nabonidus), then ruled (555-539) as the last king of New Babylonia.[24]

In practice, however, Nabunaid shared the kingship with his own oldest son Belshazzar. Belshazzar is named as the crown prince in Babylonian inscriptions,[25] and in the so-called Verse Account of Nabunaid we read the following statement concerning Nabunaid:

> He entrusted the 'Camp' to his oldest son, the first-born,
> The troops everywhere in the country he ordered under his
> command.

> He let everything go, entrusted the kingship to him
> And, himself, he started out for a long journey,
> The military forces of Akkad marching with him;
> He turned towards Tema deep in the west.

[22] For discussion of these dates see the Appendix.
[23] W. F. Albright in JBL 51 (1932), p.100; G. A. Cooke, *The Book of Ezekiel*. ICC, 1937, I, p.4; Herbert G. May in IB 6, p.68.
[24] cf. Berossos quoted by Josephus, *Against Apion*. I, 20.
[25] ANET p.309 n.5.

He started out the expedition on a path leading to a
   distant region. When he arrived there,
He killed in battle the prince of Tema,
Slaughtered the flocks of those who dwell in the city
   as well as in the countryside,
And he, himself, took his residence in Tema, the forces
   of Akkad were also stationed there.

He made the town beautiful, built there his palace
Like the palace in Babylon, he also built walls
For the fortifications of the town and. . . .
He surrounded the town with sentinels. . . .[26]

This passage states plainly that before Nabunaid started on an
expedition to Tema he divided the rule of the empire between himself and his son and entrusted actual kingship to Belshazzar. Then
he undertook the distant campaign which was probably in Arabia,
conquered Tema, established his residence there, and built that city
with the glory of Babylon. Likewise the Nabunaid chronicle contains the following statements concerning King Nabunaid:

"Seventh year: The king stayed in Tema, the crown prince, his officials
and his army were in Akkad. . . .
"Ninth year: Nabunaid, the king, stayed in Tema; the crown prince, the
officials and the army were in Akkad. . . .
"Tenth year: The king stayed in Tema; the crown prince, his officials
and his army were in Akkad. . . .
"Eleventh year: The king stayed in Tema; the crown prince, the
officials and his army were in Akkad."[27]

Each of these initial statements for the seventh, ninth, tenth, and
eleventh years of the king is supplemented by this comment: "The
king did not come to Babylon for the ceremonies of the month
Nisanu, Nabu did not come to Babylon, Bel did not go out from
Esagila in procession, the festival of the New Year was omitted."
This means that during the years mentioned Nabunaid was in
Tema and Belshazzar was in Babylon and that owing to the absence
of Nabunaid the usual New Year's festival was not observed. Since,
therefore, Belshazzar actually exercised the co-regency at Babylon
and may well have continued to do so unto the end, the book of
Daniel (5:30) is not wrong in representing him as the last king of
Babylon.[28]

26 ANET pp.313f.   27 ANET pp.305f. (ANEA p.203).
28 R. P. Dougherty, *Nabonidus and Belshazzar*. 1929, pp.105-200. Julius Lewy
(in HUCA 19 [1945-46], pp.434-450) thinks that the stay of Nabunaid at Tema began
in the fourth year of his reign and lasted at least until the eleventh year. He suggests

THE FALL OF BABYLON

In the seventeenth year of King Nabunaid, Babylon fell to Cyrus the Persian. The Nabunaid chronicle gives exact dates. In the month of Tashritu on the fourteenth day, October 10, 539 B.C., the Persian forces took Sippar; on the sixteenth day, October 12, "the army of Cyrus entered Babylon without battle"; and in the month of Arahsamnu, on the third day, October 29, Cyrus himself came into the city.[29]

The fall of Babylon is narrated not only in the Nabunaid chronicle but also in the inscription on the famous cylinder of Cyrus (Fig. 86). The latter reads in part as follows:

"Marduk . . . scanned and looked through all the countries, searching for a righteous ruler. . . . He pronounced the name of Cyrus, king of Anshan, declared him to be the ruler of all the world. . . . He made him set out on the road to Babylon, going at his side like a real friend. His widespread troops—their number, like that of the water of a river, could not be established—strolled along, their weapons packed away. Without any battle, he made him enter his town Babylon, sparing Babylon any calamity. He delivered into his hands Nabunaid, the king who did not worship him."[30]

If Cyrus claimed to be sent by Marduk, the Second Isaiah felt that the conqueror was anointed by the Lord himself for the task of releasing the Jewish exiles and returning them to their home (Isaiah 45:1; cf. 44:28). The spirit of Cyrus' decree of release which is quoted in the Old Testament (II Chronicles 36:23; Ezra 1:2-4) is confirmed by the Cyrus cylinder, where the king relates that he allowed the captives to return to their various countries and rebuild their temples:

---

that Nabunaid transferred his residence to this place because it was an ancient center of worship of the moon-god, Sin, to whom he was devoted above Marduk and all other gods. In Daniel 5:18 Nebuchadnezzar is named as the father of Belshazzar, instead of Nabunaid. It has been surmised that Belshazzar was a grandson of Nebuchadnezzar, who might then be referred to, after Semitic usage, as his father. It is also possible that, in Jewish tradition, Babylonian legends were transferred to Nebuchadnezzar which originally had to do with Nabunaid. This would be understandable inasmuch as it was Nebuchadnezzar rather than Nabunaid who figured prominently in Jewish history and was a great enemy of the Jewish people. Thus the story of how Nebuchadnezzar went mad and was driven forth from men to dwell for seven years with the beasts of the field (Daniel 4) might reflect the stay of Nabunaid in the wilderness at Tema for about that same length of time, as it was viewed by the priests of Marduk at Babylon. See Wolfram von Soden in ZAW 53 (1935), pp.84,86f.

[29] ANET p.306 (ANEA p.203); PDBC pp.13,29.

[30] ANET pp.315f. (ANEA p.206); cf. Robert W. Rogers, *Cuneiform Parallels to the Old Testament.* 1912, p.381; *A Guide to the Babylonian and Assyrian Antiquities, British Museum.* 3d ed. 1922, p.144.

"As to the region from . . . as far as Ashur and Susa, Agade, Eshnunna, the towns Zamban, Me-Turnu, Der as well as the region of the Gutians, I returned to these sacred cities on the other side of the Tigris, the sanctuaries of which have been ruins for a long time, the images which used to live therein and established for them permanent sanctuaries. I also gathered all their former inhabitants and returned to them their habitations. Furthermore, I resettled upon the command of Marduk, the great lord, all the gods of Sumer and Akkad whom Nabunaid has brought into Babylon to the anger of the lord of the gods, unharmed, in their former chapels, the places which make them happy.

"May all the gods whom I have resettled in their sacred cities ask daily Bel and Nabu for a long life for me and may they recommend me to him; to Marduk, my lord, they may say this: 'Cyrus, the king who worships you, and Cambyses, his son. . .' . . . all of them I settled in a peaceful place. . . ."[31]

8. THE PERSIAN EMPIRE, 539-331 B.C.

CYRUS THE GREAT, who conquered Babylon in 539 B.C. and reigned there from 538 to 530, was the founder of the Persian Empire. In order to understand his place in history it is necessary to indicate briefly the earlier happenings in the land of Persia.

THE EARLIER HISTORY OF PERSIA

The homeland of Persia was the western and larger part of the Iranian plateau, which stretches from the Indus on the east to the Tigris and Euphrates on the west. It is a high, arid plateau overlooked by vast barren mountain ranges. The native name of the land, and the name to which the Persian government officially returned in 1935, is Iran. This name, Airyana or Iran, means "the [land] of the Aryans,"[1] and refers to the Aryan-speaking people who settled on the highland. Before the Aryans came, aboriginal Caspians had lived on the plateau and perhaps were the first people to develop agriculture and metallurgy. Then, around 1500 B.C., the Aryans entered the country.[2]

The two Aryan tribes which were to attain the greatest importance were the Amadai or Medes and the people from the land of Parsua (west of Lake Urmia) or Persians. Both are mentioned for the first time in annals of Shalmaneser III concerning Assyrian campaigns

---

[31] ANET p.316. For the "substantial historicity" of the edict of Cyrus as given in the Old Testament cf. W. F. Albright in BA 9 (1946), p.7. See also Kurt Galling in ZDPV 70 (1954), p.7.

[1] Old Persian, *Aryanam khshathram*; Middle Persian, *Eran*. Ernst Herzfeld and Arthur Keith in *A Survey of Persian Art*. I, p.42 n.1.

[2] Ernst Herzfeld, *Archaeological History of Iran*. 1935, p.8.

in the region of the Caspian plateau.[3] The Medes occupied the north-western part of the country, now Iraq-i-ajam, with their capital at Hagmatana, known later as Ecbatana and now as Hamadan. According to Herodotus[4] Ecbatana was founded by "a clever man called Deioces" who for the first time united the nomadic Median tribes into one nation and ruled as king. Deioces was succeeded by his son Phraortes, as Herodotus further states, and he in turn by his son Cyaxares. Cyaxares (or Uvakhshatra) we have already seen cooperating with Nabopolassar in the overthrow of Nineveh in 612 B.C. (p. 219).

The Persians moved on southward and settled not far from the Elamite land Anzan or Anshan in a region to which they gave the name Parsamash or Parsumash in memory of their old homeland of Parsua. By about 700 B.C. their leader was Hakhamanish or Achaemenes whose name was preserved by the later Persian kings. Around 675 to around 640 B.C. Teispes was king of Parsumash, and he was able to extend the Persian holdings to include a region east of Anshan and north of what we call the Persian Gulf. This area became known as Parsa or Persian land. Teispes divided his empire between his two sons, Ariaramna (c.640-c.615) receiving Parsa and Kurash or Cyrus I (c.640-c.600) receiving Parsumash.

In the land of Elam, it may be explained, a series of kingdoms had been in existence for many centuries but mostly under domination by Mesopotamian rulers from Sargon (p. 46) to the Kassites. In the first quarter of the twelfth century Kutir-Nahhunte of Elam ended Kassite control and established a true Elamite Empire but by the middle of the century Elam succumbed again to Nebuchadnezzar I. Elam enjoyed other periods of dominance but finally about 646 B.C. was destroyed and depopulated by the Assyrians.[5] Thus it was possible for the Persians to acquire much Elamite territory and we find Kanbujiya or Cambyses I (c.600-c.559), the successor of Cyrus I, bearing the title "king of the city Anshan."

Up to this time the Persians had been under the domination of the Medes. Nominally Cambyses I was a king in his own right, yet actually he was subordinate to the Median king Astyages (p. 220) to whose daughter Mandane he was married. The subserviency was not to last much longer. The son of Cambyses I and Mandane was Cyrus the Great.[6]

[3] ARAB I, §581.   [4] I, 96-103.
[5] René Grousset in *A Survey of Persian Art*. I, pp.61,64.
[6] Herodotus. I, 107-130.

CYRUS II THE GREAT

Cyrus II came to the throne of Anshan around 559 B.C., and Astyages soon recognized that revolt was intended. Astyages therefore marched against Cyrus, but the Median army rebelled and Cyrus was able to proceed to Ecbatana, the capital of his former master, in triumph. Parsa henceforth was the first ranking satrapy in the entire land, Media the second, and Elam the third. The sovereignty of the Persians was definitely established although the Medes continued to have equal honor with the Persians and foreigners spoke of either "the Persians and the Medes" (Esther 1:19) or "the Medes and Persians" (Daniel 5:28, etc.).[7]

Cyrus II extended his conquests swiftly and far. He challenged Croesus, the famously rich king of Lydia, who held sway as far eastward as the Halys River, and defeated him (546 B.C.). Finally he completed his task by conquering Babylon itself (539 B.C.) as we have already seen. Thus was established the mighty Persian Empire in which Judea for the next two centuries remained a province. The new king wrote proudly: "I am Cyrus, king of the world, great king, legitimate king, king of Babylon, king of Sumer and Akkad, king of the four rims of the earth, son of Cambyses, great king, king of Anshan, grandson of Cyrus, great king, king of Anshan, descendant of Teispes, great king, king of Anshan, of a family which always exercised kingship."[8]

Throughout his extensive campaigns, and in contrast with other ancient oriental conquerors, Cyrus always was humane. The lives of Astyages and Croesus were spared and each was allotted a royal train. Babylon was not destroyed but its people won over by his mercy and the Jews were reestablished in their homeland as we have seen.

Cyrus made his capital at Pasargadae in the land of Parsa. Here he built a palace on whose ruins the repeated inscription is still to be read, "I, Cyrus, the king, the Achaemenid."[9] The royal buildings seem to have formed a group consisting of scattered individual pavilions set amidst gardens, and surrounded by a masonry wall some thirteen feet in thickness.[10] The carving shown in Fig. 87 adorned a doorway at Pasargadae and is our earliest extant Persian relief. The

[7] Cameron, *History of Early Iran*, pp.179-226.
[8] ANET p.316.
[9] E. Herzfeld, *Archaeologische Mitteilungen aus Iran.* i (1929-30), p.10.
[10] Friedrich Wachtsmuth in *A Survey of Persian Art.* i, p.309.

strange four-winged genius is believed by some to represent the deified Cyrus.

Nine years after the surrender of Babylon, Cyrus marched eastward to meet enemies and was killed in battle (530 B.C.). His body was brought back to Pasargadae and buried in a tomb which still exists and which consists of only a single small room on a foundation course of six steps (Fig. 88). Arrian (A.D. c.96-c.180) describes the tomb as follows: "The tomb itself was built, at the base, with stones cut square and raised into rectangular form. Above, there was a chamber with a stone roof and with a door leading into it so narrow that with difficulty, and after great trouble, one man, and he a small one, could enter. And in the chamber was placed a golden sarcophagus, in which Cyrus' body had been buried."[11] Plutarch (A.D. c.46-c.120) says that the tomb had this inscription: "O, man, whosoever thou art and whencesoever thou comest, for I know that thou wilt come, I am Cyrus, and I won for the Persians their empire. Do not, therefore, begrudge me this little earth which covers my body."[12]

CAMBYSES II

Cyrus was followed on the throne by his son Cambyses II (529-522) who defeated the Egyptians at Pelusium (pp. 132f.) and added Egypt to the Persian dominions. The Persian Empire was now the greatest the world had even seen. Not long after his Egyptian victories, however, Cambyses went mad and committed suicide. The new empire nearly broke up in the confusion which followed. Gaumata, a Magian, declared himself to be Smerdis, the younger brother of Cambyses (who actually had been murdered), and seized the throne. Also national kings of Babylonia, Media, Armenia, and other provinces which had been annexed by Cyrus, attempted to break away.

DARIUS I THE GREAT

It was an Achaemenid prince of a younger line, Daryavaush or Darius I the Great (521-486), son of Hystaspes,[13] who saved the empire. The name of the father of Darius, Hystaspes or Vishtaspa, is the same as that of the traditional royal convert and patron of Zoroaster. The traditional dates for Zoroaster (c.660-c.583) are too early to allow for the identification of the father of Darius with the patron of the prophet, however, and either it must be supposed that

---

[11] *Anabasis of Alexander.* VI, xxix, 5. tr. E. I. Robson, LCL (1929-33) II, p.197.
[12] *Life of Alexander.* LXIX, 2. tr. B. Perrin, LCL (1914-26) VII, p.417. cf. below p.244.
[13] Herodotus. I, 209.

the latter was an earlier Vishtaspa or else the date of Zoroaster's birth must be brought down to a later date, perhaps around 570 B.C.[14] At any rate it is well known that Darius I was a zealous worshiper of Ahura Mazda, the god preached by Zoroaster, and so were Xerxes and Artaxerxes as well.

In the Old Testament the appearance of the prophet Haggai in Jerusalem is dated (Haggai 1:1) on the first day of the sixth month of the second year of Darius, which would be August 29, 520 B.C.; and the first sermon of Zechariah is placed (Zechariah 1:1) in the eighth month of the same year or in October/November 520 B.C. Likewise the completion of the rebuilt Jewish temple is dated on the third day of the month Adar in the sixth year of Darius (Ezra 6:15), or March 12, 515 B.C.[15]

THE ROCK OF BEHISTUN

Returning now to the rebellion with which Darius I was confronted, it may be said that the new king acted swiftly. Gaumata was defeated, seized and killed, and the various provincial uprisings were suppressed. An impressive memorial of the victory over the rebels was left on the famous Rock of Behistun. This great rock looms up above a spring-fed pool of water on the old caravan-road from Ecbatana to Babylon. The rock is really the last peak (3,800 feet high) of a long narrow range of mountains which skirts the plain of Karmanshah on the east. The name by which we customarily refer to it is derived from the small village of Bisitun or Behistun which is now located at its foot. High upon the face of the rock, perhaps five hundred feet above the level of the plain, Darius I carved a large relief panel and accompanied it with many columns of inscription (Fig. 89).[16] The scene represents the king receiving the submission of the rebels. At the left (Fig. 90) we see the life-sized figure of Darius I, accompanied by two attendants. The king's left foot is placed upon the prostrate form of Gaumata, the leading rebel. In his left hand the king grasps a bow while he lifts his right hand toward the winged disk with anthropomorphic head which is the symbol of Ahura Mazda. Behind Gaumata is a procession of rebel leaders, roped together by their necks. The last one, Skunkha the

[14] Herzfeld, *Archaeologische Mitteilungen aus Iran.* II (1930), p.47; cf. A. T. Olmstead, *History of the Persian Empire [Achaemenid Period].* 1948, pp.102f.

[15] cf. Peter R. Ackroyd in JNES 17 (1958), pp.13-27.

[16] cf. E. Herzfeld, *Am Tor von Asien, Felsendenkmale aus Irans Heldenzeit.* 1920, Pl. IX.

Scythian, wearing a high pointed cap, was a later addition to the group. Beside and beneath the sculptured panel are many columns of inscription relating how Darius gained the crown and put down the rebellion. The inscription is composed in three languages, Old Persian, Elamite, and Akkadian (formerly known as Old Persian, Susian, and Babylonian), all written in cuneiform characters. Copies of the inscription were also circulated in distant provinces of the Persian Empire, as is known from the discovery of an Aramaic version of it among papyri at Elephantine in Upper Egypt (p. 239).

The great carving at Behistun was indestructible and unconcealable and hence early became known to travelers in that region. The Arabian geographical writer Ibn Hawkal, who was born at Mosul in the tenth century A.D., described it and supposed that the scene represented "a schoolhouse, with the master and the boys; further in the schoolmaster's hand is an instrument like a strap wherewith to beat."[17] In the early nineteenth century another traveler saw the monument and thought that the winged figure of Ahura Mazda was a cross, and that Darius and his officers and prisoners were the Twelve Apostles![18]

Then in 1835 and following, Henry C. Rawlinson, a British official in the Middle East, made the difficult climb up to the inscription and made copies and squeezes. He said, "The climbing of the rock to arrive at the inscriptions, if not positively dangerous, is a feat at any rate which an antiquary alone could be expected to undertake."[19] Fresh copies were made from the original in 1904 by L. W. King and R. Campbell Thompson, who were sent out by the British Museum,[20] a new photograph of the monument was published in 1943 by George G. Cameron of the Oriental Institute of the University of Chicago (see Fig. 89), and further study of the inscriptions was made by Dr. Cameron in 1948.[21]

Efforts had already been made to read cuneiform, or wedge-shaped writing, particularly by G. F. Grotefend of Germany who was able to identify in other inscriptions the names of Darius and his son Xerxes as well as the title "King of Kings." Rawlinson was finally

---

[17] G. LeStrange, The Lands of the Eastern Caliphate. 1905, p.187.

[18] E. A. W. Budge, The Rise and Progress of Assyriology. 1925, p.30.

[19] A. V. W. Jackson in JAOS 24 (1903), p.81.

[20] King and Thompson, The Sculptures and Inscription of Darius the Great on the Rock of Behistun in Persia. 1907.

[21] Cameron in JNES 2 (1943), pp.115f. and Pl. II; in NGM 98 (1950), pp.825-844; and in JCS 5 (1951), pp.47-54. See also Roland G. Kent in JCS 5 (1951), pp.55-57; W. C. Benedict and Elizabeth von Voigtlander in JCS 10 (1956), pp.1-10.

able to decipher the Persian part of the Behistun inscription and this victory at last led to the reading of the other two languages.[22] Such was the Rosetta Stone of cuneiform decipherment.

Darius I not only dealt effectively with the rebellion which he faced at the beginning of his reign but also continued to rule well the far-flung Persian territories. Indeed his genius lay most of all in the field of administration, and one of his outstanding achievements was the completion of the organization of the empire into twenty satrapies.[23] Furthermore, he undertook extensive works of construction which ranged from the digging of a canal from the Nile to the Red Sea,[24] to the erection of a new capital at Persepolis (p. 241).

Despite the fact that in so many ways Darius I deserved the title "the Great," which has been given him, the closing years of his reign saw the outbreak of the Greco-Persian wars which were to be disastrous for Persia. This conflict grew ultimately out of the fact that the conquests of Cyrus in Asia Minor had included Greek colonies, but the wars now were begun by the Greeks themselves. During the reign of Darius I, Persian armies suffered defeat at Marathon (491 B.C.) and again a few years after his death the Persian fleet was beaten at Salamis (480 B.C.). Thereafter the future belonged to Europe instead of Asia.

NAQSH-I-RUSTAM

Darius I died in 486 B.C. and was buried in a rock-hewn tomb at Naqsh-i-Rustam (Fig. 91) a few miles northeast of Persepolis.[25] The name of this place means "Pictures of Rustam," for the rock sculptures have been associated by the local inhabitants with the legendary Persian hero, Rustam. The tomb of Darius bears trilingual inscriptions which give the king's own account of his achievements and of his character. His words include the following: "Says Darius the king: By the favor of Ahuramazda I am of such a sort that I am a friend to right, I am not a friend to wrong; it is not my desire that the weak man should have wrong done to him by the mighty; nor is that my desire, that the mighty man should have wrong done to him by the weak."[26]

[22] Henry C. Rawlinson, *The Persian Cuneiform Inscription at Behistun.* 1846.
[23] CAH IV, pp.194f.
[24] Roland G. Kent in JNES 1 (1942), pp.415-421.
[25] cf. E. Herzfeld and F. Sarre, *Iranische Felsreliefs.* 1910, Pl. IV.
[26] Roland G. Kent in JNES 4 (1945), pp.39-52.

Similar tombs were later cut from the same cliff for the three successors of Darius—Xerxes, Artaxerxes I, and Darius II—and are to the right and to the left of the tomb of Darius. These tombs do not appear in Fig. 91. The carving which is seen in the lower left hand corner of the illustration is a yet later representation of the Sasanian king Shapur I (A.D. 241-272) receiving the submission of the Emperor Valerian. Not far away and facing the cliff of the royal tombs is a strange structure of stone to which the name Ka'bah-i-Zardusht ("Square [Tomb] of Zoroaster") has been attached. It is thought perhaps to have been a Zoroastrian fire temple, and may later have served as the shrine where the Sasanian kings were crowned and the crown jewels were kept.

XERXES

Darius was followed on the throne of Persia by his son Khshayarsha or Xerxes (485-465 B.C.). An important historical inscription of Xerxes discovered at Persepolis lists the numerous subject nations over which he ruled, tells of uprisings with which he had to contend at the time of his accession to the throne, and reveals his devotion to the worship of Ahura Mazda. This record reads as follows:

"Ahuramazda is the great god who gave us this earth, who gave us that sky, who gave us mankind, who gave to his worshipers prosperity, who made Xerxes, the king, rule the multitudes as only king, give alone orders to the other kings.

"I am Xerxes, the great king, the only king, the king of all countries which speak all kinds of languages, the king of this entire big and far-reaching earth,—the son of king Darius, the Achaemenian, a Persian, son of a Persian, an Aryan of Aryan descent.

"Thus speaks king Xerxes: These are the countries—in addition to Persia—over which I am king under the 'shadow' of Ahuramazda, over which I hold sway, which are bringing their tribute to me—whatever is commanded them by me, that they do and they abide by my laws—: Media, Elam, Arachosia, Urartu (Armenia), Drangiana, Parthia, Haria, Bactria, Sogdia, Chorasmia, Babylonia, Assyria, Sattagydia, Sardis, Egypt, the Ionians who live on the salty sea and those who live beyond the salty sea, Maka, Arabia, Gandara, India, Cappadocia, Da'an, the Amyrgian Cimmerians, the Cimmerians wearing pointed caps, the Skudra, the Akupish, Libya, Banneshu (Carians) and Kush.

"Thus speaks king Xerxes: After I became king, there were some among these countries the names of which are written above, which revolted but I crushed these countries, after Ahuramazda had given me his support, under the 'shadow' of Ahuramazda, and I put them again into their former political status. Furthermore, there were among these countries some which performed religious service to the 'Evil Gods' (Daivas), but under the 'shadow' of Ahuramazda I destroyed these temples of the 'Evil Gods' and proclaimed as follows: 'You must not perform religious service to the 'Evil Gods' any more!' Wherever formerly religious service was performed to the 'Evil Gods,' I, myself, performed a religious service to Ahuramazda and the *arta* (cosmic order) reverently. Furthermore, there were other things which were done in a bad way, and these too I made in the correct way.

"All these things which I did, I performed under the 'shadow' of Ahuramazda and Ahuramazda gave me his support until I had accomplished everything.

"Whosoever you are, in future days who thinks as follows: 'May I be prosperous in this life and blessed after my death!'—do live according to this law which Ahuramazda has promulgated: 'Perform religious service only for Ahuramazda and the *arta* reverently.' A man who lives according to this law which Ahuramazda has promulgated, and who performs religious service only to Ahuramazda and the *arta* reverently, will be prosperous while he is alive and—when dead—he will become blessed.

"Thus speaks king Xerxes: May Ahuramazda protect me, my family and these countries from all evil. This I do ask of Ahuramazda and this Ahuramazda may grant me!"[27]

Xerxes is no doubt the Ahasuerus[28] who is mentioned in Ezra 4:6 between Darius and Artaxerxes and who also figures prominently in the book of Esther (1:1, etc.).

ARTAXERXES I

The successor of Xerxes was Artakhshathra or Artaxerxes I Longimanus (464-424 B.C.). According to Nehemiah 2:1 the request of Nehemiah to visit Jerusalem was made in the month Nisan in the twentieth year of Artaxerxes; assuming, as is probable, that the reference is to Artaxerxes I, the date indicated is in April/May, 445 B.C.

General confirmation of a date around this time for Nehemiah is found in the Elephantine papyri, which belong toward the end of this same century and mention by name two persons connected in the Old Testament with Nehemiah. Both are named in a letter which is dated in the seventeenth year of King Darius II, 408 B.C.[29]

---

[27] ANET pp.316f.; Erich F. Schmidt, *The Treasury of Persepolis and Other Discoveries in the Homeland of the Achaemenians.* OIC 21, 1939, pp.14f.

[28] The Hebrew אחשורוש represents the Persian Khshayarsha of which the Greek form is Xerxes. In Esther the LXX (ed. Swete, II, p.755) renders the name as Artaxerxes and is followed in this by Josephus (*Ant.* XI, vi) who names Artaxerxes I as king in the days of Esther.

[29] ANET p.492. The equation of the date with 408 B.C. supposes that Egyptian custom was followed and the accession year of Darius was counted as his first regnal year.

One is Sanballat who is mentioned in connection with reference to his two sons, Delaiah and Shelemiah; the other is Johanan who is spoken of as high priest in Jerusalem. Sanballat was the leading opponent of Nehemiah (Nehemiah 2:19, etc.). Johanan was grandson of Eliashib (Nehemiah 12:23) who was high priest when Nehemiah came to Jerusalem (Nehemiah 3:1).

In Ezra 7:1, 8, it is stated that Ezra came to Jerusalem in the seventh year of Artaxerxes. If this means Artaxerxes I the date was 458 B.C. and Ezra preceded Nehemiah. Since Jehohanan the son of Eliashib is mentioned in connection with the work of Ezra (Ezra 10:6), however, it seems probable that Ezra followed Nehemiah. In this case Ezra's mission may have fallen under Artaxerxes II, the seventh year of whose reign was 398 B.C.[30]

THE ELEPHANTINE PAPYRI

The Elephantine papyri referred to above give us an interesting glimpse of one of the outlying regions of the Persian empire at this time. These documents were discovered in 1903 on the island of Elephantine at the First Cataract in Egypt.[31] They date from toward the end of the fifth century B.C. and come from a Jewish military colony which was settled here. The papyri are written in Aramaic, which was the language of diplomacy and of trade throughout western Asia in the Persian period, and which was gradually replacing Hebrew as the everyday tongue of the Jewish people not only abroad but also at home in Palestine.

The contents of the Elephantine papyri are varied, ranging from the copy of the Behistun inscription of Darius mentioned above (p. 235), to such a document as a Jewish marriage contract. In one letter, dated about 419 B.C., the Jews of Elephantine are instructed by the authority of the Persian government to celebrate the Passover according to the official practice of the Jerusalem temple as embodied in the priestly code (Exodus 12:1-20). Again we learn that there was a Jewish temple at Elephantine which had just been sacked in an anti-Jewish pogrom of around 411 B.C. As their national God, the Jews of this colony worshiped Yahweh, whom they referred

---

[30] Albright, *The Archaeology of Palestine and the Bible*, pp.169f.; R. H. Pfeiffer, *Introduction to the Old Testament*. 1941, pp.819f.,827; Norman H. Snaith in ZAW 63 (1951), pp.53-66; H. H. Rowley, *The Servant of the Lord and Other Essays on the Old Testament*. 1952, pp.131-159; and in BJRL 38 (1955), pp.166-198.

[31] E. Sachau, *Aramäische Papyrus und Ostraka aus einer jüdischen Militär-Kolonie zu Elephantine*. 2 vols. 1911; A. Ungnad, *Aramäische Papyrus aus Elephantine*. 1911; A. Cowley, *Aramaic Papyri of the Fifth Century B.C.* 1923.

to by the name Yahu. Also three other divine names appear, Eshem-bethel, Herem-bethel, and 'Anath-bethel or 'Anath-Yahu. These usually have been interpreted as polytheistic borrowings on the part of the Elephantine Jews from their pagan surroundings. It is possible, however, that they represent hypostatized aspects of Yahweh under the respective titles, "Name of the House of God," "Sacredness of the House of God," and "Sign of the House of God."[32]

Other papyri from Elephantine, which have only recently become known and been published by the Brooklyn Museum, show that the temple was rebuilt after its destruction, and contain mention of Yahu as "the god who dwells in Yeb[33] the fortress," much as Psalm 135:21 speaks of Yahweh as the one "who dwells in Jerusalem." The new papyri also show that Egypt was still under the authority of Persia in the first years of the reign of Artaxerxes II.[34]

As both the Elephantine papyri and the biblical records show, the Persian kings took an interest in the welfare and religious life of their subjects. Despite some exceptions, it may be said in general that the Achaemenids exercised a more liberal rule than any other oriental despots of the ancient world. They manifested a great capacity for administration and adhered to relatively high ethical conceptions. Under their sway peace was maintained throughout the Orient for approximately two centuries. The different civilizations which fell under their dominion were allowed to continue in existence, and the various religions were tolerated. Instead of sudden, random exactions of tribute, systematic taxation was introduced and with it civil progress was supported in many ways. Roads were repaired carefully, agriculture was protected, and justice was administered systematically and well. The attitude of the Jews is significant in this regard, for we find them, although still a subject people, displaying an appreciation of their Achaemenid masters which contrasts strongly with their resentment against all of their other conquerors, Egyptian, Assyrian, Chaldean, Seleucid, and Roman.[35]

[32] Albright, *From the Stone Age to Christianity*, p.286.
[33] The Egyptian name of Elephantine.
[34] Emil G. Kraeling, *The Brooklyn Museum Aramaic Papyri, New Documents of the Fifth Century B.C. from the Jewish Colony at Elephantine.* 1953; and in BA 15 (1952), pp.50-67. Fourteen of the new papyri bear dates, and for the evidence they provide concerning the Jewish calendar in use at this time at Elephantine see S. H. Horn and L. H. Wood in JNES 13 (1954), pp.1-20.
[35] René Grousset in *A Survey of Persian Art*. I, pp.66f.

PERSEPOLIS

The most impressive evidence of the height which Persian culture attained is to be found in the ruins of Persepolis.[36] This was the place to which Darius I transferred the main capital of Persia from Pasargadae (pp. 232, 236), and it remained from that time on the chief home of the Achaemenian dynasty. Archeological excavations have been conducted at Persepolis by the Oriental Institute of the University of Chicago under the direction of Ernst Herzfeld in 1931-1934 and of Erich F. Schmidt in 1935-1939. The location of the new capital was some twenty-five miles southwest of Pasargadae, on a spur of what is now known as the Kuh-i-Rahmat or "Mountain of Mercy," overlooking the plain now called Marv Dasht.

Persepolis was surrounded by a triple fortification system with one row of towers and walls running over the crest of the mountain itself. The chief buildings were erected upon a large, roughly rectangular, terrace. Here stood the palace of Darius, known as the Tachara (Fig. 92). It had an entrance hall opening across the entire width of the building, and a main hall some fifty feet square. It was adorned with relief sculptures which are still well preserved, and bears the repeated inscription, "I am Darius, great king, king of kings, king of lands, son of Hystaspes, the Achaemenid, who constructed this palace.[37]

A building known today as the Tripylon probably was the first reception hall of Persepolis. In its stairway reliefs, rows of dignitaries are shown ascending, and on its eastern gate jambs Darius I is shown on the throne, with Xerxes, the crown prince, standing behind him (Fig. 93). The later and greater audience halls at Persepolis were the so-called Apadana, begun by Darius I and completed by Xerxes, and the Hall of One Hundred Columns started by Xerxes and finished by Artaxerxes I. The Apadana or Hall of Xerxes was a huge room approximately 195 feet square and surrounded by vestibules on three sides. The wooden roof was supported by seventy-two stone columns of which thirteen still stand. Several of these are shown in their classic beauty in Fig. 94. The building stood upon an elevated platform which was ascended by two monumental sculptured stairways. Of these the northern one has always been partially exposed

---

[36] For Persepolis see now Erich F. Schmidt, *Persepolis*, I, *Structures, Reliefs, Inscriptions.* OIP 68, 1953; II, *Contents of the Treasury and Other Discoveries.* OIP 69, 1957.

[37] F. H. Weissbach, *Die Keilinschriften der Achämeniden.* 1911, pp.80f.

and is badly weathered, but the eastern was discovered and excavated first by Professor Herzfeld. The reliefs on the latter are very well preserved and show the opposite side of the same procession which is sculptured on the northern stairway. The chief figures are those of envoys from twenty-three subject nations who are bringing New Year's gifts to the Persian emperor. A portion of these reliefs is illustrated in Fig. 95. In the upper panel we see Parthians bringing vessels and leading a camel, in the center are Gandarans from the region of Afghanistan with a humped bull, shields and lances, and in the lower panel are Bactrians with gold vessels and another camel. The reliefs are regarded as the greatest monument of Achaemenian art, and the rhythmical arrangement of the figures in the procession and the excellent delineation of the animal forms are particularly noteworthy.[38]

The central unit of the Hall of One Hundred Columns was even more immense than that of the Apadana, being a room over 229 feet square. The roof was once supported by one hundred columns, the northern portico was flanked by huge stone bulls, and eight stone gateways were ornamented with throne scenes and representations of the king's combat with demons.

Another impressive structure on the royal terrace was the Gate of Xerxes, which stood above the stairway leading up from the plain. As in the Assyrian palaces, colossal bulls guarded the entrances of this gate. Those on the eastern side, shown in Fig. 96, are human headed, bearded, and crowned. The accompanying inscription reads, "King Xerxes says: By the grace of Ahura Mazda I constructed this gateway called All-Countries."[39]

Other buildings at Persepolis include the Harem of Darius and Xerxes, the residence of Xerxes known as the Hadish, a badly weathered palace which may have been begun by Xerxes and completed by Artaxerxes I, and the royal treasury which contains fine reliefs of Darius and Xerxes like those on the Tripylon.

ECBATANA AND SUSA

Both Ecbatana and Susa were also important centers of the Persian Empire, the former serving as a summer residence of the kings and the latter as a winter capital. Ecbatana, as we have seen (p. 231), was the former Median capital. Polybius (c.208-c.126 B.C.) says that

---

[38] Stanley Casson in A Survey of Persian Art. I, p.349.
[39] Weissbach, Die Keilinschriften der Achämeniden, pp.108f.

the citadel of the city was strongly fortified, and he gives a description of the palace of the Persian kings in which he says that "the woodwork was all of cedar and cypress, but no part of it was left exposed, and the rafters, the compartments of the ceiling, and the columns in the porticoes and colonnades were plated with either silver or gold, and all the tiles were silver."[40] Little now remains of the ancient city, but an inscription has been found there in which Artaxerxes II Mnemon (404-359) celebrated the erection of a palace.[41]

Susa became a part of the Achaemenid empire when Cyrus took Babylon and all of its provinces. The city is called Shushan in the Old Testament (Nehemiah 1:1; Esther 1:2, etc.; Daniel 8:2; ASV), just as the people there today call it Shush (p. 21) which was probably the ancient name. The greatest monument of Persian Susa is the royal palace which was begun by Darius I and enlarged and further beautified by the later kings.[42] The foundation of the building was commemorated by Darius I in an inscription in which he tells of bringing materials for its decoration from afar, including columns of stone from a town called Aphrodisias of Ogia, cedar wood from Lebanon, silver from Egypt, gold from Bactria, and ivory from India.[43]

The outline of the palace can still be traced by some rows of bricks, and bits of brick and lime remain from the pavements. The main plan included three courts of varying size, surrounded by large halls and apartments, while a great hypostyle hall stood nearby. The walls were of sun-dried brick covered with whitewash on the inside, and the paving was coated throughout with polished red ochre.

Panels of beautifully colored glazed bricks, which served in the same role as tapestries, constituted the most notable feature in the decoration of the palace. Many of the designs were executed in relief, and included winged bulls, winged griffins, and the famous spearmen of the guard—of whom two are shown in Fig. 97. Most of the extant examples of this type of decoration at Susa come probably from the reign of Artaxerxes II Mnemon, mentioned above.[44]

The splendid capitals of the Achaemenid kings were destined to

[40] The Histories. x, xxvii, 10. tr. W. R. Paton, LCL (1922-27) IV, p.167.
[41] Georges Perrot and Charles Chipiez, Histoire de l'art dans l'antiquité. v (1890), p.501; Oscar Reuther in Gunther Wasmuth, ed., Lexikon der Baukunst. II (1930), p 328.
[42] R. de Mecquenem in A Survey of Persian Art. I, pp.321-326.
[43] J. M. Unvala in A Survey of Persian Art. I, p.339.
[44] Stanley Casson in A Survey of Persian Art. I, p.351.

be looted and destroyed by Alexander the Great. Following Artaxerxes I the Persian throne was occupied by Darius II (423-405 B.C.), Artaxerxes II Mnemon (404-359), Artaxerxes III Ochus (358-338), Arses (337-336), and Darius III (335-331).[45] Then came the end.

9. ALEXANDER THE GREAT, 336-323 B.C.

In 331 B.C. Alexander the Great[1] invaded Persia after having made himself master of the entire eastern Mediterranean world including Egypt. Beyond the Tigris by the village of Gaugamela, Alexander met and defeated the armies of Darius III. Then he advanced to Susa, Persepolis, and Ecbatana, at each of which places he seized fabulous treasures. At Persepolis, according to Plutarch, ten thousand pairs of mules and five thousand camels were required to carry away the loot.[2] There at the main capital, with three thousand of his soldiers occupying the royal terrace, Alexander sealed the conquest of Persia by putting to the torch the palaces which symbolized the power of the Achaemenids.

In 324 B.C. the youthful conqueror of the world returned from India and stopped to visit the tomb of Cyrus at Pasargadae, which he found already despoiled. The man who had committed the outrage was slain, and Plutarch adds that the sight of the inscription on the tomb (p. 233) "deeply affected Alexander, who was reminded of the uncertainty and mutability of life."[3] If this is true, Alexander's forebodings were not unfounded, for he died not long after (323 B.C.) at the early age of thirty-three.

10. THE SUCCESSORS OF ALEXANDER, 323-30 B.C.

AFTER the death of Alexander the Great, his empire fell to his generals who are known as the Diadochi or "Successors." In Egypt, Ptolemy I Soter I (323-285), son of Lagus, carried on the government at first for Philip Arrhidaeus, the feeble-minded half-brother of Alexander the Great, and Alexander (II), the young son of Alexander the Great and then for the latter alone after Philip Arrhidaeus

---

[45] It was in the reign of either Artaxerxes II or Artaxerxes III that a rebellion of the Jews was put down with great severity by the king's general Bagoses (Josephus, *Ant.* XI, vii, 1).

[1] For new discoveries at Pella in Macedon, birthplace and capital of Alexander the Great, see Photios Petsas in *Archaeology.* 11 (1958), pp.246-254.

[2] *Life of Alexander.* XXXVII, 2. [3] *ibid.,* LXIX, 3.

was killed around 317. About 310 Alexander II was killed and Ptolemy assumed the title of king. His successors, the dynasty of the Ptolemies or the Lagidae, ruled Egypt until it became a Roman province in 30 B.C.[1] In the eastern provinces, Seleucus I Nicator (312-281) emerged eventually as master. He took Babylon and began his official reign in Syria in the autumn of 312. The founding of the Seleucid Kingdom was taken as the beginning of the Seleucid era, a chronological system which was long used in western Asia and among the scattered Jews.[2] The successors of Seleucus I, comprising the Seleucid Dynasty, continued to rule Syria until Pompey made it a Roman province in 64 B.C.[3]

As far as Judea was concerned, the land was ruled for a time by the Ptolemies, but around 198 B.C. was taken by Antiochus III and made a part of Syria, where the Seleucids had established their capital at Antioch. In general the rule of the Ptolemies was favorable to the

[1] The kings who followed the first Ptolemy, with their approximate dates, were: Ptolemy II Philadelphus (285-246), Ptolemy III Euergetes I (246-222), Ptolemy IV Philopator (222-203), Ptolemy V Epiphanes (203-181), Ptolemy VI Philometor (181-146), Ptolemy VII Eupator, Ptolemy VIII Neos Philopator, Ptolemy IX Euergetes II (Physkon), Ptolemy X Soter II (Lathyrus), Ptolemy XI Alexander I, Ptolemy XII Alexander II, Ptolemy XIII Neos Dionysos (Auletes) (80-51), Ptolemy XIV (51-47), Ptolemy XV (47-45), Ptolemy XVI Caesar or Caesarion (45-44). Cleopatra became queen jointly with Ptolemy XIV and dominated the closing part of this period until her death in 30 B.C. George Steindorff in Karl Baedeker, *Egypt and the Sudan.* 8th ed. 1929, pp.cxi-cxiii.

[2] The Seleucid era began in the Macedonian calendar with October 7, 312 B.C., and in the Babylonian with April 3, 311 B.C. PDBC p.20; cf. Wilhelm Kubitschek, *Grundriss der antiken Zeitrechnung* (in Walter Otto, ed., *Handbuch der Altertumswissenschaft.* I, 7 [1928]), p.70.

[3] The kings who followed Seleucus I, with their approximate dates, were: Antiochus I Soter (281-261), Antiochus II Theos (261-246), Seleucus II Callinicus (246-225), Seleucus III Soter (225-223), Antiochus III the Great (223-187), Seleucus IV Philopator (187-175), Antiochus IV Epiphanes (175-164), Antiochus V Eupator (164-162), Demetrius I Soter (162-150), Alexander I Balas (150-145), Demetrius II Nicator (145-139/38, 129-125), Antiochus VI Epiphanes (145-142/41), Antiochus VII Sidetes (139/38-129), Alexander II Zabinas (128-123), Antiochus VIII Grypus and Cleopatra Thea (125-121), Seleucus V (125), Antiochus VIII Grypus (121-96), Antiochus IX Cyzicenus (115-95), Seleucus VI Epiphanes Nicator (96-95), Antiochus X Eusebes Philopator (95-83), Demetrius III Eucaerus Philopator Soter (95-88), Antiochus XI Philadelphus (92), Philippus I Philadelphus (92-83), Antiochus XII Dionysus (87-84), Tigranes of Armenia (83-69), Antiochus XIII Asiaticus (69-64), Philippus II (65-64).

When the Seleucids neglected their Iranian possessions in favor of their Syrian territory, Persia fell into the power of the Parthians, an Iranian people whose leader Arsaces (c.250-c.248 B.C.) founded the Arsacid Dynasty which endured from c.250 B.C. to A.D. c.229. The Parthian Empire was overthrown by Ardashir I (the name is the modern form of Artaxerxes), who ruled A.D. c.224-241. He was the descendant of Sasan, and thus the Sasanian or Neo-Persian Empire was established which endured until the victory of the Arabs in A.D. 651. There is a list of the Parthian kings in PDBC p. 24, and Eduard Meyer gives a list of the Sasanid kings in EB XVII, p.583.

Jews, and Ptolemy II Philadelphus is remembered favorably for having encouraged the beginning of work by the Seventy at Alexandria on the famous Greek version of the Old Testament. The Seleucids, however, soon laid a heavy hand upon the Jews and the persecution by Antiochus IV Epiphanes (c.168 B.C.) led to the Maccabean war and the temporary freedom of Judea. This independence lasted until Jerusalem fell to Pompey (63 B.C.) and Palestine passed under the sway of Roman power.

Index of Scriptural References

General Index

All references are to pages, except where Figures, Maps, or Plans are specifically indicated.

Alexamenos, 373
Alexander I Balas, 245
Alexander I, pope, 458
Alexander II, son of Alexander the Great, 244f.
Alexander II Zabinas, 245
Alexander VII, pope, 383
Alexander Janneus, 253, 300, 308, 312
Alexander, named in inscription in Catacomb of Priscilla, 477
Alexander, son of Herod the Great, 255
Alexander the Great, 37, 42, 133, 150, 244, 310f., 336, 345, 348, 359, 388
Alexandretta, Iskanderun, Gulf of, Map 6; 339, 356
Alexandria, Maps 2, 6; 81, 246, 248, 335, 338, 346, 348, 389, 391, 406, 424, 432f., 435, 438, 446f., 533, 546
Alexandrian Text, 424, 432-441, 447
Alis, 406f., 417
Aliyan, 173
Allenby, E. H., 155, 169, 330
Alorus, 30
Alphabet, 149, 163, 165
Alps, 302
Altaku, Eltekeh, Map 3; 211
Altar of Zeus, Pergamum, 345
Altar to Unknown Gods, Fig. 126; 356f.
Alulim, 30
Amadai, 230
Amalekites, 543
Amanus Mountains, Map 6; 49, 145; Pass, 334
Amasis, 131f., 223
Amaziah, 589
ambon, 507
Ambrose, 443
Amel-Marduk, 227, 594f.
Amelon, 30
Amemit, 101
Amempsinos, 30
Amen, god, 105
Amen, or Menas, 545
Amenemhet I, 90-92
Amenemhet II, 91
Amenemhet III, 171
Amenemhet IV, 91
Amenemopet, 123-125
Amenhotep I, 97
Amenhotep II, Figs. 38, 39; 102f., 119

Amenhotep III, Fig. 41; 103f., 109, 116, 162f., 198f.; colonnade of, at Luxor, Fig. 42
Amenhotep IV, Akhenaton, Fig. 44; 104-112, 115, 149, 198f., 201
Amenmose, 134
Amen-Re, 99, 105f.
American School of Classical Studies at Athens, 354, 360
American Schools of Oriental Research, 18, 183, 308; at Baghdad, 47; at Jerusalem, Plan 1; 160, 163, 189, 268-271, 276, 313, 319
American Tarsus College, 335
Amman, 153, 277, 309
Ammenon, 30
Ammeris, 128
Ammianus Marcellinus, 521
Ammi-zaduga, 73
Ammon, Map 3; 154
Ammonites, 153, 309
Ammonius, Ammonian Sections, 403
Amor, region, 92
Amoretti, 477
Amorites, 53-55, 68, 73, 145f., 153f., 157
Amos, 187
Ampliatus, 464
Amraphel, 73
Amratians, 79-81, 143
Amreh, el-, 80
Amun, god, 90, 99f., 103, 105f., 112, 114, 116, 121f., 126, 134, 390
Amurru, 92, 114, 145f.
Amyntas, 344
Amytis, 220
An, god, 44f.
Anacletus, 514
Ananel, 262
Ananias, 263, 482
Ananos, 262f.
Ananos the son of Annas, 263
Anastasia, wife of Marinianus, 512
Anastasis, in Church of Holy Sepulcher, 529-531, 537
Anastasius I, 252
Anat, goddess, 168, 173
'Anath-bethel, 240
'Anath-Yahu, 240
Anatolia, 266
Ancient Records of Egypt, 76

Ancyra, Angora, Ankara, Maps 4, 6; 198, 344f.
Andrae, Walter, 200
Andronicus II Palaeologus, 550
Angel, earliest known representation of, 51
Anglo-Egyptian Sudan, Map 2
Angora, see Ancyra
Ani, 101
Anicetus, 514
Anio River, Plan 3; 366
Ankara, see Ancyra
Ankhesenamun, 199
Annals of Tacitus, 378
Annas, high priest, 252, 262f.
Annius Rufus, procurator, 257
Anshan, Map 4; 229, 231f.
Antakya, 337
Anteros, pope, 458f.
Anthemius, 251, 550
Anthius River, 341
Antigonus, 254, 274
Anti-Lebanon, Map 4; 336
Antioch in Pisidia, Map 6; 340-346
Antioch in Syria, Maps 4, 6; 15, 245, 248, 334, 337-340, 346, 389, 446f., 495, 539, 541f., 544
Antiochs, 16 founded by Seleucus I Nicator, 340f.
Antiochus I of Commagene, 200
Antiochus I Soter, 30, 245, 337
Antiochus II Theos, 245
Antiochus III the Great, 245, 248, 345
Antiochus IV Epiphanes, 245f., 253, 282, 335, 338, 354
Antiochus V Eupator, 245
Antiochus VI Epiphanes, 245
Antiochus VII Sidetes, 245
Antiochus VIII Grypus, 245
Antiochus IX Cyzicenus, 245
Antiochus X Eusebes Philopator, 245
Antiochus XI Philadelphus, 245
Antiochus XII Dionysus, 245, 336
Antiochus XIII Asiaticus, 245
Antipater of Sidon, 348

Antipater, son of Herod the Great, 255
Antipater, the Idumean, 253f.
Antipatris, Map 5; 312
Antiquities of Athens, 352
Antium, Map 6; 365
Antonia, Tower of, Plan 1; 317-321, 323f., 327
Antonines, 463f.
Antoninus Pius, 251, 375, 466
Antonis, Antonius, Antonis Maximus, 408
Antonis Longus, Antonius Longus, 409
Antonius, Marcus; Mark Antony, 248, 254, 258, 312, 320, 335, 350f.
Anu, god, 31f., 45, 55, 64
Anubis, god, 101
Anzan, 231
Apachnan, 95
Apadana, Hall of Xerxes, Figs. 94, 95; 241f.
Apamea, 481
Apameia, 260
Apamenians, garrison of, in Egypt, 409
Apennines, 366
'Aperu, 69
Aphrodisias, person mentioned in Letter of Hilarion, 406
Aphrodisias, town, 243
Aphrodite, goddess, 330, 335, 359, 361, 533
Apil-Sin, 56
Apion, 408f.
'Apiru, 69, 111, 119f., 167
Apocryphon of John, 414
Apollo, god, 335; so-called shrine of, at Rome, 383, 511; temple of, at Corinth, Fig. 127; 361f.; at Rome, 373
Apollonarion, 406f.
Apollonia, 345
Apollonius of Tyana, 356f.; visits Colossi of Memnon, 104
Apollonius, person mentioned in Letter of Irene, 408
Apollo Patroos, temple of, 355f.
Apophis, 95
Apostolic Constitutions, 508
Appian, Roman historian, 351
Appian Way, *see* Via Appia

Appius Claudius Caecus, 365f.
Apries, 130-132
apse, 507
Apsu, 63f.
Aqabah, Gulf of, Map 3; 137, 151-153, 181, 265f., 429
Aqsa, el-, Mosque, Plan 1; 325
Aqua Alsietina, Plan 2; 366
Aqua Anio Novus, Plan 2; 366
Aqua Anio Vetus, Plan 2; 366
Aqua Appia, Plan 2; 366
Aqua Claudia, Fig. 130; Plan 2; 365f.
Aquae Salviae, 383
Aqua Julia, Plan 2; 366
Aqua Marcia, Plan 2; 366
Aqua Tepula, Plan 2; 366
Aqua Virgo, Plan 2; 366
Aqueducts, at Pisidian Antioch, 341f.; at Rome, Plan 2; 365f.
Aquila, 493
Arabia, 48, 213, 228, 237, 264; Arabs, 9, 188, 203, 213, 245, 303, 324, 388f., 434, 443, 496
Arabian Desert of Egypt, Map 2
Arabian Nights, 10
Arabic language, 6, 46, 389
Arabic period in Palestine, 150, 189, 275, 313
Arachosia, 237
Arad, 126
Aramaic language, 46, 235, 239, 269-271, 277, 279, 281, 331, 364, 388f., 411, 446
Ara Pacis, 549
Aratus, 335
Araunah, 179f.
Arcadius, 252, 516, 547
ἀρχαιολογία, 3
Archelaus, 252, 256, 261f., 275, 310, 313
Arch of Augustus, 374
Arch of Constantine, Plan 2; 374
Arch of Severus, 375
Arch of Tiberus, 375
Arch of Titus, Plan 2; 374, 376
Archles, 95
arcosolium, 452
Arculf, 302
Ardashir I, 245, 496
Areopagus, 355-357
Ares, temple of, 355

Aretas III, 336
Aretas IV, 256, 300, 336f.
Ariaramna, son of Teispes, 231
Aristeas, Letter of, 390
Aristides, Apology of, 385
Aristobulus I, 253
Aristobulus II, 253f.
Aristobulus, high priest, 262
Aristobulus, son of Herod the Great, 255f.
Aristotle, 394, 556
Ark of the Law, 174; return of, from the Philistines, Fig. 179; 497f.; shown being carried around Jericho, Fig. 188; 526
Armageddon, *see* Megiddo
Armenia, Map 4; 9, 71, 233, 237, 245, 258, 338
Armenian Convent, Bethlehem, 534
Armenian Patriarchate, Jerusalem, 437
Arnold, J. R., 13
Arnon River, Map 5; 154, 188f., 312
Arnuwandas III, 199
Aroer, Map 3; 189
Arrian, Greek historian, 74, 233
Arsaces, Arsacid Dynasty, 245
Arses, Persian king, 244
Arsinoë Crocodilopolis, Map 2; 133, 405; Arsinoïte nome, 410
Arta, 238
Artaxerxes, 245
Artaxerxes I Longimanus, 227, 234, 237-239, 241f., 244
Artaxerxes II Mnemon, 239f., 243f.
Artaxerxes III Ochus, 244
Artaxias, general of Antiochus III, 248
Artemis, goddess, 335, 347f.
Artemision, Ephesus, 347f.
Art of the catacombs, 476-482
Arundell, Francis V. J., 341
Arvad, Map 4
Arx, Citadel at Rome, Plan 2; 372
Aryans, 29, 230, 237
Asa, 176f.
Asamoneus, 253
Asclepius, 353, 356
Ashdod, Map 3; 209, 212
Asherah, Asherat, Ashirat,

Boston Museum of Fine Arts, 251
Botta, Paul Émile, 4, 209, 211
Bouillon, Godfrey de, 330
Bouleuterion, meeting place of Council of Five Hundred at Athens, 355
Braidwood, Robert J., 12
Bramante, 512, 515
Breasted, James Henry, 76
Brickmaking, 100
Bridge, Palestine as a, 137
Brindisi, see Brundisium
Britain, 330
British Academy, 185
British Museum, 14, 19, 204, 211, 217f., 220, 235, 272, 347, 352, 392, 426, 428, 436, 438, 444
British School of Archaeology, in Jerusalem, 140, 157, 185, 308; in Iraq, 203
Bronze Age, 27, 139, 144-149, 152, 154, 157-163, 166, 169f., 175, 183f., 189, 192, 264, 279
Brooklyn Museum, 93, 240
Brugsch, H., 115
Brundisium, Brindisi, Map 6; 365
Brutus, 350
Bryn Mawr College, 335
Bubastis, Map 2; 126
Buhen, 91
Burma, 6
Burning Bush, 434
Bur-Sagale, 200
Bur-Sin, 53
Business contract from time of Hammurabi, Fig. 22
Buto, Map 2; 82
Byblos, Byblus, Map 4; 109, 144
Byzantine Institute, 550
Byzantine period in Palestine, 150, 275, 299
Byzantine Text, 432, 440, 447-449
Byzantine tradition, places Peter at right hand of Christ, 522
Byzantium, 548f.; see also Constantinople

Caelian Hill, Plans 2, 3; 367
Caelus, the Sky, 250, 490
Caesar Augustus, see Augustus
Caesar, C., legate in Syria, 258

Caesar, Gaius Julius, see Julius Caesar
Caesar, title, 258, 408
Caesarea, Maps 5, 6; 254f., 257, 275, 312, 329, 398, 437, 446f., 493, 504f., 530
Caesarea in Cappadocia, Map 6
Caesarean Text, 424, 426, 446f.
Caesarea Philippi, Banias, Map 5; 137, 255, 307
Caesarion, 245
Caiaphas, or Joseph Caiaphas, high priest and son-in-law of high priest Annas, 252, 262f.
Cairo, Map 2; 75, 82, 89, 92, 282, 405, 428, 431, 435, 444
Caius Caesar, 258
Caius, presbyter in church at Rome, 380-383, 473, 514f.
Calah, Nimrod, Map 4; 4 63, 68, 203, 205, 209, 211
Calendar, 97, 117, 128f., 130f., 200, 202, 206, 208, 218f., 222f., 227, 229, 234, 238-240, 245, 247, 250-252, 275, 293-297, 328, 407, 474, 497, 545, 552-598
Caligula, 251, 256, 261f., 337, 366, 369f., 372, 374, 513
Callistus I, pope, 458-461
Calvary, 525, 528f., 531
Calvin, 441
Cambrian period, 264f.
Cambridge University, 271, 427, 436, 441f.
Cambyses I, father of Cyrus the Great, 231f.
Cambyses II, son of Cyrus the Great, 132f., 230 233
Camel, early representation of, at Tell Halaf, Fig. 25; 67; on Apadana relief, 242; with St. Menas, 546f.
Cameron, George G., 235
Campagna di Roma, Plan 3; 365f., 485
Campo Verano, 522
Campus Martius, Plan 2; 367, 369-371, 373
Campus Vaticanus, Plan 2; 367
Cana, 488, 538
Canaan, Map 3; 67, 70-72, 113, 116, 118, 135, 182

Canaanites, 99, 146f., 149, 162, 166-174, 573f.
Canatha, el-Kanawat, Map 5; 308
cancelli, 507
cantharus, 507
Capernaum, Tell Hum, Map 5; 302-307, 312, 554; synagogue at, Fig. 111; 304f.
Capito, person mentioned in Letter of Apion, 408
Capito, who dedicated altar to unknown gods, 357
Capitol, 366, 372
Capitolias, 308
Capitoline Hill, Plans 2, 3; 367, 371f., 376
Capitoline Jupiter, 329
Cappadocia, province, Map 6; 237, 344, 356, 380, 448
Cappella della Pieta, 513
Cappella Greca, Figs. 158, 159, 160; 465f.
Captivity of Jehoiachin, 225-227
Capua, Map 6; 365, 523
Capuchin monks, 352
Caracalla, Antoninus, 251, 371
Carbon 14, 13, 57, 83, 141, 144, 272
Carcer Mamertinus, 376f.
Carchemish, Maps 1, 4; 17, 130, 199, 220f., 590
Carians, 237
Caricature of the Crucifixion, Fig. 131; 373
Carinus, 251
Carmel, Mount, Maps 3, 5; 99, 136, 139f., 266, 298
Caro, Hugo de S., cardinal, 403
Carpian, 403
Carter, Howard, 112
Carthage, Map 6; 117, 247
Cartouche, 134
Carus, 251
Caspian Plateau, 230f.
Caspian Sea, Maps 1, 4
Cassander, 351
Cassius, 350
Castel Sant'Angelo, Plan 4
Castor and Pollux, temple of, 374f.
Catacomb at Ephesus, 349
Catacomb of Calepodius, Calipodius, Plan 3; 458
Catacomb of Callistus, Figs. 157, 166; Plan 3;

Simon, son of Mattathias, 253, 282, 454
Simon the son of Kamithos, high priest, 262
Simonides, 306
Sin, god, 45, 47, 53, 204, 229, 566
Sinai, peninsula, Map 3; 91, 148, 386, 433-437; Mount Sinai, Fig. 146; Map 3; 148, 150, 581; Sinaitic Bible, 436; Sinaitic inscriptions, 148; Sinaitic Syriac, 444
Single Gate, in Temple area, 324
Sin-idinnam, 10
Sin-muballit, 56
Sinope, Map 6
Sin-shar-ishkun, 218f.
Sin-shum-lishir, 218
Sinuhe, 91f.
Sippar, Map 1; 30f., 219, 229
Siricius, pope, 517, 524
Sirita, person mentioned in catacomb inscription, 483
Siseos, person mentioned in graffito at Dura-Europos, 499
Sisyphus, 359
Siuph, 131
Skudra, 237
Skunkha the Scythian, 234
Slip, in pottery-making, 16
Smerdis, 233
Smith, George, 217
Smith, George Adam, 169
Smyrna, Map 6; 341
Snefru, 86
Socoh, Shuweikeh, Map 3; 126
Socrates, church historian, 520, 550
Socrates, Greek philosopher, 358
Soden, Hermann Freiherr von, 416
Sodom, 147
Sogdia, 237
Sol, the Sun, 250
Solem, see Shunem
Soli in Cilicia, 335
Solomon, 49, 117, 151, 179-183, 191, 323, 325, 496, 573, 588
Solomon's Porch, 325
Solomon's Stables, 322
Somali coast, 98
Soreg, wall in Jerusalem temple, 325
Soter, bishop of Rome, 380

Sothis, 564f., 566
Soviet government, 436
Sozomen, church historian, 520, 541
Spain, 248, 359, 377
Speiser, Ephraim A., 18
spelunca, 468
Spelunca Magna, 468f.
Sphinx, 88, 102
spina, 513, 515
Spon, Jacques, 352
Squeezes, 188
Stables at Megiddo, 180f.
Stadium, Roman, 156
Standard of Ur, Fig. 16; 42
Stanley, Henry, 74
Starkey, John Leslie, 161, 193
Statius, Roman poet, 365
Stauris, Mount, 339
Steckeweh, H., 163, 183
Stela of the Vultures, 43
Stela of Ur-Nammu, 51
Stela, Stele, 43
Stephanus, or Robert Étienne, 403
Stephen, first Christian martyr, 333, 522
Stephen, pictured in San Lorenzo fuori le Mura, 522
Stephen I, pope, 458f.
Stephinates, 128
Step pyramid at Saqqara, 87
Sterrett, J. R. Sitlington, 343
Stichometry, 402
Stoa Basileios, 356
Stoa Basilica, 325
Stoa of Attalos, 354f.
Stoa of the Giants, 354
Stoa of Zeus Eleutherios, 355f.
Stone Age, 139-142, 247
Stotoëtis, chief priest addressed in Letter of Mystarion, 407
Strabo, Greek geographer, 74, 104, 335, 338, 350-352, 359, 411
Straight Street in Damascus, Fig. 121; 337
Straton's Tower, 254
Stuart, James, 352
Styger, Paul, 453, 456f., 474
Suetonius, Roman historian, 372, 379
Suez Canal, Map 3
Suez, city, Map 3
Suez, Gulf of, Maps 2, 3
Sukenik, E. L., 273, 319
Sultan Dagh, 341

Sumer, Map 1; 10, 38, 43, 50, 52, 55f., 144, 216, 230, 232; Sumerians, 26, 29, 31f., 39, 42, 45f., 53-55, 62, 145, 200, 552, 566f.; Sumerian King List, 18, 28-31, 36f., 39f., 44, 46; Sumerian statues, Figs. 10, 11
Sumu-abu, 55f.
Sumu-la-el, 56
Sunium, Cape, Map 6; 353
Suppululiumas, 198f., 201
Suq et-Tawileh, Long Bazaar or Straight Street in Damascus, 337
Susanna, 466, 469, 481f.
Susa, Shush, Fig. 3; Maps 1, 4; 21f., 58, 201, 230, 242-244; enameled brick panels from, showing spearmen of Achaemenid Period, Fig. 97
Susian language, 235
Susitha, 308
Susiyeh, Map 5; 308
Swedish School in Jerusalem, 319
Sychar, Askar, Map 5; 310
Sylvester I, Silvester, pope, 459, 510f., 516, 519f.
Symbols of the four evangelists, 525
Symbolum, Mount, 350
Symmachus, pope, 517
Synagogue church, Gerasa, 539
Synagogues, 299f., 303, 306, 354, 362, 492f., 506, 539; Capernaum, 304f.; Corinth, 361; Dura-Europos, 496-498
Syncellus, George, 78
Synnada, Map 6; 479
Syracuse, Map 6; 360, 387
Syria, Maps 4, 6; 15, 47, 49, 69, 92, 104, 109, 114, 116, 119, 121f., 130, 135f., 144-146, 171, 198, 204f., 207, 215, 221, 223, 245, 248, 252f., 256-262, 308, 329, 336, 338, 344-346, 354, 358, 478f., 496, 508, 539, 543f., 579; Syrians, Fig. 40; 103, 186
Syriac language, 46, 280
Syrian Gates, Map 6; 334